HISTORY, RELIGION AND IDENTITY
IN MODERN BRITAIN

HISTORY, RELIGION AND IDENTITY IN MODERN BRITAIN

KEITH ROBBINS

THE HAMBLEDON PRESS

LONDON   AND   RIO GRANDE

Published by The Hambledon Press 1993

102 Gloucester Avenue, London NW1 8HX (U.K.)
P.O. Box 162, Rio Grande, Ohio 45674 (U.S.A.)

ISBN 1 85285 101 5

A description of this book is available from
the British Library and from the Library of Congress

Phototypeset by The Midlands Book Typesetting Company

Printed on acid-free paper and bound in Great
Britain by Cambridge University Press

Contents

Acknowledgements

The articles reprinted here first appeared in the following places and are reprinted by the kind permission of the original publishers.

1 *History*, 66 (1981), pp. 413–25.
2 *Nuchdenken über Geschichte: Beiträge aus der Ökumene der Historiker in Memoriam Karl Dietrich Erdmann*, ed. Hartmut Boockmann and Kurt Jürgensen (Karl Wachholtz, Neumünster, Germany, 1992), pp. 397–408.
3 *History*, 75 (1990), pp. 369–87.
4 The Stenton Lecture (University of Reading, 1990).
5 This essay appears here for the first time.
6 *Studies in Church History*, 11, *Materials, Sources and Methods* (Oxford, 1975), pp. 355–65.
7 *Studies in Church History*, 18, *Religion and National Identity* (Oxford, 1982) pp. 465–88.
8 *Studies in Church History: Subsidia 7* (Oxford, 1990), pp. 281–96.
9 *Edwardian England*, ed. D. Read (Croom Helm for the Historical Association, London, 1982), pp. 113–33.
10 *Journal of Ecclesiastical History*, 30 (1979), pp. 261–76.
11 *Baptist Quarterly*, xxvii (1978), pp. 346–57.
12 *Journal of Ecclesiastical History*, 21 (1970), pp. 149–70.
13 *Studies in Church History*, 12, *Church Society and Politics* (Oxford, 1975), pp. 419–53.
14 *History, Society and the Churches: Essays in Honour of Owen Chadwick*, ed. D. Beales and G. Best (Cambridge, 1985), pp. 279–99.
15 *Friends of Lambeth Palace Library Annual Report* (1991), pp. 17–29.
16 This essay appears here for the first time.
17 *Proceedings of the British Academy*, 1xx (1984), pp. 275–97.
18 *Cultural Traditions in Northern Ireland*, ed. Maurna Crozier (Belfast, 1990), pp. 4–18.
19 *Transactions of the Honourable Society of Cymmrodorion* (1985), pp. 57–69.
20 *Journal of Contemporary History*, 15 (1980), pp. 81–95.

Preface

The essays in this collection have been written over a period of twenty-five years. They were composed, in many instances, in response to particular requests and for specific occasions. At the time, they seemed self-contained pieces, designed in most cases to address discrete issues in isolation. Even so, in aggregate, the topics turn out to reveal more about the underlying concerns of the writer than he himself would have realized at the moment of their individual composition. They display a fascination, perhaps an obsession, with the question of 'British Identity' in the twentieth century. The great empire of the Victorian Age now seems distant but imperial echoes remain. What is 'Britain' now that the Empire is no more? Is it 'just another European state', perhaps of a rather peculiar kind? Is it a confused assemblage of peoples and cultures on the point of fragmentation? Is it a 'Christian country' but one divided as much as united by religion? What was at stake in 1940? In short, while the topics are indeed different, they are more closely related than might at first sight appear.

In the first group, I consider how British historians, and their organizations, have both shaped and reflected the national understanding of the British past and its significance for the present. What is the public function of history? Have we reached the end of 'British history' in the age of European integration? Alternatively, is a strong sense of national identity both desirable and inevitable even in a 'common European home'? If so, can there be a recognition of the 'foreign' without xenophobia? In the second group, attention is concentrated on beliefs and values. In a domestic context, essays look at the ways in which the churches in the British Isles have preserved and reinforced distinct national insular identities. In an external context, essays on English interpretations of the German *Kirchenkampf* in the 1930s bring out the tensions between nationalism and a faith which transcends the nation-state. In the British context it is explored at a different level in examining the relationship between successive Prime Ministers and successive Archbishops of Canterbury. At a deeper level still, questions are posed concerning the application of 'prophecy' to political life. In these circumstances, it is not difficult to see both the attraction and the difficulty inherent in the concept of a 'Christian Civilization' as it appeared in Britain at the outset of the Second World War. The third group concentrates upon regional and national relationships within the British Isles, culminating in studies which consider 'state' and 'nation' after 1945 in the context of decolonization. Two of the essays (5 and 16) have not previously been published. They were prepared, respectively, for a Council of Europe symposium in Strasbourg and for a conference on the History and Methodology of International Relations held in Spoleto, Italy.

A fledgling author was assisted in 1966 by the dedicatee of this volume in the preparation of the first of these essays to be written. The dedication reflects a continuing gratitude and inspiration.

Lampeter

April 1993

This volume is dedicated with respect to

Owen Chadwick OM, KBE, FBA

1

History, the Historical Association and the 'National Past'

It is curious that historians, even those who have been connected with the Historical Association, have been reticent about its own history.[1] Yet an investigation of the opinions that have been expressed by distinguished members since its foundation in 1906 tells us a great deal about the attitudes to the national past which are to be found in twentieth-century Britain. Many of the questions which were asked at the outset have been repeated in succeeding generations, though the answers have not been unanimous. Do writers and teachers of history have a particular responsibility to the society in which they live to help it come to an understanding of its past? Even amongst themselves, can they reach agreement on its significant features? Is there a 'common core' which every citizen can grasp and to which he can relate his own experience? Is there a 'national character' and, if so, is it important that it should survive?[2] If we welcome the demise of nationalist historiography in a crude sense does that mean that the national past has no particular claim on the attention of a national Historical Association?[3] Does the historian have nothing to contribute to what Maurice Cowling would call 'public doctrine', though his recent book only concerns itself with England (that is to say with the University of Cambridge!).[4] The United Kingdom has no less than four capital cities, each with a distinct flavour and ethos, but after centuries of political union, has our historiography even begun to grapple with the complexities of distinct national pasts? In recent decades, we have been frequently told that we have lost an Empire and not yet found a role and part of that process may entail a reconsideration, in a fundamental way, of the history of the British Isles as a whole.[5] At a humble level, it might mean that schoolchildren in England might know the names of two Scottish monarchs besides Mary Queen of Scots and James VI and I. At a higher level, it might involve English universities in the serious teaching of British history for the first time. I find it a little sad that, under the potent influence of my old tutor, the Association's anniversary

---

1. *The Historical Association, 1906–1956* (London, 1957). E.W.M. Balfour-Melville, *Reminiscences of our First Fifty Years* (Edinburgh, 1962).

2. D.M. Potter, *People of Plenty: Economic Abundance and the American Character* (Chicago, 1954). E. Barker, ed., *The Character of England* (Oxford, 1947).

3. P.M. Kennedy, 'The Decline of Nationalistic History in the West, 1900–1970', in W. Laqueur and G.L. Mosse, ed. *Historians in Politics* (London, 1974), pp. 329–52.

4. M. Cowling, *Religion and Public Doctrine in Modern England* (Cambridge, 1980).

5. See below, chapter 20, pp. 281–92.

lectures are to consider Edwardian *England*. Such a reconsideration of the past is already beginning in Ireland where the burden of history, as F.S.L. Lyons puts it, is more tragically and dramatically present.[6] If the cultural complexity of the national past can be unravelled in Ireland there is even less excuse for a failure to do so in the United Kingdom. National disorientation may be, at least in part, a consequence of loss of Empire but the substantial immigration that accompanied and has followed its demise raises further questions, which would not have been dreamed of in 1906, about how the national past can be presented in a multicultural environment. To take one further illustration, we struggle on very often, at many different levels of education, with the teaching of 'British' and 'European' history in different compartments, faithfully reflecting and perpetuating the assumption that our national past is distinct from the past of Europe. Yet if the national future is to be a European future it is precisely the contact — revealing both similarity and distinctiveness — that needs the most careful consideration. The answers to these questions are more difficult than might be supposed and all I hope to do is to clear the ground. The Historical Association is itself a part of the past. Its members, most notably its presidents, have by their own words and writings in part made the past which we seek to understand. *History* has been an important vehicle for such debate and discussion. The articles selected by its editors can be seen to have reflected, to some degree, a national mood or obsession. Such choice may well be made unconsciously. Certainly, I have never been asked to swear an oath of loyalty to the Association. It has no general view of an overtly political character. Yet its presidents are, and have been, public men and so also, but much more modestly, are its editors. In what sense they are 'representative' men is rather more difficult to determine. It may now be impossible to establish why particular individuals assumed office when they did but it would be wrong to presume that the roll of honour is totally fortuitous and without historical significance. Even if I can lay claim to being '*History* speaking', I do so on this occasion with due modesty and an awareness of the limitations of the evidence at my disposal.

'I am not very keen on the proposed Historical Association', wrote one historian to A.F. Pollard in the month before the inaugural meeting, 'because I am not much of an historical teacher myself and look forward to being less of one'.[7] Pollard, a young man of thirty-six, recently-appointed professor of constitutional history at University College, London, poorly paid but rich in self-confidence, was not deterred by such rampant apathy. His correspondent was not the only one to wonder whether it had any function to fulfil. There was, after all, the Royal Historical Society, which had survived since 1868 and must therefore have performed a scholarly purpose.[8] There was the *English*

6. F.S.L. Lyons, *The Burden of our History* (Belfast, 1978). D.W. Harkness, *History and the Irish* (Belfast, 1976).
7. R. Lane Poole to A.F. Pollard, 28 April 1906, Pollard MSS, University of London.
8. R.A. Humphreys, *The Royal Historical Society, 1868–1968* (London, 1969).

Historical Review, founded in 1886, about which the same comment might be made. However, to middle-aged men around the turn of the century, the mature generation of those who had shared in the expansion of historical studies at Oxford and Cambridge in the 1870s and beyond, existing arrangements were inadequate for the advancement of that study of history which they believed to be of national importance. Many of them had spent part of their academic youth in Germany and were well aware of the standing of historical studies in German universities.[9] Pollard, gearing himself up for that sustained assault on the University of London which was, by one means or other, eventually to lead to the establishment of the Institute of Historical Research, bitterly attacked the treatment of modern history in the capital of the British Empire. In a lecture in October 1904 he described it as the Cinderella or, more properly, one of a number of Cinderellas, awaiting the beneficent advent of some fairy prince. It was with Germany that he made his comparisons. Discussion of German scientific and technological education was widespread as part of the post-Boer War alarm about 'National Efficiency'. Pollard pointed out that proficiency in applied mathematics or science in Germany was not achieved by the neglect of 'pure scholarship'. The glorious University of Berlin had six professors of modern history and, an even more splendid being, a professor of the methods of historical research. The United States, which had drawn deeply from the German well, was not far behind in its provision. He also noted that German interest in modern history was not confined to universities. Each kingdom or duchy had its commission for the publication of its own historical records. Most districts had their *Verein* or *Gesellschaft* to promote historical research. There were some 200 regular periodical publications devoted to historical research, against which only the *English Historical Review* could be set. It was true that German zeal might not always be tempered by wisdom, but the zeal was admirable. In London, however, the fund to establish a Chair of Modern History in memory of Bishop Creighton had failed to attract sufficient subscription. He contrasted this failure with a contemporary success in Cape Town. It was a poor reflection on the heart of Empire. London, he believed, could specialize in three subjects for a school of research in English History. First and foremost was Naval History — the British Empire was the greatest naval power the world had ever known with 'the longest and most glorious naval history on record' and its continued existence depended upon sea power. It was therefore vital that there should be 'a true interpretation and appreciation of the lessons of naval history'. Closely connected with naval history was the teaching of the history of war. If the nation and its rulers had gained a better appreciation of what that subject had to teach then many lives and millions of pounds might have been saved in the late war. Pollard then

9. K. Dockhorn, *Der deutsche Historismus in England: ein Beitrag zur Englischen Geistesgeschichte des 19, Jahrhunderts* (Göttingen, 1950). C. Harvie, *The Lights of Liberalism* (London, 1976).

mentioned the history of London itself. He also revealed his distress that half of the candidates who had attempted a matriculation examination question on Imperial Federation had not the ghost of a notion what it meant. He was certain that they ordered these things better in France where contemporary history was given due weight — that is to say treated as superior to any other kind.[10]

Knowledge of the national past as an element in national or imperial survival was not a new theme, but in the early years of the century it had an immediate appeal across Europe. But, in alluding to Germany and France, Pollard was not apparently interested in any historical explanation for the lavishness of Berlin and the parsimony of London. It was sufficient, for his propagandist purposes, to allude to these startling facts, though he was not the first or only historian to allude to them. It may be suggested, however, that historians did not flourish in Germany because of the climate or some inherent weakness for the discipline. The resources devoted to the study of history, the nature of the historical profession, the relationship of the universities to the state all had a specific historical and sociological context. Even if, by the end of the century, historians were less involved in politics, the political implications of their writings remained important. Broadly, after 1871, the English ideal which had been so influential became irrelevant. In a new state, the task of the historian was to stimulate an integral nationalism and the political order was broadly acceptable. To suggest that they conceived themselves to have a 'national mission' would be going too far in most cases but one historian comments that it was clearly 'the German national state which provided the secular standpoint from which they judged past and present'. The voice of Prussian historiography became predominant in post-1871 Germany. To be 'called to Berlin' was the 'ultimate flattery' for a German professor. Freiburg, Göttingen and Leipzig crumbled before the majesty of the capital where the national past was now newly distilled.[11] Even so, the profusion of periodicals and local commissions to which Pollard referred allowed the survival of a kind of professional particularism.

In France, on the other hand, in the last decades of the century, the defeat of Sedan 'weighed particularly heavily on the young historians who began their careers in the last years of the Second Empire'. 'The study of France's past, which will be the principal part of our task, has a national importance at this moment', wrote Gabriel Monod, founder of the *Revue historique* in 1876. 'Through it we can provide our country with the moral unity and vigour that it

10. A.F. Pollard, *Factors in Modern History* (London, 1907), pp. 262–87. V.E. Chancellor, *History for their Masters: Opinion in the English History Textbook, 1800–1914* (Bath, 1970). C. Parker, *History as Present Politics* (Winchester, 1980).

11. C.E. McClelland, *The German Historians and England* (Cambridge, 1971) pp. 230–5. F.K. Ringer, *The Decline of the German Mandarins: The German Academic Community, 1890–1933* (Cambridge, 1969). A. Dove, *Der Wiedereintritt des nationalen Prinzips in die Geistesgeschichte* (Leipzig, 1898).

needs . . .'[12] In comparison with Germany, however, he could not disguise the malaise that afflicted French scholarship. He knew also that the past hundred years of French history might not exactly display the moral unity he sought. But a journal should eschew partisanship, take up no banner, profess no creed and gain its unity in the adoption of a strictly scientific standpoint. History teaching and research in France, particularly in Paris, was transformed during these years so that by the early 1880s one foreign observer wrote that none of the great German universities could boast of so many historical courses as were scattered among the various institutions of the capital. Yet, latent in this proliferation of facilities, was a conflict which could not be resolved. Did all this historical study have a patriotic function or was it something to be undertaken for its own sake? As a study of the French historical profession has noted, the content of its historical instruction 'harmonized so perfectly with the universally accepted value system that the republicans had adopted to replace the authoritarian, clerical traditions of the past'.[13] In fact, the academic historical profession did not rally *en masse* to the Dreyfusard banner. By the turn of the century, however, a fresh emphasis is detectable in some French historical circles. For example, Langlois, one of the Sorbonne *savants*, declared in 1904 (in Chicago) that all the universities of the world were now working fraternally.[14] No historian could rest content with his national literature. The previous year, in Rome, an informal gathering of historians adopted the name Congrès Internationale des Sciences Historiques and speeches were delivered against the writing of history with an excessively nationalist flavour.

Given this general background, it is not sufficient to account for the formation of the Historical Association by referring to Pollard's righteous indignation confronted by ignorance of Imperial Federation. 'Subject' associations were much in vogue. The Mathematical Association had been founded in 1870, the Geographical and Modern Language Associations in 1893, the Classical Association in 1903 and English Association in 1906. In this aspect, the Historical Association must be seen as another 'professional' body.[15] Likewise, concern that the United Kingdom did not possess a body of sufficient standing to develop contacts with foreign academies led to the foundation of the British Academy in 1903, with historians prominent in its ranks. It was, perhaps, the foundation of the Automobile Association which gave historians the final inducement to move with the times. It was, however, questionable whether the separate disciplines on their own would make the

12. W.R. Keylor, *Academy and Community: The Foundation of the French Historical Profession* (Cambridge, 1975), pp. 40–1. Ch.-O. Carbonell, *Histoire et historiens: une mutation idéologique des historiens français, 1865–1885* (Toulouse, 1976).

13. Keylor, *Academy and Community* p. 100.

14. Ibid., p. 160.

15. W.J. Reader, *Professional Men: The Rise of the Professional Classes in Nineteenth-Century England* (London, 1967). Tout told Pollard that he was rather sick of pedagogics but was of opinion that 'historians should organise with the rest'. T.F. Tout to A.F. Pollard, 25 April 1906, Pollard MSS.

impact on politicians and schools that they desired. Informal talks took place among the associations but it was only in 1916 that their representatives met and agreed on a general statement about the place of humanistic studies in any comprehensive system of national education. The following year, in conjunction with the British Academy, a Council of Humanistic Studies was formed, with Lord Bryce as President. Even so, when discussion moved beyond bland generalization, each subject association was convinced of the unique importance of its own discipline.

In this connexion, for historians, the relationship between the new Association and the Royal Historical Society was still a source of some embarrassment. G.W. Prothero, editor of the *Quarterly Review* and a former President of the Royal Historical Society, gave a lecture, published by the Association in January 1912, on the organization of historians in the United States.[16] He noted that the American Historical Association had been founded in 1884 and chartered five years later. The *American Historical Review* had been started in 1895 — its constitutional position was distinct from the Association though, as Prothero noted, in practice the same people ran both. He then distinguished four main differences between the American and the English Associations. The American was much larger, richer and more fully representative. It enjoyed some state support, the advantages of this arrangement being greater than the drawbacks. Thirdly, he thought the Americans combined research and the publication of documents with the discussion of practical assistance for teachers more vigorously than happened in England. Finally, in effect, the American association did have its journal. In short, he suggested, the American Historical Association was the Royal Historical Society, the Historical Association and the *English Historical Review*, all combined in one body. It was worth considering whether such a combination was 'an ideal at which we should aim'. If so, it was not to be realized.

The particular, though perhaps not exclusive function of the new association was to concern itself with instruction. Persons were eligible for membership who were either engaged or interested in the teaching of history. At the first annual meeting held in London in February 1907 the speaker was the veteran historian, lawyer and Liberal politician, James Bryce, shortly to leave the Cabinet and take up his post as Ambassador to the United States. His theme was indeed 'The Teaching of History in Schools'. Welcoming new trends, in particular the tendency to send students to sources, he nevertheless wondered whether there ought not to be more unity and co-ordination in the teaching of history across the country. He stopped short, however, of advocating a regular and uniform system. Beyond stating that history should be studied over many centuries in order to appreciate change over time, Bryce had singularly little to

16. G.W. Prothero, *The American Historical Association*, leaflet no. 27, London, 1912.

say about the importance of history to the nation.[17] Yet it is evident from the early leaflets of the Association that schoolteachers were very concerned about this aspect. Speaking to the London branch in February 1909 on *The Teaching of Civics in Public Schools*, G.T. Hankin stated that his task was to bring the realities of the existence of the nation and the empire within the mental grasp of the schoolboy. He was trying to build up 'as the foundation of my boys' budding beliefs, that they are a real part of the Empire, that they will have a real duty to perform as citizens . . .'[18] Historical Association Leaflet No. 17 was a paper read by Miss Mercier, *An Experiment in the Teaching of History* — before the Manchester branch in January 1909. 'Teachers of History', she declared, 'should interpret the national character, the national ideals, and educate their pupils in the ethos of their own race. Nations, no more than individuals, can[not] afford to dispense with their own peculiar characteristics. Individuality is as salt among virtues . . .'[19] Against this concern, Tout declared from the presidential chair at the fifth annual meeting in January 1911: 'What is the use of forming the Historical Association unless the Historical Association make up its mind as to a definite policy with regard to History, and the place it should occupy in our school curriculum?' It did not prove too difficult to agree that in every school of sufficient size there should be at any rate one teacher specially qualified to supervise history teaching. But the curriculum proved more difficult and a decision had to be postponed. Miss Burstall, Headmistress of the Manchester High School for Girls and President of the Head Mistresses' Association, moved that all school-leaving, matriculation and professional entrance examinations should include, as a compulsory subject, the outlines of British history up to the present, including such European history and geography as were essential to the understanding of history. She argued that the purpose of teaching history in schools was not that the pupils should learn history, but that they should receive a training in citizenship — which, since they were British citizens, they could not receive except by studying British history. This was too much for two professors — Grant of Leeds and Harte of Exeter. 'The man who had only knowledge of British history', the former declared, 'was a poor British subject indeed.' Harte thought that the teaching of European history 'need not undermine patriotism at all, but on the contrary put it on the right lines. We want to feel that our ideas with regard to England are the result of comparisons of the history of our country with that of other countries.' Grant's amendment, suggesting papers in ancient, European, or even social history in addition to British, did not receive much support. No doubt, the speakers in this debate addressed themselves to what they considered the pedagogic arguments, but few members present could have

17. J. Bryce, *The Teaching of History in Schools*, leaflet no. 4, London, 1907. Keith Robbins, 'History and Politics: the Career of James Bryce', *Journal of Contemporary History*, 7, nos. 3 & 4, (July–Oct 1972), pp. 37–52.
    18. G.T. Hankin, *The Teaching of Civics in Public Schools*, leaflet no. 15, London, 1909.
    19. Miss W. Mercier, *An Experiment in the Teaching of History*, leaflet no. 17, 1909.

been unaware of the wider implications of the topic.[20] Spenser Wilkinson, first holder of the Chichele Chair of the History of War at Oxford, addressed the seventh annual meeting in January 1913 on *Some Lessons of the War in the Balkans*. He asked whether, in the event of an Austrian and German war against Serbia (which would in turn receive French and Russian support), Great Britain could 'remain neutral consistently with her own self-respect and with the position she had hitherto held as a European Power. That was the issue which made it desirable that Englishmen should make up their minds while there was time regarding the country's duty to Europe and concerning the necessity of national organization for war.'[21]

It was not to be expected that the Historical Association could or should answer this question. The notion that the study of history could provide the state with the answer to pressing problems had received a devastating blow in the disputes in the mid eighties over Home Rule for Ireland. John Seeley, for example, wrote to his erstwhile friend Oscar Browning that in his view a Gladstonian Home Ruler was someone who had renounced all that was most certain and elementary in politics. Joint literary projects, which they had contemplated, would be impossible. More fundamentally, he had to admit that 'My favourite notion of making politics a matter of teaching seems to me to suffer a humiliating *reductio ad absurdum*, when two men who united in advocating it are led by their historical studies to adopt views of politics so extremely opposite . . .'[22] Fearing that 'the disruption of the Empire' might emanate from the Irish issue, Seeley still pinned his hopes upon imperial federation. Liberal Unionism was predominant among Cambridge historians — mentioning simply Creighton and Prothero. When the Historical Association was formed Liberal Imperialism was still a cause which engaged the emotions and energies of many historians of that generation and vintage.[23] The Balliol diaspora carried the same message from Oxford to the far-flung parts of the United Kingdom whither it went in search of history chairs in the new departments and universities of that period. Richard Lodge, professor at Edinburgh university, as soon as his academic duties ended for the year, as they happily did in April — a situation which no longer obtains — set off on speaking tours in Scotland on behalf of the Liberal League.[24] Imperialists and unionists, as far as I am able to judge, preponderated amongst the early vice-presidents and council of the Historical Association; nevertheless, it could not be supposed that 'history' only spoke through them on the concern of the present.

The outbreak of war in 1914, however, placed historians in a position of special importance, though it could not be claimed that as a breed they showed

20. *Proceedings of the Fifth Annual Meeting . . . 7 January, 1911*, leaflet no. 24, 1911.
21. *Report of the Seventh Annual Meeting . . . 10–11 January, 1913*, leaflet no. 31, 1913.
22. D. Wormell, *Sir John Seeley and the Uses of History* (Cambridge, 1980), p. 173.
23. H.C.G. Matthew, *The Liberal Imperialists* (Oxford, 1973).
24. M. Lodge, *Sir Richard Lodge* (Edinburgh, 1946).

any particular perspicacity in anticipating its outbreak. Sir George Prothero, for instance, had been on a tour of European capitals in May/June 1914 but did not find the atmosphere disturbing. It was only the Austrian ultimatum to Serbia in late July that alarmed him. He had no doubt that historians had a duty, as he put it in a letter to *The Times* on 20 August 1914, to explain in lectures and in print why Britain should join in 'a fight to a finish'.[25] The historians at Oxford swiftly engaged in extensive exercises of explanation in a well-known series of pamphlets. Lodge was given leave by the University of Edinburgh to engage in the organization for Scotland of the Prince of Wales's National Relief Fund. Twenty years earlier, in his inaugural lecture in Glasgow as the first Professor of History, he had claimed that the fundamental distinction between right and wrong survived all allowance for differences of age and climate and ethical ideals. There was no lesson which history so conclusively taught as that the only sound basis for national greatness was the character of the people and the advance of moral degradation was invariably followed by disaster and decline.[26] Such beliefs dictated his behaviour in 1914. Most prominent historians, even if they retained pleasant memories of Germany and individual Germans, were of like mind. G.M. Trevelyan, who felt on 28 July 1914 that the worst danger to the country was the possibility of following France to war — 'Our whole British civilisation may be made or marred by its decision' — wrote a week later that he supported the war 'not *merely* for our own survival but because I think a German victory will probably be the worst thing for Europe, at any rate in the West'.[27] His reservation about German expansion in the East was, in effect, expressed another way by the economic historian, John Clapham, when he wrote that, notwithstanding his support for intervention, he was a Teuton not a Slav.[28] Another future president of the association, G.P. Gooch, with a German wife and a warm appreciation of certain aspects of German culture, felt the crisis most acutely. It is reported that he could not do any work for months — a measure of his disturbance. Like many other academics Liberals he eventually resolved his dilemma by giving general support to the war substantially in the hope that some good could come of it, particularly for the nationalities of the Habsburg Monarchy.[29]

A world war so soon after its foundation naturally placed the Historical Association in some difficulty. Its membership dipped below the thousand mark under the impact of events. Even so, there was sufficient resilience and confidence to take the journal *History* into the hands of the association in

25. C.W. Crawley, 'Sir George Prothero and his Circle', *Transactions of the Royal Historical Society* (1970), pp. 122–3.
26. R. Lodge, *The Study of History in a Scottish University* (Glasgow, 1894).
27. M. Moorman, *George Macaulay Trevelyan* (London, 1980), p. 125.
28. Cited in H. Butterfield, 'Sir Edward Grey in July 1914' *Historical Studies*, v (1963).
29. F. Eyck, 'G.P. Gooch' in Laqueur and Mosse, ed., *Historians in Politics*, p. 179, and K.G. Robbins, 'Lord Bryce and the First World War', *Historical Journal*, x (1967), pp. 255–77: Ramsay Muir, *An Autobiography* (London, 1943), pp. 108–9.

1916. 'Our aim', stated Pollard, the first editor, 'is to bring the gods into contact with those men and women who have to save historical truth from sterility by propaganda.' He hoped 'to bring the light of history to bear in the study of politics, and to supply in some measure that notable void in British intellectual equipment, the absence of any review which systematically endeavours to link the past with the present and to test modern experiment by historical experience'. He added, significantly, that he hoped *History* would remain a means of communication and exchange of ideas between all parts of the King's dominions. The Tenth Annual Meeting in January 1916 began, again significantly, with a paper from Sir Charles Lucas on 'The Teaching of Imperial History' and the entire meeting was dominated by discussion of that topic and of naval history. With characteristic astringency, Pollard noted that if 'democratic control' were to be exercised over the navy with the existing level of popular ignorance then it would be political suicide. The Headmaster of St Peter's School, York (later to be Chairman of the Historical Association Council during G.M. Trevelyan's presidency in the years just after the Second World War) remarked that before the war teachers were inclined to treat British history merely as a school subject. However, it was clearly more than that: 'It should lay the foundation of the outlook upon national life.' Pollard was greatly relieved that the University of Cambridge saw the light and established the Vere Harmsworth Professorship of Naval History (which later added Imperial to its title). He hoped that other universities would soon follow its example. In early 1918, J.W. Headlam contributed an Open Letter to *History* on 'The Effect of the War on the Teaching of History', stressing the place of the Empire but also mentioning that American and European history was gaining in significance. Even so, he concluded, 'above all, we must always keep in our minds the history of England as a whole and the English nation from the early times, the development of the British Constitution and the character of British nationality'.

The ease with which Headlam moved from the 'history of England' and the 'English nation' to the 'British constitution' and the 'character of British nationality' was typical, but it did not go unchallenged. What was needed, Ramsay Muir argued, mindful of the fact that he had been Professor of History in Liverpool, 'was a treatment of British history which should not be merely a history of England, but should include Scotland and Ireland in an adequate way'; though at the same time treatment of British history should always keep in mind the ultimate result — the world-wide Commonwealth — 'and should reduce to due subordination all episodes which did not help to explain how that had come about'. Sidney Low regretted that students were not induced 'to pay attention to the history, not only of the British Empire, but even of the British Islands as a whole. They did not even learn in the true sense British history — they were so absorbed in the history of England that they had a very limited acquaintance even with that of Scotland and Ireland.' Pollard was happier returning to the view that the history of Great and Greater Britain were inseparable 'because Greater Britain is the completion and perfecting of Great Britain, and in Greater Britain Great Britain is realizing and expressing itself'.

In fact, history other than the history of England was making some progress. Lodge became the first president of the Historical Association of Scotland in 1911. It too concerned itself with trying to improve the meagre provision for history in Scottish schools but it also naturally concerned itself with the issue of Scottish history. 'A nationality that is not based on institutions but on sentimental and historical reminiscences', wrote Mackinnon, the first lecturer in History at St Andrews, 'can with difficulty continue to differentiate itself from that of the great nation with which we are united.'[30] The Fraser Chair was established in Edinburgh in 1901 in large measure in the belief, as a latter-day holder of that chair has put it, that 'History . . . undoubtedly helped to create the nation; and it is still history which maintains the identity of the nation'.[31] But Lodge (who forsook the foul fog of Glasgow for the cold winds of Edinburgh) has not invariably received an encomium for the syllabus he established in either Glasgow or Edinburgh. 'Academic history', Bruce Lenman writes, 'was primarily the corporate worship of the origins and development of the contemporary parliamentary establishment at Westminster . . .' Medley, Lodge's successor in Glasgow, strongly opposed the establishment of a Chair of Scottish History in the university. However, an exhibition of Scottish history, art and industry at Kelvingrove in 1911, designed to raise funds for the chair, was successful and led to his defeat.[32]

It was a singular circumstance — in view of events in Ireland in 1916 — that Pollard's successor as president of the association in 1915 was Alice Stopford Green. Her writings on Irish history were well-known and she strongly criticized the inattention given to Irish history on both sides of the Irish Sea. She attacked Trinity College, Dublin for its failure to give a living wage to an Irish historian.[33] It is worth noting too, in this connexion, that it was not until the 1930s that Irish history took a regular and formal place in the teaching of the History department at Queen's.[34]

Despite the fact that later in 1916 the United Kingdom was to acquire its first Welsh-speaking Prime Minister, that was no mention in the discussion of the history of Wales. The early connexions of the association with the principality were not strong. Sir Harry Reichel, Principal of the University College of North Wales, Bangor, was the only initial member of Council from Wales,

30. Cited in R.G. Cant, *The Writing of Scottish History in the Time of Andrew Lang* (Edinburgh, 1978).

31. G. Donaldson, *Scottish History and the Scottish Nation* (Edinburgh, 1964), p. 13.

32. B.P. Lenman, 'The Teaching of Scottish History and the Scottish Universities', *Scottish Historical Review*, 52 (1973), pp. 174–77.

33. Mrs J.R. Green at the Sixth Annual Meeting 1912. Leaflet no. 30, 1912. R.B. McDowell, *Alice Stopford Green: A Passionate Historian* (Dublin, 1967). In 1916, she took the drastic step of uprooting herself from London where she had lived for forty years and settling in Dublin. McDowell does not mention the Historical Association.

34. J.C. Beckett, *The Study of Irish History* (Belfast, 1963).

making way for the Professor of History there, Sir John Lloyd, in 1912. It is noteworthy, however, that T.F. Tout, second president of the Association, had been Professor of History at Lampeter from 1881 to 1890. That he took an interest in Welsh history can be judged by the fact that he wrote articles on no less than eighty-two Welsh personalities for the DNB. And A.G. Little, president 1926–29, went to Cardiff in 1892 and became the first Professor of History there in 1898. Attention has recently been drawn to the importance of his small book on medieval Wales. A Chair of Welsh History was established in Bangor in 1930 (though Lloyd can hardly be said to have neglected Welsh history) after a public controversy.[35]

At the close of war, therefore, two tendencies can be discerned in the Association. On the one hand, the stress upon the national past as an imperial past remained strong — *History* had stated during the war that 'the Historical Association knows no geographical limits less extensive than those of the British Empire' and branches were established after 1918 in Colombo, Rangoon, Pietermaritzburg and Montreal, amongst other cities. On the other hand, a letter in the first issue of *History* which urged that, in the light of the war, the rising generation should 'understand clearly the position in which we stand relatively to other European nations', represented a view that was gaining ground. A.J. Grant and G.P. Gooch, presidents 1920–23 and 1923–26 respectively, both happened to be modern historians with strong European interests. Gooch published a *History of Modern Europe, 1878–1919* in 1923. Grant and Temperley published their *Europe in the Nineteenth Century* in June 1927. Temperley was chairman of the Historical Association Publications Committee from 1924 to 1927. He and Gooch (described by the then Prime Minister Ramsay MacDonald as 'by far and away our ablest historian') were appointed to take charge of the publication of the British documents on the origins of the war. F.S. Marvin, energetic chairman of the significantly-named Propaganda Committee from 1918 to 1943 (with a brief intermission from 1929 to 1931 when he departed to be Professor of Modern and Contemporary History in the University of Egypt), was the persuasive editor of a series of volumes appearing during and just after the First World War. Their titles — *The Unity of Western Civilization; Progress and History; Recent Developments in European Thought;* and *The Evolution of World Peace* — give an indication of his purposes. In the last volume he published a paper by Eileen Power on 'The Teaching of History and World Peace' which argued that no child ought to leave school without knowing something of the history of the world; it is just as important that he should understand the place of his country within the larger whole of mankind, swept by great movements common at least to Europe, as that he should understand the place of Whigs and Tories in the politics of his country'. Talking a good deal about the League of Nations, she concluded that 'the only way to cure the evils which have arisen out of purely national

---

35. G.O. Pierce, *A Matter of Primary Urgency* (Cardiff, 1979).

history . . . is to promote a strong sense of the solidarity of mankind as such'.[36] In April 1929, *History* published R.W. Seton-Watson's Creighton Lecture, 'A Plea for the Study of Contemporary History', in which he stated that he was not so 'foolish as to plead for the enlistment of historians as mere propagandists of this or that campaign of pacifism or disarmament; but it is self-evident that they have a special function to perform in promoting that scientific study of recent times which is one of the essential foundations on which a new world and a new mentality must be constructed'. C.K. Webster, whose inaugural lecture as the first Stevenson Professor of International History at the LSE was published in *History* in July 1933, drew public attention to the stipulation in the trust deeds that the holders of the Stevenson Chairs should, so far as possible, eschew national bias.

This new emphasis was not without its critics. Before his death, Tout had some tart remarks to make about text-books being written from the stand-point of the League of Nations Union.[37] And, as the international situation deteriorated in the later 1930s, L.B. Namier and A.J.P. Taylor launched a fierce attack on the picture of Germany and on the origins of the First World War perpetrated by Gooch. For a foreigner, Sir Ronald Wingate wrote of Namier in 1919, 'his knowledge of history' was 'outstanding'.[38] Drawing upon the complexities of his own inheritance and experience, he found what passed for 'European' or 'League of Nations' history spurious and superficial. And, after war had broken out, *History* published in September 1940 a vigorous attack on the domination of historians who had become bemused by the League. J.D. Mackie, Professor of Scottish History in Glasgow, declared that 'It must have been obvious to all that although the "nation" was professedly the essential element of the League, some of the League's supporters preached an "internationalism" which was really "anti-nationalism"'. British historians should have done something 'to keep the nation in touch with reality'. Gavin Henderson, with a renewed plea for the study of contemporary history in June 1941, feared that historians were selling their birthright — the birthright won for them by Thucydides — for a mess of potage, for a quiet academic existence far from the madding crowd, for a reputation of amiability and absent-mindedness and general futility.

Perhaps, indeed, that is what we have settled for. At any rate, although *History* did publish in March 1946 a contribution from Arnold Toynbee arguing that national history was a comparatively recent field of study and that what was now needed was an approach which would enable world history to be viewed as a whole, the issues which I have been considering largely disappeared from the columns of *History*, although the nation state was a topic

36. F.S. Marvin, *The Evolution of World Peace* (London, 1921), pp. 181–82.

37. B.J. Elliott, 'The League of Nations Union and History Teaching in England: A study in Benevolent Bias', *History of Education* 6 (1977), pp. 131–41.

38. N. Rose, *Lewis Namier and Zionism* (Oxford, 1980), p. 12. C.J. Wrigley, *A.J.P. Taylor: A Complete Annotated Bibliography of his Historical and Other Writings* (Brighton, 1980), pp. 13–15.

central to Cobban's concerns. Decolonization after 1945 steadily rendered irrelevant that imperial theme which had once been dominant. Consideration of the League of Nations and the United Nations tempered the kind of enthusiasm among historians which was so evident in the 1920s. Perhaps, too, it engendered a certain scepticism about the value of the advice of even the best-informed diplomatic historian.[39] Although during the Second World War Butterfield had meditated fruitfully on 'The Englishman and his History' his presidency of the association twenty-five years ago did not see a development of this particular theme. *History* itself sounded a more severely 'professional' note in its articles and contributions. Its editors proved much more nervous about bringing the light of history to bear upon the politics of the present than Pollard would have thought likely. Whether the Historical Association should again consider what kind of national past is 'usable' in present circumstances may be contentious, but it can only do so in the light of its own history.

39. P.A. Reynolds and E.J. Hughes, *The Historian as Diplomat: Charles Kingsley Webster and the United Nations, 1939–1946* (London, 1976).

2

History, Historians and Twentieth-Century
British Public Life

'In these days every man is a citizen; he has a share in the responsibility, not only for local administration, but also for the government of a vast empire', declared the youthful Richard Lodge when he came from Oxford in 1894 to become Professor of History in the University of Glasgow. Many distinguished men over centuries in the university had concerned themselves in one way or another with historical enquiry, but it was not until this date that a Chair was formally established. 'A University', Lodge continued in his inaugural lecture, 'would be ill-advised which neglected the training of its students for the fitting discharge of their civic duties. And from this point of view the study of History is, I contend, of inestimable importance.'[1] He had made his reputation with a text book on *Modern Europe* and had jointly translated Bluntschli's *The Theory of the State*. The development of a theory of citizenship was a major preoccupation of Glasgow's moral philosophers of this time. What was now needed was the contribution which the study of History could provide.

The connexion between scholarship and public life was emphasized in Glasgow in 1897 by the election of Joseph Chamberlain, the Colonial Secretary, as Lord Rector of Glasgow University — the latest in a long line of major British politicians to hold this temporary office. And, two years later, on the outbreak of the South African War, Glasgow students could perhaps learn from their Rector some lessons on 'the fitting discharge of their civic duties'. Lodge himself moved to the Chair of History at the University of Edinburgh in 1899 and he did not hesitate to hide his Liberal Imperialist convictions. He took great interest in the development of the British Dominions overseas and ensured that the subject was fully taught in the syllabus. At the same time he delivered many lectures on naval history and the importance of seapower. He threw himself into the activities of the Liberal League in Scotland and soon found himself a welcome guest at Lord Rosebery's house at Dalmeny outside Edinburgh. The two men greatly enjoyed each other's company. The former Prime Minister's enthusiasm for studying history was well-known — his study of *Napoleon: The Last Phase* (1900) was much admired — and his brilliant speechmaking drew sustenance from historical analogy. The two men conversed deep into

1. M. Lodge, *Sir Richard Lodge: A Biography* (Edinburgh and London, 1946), p. 125.

the night shortly after the signing of the 1904 Anglo-French agreement (which Rosebery opposed). Afterwards, the Professor of History told his wife: 'If you had heard what Lord Rosebery has been prophesying about the future of Europe you would never sleep tonight.'[2]

This particular personal relationship between a former Prime Minister and a Professor of History was fortuitous, but it was not an exotic and peculiar Scottish development. Here was a Caledonian flourishing of the theme which J.R. Seeley had elaborated in his celebrated *The Expansion of England* (1883): that politics and history were only different aspects of the same study. There was 'a vulgar view of politics which sinks then into a mere struggle of interests and parties, and there is a foppish kind of history which aims only at literary display ... These perversions, according to me, come from an unnatural divorce between two subjects which belong to each other'. History had both to pursue a practical object and be scientific in its method. It was possible both to instruct the statesman and inspire the citizen. English history, he believed, 'instead of being valued as a stirring, or flattering, or romantic story, would become a source of the most potent practical influence, a principal and fundamental instrument of culture'. His view of the function of history in education can be summed up in the well-known phrase that it was 'a school of statesmanship'.[3]

The Rector of Glasgow University in 1897 had never been to a university himself but he was determined to lay the best possible educational foundations for his eldest son. Joseph Chamberlain wrote to Austen Chamberlain's housemaster at Rugby in 1882 that there was 'no doubt about the interest of the subjects included in the History Tripos and his work will not be thrown away in after life.'[4] Accordingly, Austen went up to Trinity College, Cambridge in that year to study history — though the young man also took a prominent part in under-graduate politics. Apparently, his historical studies did not extend in time beyond the Peace of Amiens of 1802 and his father then arranged for him to follow further lectures in Paris (amongst others from Sorel) and in Berlin. Austen Chamberlain was alarmed by what he understood of von Treitschke's lectures on Prussian history. There were, therefore, few other young men in the House of Commons when Austen Chamberlain was elected in 1892 who possessed such a good grounding in Modern History. It seemed obvious that Austen would become a statesman, whereas his younger half-brother Neville was sent to study commerce, metallurgy and engineering design and then despatched to develop sisal production in the obscurity of the Bahamas.

One other West Midlands industrialist had a son who went up to Trinity College, Cambridge in the mid 1880s. Stanley Baldwin quickly switched to the

2. Ibid., p. 168.
3. J.R. Seeley, *The Expansion of England*: D. Wormell, *Sir John Seeley and the Uses of History* (Cambridge, 1980).
4. D. Dutton, *Austen Chamberlain: Gentleman in Politics* (Bolton, 1985), p. 15.

study of History and gained a First Class in the First Part of the Tripos, but the quality of his work thereafter declined and he gained an undistinguished Third Class at the conclusion of his studies. He did not seem to take the school for statesmen very seriously and went back to the West Midlands to work in his father's iron business and, like Neville Chamberlain, study metallurgy in Birmingham. When he was elected to Parliament in 1908 there was no evidence that he had allowed himself to be bothered with the problems of statecraft which had troubled Seeley.

Austen Chamberlain's career made rapid progress. He was in Balfour's Cabinet in 1902 and became Chancellor of the Exchequer in the following year. When the Conservative government collapsed in December 1905 there were many who thought that Austen Chamberlain would be the man to lead them in the future. The Prime Minister, Balfour, exercised his mind by engaging in philosophical speculation, but his critics supposed that this led merely to an irritating capacity to see all sides to every question. Historians were at least supposed to reach conclusions.

Sir Henry Campbell-Bannerman, the incoming Prime Minister, had dabbled a little in Classics at Glasgow and Cambridge universities fifty years earlier, but he had never aspired to write historical essays of the brilliance achieved by his sulking rival Lord Rosebery. The new Cabinet did not contain a galaxy of historians. As a boy, Sir Edward Grey, the new Foreign Secretary, had received some lessons from the distinguished ecclesiastical historian Mandell Creighton but as an undergraduate at Balliol he had shown little interest in academic study. He obtained a very poor degree. Asquith's academic career, by contrast, had been brilliant but he had studied classical literature, history and philosophy. He and Haldane (a philosopher) had then proceeded to earn substantial incomes at the Bar. Lloyd George was a small-town lawyer who had never been to university.

There was, however, one man who did stand out as a remarkable scholar — James Bryce, the new Chief Secretary for Ireland.[5] His original academic distinction at Glasgow and Oxford had been in classical studies, but he then turned to that borderland between history, law and politics. He had served as Under-Secretary at the Foreign Office in 1886 and was subsequently the author of such well-known studies as *The American Commonwealth* (1888). There were many who supposed that his range of historical knowledge and first-hand experience — he was an inveterate traveller — ideally equipped him for the Foreign Office. He was a better pupil in the 'school for statesmen' than Sir Edward Grey — but he did not receive the appointment. Instead, in 1907 he went to Washington as British Ambassador and spent six successful years there. He remained throughout an obvious conduit between the academic and political worlds. He took a keen interest in the newly-formed Historical

5. K.G. Robbins, 'History and Politics: the Career of James Bryce' in W. Laqueur and G.L. Mosse, ed. *Historians in Politics* (London, 1974), pp. 113–129.

Association and, prior to leaving for America, remarked that in his judgement the organization of historical studies in Britain was 'incomparably better and more promising than that which prevailed half a century ago'. On his return from America, he was the obvious man to address the International Congress of Historical Studies when it met in London in 1913. As a result of his own extensive travels, he was convinced that world history was becoming one history. Historians could play their part in this process because they knew how few wars had been necessary wars. They also knew that all great people had both characteristic merits and characteristic faults.[6]

The expansion of history as an academic discipline over the previous few decades had been remarkable. There was scarcely a university left which was without a Chair of History and political history occupied a dominant place in history syllabi. There was much talk about the virtues of intellectual detachment as the essential element in historical enquiry.

Then came August 1914. Within six weeks, the Clarendon Press published *Why We Are At War: Great Britain's Case* by a group of Oxford historians. 'We are not politicians', they declared, '. . . We have some experience in the handling of historic evidence and we have endeavoured to treat the subject historically.' They were subsequently joined by the many contributors to the long series of *Oxford Pamphlets* on the war. Of course, this was not merely an Oxford enthusiasm. Professors of History rushed into print throughout the country and they invariably asserted their professional integrity. 'Despite the difficulty of maintaining an attitude of aloofness and impartiality during a great war', wrote Professor Ramsay Muir lately of Liverpool and newly of Manchester, "I have honestly tried . . . to see the facts plainly, and never to tamper with them." Such an intention did not prevent him from suggesting that Alaric's sack of Rome faded into insignificance beside the bombardment of Louvain. The title of his study, *Britain's Case against Germany* (1914) indicates that he was still some distance from accepting the venerable A.V. Dicey's advice 'to look upon the war from something like the point of view from which it will be regarded by a fair-minded historian writing in A.D. 2000'. Certainly, Dicey's friend R.S. Rait, Professor of Scottish History at Glasgow, used his expertise in this field to explain *Why We Are Fighting Germany: A Village Lecture* (1914). It was clear to him that 'Germany's real aim is to seize not French colonies and dependencies, but British colonies and dependencies'. His colleague Professor Dudley Medley explained *Why Britain Fights* (1914) with a little more circumspection. Indeed, the willingness (and apparently the ability) of all these new professors to explain what the war was about and why it was so necessary to fight was most impressive.

It is easy, as a fair-minded historian writing in the 1990s, if not in 2000, to be scornful of the crude simplicity of some of these comments and it has not been difficult for some writers to do so. Yet there did still remain a pervasive

6. See above, pp. 1–14.

sense of an inescapable duty 'to see the facts plainly' but it was combined with a perceived need to perform a public social function. So much had been said over the previous few decades about the utility of history that a professional silence at such a crisis would have been inconceivable. There was a need for an explanation and historians had to supply it or forfeit their claim to credibility. In his inaugural lecture in 1915, 'The Study of Nineteenth Century Diplomacy' C.K. Webster nevertheless argued for what he termed 'enlightened patriotism'. He considered that there had been some public acceptance of the view that historians best served the interests of their country if they tried only to serve the interests of truth. False ideals of patriotism might make that difficult in wartime but even so, it was better that it should be done badly than not at all: 'The difficulty increases indeed the responsibility of the historians of every country.'[7]

But where did 'enlightened patriotism' begin and end? It seemed most unlikely that historians would stay quietly in their studies for the duration of the conflict. Professor Lodge of Edinburgh immersed himself immediately in a range of public activities which earned him a knighthood. His predecessor, G.W. Prothero, now editor of the *Quarterly Review* wrote to *The Times* on 20 August 1914 expressing the view that large and influential sections of the population did not regard the war with whole-hearted approval, or indeed, approval at all. They clearly needed to be enlightened without delay. To put it at its lowest, historians could provide the public with necessary information on Belgium and Serbia. And there were unexpected young men like L.B. Namier who knew facts about obscure areas of Central Europe. There were places for historians in Admiralty Intelligence (Wickham Legg, R.B. Mowat); War Office Intelligence (R.G.D. Laffan, K. Pickthorn, B.H. Sumner, H. Temperley, C.K. Webster); War Trade Intelligence Department (H.W.C. Davis, F.M. Powicke, R.S. Rait, W.T. Waugh); and, in various other capacities, for Z.N. Brooke, G. Butler, C. Oman and J.H. Clapham — and that list is not exhaustive[8]. G.P. Gooch's very considerable erudition was put to limited use. His specific war service consisted in preparing handbooks for the Historical Section of the Foreign Office on matters which might be useful for the eventual peace negotiations. He dealt with French claims in the Levant and contributed to a brochure on the Anglo-French condominium in the New Hebrides[9]. Other historians with passionate interests in particular parts of Europe saw their opportunity. R.W. Seton-Watson, for example, threw himself into his periodical *The New Europe*[10]. Historians tended to think they

7. K. Hamilton, 'The Pursuit of "Enlightened Patriotism". The British Foreign Office and Historical Researchers during the Great War and its Aftermath', *Historical Research*, lxi (1988), pp. 316–344.

8. See the chapter 'Historians and the War' and pp. 238–40 in S. Wallace, *War and the Image of Germany: British Academics, 1914–1918* (Edinburgh, 1988).

9. F. Eyck, *G.P. Gooch: A Study in History and Politics* (London, 1982), p. 261.

10. H. and C. Seton-Watson, *The Making of a New Europe: R.W. Seton-Watson and the Last Years of Austria-Hungary* (London, 1981).

were too important to be called up to fight. Gooch congratulated Seton-Watson on his transfer to the Intelligence Bureau in these terms: 'I am so glad you after all escaped what I call the body-snatchers, and are still able to utilize your gifts and knowledge'. In the spring of 1915 G.M. Trevelyan used his gifts in a lecture tour in American universities about Serbia. 'It was not an attempt to enlist American support for the European War with Germany', declared his daughter, "for America was still neutral . . . and it was necessary still to avoid anything like propaganda for our own cause."[11] This disclaimer is not very convincing.

This list of activities engaged in by historians is not meant to be exhaustive, but it does reflect a professional consensus. British historians, with remarkably few exceptions, experienced no conflict between their conception of themselves as 'professionals' with austere standards of evidence and their commitment to a 'public service' role for themselves and their subject. The *Bryce Report* of May 1915, however, is an example of the latent tension (if not open conflict) between these two aspirations. In December 1914 the Liberal government appointed a committee to investigate charges that German soldiers, either directed or condoned by their officers, had committed atrocities in Belgium. Lord Bryce agreed to chair the committee and his academic and personal reputation seemed guaranteed to ensure a fair enquiry. Indeed, in June 1915, Bryce was told by C.F.G. Masterman, who was responsible for British propaganda, that the report had swept America: 'As you probably know even the most sceptical declare themselves converted, just because it is signed by you.' Bryce had initially found it difficult to support British intervention in the war and he could certainly not be described as a 'jingo'. The violation of Belgian neutrality had been of crucial importance in his own support for the war. It was apparent, therefore, that anything which highlighted German behaviour in Belgium was ripe for exploitation. There were many tales in circulation which purported to tell of German outrages against Belgian civilians. Confirmation that they were true would undoubtedly strengthen the British case — but it was equally the case that scepticism about them would weaken the moral appeal which Belgium had. Consciousness of this dilemma led most members of the committee and its chairman to seek to avoid verifying the evidence. Bryce himself neither confronted nor cross-examined the persons upon whose unsworn statements he was prepared to convict Germany of unparalleled 'Murder, lust and pillage' in time of war. Other evidence suggests, on the other hand, that he did not consciously intend to deceive. The most recent investigation of the affair concludes that 'Bryce did not have the choice of telling the truth or telling falsehood. If he proved so scrupulous in his investigations that he might have to deem the tales of sadistic crimes unproven, then — inadvertently but inescapably — he would be helping to propagate a much larger untruth:

11. M. Moorman, *George Macaulay Trevelyan* (London, 1980), pp. 134–135.

that the whole notion of deliberate and calculated atrocity by Germany upon Belgium was unfounded.'[12]

Work for the Bryce Committee proved to be a further step in the temporary transmogrification of H.A.L. Fisher from historian to Cabinet Minister. At the outbreak of war he had just left Oxford, where he had been lecturing on 'Foreign History', to become Vice-Chancellor of Sheffield University. He was the historian amongst the lawyers on the Bryce Committee and his work in this respect was noted with approval. By the autumn of 1916 he was attending Lloyd George's famous breakfast parties and was making wise suggestions for the future of Europe at the end of the war to ears that he thought were receptive. At Winchester, where he had been at school, he had won the Queen's Medal for an English essay on 'The Insular Position of Great Britain' and he had been Edward Grey's 'fag' before proceeding to Oxford and academic distinction in classical philosophy before switching to History and further studies in Paris and Göttingen. He too took a broad view of the mission of the historian and his only consolation for the fact that he was not successful in his application to become Professor of History at Glasgow in 1894 was his suspicion that the electors took 'a narrow and illiberal view of the requirements of historical study'. By 1916 it was not the Foreign Secretary, his ailing erstwhile schoolmate Grey, but the unlettered Lloyd George to whom he attached himself. In turn, in December 1916, the new Prime Minister brought Fisher into the Cabinet as President of the Board of Education. His particular brief was educational reform — which led to the Education Act of 1918. However, at least in the eyes of his biographer, the Prime Minister found Fisher a mine of information about Europe and foreign affairs. Lloyd George, allegedly, was somewhat shy of brilliant products of Balliol and Cambridge, such as Balfour and Curzon, and took to his heart Fisher, the humane humanist. For his part, Fisher admired the vision and energy of a great national leader and relished the unexpected role he had come to play in affairs. His *Studies in History and Politics* (1920) had begun life as donnish pieces, but they had been embellished in odd moments of leisure snatched by a Minister of the Crown.[13]

In general, therefore, academic historians might be numbered among the 'hard-faced' men who had done well out of the war. It took many of them into spheres of activity in which they would not otherwise have operated. Some of them never returned to the routines of academic life. Others who did, for example H.W.C. Davis, had become convinced of the importance of modern history and shifted away from their former specialization in medieval studies. Ramsay Muir lasted as a Professor of History until 1921, but then decided, in his fifties, to embark on a political career with the decaying

12. T. Wilson, 'Lord Bryce's Investigation into Alleged German Atrocities in Belgium, 1914/15', *Journal of Contemporary History*, 14 (1979), pp. 369–383.

13. H. Fisher, *Studies in History and Politics* (Oxford, 1920): D. Ogg, *Herbert Fisher, 1865–1940* (London, 1947).

Liberal Party. It was not successful. Bryce died in ripe old age in 1922 and his place in public life as historian/politician was taken by Herbert Fisher who returned to Oxford as Warden of New College — and, amongst other things, wrote a two-volume biography of Bryce. Yet Fisher could not quite take Bryce's place. The latter's last book *Modern Democracies* (1921) showed considerable pessimism about the values which would inform societies in the post-war world. Would there still be a public role for historians?

There was a certain irony too, in the fact that politicians themselves now began to present themselves before the public as historians, at least insofar as they were under pressure, which they showed little disposition to resist, to publish their memoirs, particularly concerning the Great War. Few of the leading politicians showed any desire to hand over this entire task to professional or academic historians. Edward Grey was helped by the journalist J.A. Spender but retained control over the enterprise. So did Winston Churchill, who did not need to be convinced of his own skill as a writer and historian. It was Lloyd George, however, who proved to be the supreme impressario. The project of his *War Memoirs* was controversial from the outset. It was a task which eventually took six volumes and a million words. He had considerable assistance from military historians, particularly from E.D. Swinton and B.H. Liddell Hart, but he was not inclined to hand over the grand strategy of the volumes to professional historians. Indeed, the latter records one occasion in which Lloyd George shouted 'Who's writing these memoirs — you or I?' Even so, it is not altogether easy to disentangle precisely who wrote what. There can be little doubt, however, that the *War Memoirs* had a major impact on British political opinion in the mid and late 1930s. Each volume was very widely reviewed. However, reviewers were not agreed on whether the result was 'history' or 'polemical pamphleteering'. *The Times* on 27 November 1934 gave prominence to a critique by Harold Temperley which claimed to have discovered serious historical defects. It had to be admitted, however, that the former Prime Minister displayed great brilliance in his characterization. He possessed great power of discernment and verbal organization; his literary skill exceeded that of many historians, though they were reluctant to admit it. Somewhat to the consternation of the 'professionals', it was a man totally without a university training in history who seemed to put historians in their place[14].

After the First World War, therefore, it became clear that academic excellence in the 'school for statesmen' by no means guaranteed that historians would become statesmen. Members of Parliament who had undertaken a serious academic study of history were not very conspicuous in the higher reaches of post-war British politics dominated, at least for a time, by Lloyd George and Bonar Law. The rise of the Labour Party in turn saw the emergence

14. G.W. Egerton, 'The Lloyd George *War Memoirs*: A Study in the Politics of Memory', *Journal of Modern History*, 80 (1988), pp. 55–94.

of Ramsay MacDonald and Arthur Henderson. They were undoubtedly intelligent but they did not have a History degree to instil statesmanship into them! They had to manage as best they could without its famed advantages. It was also the case that the academic brilliance of Lord Curzon did him no good in the contest for the premiership and it was Baldwin (who had done shown little interest in remedying his poor Cambridge Final History Tripos in the interval since graduation), who became Conservative Prime Minister in May 1923. On the other hand, it could be argued that Austen Chamberlain, during his tenure of the Foreign Office from 1924 to 1929 did put to effective use the knowledge of modern European history which he had acquired at Cambridge and subsequently. It is, of course, easy to exaggerate the extent to which his foreign policy was 'European' in orientation but he had an unusual grasp of underlying European realities for a British politician — which may conceivably be attributed to his historical training. And, when he became Foreign Secretary in 1935, there were some who supposed that Sir Samuel Hoare would similarly show the advantages of a training in academic history. Thirty years earlier, he had been a pupil of H.A.L. Fisher at New College, Oxford, and had taken a First in History — having previously gained a First in Classics[15]. Instead, within a short time, he had to resign because the 'Hoare-Laval Pact' which aspired to find a solution to the Abyssinian crisis produced a public outcry. Anthony Eden, his successor, who had studied Persian Language and Literature at Oxford, might survive rather longer.

In any case, the political ascendancy rested with Neville Chamberlain who had not been groomed by his father with appropriate historical studies. It should not be supposed, however, that he was indifferent or hostile to the work of historians. Catherine Cline has recently argued that most British historians by the later 1920s had come to the conclusion that responsibility for the war of 1914 could not be placed uniquely upon Germany and they advocated a revision of the Versailles peace settlement. G.P. Gooch — who enjoyed a close relationship with Ramsay MacDonald — was particularly influential in this respect. After 1933 he was not sympathetic to Nazism, but was still arguing in 1937 that it would be a great mistake to resist Hitler's territorial demands. By this date, however, other historians with rather different sympathies, notably R.W. Seton-Watson, were drawing different conclusions. It has been noted indeed that at time historians dominated the correspondence columns of leading newspapers[16]. Prominent among these contributors was Harold Temperley, now Master of Peterhouse, Cambridge and author, amongst other works, of *The Foreign Policy of Canning*. In a letter to *The Times* on 27 August 1937 he argued that study of Castlereagh's

---

15. J.A. Cross, *Sir Samuel Hoare: A Political Biography* (London, 1977), pp. 5–6. It is a little difficult, in the light of this information, to understand A.L. Rowse's comments in *All Souls and Appeasement* (London, 1961) that the appeasers had 'no knowledge of Europe, its history or its languages . . .', pp. 19–20.

16. C.A. Cline, 'British Historians and the Treaty of Versailles', *Albion* (1988).

European policy, followed by an examination of Canning's, offered great insight into contemporary circumstances. In July 1938 he drew attention, in a further letter to the newspaper, to a close parallel between words recently spoken by Chamberlain and some uttered a century earlier by Canning. He followed it up by sending a copy of his book directly to the Prime Minister who promised to read it. In early September 1938 he wrote to the author confessing that he had not hitherto studied much history but stating that he drew great 'encouragement and fortification' from the fact that ideas which he had arrived at empirically had also underpinned the thinking of such a great man. John D. Fair, who has written on the relationship between politician and historian at this critical juncture, argues that Chamberlain drew considerable encouragement from the weighty advice of a distinguished Cambridge historian. Needless to say, some of Temperley's Cambridge historian colleagues were less impressed by the historical analogies that were being so assiduously drawn.[17] In any event, it does not seem that the Foreign Secretary was drawn into the historical debate — though he was a historian by training. It was back in 1903 that Edward Wood (as Lord Halifax then was) gained a First in History at Oxford. His father was delighted, having written to his son some years earlier in these terms: 'You know when you are big you are to get a First Class in History at Oxford and do all sorts of grand things.'[18] It is true that in September 1938 he did occasionally have reservations about the Prime Minister's policy, but those reservations did not appear to rest on historical analogy.

The Prime Minister's principal domestic political opponent at the time of Munich was more than an occasional reader of volumes by Cambridge historians. Winston Churchill wrote history. Indeed, speaking of Neville Chamberlain, he said: 'History will judge him harshly; I know, because I shall write it.' He published the life of his ancestor Marlborough in four volumes between 1933 and 1935. He employed a research assistant on this task and corresponded with professional historians. He felt he had something to tell them as well as receive from them. 'One of the most misleading factors in history', he wrote to L.B. Namier, 'is the practice of historians to build a story exclusively out of the records which have come down to them.' These records constituted only a very small part of what took place and he felt that he could visualize how leading men of affairs actually passed their time with more authority than many historians who had little personal experience of high politics. In the later 1930s, out of office, Churchill turned his attention, largely for financial reasons, to writing, *The History of the English-Speaking Peoples*. To some extent, it seemed another maverick enterprise — the historical swansong of a failed politician. Professional historians again gave him some

---

17. John D. Fair, 'The Chamberlain-Temperley Connections; Munich's Historical Dimension', *The Historian*, 48 (1985), pp. 1–38. Peter Fraser, 'Cabinet Secrecy and War Memoirs', *History* (October 1985), pp. 397–409.
18. The Earl of Birkenhead, *Halifax: The Life of Lord Halifax* (London 1965), p. 49.

assistance, but the vision of the English past was Churchill's own, reflecting, as Sir John Plumb has noted, his conviction that 'English history was a progression, a development of inherent national characteristics, a process whereby the Englishman's love of liberty, freedom, and justice gradually, by trial and error, discovered those institutions of government which were apt to his nature'. In 1939 Churchill was fully aware that the concept of the work he had in mind 'has a current application'. Of course, it was a view of the past which was intensely usable and, as Plumb puts it, 'Churchill used it constantly'. His conflict with Chamberlain stemmed from a deep conviction that the policy of appeasement was a denial of England's historical destiny. Hitler should study English history and realize the nature of the opponent he would face.[19]

It was this man, with his vivid but idiosyncratic view of English history, who became Prime Minister in 1940 at the moment of supreme national crisis. He was himself a living embodiment of English tradition. He was both 'making history' and reflecting the essential character of England, as he perceived it. His sense of continuity sustained him in dark days. He nourished himself and the British people on the remarkable achievements of 'our island race'. It was not that a sense of the past provided particular and specific guidance in the present. Rather, his historical consciousness reinforced his sense of mission and provided the essential context for all decisions, implicitly or explicitly. These were glorious and tragic days in which past and present overlapped. Churchill orchestrated that sense in splendid words and phrases, though even at the time of their impressive delivery there was a certain archaic quality about them.

His defeat in the General Election of 1945 provided Churchill with time and space to embark on his *The Second World War* which was to appear in six volumes between 1948 and 1954. For the first he was awarded the Nobel Prize for Literature. In the initial preface he was careful to claim that what he was writing was not history, for that belonged to another generation, but he vigorously asserted that it was a contribution to history. So it has remained. It is not difficult, at this juncture, to point to certain shortcomings, nevertheless it remains a distinctive work of participatory history. The Second World War had of course interfered with the *History of the English-Speaking Peoples* and, much revised, it began to appear in 1956 and was a considerable commercial success.

Even so, it is possible to argue that Churchill's entire oeuvre represented the end of a tradition. *The History of the English-Speaking Peoples* was a remarkable achievement but, as Plumb puts it, 'it was like an apparition from the nineteenth or early twentieth century'. Churchill had consulted historians

---

19. M. Gilbert, 'Winston Churchill', in J. Cannon, R.H.C. Davis, W. Doyle, and J.P. Greene, ed., *The Blackwell Dictionary of Historians* (Oxford, 1988), pp. 79–81: 'Churchill', in J.H. Plumb, *The Making of an Historian: The Collected Essays of J.H. Plumb* (New York and London, 1988), pp. 225–242.

on points of detail but it was not a work which reflected contemporary historiography as it was perceived by 'professionals'. And it was not only the past which Churchill served which died with him. No one in the mainstream of British politics sought to emulate him and professional historians wrapped themselves ever more closely in the cloak of their own professional organizations and concerns. Attlee, Churchill's immediate successor as Prime Minister in 1945, had read History at Oxford, but he was not a man to express himself at length on broad historical topics, or indeed on anything. No subsequent British Prime Minister could be described as a historian by academic background, though R.A. Butler came close. That is not to say that there have not been individuals who have been prominent in British politics who have been interested in history and, in some instances, written monographs or historical biography. Perhaps the most conspicuous example is Lord Jenkins of Hillhead (Roy Jenkins) but he has himself commented in an essay on the decline of the historian/politician in post-1945 British politics.

In conclusion, three inter-linked reasons may be advanced for this state of affairs. Firstly, it has increasingly come to be argued that if politicians can be held to benefit from expertise in a particular academic discipline that discipline should be Political Science itself or Political Economy broadly conceived. It was the Oxford school of Politics, Philosophy and Economics — itself a new degree of the inter-war period — which trained Harold Wilson and Edward Heath, not the school of History. James Callaghan did not go to university, but it was in politics and economics that he sought to school himself. Mrs Thatcher, too, schooled herself in these disciplines and was the first British Prime Minister to graduate in a science subject (chemistry). None of these Prime Ministers has studied history in a sustained or systematic fashion.[20] Secondly, the fragmentation of 'history' as an academic discipline in Britain since 1945 had seen the emergence or consolidation of research emphases which have often taken students and their teachers far away from the political/constitutional framework which once constituted the core of the subject. Historians themselves have shown little desire to recruit readers or students on the grounds that their subject was indeed particularly useful as a school for statesmanship or citizenship. Finally, the historical experience of Britain since 1945 has inexorably eroded many of the assumptions about the character of British history and of Britain's place in the world which could still inform the writing of Churchill. In these circumstances, the extent to which historians *qua* historians should seek to play a serious role in public life has become contentious and controversial; but, on further reflection, perhaps it always has been.

20. Keith Robbins, ed., *The Blackwell Biographical Dictionary of British Political Life in the Twentieth Century* (Oxford, 1990).

3

National Identity and History: Past, Present and Future

The present condition of 'Europe' has produced a crisis of historiography which matches the tensions and opportunities of the continent. We seem to be confronted by two tendencies which may or may not, be in conflict. Historians find themselves drawn into debate and political prominence, sometimes against their inclination and better judgement. They have been forced again to wrestle with their interpretation of the past, their own status and activity in the present, and their own hopes for the future.

On the one hand, in the laborious, protracted and still problematic creation and extension of the 'European Community' we have witnessed over three decades the gradual establishment of a structure which has no precise parallel in European history. This is not the place to attempt to describe that structure precisely; suffice it to say that its definition goes beyond many of the terms habitually employed by historians and political scientists. It is, at present, *sui generis*; a 'community' which is something more than the sum of its parts but which is not yet, and may never be, a state capable of evoking the kind of loyalty which nation-states have been able to rely on in the past. It is a 'community' whose identity is uncertain and precarious.

On the other hand, alongside this process of integration we find the continuing assertion of an identity which is national and which shows little sign of disappearing. Indeed, 'Europe' may offer some 'nations' an opportunity to assert a national identity which is undervalued, ignored or suppressed by the existing state structures. The Scottish National Party, for example, now wishes to campaign under the slogan 'Scotland in Europe' and has retreated from its previous hostility to the Community. In Eastern Europe and what was the Soviet Union, it scarcely needs to be said that 'national' problems constantly grow in frequency and gravity in the Baltic republics, Moldavia, Armenia, Bulgaria, Yugoslavia and elsewhere. The notion that the 'Age of Nationalism', so beloved of textbook writers, came to an end in 1945 seems at least premature.

It is difficult, therefore, to escape the problem of 'identity' in contemporary Europe, and in this situation historians in particular often find themselves with 'divided loyalties'. They can find themselves torn between their sense of individual and professional integrity on the one hand, and the expectations and demands of the society which pays them on the other, a society which has certain expectations of what a historian should be doing.

It has come to be accepted, generally, that academic historians are indeed 'professionals'. The value placed upon their activities fluctuates from country to country, and so do their numbers and the precise conditions of their employment. 'Professionalization' has manifested itself in many forms in this century, particularly since 1945. Historical journals devoted to particular specialisms have mushroomed and specialist societies have proliferated. Various forms of 'new history' have come, and some have gone. Certain methodological approaches have been dominant in particular countries — the influence of the *Annales* school in France, for example — but they have rarely remained within national professional boundaries. The International Historical Congress, held every five years, most often in Europe, has become, in the words of its historian, the 'Oekumene' of historians. It has in turn been accompanied by a plethora of international professional gatherings and conferences as travel has become easier and finance sometimes more plentiful. At this level, it is possible to speak of the 'internationalization' of history.[1]

Such internationalization might, however, have been restricted to a purely organizational level. It has, however, gone deeper than that. We have witnessed what Paul Kennedy has described as the decline of nationalistic historiography in the West.[2] That is to say, the assumption that a historian of a particular nationality had a responsibility, which often accorded with inclination, to present the history of his country in a particularly favourable light, has diminished. Historians used to talk intimately of 'our country' rather than of 'British' or 'French' history in the impersonal and detached fashion that is now common. 'National' history perhaps found its apotheosis in the First World War, though it was still commonplace in the inter-war years.[3] In Britain, however, there was a strong reaction against the 'patriotic' role played by some British historians during that conflict. Indeed, it has recently been argued that British historians played a major role in undermining the initial public approval of the Treaty of Versailles by arguing that 'war guilt' could not in fact be placed exclusively on Germany.[4] Certain historical works — Taylor's *Course of German History* among them — were influential in creating during the Second World War a view of the German past which had a bearing on post-war planning, though their authors did not specifically set out to be 'patriotic' in their interpretations.[5]

1. K.D. Erdmann, *Die Oekumene der Historiker: Geschichte der internationalen Histor-ikerkongresse und des Comité International des Sciences Historiques* (Göttingen, 1987); Akira Iriye, 'The Internationalization of History', *American Historical Review*, xciv (February, 1989).

2. P.M. Kennedy, 'The Decline of Nationalistic History in the West, 1900–1970', in W. Laqueur and G.L. Mosse, ed., *Historians in Politics* (1974), pp. 329–52.

3. S. Wallace, *War and the Image of Germany: British Academics, 1914–1918* (Edinburgh, 1988).

4. C.A. Cline, 'British Historians and the Treaty of Versailles', *Albion*, xx (Spring 1988).

5. D. Cameron Watt, 'Every War Must End: War-time Planning for Post-War Security in Britain and America in the Wars of 1914–18 and 1939–45. The Roles of Historical Example and of Professional Historians', *Transactions of the Royal Historical Society*, 5th ser., xxviii (1978), pp. 169–70.

The nature of the Second World War accelerated these historiographical trends. After 1945, German historians neither desired nor were able to defend their country's action in 1939 after the manner in which a previous German generation had been able to defend 1914. To some extent the onset of the Cold War did freeze historians into 'Western' or 'Eastern' camps, but not completely. Differences of interpretation reflected ideological rather than national predilections. The return of Western European prosperity enabled research to take place across national frontiers on an ever-increasing scale, though it was only the West German historical community, with government support, which was able specifically to establish historical institutes in major centres abroad — London, Paris, Rome, Washington. Such institutes, by their very presence, promoted historical dialogue. They were the expression of a desire for enhanced mutual understanding as part both of the process of reconciliation and of 'building Europe'. A further symbol of this desire within the Community was the establishment of the European University Institute at Florence. Another example was the pioneering work undertaken at Brunswick into 'bias' in textbooks. The integration of the 'community of historians', therefore, was both an expression of, and a contribution towards, greater European unity.

Inevitably, however, this process of mutual exchange and communication has been partial and, in some respects, superficial. One of the drawbacks in the 'professionalization' of history has been a tendency, more marked in some countries and in certain quarters than others, for historians to be content merely to review each other's books and articles in an ever-diminishing circle of attention. Subsidies from government or private foundations have permitted the production of volumes with a substance and in a style that only professional historians could digest. There is nothing in itself surprising about the professionalization of historical study; it has been paralleled in many other disciplines. In the case of history, however, its subject-matter is to some degree or other of universal interest. It is not in principle arcane or remote. Other non-academic writers have continued to produce history books and, indeed, to regard their activities as full-time, whereas academics are merely part-time authors. Such writers may actively see themselves as rivals or merely set out to communicate to that wider audience neglected or despised by more austere scholars. In turn, 'the people' have wanted a kind of history, even if it is not the variety which professional historians think they ought to have. The social function of historians has become uncertain in this context of 'denationalization' and 'professionalization'.

There has also been much agonizing, in Britain and elsewhere, about the nature of history itself and the purpose of historical enquiry. An attempt at 'total' history entailed the rescue of individuals and groups who had been overlooked by a condescending posterity. Some writers believed that they had discerned the wave of the future and were happily riding along on its crest. Other historians, however, were only too eager to dismiss the notion that history was a school for statesmen. In their view it offered no guidance and afforded no vision of the future. In other quarters, on the contrary, history became quite meaningless if its students drifted aimlessly through time and space without any sense of development or location, at least for a while, in particular places. Meanwhile, a not inconsiderable section of the population distanced itself from history altogether. An obsession with the past, supposedly encouraged by historians, stood in the way of 'modernization' and change. As the pace of change itself accelerated in the post-1945 world, 'lessons from the past' seemed more and more implausible. 'The past' simply got in the way of what the future would be. It was lumber to be discarded.

It is in such a context that we turn to the present. It is now a commonplace to find articles and books throughout the continent that wrestle with the issue of 'identity', usually inconclusively. 'Europe seeks identity for new political age' is the kind of headline to be found in newspapers across Europe.[6] Historians have again turned their attention to the problem of seeking to define Europe — at a time when the speed and scale of change in Eastern Europe offers a perspective which has not been available for decades. Before the collapse of the Soviet Union, Gorbachev spoke of 'our common European homeland', whatever that might mean. Developments throughout Central and Eastern Europe, in different ways, entail a fundamental reconsideration of the European state system as it has existed since 1945.

In such exciting but potentially dangerous times historians can find them-selves in exposed and difficult positions. There may be some, but not many, amongst their number who have an unreconstructed enthusiasm for nationalism and who relish the chronicling of national liberation and the refurbishment of national myths. Most, one suspects, particularly those drawn from the increasingly influential generation of historians who have no personal memory of the Second World War, have become too 'internationalized' by professional formation and personal inclination to wish to become 'autarkic' once again. On the other hand, what constitutes the essence of European history remains contentious and unclear. European history may be more than the sum of its parts, but it cannot be built except by studying those parts in their full idiosyncrasy. Historians cannot be used to provide a simple usable pedigree for the present membership of the European Community, much less to suppose that it represents the inevitable climax of all European history. It seems that we are reaching a state at which we cannot be content with national history, but 'pan-European' history, in which all members' national histories are on a par, for didactic or research purposes, is not easily achieved. Historians from member-countries of the Community, and beyond, can only approach 'Europe' from the perspective of their own personal and national experience.

It is not surprising, therefore, that in country after country we find an emphasis on the particular which only links uneasily with an awareness of the general. In his old age, with a ripe understanding of the links and patterns

---

6. See the discussion in William Wallace, *The Transformation of Western Europe* (London, 1990) and the collection of papers he has edited, *The Dynamics of European Integration* (London, 1990).

of the Mediterranean world about which he had written with such brilliance and perspicacity, Fernand Braudel turned to examining the identity of France in what were intended to be four volumes. In the event, he completed two, the first of which has recently been translated into English.[7] It is clear, however, that even Braudel has not been able to distil the essence of France. There are many Frances, and indeed many Burgundies, Provences, Lorraines etc. We learn, perhaps without great surprise, that France is a country of diversity and that conventional criteria, such as 'natural' boundaries or language, do not explain the 'unity' of France. Braudel has not been alone in this concern with French identity, as studies by Pierre Chaunu and other historians in France and abroad demonstrate.[8] It is also problematic whether an investigation of French identity must restrict itself to the current territory of European France. France *outre-mer* may be marginal, but it does exist. Does *une certaine idée de la France* entail a continuing vision of a *monde francophone* from Quebec to the Ivory Coast? And there is also the continuing significance of the Algerian past, both in respect of French colonists reabsorbed into metropolitan France, and of the Algerian community in contemporary France. Even so, to outsiders it can appear that 'The French image of their history does not change; the slogans, eras, names and assessments are immovable, a sedimentary rock in the collective consciousness upon which unity and identity are founded.'[9]

In comparison with 'Germany', French identity seems confident and straightforward. In the Federal Republic there is, one might say, almost an obsession with 'identity', expressed on the one hand by Richard von Weizsäcker[10] and on the other in the *Historikerstreit* conducted by the German profession. The vigorous and sometimes vitriolic debates have focused once again on the allegedly peculiar path of German history and how to approach the history of the German nation 'after Hitler'.[11] The literature on this topic threatens to become overwhelming and is not likely speedily to diminish. 'Today a unified, streamlined picture of German national history can no longer be drawn', one writer concludes; 'Breaks in tradition and discontinuities make this impossible, as does the knowledge that in a pluralistic and democratic society, a unified national view of history is ineffective.'[12] Nevertheless, there remain difficult and divisive questions of balance and emphasis. Is there a 'West German' identity (or, for that matter, an 'East German') and how does it relate

7. F. Braudel, *The Identity of France, History and Environment* (London, 1989).

8. Hans Boll Johansen, (ed.,), *L'identité française* (Copenhagen, 1989). See the essay by Peter Burke, 'French Historians and their Cultural Identities', in E. Tonkin, M. McDonald and M. Chapman, (ed.,), *History and Ethnicity*, London, (1989), pp. 157–67.

9. Hagen Schultze, *Is there a German History?* (London, 1987), p. 8.

10. R. von Weizsäcker, *Die Deutschen und ihre Identität* (Kiel, 1985).

11. The literature on the *Historikerstreit* is now very large and the mention of two contributions by Geoff Eley should not be taken to imply that he has said the last word on these matters. G. Eley, *From Unification to Nazism: Reinterpreting the German Past* (London, 1986) and 'Nazism, Politicians and the Image of the Past', *Past and Present* cxxi (1988); Harold James, *A German Identity, 1770–1990* (London, 1989).

12. Schultze, *German History*, p. 31.

to the 'German' past and to the future which has so unpredictably opened up? A small section of German intellectuals does indeed advocate an anti-'western' nationalism, but most writers argue, as Maier puts it, that 'If there is to be a positive, and not merely a passive, historical identity forged for the Federal Republic, then it must be as a component of a transnational system of values.' Yet the disputants diverge over what system of values should form the basis for a 'Germany-in-Europe'. Some wish to anchor Germany to an alliance of nation-states, others to a 'community of liberal values' and yet others to a notional 'social' Europe.[13] 'History' in itself cannot answer these questions, but historians can offer informed assessments to their publics, governments and society at large.

The problem of a German 'usable past' is obviously particularly difficult and contentious in present circumstances, but the search for identity goes on throughout the Community and beyond. A Spanish history has to cope with the myths of a civil war, Basque and Catalan identities, and a 're-entry' into the mainstream of European development after decades in which the peninsula has appeared to be on the sidelines. An Italian history has to come to terms with a potent myth of national 'reunification' on the one hand and continuing (and arguably increasing) regional divisions on the other. And so on. In each case, however, the framework can no longer be solely 'national'; there is a European dimension to the discussion, varying in strength and attractiveness from state to state. The paradoxes are readily apparent. Brussels may in a certain sense be the 'centre' of the Community, but it is also the capital of a small country still riven by cultural and linguistic divisions of fierce intensity.[14]

'British' history does not have to wrestle with some of the recent bitter experiences common to many of the present members of the Community: civil war, military defeat, occupation, revolution. Its political and institutional continuity with its nineteenth-century past — a continuity without foreign invasion — is unique within the Community and very exceptional within Europe a a whole. For this reason, until recently British historians have rarely found it necessary to ask themselves any questions about the nature of the state whose history they were writing. British identity was self-confident and self-evident. The *Encyclopedia Britannica*, for example, saw no occasion to waste valuable space by allowing even a line of print to the term 'nation'. Identity was rendered secure by insularity. The 'island race', however, did not confine itself to its own islands but spread across the globe, either in settlement or conquest, in a manner and on a scale not paralleled by any other European people. In their different ways New England, Nova Scotia and New South Wales all testified to a kind of Britishness across the world — and they were only the tip of the iceberg. Britain was a part of Europe, but had so many other

13. C.S. Maier, *The Unmasterable Past: History, Holocaust and German National Identity* (London, 1988), pp. 147–88.

14. W.R. Lorwin, 'Belgium: Religion, Class and Language in National Politics', in R.A. Dahl, (ed.,), *Political Oppositions in Western Democracies* (New Haven, CT, 1966), pp. 147–87.

links and connections in distant lands that its destiny could not be confined to the neighbouring mainland.[15]

This 'Expansion of "England"' was so significant that no historian of Britain could ignore it. British history, by definition, was both global and insular. It was not continental. Sometimes, after 1919, British historians did begin to feel that Britain was primarily part of the European continent, but that had little discernible impact on the framework of their historiography. The Second World War reinforced that sense of being a great little island which was the hub of a worldwide association. There was no rupture, no tragic discontinuity, merely heroic endurance. It was not conceivable that this island story (as a discrete phenomenon) would come to an end. If its history had to be thought of as bound up with an adjoining entity, that 'neighbour' lay on the other side of the Atlantic. On the whole, therefore, certainly until after the end of the Second World War, British historians wrote about a kind of Britain that they themselves had been brought up to believe in and which appeared to correspond with their own experience. European intellectuals who settled in Britain had a profound influence on the development of some disciplines, but what attracted Sir Lewis Namier was the Englishness of English history. He retained a sharp sense of 'European' history, but the English were so marvellous, at any rate in his eighteenth century, because of the way they handled politics; that is to say, not like Europeans. Historians like Christopher Dawson who wrote *The Making of Europe* (1932) and talked of developing a common European consciousness, and who urged. 'We must rewrite our history from the European point of view', were not highly regarded within the academic world and were apt to be Roman Catholics.[16]

British decolonization after 1945 was not without its difficulties, but it was not accompanied by defeats on the field of battle of a kind which sapped the morale of other countries in mainland Europe. There was a certain smugness, indeed that the British ordered these things so much better than the French, Dutch, Belgians or Portuguese. Both Labour and Conservative governments were anxious to create and maintain a Commonwealth which at first preserved the prefix 'British' — and which still did in letters written to the press by Mr Graham Greene when he wished to express his wrath at the American intervention in Grenada. And, even in 1990, the University of Oxford has filled the Beit Chair of the History of the British Commonwealth. As its membership expanded and its character changed, however, it became steadily more difficult to regard this Commonwealth as that extension of the personality of Great Britain so beloved of many historians before 1914. Canadians or Australians could not see themselves in that guise either. It is not possible to give a precise date when 'British history' in this mode died, since there were no formal acts of dissolution, but it was no longer a lively option by the mid-1970s. Of course,

15. See below, pp. 45–58.
16. C. Scott, *A Historian and His World: A Life of Christopher Dawson, 1889–1970* (London, 1984), p. 102.

all sorts of links between Britain and its former dominions and colonies remain and the Commonwealth still survives, but what had given unity, purpose and coherence to British history has faded away.

Coincidentally and according to some, causally, there was a reawakening of 'national' consciousness within the British Isles. In Wales and Scotland, Plaid Cymru and the Scottish National Party respectively gained spectacular by-election victories and made some more solid and sustained political progress. In addition, over the same period, Northern Ireland became bitterly and violently torn in a struggle which may, or may not, be accurately characterized as being between an 'Irish' and a 'British' identity. The break-up of the United Kingdom has been confidently predicted. There has been a welter of proposals for constitutional reform, but no general unanimity on the way forward. A majority probably regards such proposed 'advances' as retrogressive.

In addition, alongside this reassertion of national identity — albeit patchy and internally divided — on the part of the 'historic' nations of Britain has come the substantial post-1945 immigration into the United Kingdom of peoples from Asia, Africa and the Caribbean, largely from former 'British possessions'. The British empire has ended but, through migration, the identity of many of these peoples has become much more a reality to the 'indigenous' population than was ever the case during the days of formal empire. In some cases, the linguistic, cultural and religious background of this new British population is of such a character as to make 'assimilation' problematic. The scale of this presence varies very considerably in different parts of the United Kingdom, making even more acute the problem of reconciling a local communal identity with a national one. The resonances evoked by teaching 'British history' in Brent and Bradford on the one hand, and Bridgwater and Bridgnorth on the other, are likely to be very different.

Finally, after a long and tortuous journey, British membership of the European Community was confirmed in the referendum of 1975. 'British history' in another sense had arguably come to an end, whether the creeping and creaking integration that was to follow was interpreted with hope or despair. In ways which it is unnecessary to list, the Community has come to loom ever larger in British political, economic and intellectual life. The successful completion of the Channel tunnel and the operation of the 'single market' in 1992 are likely to have a very significant impact on 'British consciousness', whatever the political shape of Europe turns out to be.

The combination of these developments places historians — 'British' or 'European' — in a situation which is both exciting and difficult. Just over a century ago, in very different circumstances, Sir John Seeley set out in *The Expansion of England* explicitly 'to exhibit the general tendency of English affairs in such a way as to set us thinking about the future and divining the destiny which is reserved for us'.[17] In the interval that has elapsed it has become apparent that historians do not invariably divine that destiny

17. J.R. Seeley, *The Expansion of England* (Cambridge, 1884), p. 7.

correctly. Some despair at their failure; some shudder at even attempting to talk about the future. During the long decades when British membership of the Community was being sought and consolidated, eminent historians were to be found in the 'pro' and 'anti' camps. Yet, whether they like it or not, the writings of historians do have influence in the mass of exchanges that combine mysteriously to create any society's sense of its past, present and future. Their frameworks, whether consciously contrived or fortuitous, do have implications from which they cannot escape.

It is on the school curriculum that most attention is currently focused in many parts of Europe, as individual countries try to find a way of coping with the past that obstinately obtrudes into their present. In what was the Soviet Union, there was the obvious difficulty of dealing with Stalinism, a problem so complicated that one understands that the teaching of history had to be temporarily suspended.[18] In Germany, the debates amongst historians and political scientists which have already been referred to are not merely arcane academic exchanges. They too have implications for schools. They have aroused a new interest in history amongst the public at large.[19] The unexpected achievement of German reunification has in turn produced further questions about German identity and its relation to European unification in the era of Maastricht. One might say that it is because the people of West Germany have at length found it impossible to repress history in their pursuit of high growth rates and prosperity that they have asked historians for answers. It is worth recalling that in the 1970s several SDP-governed *Länder* had removed the teaching of history from school curricula and in other *Länder* the curriculum provided nothing but medieval history or nothing but German history from 1919 to 1945. In consequence, many German schoolchildren proved unable to put Hitler, Frederick the Great, Bismarck and Luther in their correct chronological sequence.[20]

A similar lack of grasp of certain 'basic facts' about French history amongst French schoolchildren was also being remarked upon in France. It led to complaints that the methods and procedures of the dominant French school of historiography contributed to this ignorance. President Mitterrand was not alone in believing that a country that lost its collective memory lost its identity. Historians in France did indeed find it alarming that only a third of the children entering secondary schools could give the date of the French revolution — this was a few years before 1989! Various scholars, among them Jacques Le Goff and René Girault, were brought in in order to try to 'rectify' the position. The gap between what professional historians thought they were doing and what 'the public' wanted as 'history' had become too wide in France.

18. For the problems of Soviet historiography in present circumstances see Takayuki Ito, (ed.,), *Facing up to the Past: Soviet Historiography under 'Perestroika'* (Sapporo, Japan, 1989).

19. Hans-Ulrich Wehler, 'Das neue Interesse an der Geschichte', in *Aus der Geschichte Lernen?* (Munich, 1988).

20. I am indebted to a paper by Dr B. Heuser, 'Museums, Identity and Warring Historians: Observations on History in Germany'.

It is against this background that we must consider the present position in the United Kingdom. In the late 1960s, it seemed to many that History was in danger in schools. A 1968 Schools Council report on *The Young School Leaver* showed that the subject was near the bottom of the list in the eyes of young people, in terms both of interest and of value. The so-called 'New History' sought to remedy this position by switching the emphasis from 'learning facts about the past' to teaching pupils how to think historically. They were exposed to many types of evidence in the process. Even so, numbers opting to study history at fourteen and sixteen continued to fall over the next couple of decades.[21] A paradox seemed to be emerging. History was declining in schools but the general public interest in 'the past' had perhaps never been greater. In the press and on television a very great deal continued to be said about history, and particularly about British history. A body like the Historical Association, whose membership contains historians in higher education and in schools, and 'lay' people with a general interest in history, tried to bridge the gap. Sir Keith Joseph, then Secretary of State for Education and Science, was persuaded to speak to a conference organized by the Association in January 1984 and gave a measured and thoughtful address on the importance of history.[22] His remarks gave encouragement to historians in general and, indirectly, led to a place for history being guaranteed under the proposals to establish a national curriculum. As has been pointed out, the impetus behind this step has been political and there has been a vigorous and proper debate about 'what should be taught'.

In late 1988 HM Inspectorate produced a considered paper on *History from 5 to 16* as a contribution to these issues. It was pointed out that one of the main reasons for offering a course in history was that the school curriculum provided 'one of the fundamental ways in which a society transmits its cultural heritage to new generations'. Novelists, professional historians and columnists in the press have been keen that the transmission of this cultural heritage should not be accompanied by breast-beating. It should be accompanied by an unaffected pride which would lift national morale and be an occasion for general rejoicing. The HMI paper, however, went on to point out that the concept of 'heritage' is complex and problematic. What have British people in common and how is local history to be fitted in on the one hand and global history on the other? The document goes on to suggest that the content of history courses cannot be fixed for all time.[23] The problem, however, is that there are so many things that are desirable; so many skills have also to be mastered; and time is limited. It is stressed, however, that chronology should not be ignored. Over however long a span, it is important to grasp change over

21. J. Slater, *The Politics of History Teaching: A Humanity Dehumanized* (London, 1989), pp. 2–3.

22. Lord Joseph's speech, in which he firmly distinguished between a proper emphasis on national history and nationalistic history, was printed in full in the 'house magazine' of the Historical Association, the *Historian*, no. 2, 1984.

23. *History from 5 to 16*, Curriculum Matters 11 (1988), p. 1.

time. Tentatively, they produce 'outcomes' of a course of history. By the age of sixteen, pupils should know something about a range of topics from hunter-gatherer societies to the world after 1945. However, the paper does specifically address 'the British dimension' and urges that children should become well acquainted with British history, including the particular history of their own locality. There should be no attempt to cover all British history, but any selection should include local history, the origins and historical developments of the British peoples up to the present day (with their religious, cultural and ethnic variety), their institutions (in particular of parliamentary democracy) and the major changes in British political, economic and social life. Courses should help young people to understand the part played by British people in other parts of the world 'as well as the influence of Europe and the wider world on the development of Britain.'[24]

The working group set up to consider what 'History' in the national curriculum should be has published both an interim report and its final report. Individuals and groups have been free to communicate their own ideas on what they believe the History curriculum should contain. The initial document submitted by the Historical Association ranges widely over many aspects but reiterates the view that the study of history is 'essential if our future citizens are to understand their own country, its culture and its institutions, to identify what is distinctive about Britain yet simultaneously to appreciate our past and present relations with other societies, both in Europe and further afield'.

The terms of reference of the working group, amongst other things, required it to identify, with programmes of study, 'the key elements' considered 'to be *essential* at each key stage for children throughout England and Wales, bearing in mind the need for a balanced history curriculum for all pupils and, in Wales, the need to allow room within that curriculum for appropriate attention to the History of Wales'. The supplementary guidance to the chairman adds further that 'The programmes of study should have at the core the history of Britain, the record of its past and, in particular, its political, constitutional and cultural heritage.'[25]

The business of determining what is 'essential' and what constitutes a 'balance' in terms of content is formidably difficult. Of course, content will not be the only thing that matters and there is no need to presuppose a fundamental clash between 'skills' and 'content'. For my personal purposes, that aspect can be left on one side. The central problem is 'British history'.[26] Some, though I am not among them, would deplore a return to any emphasis upon the national past as such. They would prefer the curriculum to have no core

24. Ibid., pp. 8–9.

25. Department of Education and Science, circular 13/89, 13 Jan. 1989, and accompanying papers.

26. See below, chapter 17, pp. 239–58. Keith Robbins, *Nineteenth-Century Britain: Integration and Diversity* (Oxford, 1988; paperback as *Nineteenth-century Britain: England, Scotland, and Wales: The Making of a Nation* (Oxford, 1989); J.G.A. Pocock, 'British History: A Plea for a New Subject', *Journal of Modern History*, xlvii (1975), and 'The Limits and Divisions of British History: In Search of a New Subject', *American Historical Review*, lxxxvii (1982). See also below, pp. 259–70.

at all. However, it is not to decry the importance of 'world history' to argue that an emphasis upon national history is proper. We may assert that pupils, as future citizens, should have an understanding of the evolution of their own country. In addition, it is arguably only by gaining a relatively detailed 'base' in one particular society that pupils and adults can encounter other societies and cultures in a creative fashion. A syllabus that wanders across the globe but is anchored nowhere can leave a student with an inadequate feel for the peculiarities and distinctive qualities of any society. From a pedagogical standpoint, national history also has the conspicuous advantage that the visible traces of the past lie all around. A phrase in the interim report expresses the whole matter neatly, but perhaps not altogether clearly: 'We have placed British history at the core of our proposals, but that does not mean that it has to be the centre of gravity.' In its final report the Working Group would appear to have met the Secretary of State for Education's request for an increased emphasis on British history.[27]

The paper on *History from 5 to 16* refreshingly recognized that British history is 'seriously limited if it is confined to the history of England or Wales, and fails to take into account the histories of Scotland and Ireland'.[28] However, it is one thing to recognize this necessity and another to deal with it adequately in the curriculum. In the first place, this is because there has been very little systematic attempt to produce what might be termed 'inter-British' history. Secondly, there is an unavoidable but unfortunate paradox about the entire exercise. Although the London-based press seems largely oblivious to the fact, the 'national curriculum' that is currently being produced is not 'British national' because the Scottish curriculum is separate. There is therefore no formal possibility as things stand of a pan-British agreement on how 'British history' should be approached in schools. Similarly, while there is reference to the need to 'take into account' the history of Ireland, it is far from clear how 'Irish history' should be viewed. Is it the entire island's history — down to the present — or that part of it which adheres to the United Kingdom and which might therefore be considered to be part of 'British history'?[29] Even more fundamentally, ought we to be looking for content which grapples over time with the 'totality of relationships within these islands' and is sceptical about the extent to which we are dealing with four discrete and monochrome nationalities? The Working Party's Interim Report is to some extent sensitive on these matters and stresses the importance of 'a broad and eclectic view of British history'. The final report maintains this emphasis and its provision of a study unit on Irish history is welcome, but such separate treatment side-steps the question of relationships between 'Britain' and 'Ireland'.[30]

27. National Curriculum History Working Group, *Interim Report* (1989); *Final Report* (1990), p. 17.

28. *History from 5 to 16*, p. 8.

29. See the essays in P.J. Drudy, (ed.,), *Ireland and Britain since 1922*, Irish Studies 5 (Cambridge, 1986).

30. *Interim Report*, p. 17: See also National Curriculum History Committee for Wales, *Preliminary Advice to the Secretary of State for Wales* (1989).

This issue is related to an even wider one currently troubling historians in higher education. Nearly a decade of staff losses and 'restructuring' has seriously undermined the range of options now available in most British universities, though the pattern of losses has been arbitrary and without regard to the balance of departmental specialisms. In this situation, universities have been forced to reconsider the syllabus they can teach. Inevitably, serious questions have been raised about the balance and direction of historical studies. Before he departed to take up a post in the United States, David Cannadine raised some of these issues in an article deliberately designed to provoke with the title 'British History: Past, Present — and Future?'[31] His criticisms ranged far and wide and have provoked vigorous rejoinders from other members of the profession. However, part of Cannadine's complaint related to 'professionalization'. The lay audience for history was pushed on one side as ever more arcane topics of research were pursued. In many cases it could indeed be said that graduates emerged with a patchwork of knowledge. There would have been little attempt to determine how it all 'added up'. What 'British heritage' might be would not have been systematically addressed, but students would have had glimpses *en passant* arising from various British history courses which they might happen to have done. The only 'lesson' to be drawn was incoherence. In consequence, Cannadine argued, 'At the universities, as in the schools, the belief that history provides an education, that it helps us to understand ourselves in time, or even that it explains something of how the present world came into being, has all but vanished — on the part of those who teach no less than on the part of those who are taught.'[32] This picture has been strongly attacked and, in my judgement, it overstates the position substantially. Nevertheless, it does return us to the central problem with which we have been concerned: the use and abuse of history and the social function of the historian in the United Kingdom and in Europe as a whole.

British professional historians do not have a single body which even purports to say what they think *qua* British historians. By no means all academic historians, alas, are members of the Historical Association, and we have always been proud to have many non-academic members who are simply interested in history.[33] The Royal Historical Society is a scholarly body which elects its fellows and is therefore by definition restrictive, though in practice it does contain a large number of academic and some non-academic historians. A History at the Universities Defence Group (HUDG) has been established, together with an equivalent public-sector body (PUSH), but their concern is primarily with the problems of the subject in their respective institutions, though larger issues impinge. Many other societies have come into existence

---

31. D. Cannadine, 'British History: Past, Present – and Future?', *Past and Present*, cxvi (August 1987), pp. 169–91; and rejoinders by P.R. Coss, W. Lamont and N. Evans, in 'Debate: British History: Past, Present and Future', *Past and Present*, cxix (May, 1988), pp. 171–203.
32. Cannadine, 'British History', p. 180.
33. See above, pp. 1–14.

in recent decades to further the study of particular branches of history — an illustration at once of the liveliness of the discipline and of its fragmentation.

The nearest thing there is to an 'annual meeting' of British historians is the long-standing annual conference arranged by the Institute of Historical Research in London each year, but this is an 'Anglo-American' conference. In short, there is no mechanism which makes it possible for British historians to speak either to government or to society at large about what it is that they think they are doing or, to be more precise, what they think in present circumstances 'British history' should be seen to be. However, even if an institutional means existed, there would be many historians who would not want it to express a public view at this juncture, for fear that it would establish an orthodoxy, or at least an orthodoxy which they would not like. Perhaps also there is a suspicion that someone might suggest that the 'core' of a university history syllabus should also be British history.

I imagine that there are few academic historians who would want to accept appointment simply as story-tellers to the tribe, yet they cannot exist in isolation from the society in which they exist and which pays for them to research and write.[34] There is a present from which the historian cannot escape. The 'agenda' emerges from a complex interplay between his or her creative skills and the needs, drives and aspirations of society at large. Sometimes that relationship is explicit and sometimes it is covert. In 1961, for example, E.H. Carr told us that it was the 'duty' of a university to correct the popular distortion that the history of the English-speaking world over the last four hundred years was the centre-piece of universal history. It was a great period, but it was not that.[35] This injunction was so enthusiastically taken up in some quarters that it was British history that could appear of peripheral significance. Such advice both matched and contributed to (who can tell in what proportion?) a national loss of confidence for two decades. However, while a self-flagellating historiography might have constituted a 'duty' of one kind, a government committed to reversing decline and defeatism was not likely to relish it. A revival of national self-esteem could not go hand in hand with historical self-depreciation. There is no need to elaborate the point further. It reminds us that no syllabus can ever be completely value-free in its implications or thrust, however much care is taken to look at issues from different standpoints.

That said, how are we to approach 'British history' today and what are the implications behind the various options before us?

We cannot be content with any notion that 'British identity' is a fixed element which is merely transmitted across the centuries. The essence of a

34. Many of the observations concerning the 'crisis of history' in the United States in T.S. Hamerow, *Reflections on History and Historians* (Madison, WI, 1987) can be applied *mutatis mutandis* to the present problems of history and historians in the United Kingdom.

35. E.H. Carr, *What is History?* (2nd edn, London, 1986), p. 151. See also the comments in the introduction to this second edition by R.W. Davies, pp. xxxvi–xxxvii.

tradition is that it changes. 'National character' — in so far as we can accept the concept — emerges from the subtle interrelationship between ideas, customs and institutions. Likewise, the 'national interest' is not unchanging. It emerges from the constant evaluation of the domestic and external environments.

Of no country in the twentieth century is this more true than the United Kingdom. The pace and scale of change is such that different generations presently living are liable to have very different notions of British identity and the history that reinforces it. It is worth spelling this out.

A diminishing senior generation still retains a knowledge of the British Empire as a viable global system. It is a generation whose leaders tried to find points of stability by appeals to history. Churchill appealed to that generation in its youth with fine rhetoric, yet in his last years was perhaps imprisoned in that past. He was at least a kind of European, but could not bring feelings and action into line. The British, Eisenhower was inclined to feel when he became US president, had so much history, and so much to be proud about in their history, that they had got stuck in the past. Anthony Eden, for example, spoke movingly of the 'open sea' which instinctively attracted the islanders. They knew 'in their bones' that they could never be drawn into a continental system. He believed that if you looked at the postbag of any English village and examined the letters coming from abroad to the whole population, 90 per cent of them would come from way beyond Europe.[36] The British were insular and global: they were not continental. Harold Macmillan in 1949 was less clear-cut and the awkward sentences that follow betray conflicting concepts of identity: 'The Empire must always have first preference for us: Europe must come second in a specially-favoured position. Politically, strategically and economically, Britain is part of Europe, though she is also head of the Empire. We cannot isolate ourselves from Europe.'[37] Even more dramatically, Hugh Gaitskell in 1962 spoke of the end of '1,000 years of British history' if Britain were to join the EEC.[38]

A middle generation — roughly between the ages of forty and fifty-five never knew the British Empire as a secure reality but grew up in the age of decolonization and the agonizing reappraisals that followed. Where did Britain 'belong'? Was it an American province? Did the future lie with the Commonwealth? Could Britain 'join Europe'? The possible permutations are

---

36. Sir Evelyn Shuckburgh in Michael Charlton, ed., *The Price of Victory* (London, 1983), p. 187.

37. Cited in A. Horne, *Harold Macmillan, 1894–1956* (London, 1988), p. 321.

38. Gaitskell spoke in these unhistorical terms to the 1962 Labour Party conference. In citing the speech, in his article 'What Price Independence? Sovereignty and Interdependence in British Politics', *International Affairs*, lxii (Summer 1986), p. 383 n. 31, William Wallace adds correctly that Gaitskell had strong family imperial links, but also remarks that Gaitskell had little personal experience of the European continent. Even so, it is worth remarking that the time Gaitskell spent in Vienna was very important in his political development. He also achieved a competent command of German. Indeed, he is the only leader of the British Labour Party to have resided on the European mainland for any continuous period.

too familiar to need elaboration. Each alternative had advocates and it was possible to posit a new British identity with some plausibility in each instance.

In the case of the generation under forty, however, even decolonization is a marginal memory and Britain's membership of the EEC has been, largely, a fact of life. With or without enthusiasm, individuals and parties have come to accept the EEC as the only home for the United Kingdom. A successfully completed Channel tunnel will in one sense constitute the end of 'our island story'. The 'single market' lies ahead and much emphasis is rightly placed upon trying to impress its implications upon the business community and the nation at large.

It is in this context that we should be considering the provision of a history curriculum *in the 1990s* for pupils aged five to sixteen.[39] The *Interim Report* of the Working Party notices coyly that the 'links between Britain and her immediate European neighbours are currently growing closer' but draws no dramatic historiographical conclusion. The final report goes so far as to speak, guardedly, of Britain being 'part of Europe', but proposes that twentieth-century Britain and Europe post-1945 are to be tackled in separate study units.[40] Yet it is a 'Britain-in-Europe', one supposes, that will constitute the political reality of the children who will be taught, however that will be formally defined in constitutional terms. Few now believe, however, that 'national identity' either will or should disappear. There will be a 'national identity' and a 'Community identity' which will coexist (as they already do on a modest scale) within individuals and institutions, varying in proportion and significance from case to case.[41] There is a danger that this dual identity will only be carried by a transnational elite. Sir Michael Howard has pointed out that such an 'overclass' shows up 'a semi-educated and resentful underclass which defiantly takes as its symbols the national flags abandoned by the elites . . . and displays them on new and less glorious battlefields'. This danger can be in some measure avoided, though expectations should not be too high, if it is a duality which permeates the approach to British history throughout the educational system.[42] It must be stressed that 'British history' should not disappear in some bland 'Eurohistory' which wilfully or casually eliminates the differences between European peoples — though it should be noted that it is becoming increasingly difficult in the United States to sustain 'British history'

---

39. Concerning the world since 1945, the 'outcomes' which it is suggested that pupils should know about by the age of sixteen are listed as 'the superpowers, high technology societies, the welfare state, the Commonwealth, Britain as a multi-ethnic society, the accelerated development of the world economy, the "third world"'. *History from 5 to 16*, p. 13. The EEC is not even mentioned.

40. *Interim Report*, p. 19; *Final Report*, p. 17.

41. C. Tugendhat, *Making Sense of Europe*, (London, 1986), p. 279.

42. 'Ideology and International Relations', *Review of International Studies*, xiii (1) (January 1989), 9. Sir Michael commented in an interview on his retirement from his Oxford Chair that if he were to be setting out a new speciality at this juncture 'It would focus on the problem of maintaining a sense of identity and consensus in multi-cultural communities in a world of instant communications', *Independent*, 21 July 1989.

as a discrete entity separate from the history of Europe.[43] All European nations need to find a way of balancing their continuing proper concern with their own past, with which we began, with their problematic common future. British history should not be left out of this process. Its framework should be as different from that of 1914 as the European engagement diary of Mr Douglas Hurd is different from that of Sir Edward Grey.[44]

It is a task which is being tackled energetically in England and Wales and it is encouraging that the matter is being given serious and careful attention by the government. It is equally evident that a partisan curriculum would not work. The attention which the issue has received in the press is encouraging. So are the steps which have been taken to allow 'professionals', be they authors or teachers, to express their views on the shape and structure of a curriculum which should give more pupils a lengthier, more coherent and more stimulating historical formation than has ever been systematically attempted before.

It may even have the desirable consequence, in the future, of creating a generation which, at the very least, has a broader historical consciousness than appears to be the case in the age-group between twenty and forty in Britain today, only a minority of whom, it seems, could name the French port from which British forces hurriedly evacuated in May 1940 or knew what or when the 'Battle of Britain' was.[45] It may even be that politicians will become better informed and therefore will cease to believe that there ever was a thousand years of 'British history' or whose views on Magna Carta or the French Revolution do not seem to be earthed in very rich historical soil.[46]

Of course, there is always the danger of 'presentism'. Historians may become so conscious of their civic duty that they neglect the *longue durée* and their particular task to submit even the most well-intentioned politico-historical 'myths' to critical scrutiny. The history of 'Britain-in-Europe' could neglect or downplay those periods when Britain has emphatically not seen its destiny

43. I have been privileged to be the British 'critic' in a European team of historians who have offered their comments on the text of *Europe: A History of its Peoples* (London, 1990) which has been written by J.B. Duroselle. While not disputing the peculiarities of 'national' history, it tries to see European development *as a whole*, though inevitably what constitutes 'Europe' is itself contentious.

44. It scarcely needs to be said that Sir Edward Grey's 'European engagements' would not have occupied half a page during a tenure of office which lasted for a decade. Keith Robbins, *Sir Edward Grey* (1971), pp. 126–27. When Selwyn Lloyd became Minister of State at the Foreign Office in 1951 he had to admit that he did not speak any foreign language, had never visited a foreign country except during the war and, just to clear up any remaining doubts, did not like foreigners. Apart from modest intervening travel, little had changed by the time he became Foreign Secretary. Selwyn Lloyd, *Suez 1956: A Personal Account* (London, 1978), p. 4. See also below, pp. 59–74.

45. According to an NOP poll reproduced in the *Daily Mail*, 26 Aug. 1989.

46. Much the best attempt to engage with the problem of history and policy is Ernest R. May, *'Lessons' of the Past: The Use and Misuse of History in American Foreign Policy* (New York, 1973). There is no British equivalent. Lord Jenkins, while able to think of one exception, has pointed to the almost complete disappearance of historians from the front benches of British politics in recent decades. R. Jenkins, 'Should Politicians know History?', in *Gallery of Twentieth-Century Portraits* (Newton Abbot, 1988), pp. 255–60.

as 'European'. It could also ignore the historical significance of the role of non-European ethnic minorities. Steps would need to be taken to guard against both dangers. In addition, the future may take a very different shape from what we suppose. Our educational system may then have been preparing itself for a future that does not work. That is a risk, but a necessary one. On the other hand, serious reflection on national identity, national history and foreign policy, arising out of current curricular discussions, could contribute a fresh impetus to the study of history in Britain and assist in the creation of a new generation better equipped than their parents for life in the European future that lies ahead of them.

4

Insular Outsider? 'British History' and European Integration

Empathy, as we all know, is a dangerous business. I should like to begin, however, with an imaginary conversation, though one, apparently, which is not altogether implausible. Picture Queen Victoria and Prince Albert travelling together near Lichfield. The Queen remembered that as a young girl she had been told that Lichfield Cathedral was unique. It had three spires. There was, she told him, no other like it. Prince Albert agreed that the cathedral was indeed beautiful; but he could not help thinking of Bamberg, Gelnhausen and Worms.[1]

I follow that parable with an authentic quotation from a very different source. Clifford Allen was leader of the Conscientious Objectors in Britain during the First World War. His 'absolutist' principles resulted in a term of imprisonment, from which his health suffered. He was allowed a period of convalescence in 1918 by the seaside. He watched with emotion the swelling of the waves and the ebb and flow of the tides. His love for the sea was boundless. 'I am glad — unashamedly glad,' he wrote, 'that this virile sea-girt country is my native country.' A Conscientious Objector was not without love of country, indeed he felt it passionately. 'No wonder there cannot be conscription for the Navy', Allen concluded. 'A moment by the sea will show why'.[2]

Insularity is such a fundamental determinant of British history that it is surprising how little attention historians have paid to it. In century after century, we can find expressions of pride in the mere fact of belonging to a 'sea-girt' country. The sea might not give its inhabitants a guarantee that they lived in a Shakespearean 'demi-paradise' but even in the early twentieth century there was something special about insularity. Most major states in the world had access to the sea and a maritime commerce of considerable significance. Nonetheless, they were not surrounded by sea. They also had land frontiers, together with all the problems of defending them against neighbours. Only Japan, of major states, shared the British characteristic. It is significant that the conclusion of the treaty of alliance with Japan in 1902 was accompanied by a good deal of loose talk about the common interests and perceptions of two 'island-empires'. It was implied that islanders understood each other in a

1. Winslow Ames, *Prince Albert and Victorian Taste* (London, 1967), p. xvii.
2. Martin Gilbert, *Plough My Own Furrow* (London, 1965), p. 105.

fashion beyond the comprehension of those who inhabited land masses remote from or devoid of coast.

The celebration of the sea and those who sailed upon it had long been a national pastime. There were Marlboroughs and Wellingtons, but naval heroes occupied pride of place. Trafalgar Square constituted a perpetual reminder of the sea at the heart of the capital. Yet naval power was also unobtrusive in the civil polity. Even radicals of a pacifist disposition found something reassuring and wholesome in the presence of the Royal Navy patrolling the oceans of the world. George Orwell made the point rather later when he remarked that there were military dictatorships everywhere but there was 'no such thing as a naval dictatorship'.[3] To judge by the enthusiastic reception of John Masefield's 'Sea Fever' in his *Sea-Water Ballads* collection (1902) it seemed that the entire nation shared John Masefield's longing to go down to the seas again at every possible opportunity. Indeed, no part of the country was remote from the coast. Railway trains took excursion passengers in their thousands for an annual encounter with sand and sea-breezes. Marine artists were fascinated by the endlessly varied encounter of sea and sky and a coastline full of spectacular surprises. 'Sea Pictures' also attracted composers, climaxing in the dramatic intensity of 'The Sea' in Vaughan Williams's *A Sea Symphony* first performed at the Leeds Festival in 1910.[4] Sir Henry Newbolt, who banged *Drake's Drum* so resonantly in 1896, was in fact a child of the Midlands but he had been at school in Clifton 'Where the Downs look out to the Severn Sea'. Many of the poems collected triumphantly in 1898 under the title *The Island Race* had naval themes and were enormously popular. It seemed that whatever else the British people might or might not be,[5] they were indeed 'the island race'.

This sense was all very splendid and deeply-felt, but the twentieth century has not been kind to it. The cruel sea has itself suffered some cruel blows and the island race has been floundering. Of course, the sea has not departed. More and more people take to their boats, and marinas are sprouting up all around the coast, crammed with craft of all shapes and sizes. Marine disasters still occupy the headlines. The superb skill displayed in the despatch of naval forces to the South Atlantic during the Falklands War in 1982 revived a pride that had been dormant since the Second World War. The naval tradition was not, after all, a thing of the past.

Even so, the glory has departed. Some of the signs that this was so were, of course, apparent before 1914. The sea only offered protection so long as British naval supremacy was maintained. The strain of competitive naval building in an age of technological improvement has frequently been commented on. 'Scaremongers' were frightened by the German naval programme specifically and by the configuration of global naval power generally.[6] It seemed to some

3. George Orwell, *The Lion and the Unicorn* (London, 1941), p. 20.
4. Michael Kennedy, *The Works of Ralph Vaughan Williams* (Oxford, 1964), pp. 97–99.
5. Derek Winterbottom, *Henry Newbolt and the Spirit of Clifton* (Bristol, 1986), pp. 42–45
6. A.J.A. Morris, *The Scaremongers: The Advocacy of War and Rearmament, 1896–1914* (London, 1984).

that the era of Pax Britannica was coming to an end.[7] Difficult decisions had to be taken concerning the respective roles of army and navy. Was it sufficient to safeguard the English Channel, as some 'Blue Water' advocates maintained, or was some rudimentary continental commitment of a military kind required? These issues were anxiously debated in the Committee of Imperial Defence and elsewhere. In the outcome, it seemed that insularity was not enough, though no one could tell precisely what the future would bring. The cry of 'We want eight and we won't wait' may now seem hysterical, but the passions aroused reflected public anxiety that the 'seagirt island' was no longer as secure as had been popularly supposed.

On 17 December 1903 the Wright brothers made the first free flight through the air in a power-driven machine. Here was a remarkable achievement, but it was variously assessed in Britain. Alfred Gollin has traced the story of the relations between the brothers and the British government in fascinating detail. The War Office would not purchase their invention. The cost was too great. For his part, however, Lord Northcliffe was convinced that Britain was falling behind in aeronautical research. On hearing in November 1906 that Santos-Dumont had succeeded in flying 722 feet he told the editor of the *Daily Mail* that the news was not 'Santos-Dumont flies 722 feet' but 'England is no longer an island ... It means the aerial chariots of a foe descending on British soil if war comes'. The prospect of Zeppelins was very frightening. Lord Montague of Beaulieu, a founder member of the Aerial League of the British Empire, forecast that airships 'would come so swiftly and strike so directly at the centres that the nation would be almost paralysed before armies or navies could come to her aid'.[8] The nerve centres and all the main communications of the country could be almost instantly destroyed. The possibility of invasion had become almost a commonplace; now it was gaining an entirely new significance.[9] In the years before 1914 government and people began to wrestle with the implications of the discovery that their country was no longer an island.

The 1914–18 war certainly accelerated yet further the progress of flight, though some of the pre-war visions concerning the potential of aircraft and airships proved at least premature. For the first time in history, however, Britain did experience air-raids.[10] The Royal Navy had not inflicted spectacular and crippling defeat on the German Navy, but there had been no invasion, merely some disagreeable naval bombardment. On the other hand, the U-boat campaign had come perilously close to starving the country into submission. There were clearly disadvantages as well as advantages in being an island.

7. Bernard Semmel, *Liberalism and Naval Strategy: Ideology, Interest and Sea Power during the Pax Britannica* (Boston, 1986).

8. Alfred Gollin, *No Longer An Island: Britain and the Wright Brothers, 1902–1909* (London, 1984), p. 193 and pp. 457–48.

9. Alfred Gollin, *The Impact of Air Power on the British People and their Government, 1909–14* (London, 1989).

10. H.G. Castle, *Fire over England: The German Air Raids in World War I* (London, 1982).

The most striking breach with insularity, however, was not invasion but exodus. The rapid expansion of the British army and its despatch to France propelled millions of men from their island home to fight in alien surroundings. It is the scale of this enterprise rather than its novelty that is significant. Young men rushed from distant parts of the United Kingdom to a foreign death. The graveyard at Aberdaron, on the tip of the Lleyn peninsula, for example, records the early death of the volunteer son of the local vicar in France in surroundings that could scarcely be more different from those of his home. There were to be many corners of foreign lands which were to be for ever 'England'.

Indeed, while in no sense underestimating the grimness of the war, there were occasions when the experience provided many thousands of working men with their closest approach to tourism. It is true that in Edwardian times even members of the Toynbee Workmen's Travelling Club were being told that the expense of a visit to the continent was probably less than that of a week at Margate; nevertheless the great bulk of the 660,000 travellers who left England by the Channel ports in 1913 were drawn from the superior classes.[11] These classes, as John Pemble puts it, were the travelling classes. They were brisk Britons, confident and even arrogant in their pursuit of foreign sun. Edward Elgar was busy composing his overture *In the South* and urging his wife, out loud, to call their local shopkeeper 'a squinting pirate'.[12] For one reason or another, therefore, more Britons temporarily left their home islands in the first two decades of the twentieth century than had ever done in a comparable period before.

The legacy of this experience, however, if one can make so broad a generalization, was not to cement a strong sense of European identity. On the contrary, the war reinforced a feeling of insularity. It had proved possible to collaborate with the French, but little sense of a deep and abiding solidarity emerged. There was no feeling that the war constituted a turning point, entailing no less than a total *bouleversement* in the British attitude to 'the Continentals'. Economic and political pressures combined to make impossible the maintenance of a major army to underpin a leading role in European diplomacy. It had probably been right to intervene in the European war in 1914, but such intervention should never happen again. Of course, there was a European role to be played, but it was only one of many. It was the British Empire which should still be the focus of national attention and enthusiasm.

Even so, some historians were worried and so, to an extent, was the Historical Association. G.M. Trevelyan had spent part of the war in Italy and read a paper before the British Academy in June 1919 on 'Englishmen and Italians'. He naturally had particular things to say about the Anglo-Italian relationship, but suggested that connections with Italy were only part of the whole question of British cultural and personal relations with Europe. British

11. John Pemble, *The Mediterranean Passion: Victorians and Edwardians in the South* (Oxford, 1987), p. 1.
12. Jerrold Northrop Moore, *Edward Elgar: A Creative Life* (Oxford, 1984), p. 425.

public men, immersed in home problems, gave what leisure they had to the colonial and transoceanic world which was Britain's peculiar heritage. Before the war, they had no time to spare for their neighbours in Europe. Their education had not helped them. They had been brought up in school and college 'in that insular ignorance of recent continental history which is one of the hall-marks of English education'. He supposed that hardly one educated Englishman in fifty knew whether or not the Magyars were Slavs or could give an intelligible account of what had occured in Europe in 1848. His experience during the war suggested the continental army officers had a far superior grasp of continental history than British officers, whether professional or war-time soldiers. The events of 1789–1815, of 1848, of 1860–70 were familiar and important to them 'as no historical events seem to the inhabitants of our old-fashioned island fortress'.It was time to wake up to the fact that England was no longer a world by herself. 'Since the war', he concluded, 'we are, whether we like it or not, a part of the Continent.' The time had gone when the British could lecture other lands so safely from their island pulpit. He listed linguistic ignorance and racial isolation as the greatest national dangers in the era opened out by the war. It was simply not possible to stand apart from Europe, yet the British were quite untrained to mix with their neighbours, or even talk to them. No people ignorant of its neighbours could have a sound foreign policy. National prosperity, even national survival required the study of modern languages and modern history.[13]

It is a powerful message and one which has not lost its force. That such a plea still needs to be made, however, testifies to the difficulty of moving from analysis and prescription to action and achievement. It might be Trevelyan's conviction that 'England' was part of the Continent but in the sense in which he conceived it his opinion was not generally shared. Indeed, G.P. Gooch wrote in May 1930 of his detestation of 'the Conservatives' idea that England is not part of Europe but only part of the British Empire'. He favoured British participation in any viable inter-European organisation that might be created.[14] Gooch deceived himself, however, in supposing that the idea which he so disliked was merely Conservative. Arthur Henderson, Foreign Secretary in the 1929 Labour Government, reacted with hostility to the Briand proposals for closer union in Europe. Whatever historians like Trevelyan might think, the British people were still insular in sentiment and outlook. In 1919 Trevelyan gave as an example of prevailing ignorance the lack of knowledge in Britain of the races which inhabited Bohemia. In 1938 Neville Chamberlain spoke accurately about Czechoslovakia as a far-away country of which the British people knew nothing.

Historians wrestled with these difficulties, but could do little to close the gap. Grant and Temperley published their *Europe in the Nineteenth Century*

---

13. G.M. Trevelyan, 'Englishmen and Italians', *Recreations of an Historian* (London, 1919), pp. 240–42.
14. Frank Eyck, *G.P. Gooch: A Study in History and Politics* (London, 1982), p. 407.

in June 1927 and Gooch published his *History of Modern Europe, 1878–1919* in 1923. Grant and Gooch were successively presidents of the Historical Association from 1920 to 1926. Both of these works helped to meet the need to which Trevelyan had alluded. They were endlessly reprinted and when I first studied modern European history in 1955–57, for 'A' level, Gooch and Temperley's book was issued to us, albeit supplemented by other texts. It had reached a fourth edition by 1932 at which point the title was changed to *Europe in the Nineteenth and Twentieth Centuries*. Temperley died in 1939 and Grant in 1948. Dame Lillian Penson was entrusted with a revised sixth edition which appeared in 1952. Agatha Ramm produced a seventh edition of *Grant & Temperley's Europe in the Nineteenth and Twentieth Centuries* in two volumes in 1984. Rarely has a single text had such an enduring and influential life. Of course, the revisions have been substantial. Miss Ramm readily concedes that: 'It is impossible nowadays to write of the continent of Europe as if it were seen by a more politically aware country with her revolution in the past and her parliamentary system the model for all to follow, or as if it were seen by the immensely powerful country that Britain still was in 1939.'[15] The perspective conveyed by the initial authors was indeed firmly insular. They were learned and informed, but they were British outsiders, not members of the European Club. Continentals had to be made aware that there was an offshore guiding light beckoning them in the right direction, if only they would look. 'England' could not be kept out of the story altogether, but her history was distinct.

Trevelyan himself, meanwhile, largely returned to 'British' history, despite his plea that 'foreign' history should be given increased attention. After finishing *Lord Grey of the Reform Bill*, he published *British History in the Nineteenth Century* in 1922. It was an instant success, selling 13,000 copies in two years and being heavily used thereafter by schools, universities and 'general readers'. What did Trevelyan take 'British History' to be at this juncture? He certainly saw that there was a problem of terminology. 'British History' meant more than the 'History of Britain', though he did not claim to have written a History of the Empire. It was right to have covered events in India, Canada, Australia and Africa in a volume which began with Pitt's ministry in 1782 and ended with the death of Queen Victoria. There is little sign here that the United Kingdom was 'part of the Continent' in Trevelyan's own phrase, though naturally 'the Continent' impinged from time to time even in this conception of British History. Trevelyan's emphasis would certainly have commended itself to A.F. Pollard, the editor of *History*, who took the view that the history of Great and Greater Britain were inseparable 'because Greater Britain is the completion and perfecting of Great Britain, and in Greater Britain Great Britain is realizing and expressing itself'.[16]

15. Agatha Ramm, *Europe in the Twentieth Century, 1905–1970 (Grant & Temperley's Europe in the Nineteenth and Twentieth Centuries)* (London, 1984), p. xv.
16. Cited above, p. 11.

Unfortunately for Pollard, and to some extent for Trevelyan, it became apparent over the next decade that the self-governing Dominions were ceasing to see their own identity in terms of 'Greater Britain'. The war had given considerable impetus to national self-awareness and imperial conferences in the early 1920s wrestled with problems of constitutional definition. The result was the Balfour formula agreed at the 1926 conference and subsequently codified in the 1931 Statute of Westminster. However, when a second edition of Trevelyan's book appeared, taking the story up to 1919, there was no change in perspective. It became steadily more apparent, nevertheless, that the history of Great and Greater Britain would have to be separated, even though the changes in the relationship appeared evolutionary rather than revolutionary. Pollard's grand teleology was coming unstuck. It was too early to say whether Great Britain might desire (or be compelled) to 'realize and express' itself in some other context.

The imperial destiny of Great Britain was not the only possible casualty of the First World War. The concept of the 'Island Race' was itself somewhat shaken. The Easter Rising in Dublin in 1916 was followed by years of bitter struggle before the settlement was reached which established the Irish Free State and a devolved government in Northern Ireland, part of the United Kingdom. Singulars were having to be replaced by plurals. There was now manifestly not 'one Island' and there was not 'one Race'. Of course, there never had been 'one Island', except for rhetorical purposes. The 'Eastern Atlantic Archipelago' — viewed from the United States — was made up of a cluster of islands ranging in size from Ireland and England/Scotland/Wales as a whole to the Northern Isles (Orkney and Shetland), Anglesey and the Isle of Wight, not to mention the Isle of Man and the Channel Isles.[17] They were all in a sense 'British Isles', but quite in *what* sense was becoming contentious. Trevelyan had listed Ireland as one area to be covered in his *British History* but, significantly, alongside Australia and Canada rather than as one element in the complex history of the British Isles themselves. Under whatever guise, however, it was unlikely after 1922 that any future historian writing British History in the Twentieth Century would deem it appropriate to include the history of the Irish Free State (and whatever its successor might be) as 'British History', notwithstanding the continuing close links between Southern Ireland and Great Britain. Whether the subsequent history of Northern Ireland could be categorized as 'British history' was problematic and probably best ignored. In any event, what had happened in Ireland dented the notion that the erstwhile United Kingdom of Great Britain and Ireland was a single sea-girt country immune from the vexatious issues of national identity which were troubling 'Europeans'. In this respect, at least, British history might not be so very distinct from European history after all.

Some historians at the time suggested that adjustments had to be made. Ramsay Muir, who knew at first hand that Liverpool was not a very English

17. Richard Tompson, *The Atlantic Archipelago: A Political History of the British Isles* (Lewiston/Queenston, 1986).

city, wanted 'a treatment of British history which should not be merely a history of England, but should include Scotland and Ireland in an adequate way'. Even so, it was the ultimate apotheosis of British history — the world-wide Commonwealth — which the historian should keep in mind. History books 'should reduce to due subordination all episodes which did not help to explain how that had come about'. Sidney Low likewise regretted that students were not induced to pay attention to the history of the British Islands as a whole. 'They did not even learn in the true sense British history . . . they were so absorbed in the history of England that they had a very limited acquaintance even with that of Scotland and Ireland.'[18] Such pleas, however, were largely ignored. In their *European History* Grant and Temperley stuck firmly to the view that the name of the state was 'England'. Temperley had written a short history of gallant little Serbia, but he was not bothered about gallant little Scotland. Even in 1952, Dame Lillian Penson was untroubled. In 1984, however, Miss Ramm conceded that 'it is difficult nowadays to write so often of "England"'. She avoided the 'modern usage' of 'the United Kingdom' and preferred instead a consistent use of 'Britain'.[19]

Trevelyan himself, however, abandoned 'British' history and reverted to a concern with the English, a concern which had been closest to his heart anyway. It was when he was in Italy in 1922–23 researching and writing the last volume in his series on the Risorgimento, *Manin and the Venetian Revolution of 1848*, that he had a vision. It was when he was living in Europe that he saw English history most clearly. He was quite certain that Fascism was neither possible nor necessary in England, and the reason was long and complicated and historical. He saw in his mind's eye a vision of the evolution of English society, character and habit 'down the ages' and was minded to put it on paper. It would be a one-volume History of England and the 'unlearned' would like it. Published in 1926, he again had a best-seller on his hands. The genesis of the idea in Italy (and a trial run as lectures in the United States) was important. It was important to be among foreigners not simply to write their history but in order to write the history of one's own country. 'Their differences from us', he wrote, 'interest me largely because they *are* differences, making one feel the value — or the curiosity — of English institutions one always before took for granted.'[20] And it was not only in the curiosity of English institutions that he was interested. He then turned to the biography of a very English person — Sir Edward Grey — a classically insular Foreign Secretary whose distinguished tenure of office had been untroubled by personal first-hand knowledge of the European countries with which he had so frequently to deal. As the book was being written, Europe again appeared to be turning sour. The march of events drove him not to an analysis of European history but to another recounting of the 'amazing story' of the

18. See above, p. 10.
19. Ramm, *Europe in the Twentieth Century*
20. Mary Moorman, *George Macaulay Trevelyan: A Memoir* (London, 1980), p. 198.

English Revolution, 1688–89. In that episode, he supposed, the English had done something of profound importance for their subsequent development. The book was published a week after the signature of the Munich Agreement in 1938. As he looked out over Europe from his fenland and Northumbrian vantage points, he came increasingly to believe that the successful stability of England, which stood out in such stark contrast to the experience of other major European states, could only be explained, in the end, by the character of the English people. He gladly turned his attention to writing an *English Social History*. It was the English he was interested in, though there were walking-on parts for other inhabitants of the British Isles.

It was a book composed for an embattled people. The circumstances of 1940 in particular gave fresh life to 'Our Island Story'. In 1915 E.M. Forster had been depressed by insularity. England seemed to him 'tighter and tinier than ever . . . almost insistently an island'.[21] There were times when one longed to sprawl over continents, as formerly. In 1940, however, tightness was rather glorious. 'We are at bay in our tight little island', J.B. Priestley broadcast to the Americans, but the people were better than ever because they had no one else to depend on but themselves.[22] The further advances in flight between 1919 and 1939 in one sense had given fresh validity to Northcliffe's early perception that England was no longer an island. The notion that the bomber would always get through had a substantial impact on public opinion; insularity did not mean invulnerability. Even so, Baldwin had not been very successful in trying to inculcate the notion that the British frontier stood on the Rhine rather than at the Channel. It was only with great reluctance that the British government and British people could be brought to contemplate the prospect of another military intervention in a European war. The 'public men' of the 1930s, with minor exceptions, had no more time to spare for their neighbours in Europe than their predecessors had in the decade before 1914. And they were all too old to have been weaned on Grant and Temperley. Their notions of the goal and purpose of 'British History', where they existed in any developed condition, had been formed in the world before 1914. And, as a querulous Cornish Celt was subsequently to point out, their grasp of European history was dangerously rudimentary.

The Battle of Britain was therefore a gratifyingly insular affair. There had been some odd attempts at 'Franco-British' union but it was a relief that they had come to nothing.[23] Dunkirk was a triumph rather than a disgrace. King George VI was not alone in feeling that it was better to be on our own rather than to have to bother about foreigners. He wrote to his mother that he felt happier now that there were no allies to be polite to or pamper. Churchill honed insular pride and defiance to a fine pitch. 'We shall defend our island',

21. P.N. Furbank, *E.M. Forster: A Life* (London, 1978), ii, p. 18.
22. Cited in Peter Lewis, *A People's War* (London, 1986), p. 25.
23. D. Dilks, 'The Twilight War and the Fall of France: Chamberlain and Churchill in 1940', TRHS, Fifth Series, 28, (1978), pp. 61–86.

he declared on the day after the Dunkirk evacuation was completed, 'whatever the cost may be.' A fortnight later he proclaimed that Hitler knew that he would have to break us on this island or lose the war. Of course, all sorts of peoples joined the island race in their struggle — Norwegians, Poles, French, Dutch among them — but they could not be partners. The British were in control. Trevelyan's *English Social History* appeared in 1944 (having appeared in the United States two years earlier) and was an enormous success. By Festival of Britain year, 1951, 400,000 copies had been sold. It was a good book for a victorious people to have.

But did it help them orientate themselves in the uncomfortable post-war world in which they had to exist? What was 'British history' now? Churchill had proudly stated that he had not become the King's First Minister to preside over the liquidation of the British Empire but under his successor that process was begun and could not be reversed. A kind of British Commonwealth might survive, and many people thought it very important that it should, but independent Indians and Africans were even less likely than Canadians or Australians to see such a structure as the 'completion and perfecting of Great Britain'. During the war there had been some interest in academic circles and elsewhere in the notion of 'Federal Union'. Britain should play its part in a Federal Europe. Such schemes, however, seemed to sensible men to be utopian and indeed absurd in the circumstances of Europe after 1945. Churchill, now in Opposition, talked eloquently on the Continent about a United States of Europe, but it was not a body which Britain could possibly join. The Labour government, under Bevin's guidance, had various plans for 'co-operation' in western Europe but it would go no further.[24] In prevailing post-war circumstances, it might make more sense to see 'British history' as a subordinate element in that *History of the English-Speaking Peoples* to which the half-American Churchill was to return. In the meantime, little more could be done than to muddle on within the old historiographical boundaries.

It was a confusing but not overwhelmingly troublesome situation for a boy beginning school in 1945. Not having the benefit of a structured national curriculum, I must have picked up miscellaneous bits and pieces of British history over the next half-dozen years. However, I have to admit that between twelve and fifteen I studied the history of classical Greece and Rome, in a modest manner, rather than anything 'British' or 'European'. Over the next couple of years I absorbed sufficient British and European nineteenth-century history — from different books and from different masters — to gain a demyship at Magdalen and sit at the feet, amongst others, of A.J.P. Taylor. The University of Oxford only purported to offer English History and my tutor was not the man to quarrel with its judgement in this matter. In any event, since English History came to an end in 1914 — just at the point when the problem of British history becomes interesting — there was no need to

24. See, for example, J.W. Young, *Britain, France and the Unity of Europe, 1945–1951* (Leicester, 1984).

be concerned. Books like Keith Feiling's *History of England* were a product of the system and reinforced it. Sir Robert Ensor had said the last word about the Irish question in his volume in the 'Oxford History of England', so anything that might have gone on since in the sister-island was quite mysterious. There was, however, opportunity to study constitutional documents on the evolution of the British Empire under the expert guidance of A.F. Madden. That took us in an exhilarating gallop down to 1951. It was also possible to tackle periods of foreign history and I edged my way through European History — undoubtedly foreign — from 1919 to 1939. Mr Taylor was rumoured to be contemplating a book on something as recent as the origins of the Second World War. He knew a vast amount about European History but he was not interested in 'Europe'. Nobody ever tried to explain how any of these courses related to each other. I was quite uncontaminated by American history. It was impossible, except as a private eccentricity, to discover whether any of the 'European' developments corresponded to or diverged from even an 'English' pattern, let alone a 'British' one. It was on the whole an enjoyable experience but not one which helped me to make sense of the period in which I had grown up or to decide what course I thought British foreign policy ought to follow. Perhaps that is not the business of a history syllabus anyway. And it is unfair to heap criticism upon the University of Oxford since the structural fog about what modern British history might be was itself a reflection of a wider political paralysis concerning the future of Britain.

The perversity of my education, as I supposed, led me to seek to remedy its deficiencies. I wanted to research 'British' history since 1914 and, if opportunity arose, to teach it and 'European' history alongside each other. Within a very few years, by choice and accident, I was able to do both. Appointment at a new university at a time when there was some enthusiasm for redrawing the map of knowledge, took 'Britain' into the 'European' syllabus. Contact with Gwyn A. Williams as a colleague developed an already existing interest in Welsh History — which may or may not be due to having a Welsh sea-captain as a great-grandfather. That in turn has led to a career which, by choice and accident, has enabled me to teach British history in Wales and Scotland — though not Welsh History or Scottish History. It has been a personal vantage point which has led to the inexorable erosion of the Anglo-centric history of my early education, though I am equally no more enamoured of a Scottish, Irish or Welsh historiography which is Brito-phobic.

There is, it seems, an increasing recognition that a subtler and more variegated modern 'British' history is necessary. Now that Trevelyan's assertion that Britain was at the centre of an association of peoples is no longer true, a period of historical introspection is almost inevitable. Of course, there is always an historiographical time-lag. The three standard books published in the mid sixties which I recommend to students — A.J.P. Taylor's *English History, 1914–1945*, David Thomson's *England in the Twentieth Century* and W.N. Medlicott's *Contemporary England, 1914–1964* — were all admirable in their way but their titles reflected an indifference, or perhaps a perversity, concerning the identity of the state about which they purported to be writing.[25] I suspect this is largely a matter of generation and location. Certainly, when I came to write a comparable text in the early 1980s my *Modern Britain*, however inadequately, at least attempted to grapple with the 'essence' of Britain in the period from 1870–1975.[26] Others have made comparable efforts and undoubtedly more will follow, though no one would claim that there is a simple or single framework which should be adopted.[27]

The relationship between 'British' and 'European' history is even more problematic. My own decision to conclude my book in the year 1975 was not accidental. In one sense, 'British history' has come to an end with the confirmation in that year of the United Kingdom's membership of the European Economic Community. The long winding post-1945 trail had presumably reached its necessary, if not perhaps altogether desirable, home. It is not my purpose, at this juncture, to embark on an extended reflection on the nature of 'Europe' or a prediction concerning the future of the present European Community. However, I have no doubt that historians in Britain should be working harder than they appear to be doing to establish in their writing and their teaching a way of doing 'British History in Europe'. 'The term European history means in Britain, Continental history', Eva Haraszti has recently noted. 'For Continental historians European history includes the history of Great Britain as well.'[28] One might add that it has also been the inexorable tendency in recent decades for historians in the United States to include Great Britain within European history.

At present, in this country, when one picks up a book by a British author with a title which refers to Modern Europe it is impossible to tell in advance whether its author will include Modern Britain within its scope or not. Authors, in turn, quite apart from their own personal predilections and methodological assumptions, do not know quite what their market expects or desires. We can assume that the label 'British History' is going to be firmly attached to at least half of the history to be taught in schools in England and Wales under the current proposals for History in the National Curriculum. There is also to be provision for 'European' history, though far less comprehensive. The interim report of the Working Party refers to the fact that 'links between Britain and her immediate European neighbours are currently growing closer' as a justification for teaching European history.[29] One supposes that this must

25. Published in 1965, 1965 and 1967 respectively.

26. Keith Robbins, *The Eclipse of a Great Power: Modern Britain, 1870–1975.* (London, 1983).

27. It is instructive, for example, to compare Edward Royle, *Modern Britain: A Social History, 1750–1985* (London, 1987), with Trevelyan's *English Social History.* This tendency is not universal, however. Harold Perkin's *The Rise of Professional Society: England since 1880* (London, 1989) makes occasional references to Glasgow, though he locates Kelvinside, and its 'refained' accent, in Edinburgh, p. 268.

28. 'What is European History?' in J. Gardiner, ed., *What is History Today?* (London, 1988), p. 151.

29. Department of Education and Science, *National Curriculum: History Working Group: Interim Report* (1989), p. 19.

be taken for a coy reference to the European Community. Its tepid quality suggests that even in the final decade of the twentieth century the historical reality of 'Britain-in-Europe' is not going to be taken seriously, despite the construction of the Channel Tunnel and the creation of the European Single Market.

There are, of course, obvious dangers in seeking to remove existing historical barriers. No one is required to believe that the present composition of the European Community is the climax of all European history. There is 'Europe' beyond the present Community. It is indeed true that Britain has a very remarkable and distinctive history which should not be smoothed over in some bland but bogus 'Euro-history'. Insularity has been and to an extent still remains a fundamental aspect of its culture and politics. On the other hand, its major language is the world language; its global acceptance makes other European languages seem almost parochial. History and geography make the United Kingdom still a bridge to the Americas. Yet Britain is not peculiar in its particularity. There is no single European history but diversities and commonalities jostling against each other in uneasy tension. British history is the awkward sum of the individual histories of the English, the Welsh, the Scots and the Irish (all of them, in turn, mongrels rather than thoroughbreds). It exists and yet it does not exist. So with British History in European History: now you see it, now you don't. The task of the historian is to discern distinctive modes and manners, to give them their due weight, but not to succumb too readily to the notion that they are quite without parallel in our 'common European home'. The three spires of Lichfield Cathedral are very beautiful, *Liebchen,* and they are English, but they are not unique.

5

Images of the Foreigner in Nineteenth- and Twentieth-Century Britain

I propose to outline in this essay some topics in this broad field which have already interested British historians and to indicate some areas where there is a clear need for further study and reflection. It does not require to be argued that this subject, quite apart from its intrinsic interest, is one of great practical relevance in the Europe of today. It is not frivolous to suggest, at the outset, that we should remind ourselves of the crucial role, frequently, of our own profession in the formulation and transmission of images of the foreigner. That inevitably involves consideration of how the historical profession emerged in Britain and the assumptions it carried with it.

I am not suggesting of course that historiography is only a creation of the nineteenth and twentieth centuries. Nevertheless, it is in our period that academic history, as we would understand that term today, emerged in the United Kingdom. There has been a good deal of scholarly interest in the expansion, from the latter decades of the nineteenth century onwards, of historical studies in universities and colleges, both with regard to the syllabi that were taught and in the professional journals and organizations that emerged. This scholarly interest is also perhaps an oblique reflection on our current concern with our own purpose and function.

In Britain, 'professionalization' was comparatively late.[1] Let me give three brief examples. It was not until 1886 that the *English Historical Review* was founded to provide a journal for scholarship which was on a par with German or French standards. It was not until 1903 that the British Academy was established as a body of distinguished scholars in the field of the humanities on a par with foreign academies. It was not until 1906 that the Historical Association was founded, seeking to bring together academic historians, schoolteachers and 'lay' people with the purpose of advancing the study of history generally throughout British society.[2]

In pointing to these developments, I am certainly not wishing to claim either that all British historical scholarship before the 1880s consisted of the mere retelling of myths and fairy-tales, with no regard for evidence or attempt at objectivity, or that the 'professionals' who did emerge were *ipso*

---

1. R. Sofer, 'Nation, Duty, Character and Confidence: History at Oxford, 1850–1914', *Historical Journal*, 30 (1987), pp. 77–104: P. Slee, 'Professor Sofer's "History at Oxford"', ibid., pp. 933–42.
2. See above, chapter 1, pp. 1–14.

facto immune from prejudice and national pride. The picture is clearly very much more complicated than that. Perhaps we all know that while we might all seek to remove crude bias from our work there is no such thing as totally dispassionate and unprejudiced historiography. We all start somewhere.

Professor Owen Chadwick has recently noted that most nineteenth-century British historians wrote about British history or, to be more precise, about English history. That is not to say that there was no interest in 'European' history, but neither in scale nor in scope was it comparable to the kind of work that was being attempted in British history. Sir John Seeley wrote a scholarly study of Stein, but he was unusual and it was his *The Expansion of England* for which he was much better known. The conspicuous exception was Lord Acton who developed a detailed familiarity with many European archives and, in his customary way, began making notes for great projects which escaped the confines of national boundaries. Acton was almost unique amongst his contemporaries in the extent of his contacts and connexions. He was, after all, an aristocrat.[3]

To draw attention to this point is not to suggest that all British historians before 1914 were infected by rampant xenophobia. Some undoubtedly were, but most might best be described as mere carriers of assumptions about the external world and its inhabitants which they found in the country at large and in the particular society in which they privately mingled. British historians of this period were not part of an intellectual community alienated from their contemporaries. Indeed, it may be questioned whether we can speak of a 'British intelligentsia' at all as a distinct social category. It therefore comes as no surprise to find that on the outbreak of war in 1914 most British historians had little difficulty in assigning responsibility for the outbreak of war elsewhere. A recent book has explored the opinions of British historians and other scholars at the time in detail.[4] The author concludes, perhaps a little too sweepingly, that disinterested assessment succumbed swiftly to patriotic emotion. However, it followed that the re-establishment of academic relations between Britain and Germany after 1919 was very difficult — as can be seen from a perusal of the history of the British Academy, to mention only one body.

Then, rightly or wrongly, a certain reaction against the role of British academics in the war did set in. J.A. Hobson, for example, the freelance economist and social theorist, wrote disparagingly about professors. They were, he wrote, not so much 'the intellectual mercenaries of the vested interests, as their volunteers'.[5] Gilbert Murray, the Liberal classical scholar who had denounced the Germans, now devoted much time to promoting

3. J.W. Burrow, *A Liberal Descent: Victorian Historians and the English Past* (Cambridge, 1981): D. Wormell, *Sir John Seeley and the Uses of History* (Cambridge, 1980); O. Chadwick, 'Acton and Butterfield', *Journal of Ecclesiastical History*, 38 (1987), p. 393.

4. S. Wallace, *War and the Image of Germany: British Academics, 1914–1918* (Edinburgh, 1988).

5. Cited ibid., p. 199.

international intellectual cooperation under the auspices of the League of Nations.[6]. Historians themselves, speaking generally, came increasingly to feel that Germany had been harshly treated by the Treaty of Versailles.[7] They sought to escape from the oversimplification of the 'image' of Germany which they had helped to develop. There was a certain shame at the way in which even scholars had talked about the 'Huns' twenty years earlier. It was increasingly believed that 'international anarchy' rather than German policy was responsible for the war. In such a context, it was frequently difficult to know how to explain the success of Nazism and how to react to it without slipping again into stereotypes which had but lately been abandoned. This historical embarrassment is one element in the complex phenomenon of 'appeasement'.[8] However, a younger generation of British historians was prepared at least to flirt with analyses of Nazism which saw it as a further manifestation of distasteful German attributes. It is an underlying attitude which appears, for example, in A.J.P. Taylor's *The Course of German History* (London, 1944).[9] On the other hand, certain other writers struggled to maintain a distinction between 'Nazism' and 'Germany'. It scarcely needs to be said that this division of opinion was pregnant with political implications for the post-war treatment of Germany. It also had immediate consequences for German exiles living in Britain on the outbreak of war. Were they to be interned or were German Christians or Socialists immune from the virus which afflicted their native land?[10]

The post-1945 situation in Europe made academic many of the wartime debates in Britain concerning Germany and the Germans. The painful process of West European integration and reconciliation slowly got under way. Some British historians who were involved in or advisers on 're-education' in Germany believed that one aspect of that process would be the reexamination of the stereotypes which existed, throughout Europe, in school text books.[11] It was imperative that the new generation should be spared the crude notions which had been widespread. One product of this movement was the institute which has been established for many years in Braunschweig. Over the years since 1945, scholars from various European countries have patiently worked through thousands of books comparing and contrasting the treatment of various central questions in modern European history. The Council of Europe is only one of a number of bodies which have assisted historians post-1945 in liberating themselves from their own national preconceptions in considering

6. M. Sanders and P.M. Taylor, *British Propaganda during the First World War, 1914–18* (London, 1982), p. 39.

7. C.A. Cline, 'British Historians and the Treaty of Versailles', *Albion*, 20 (1988).

8. K.G. Robbins, *Appeasement* (Oxford, 1988)

9. A.J.P. Taylor, *A Personal History* (London, 1983), p. 172.

10. G. Hirschfeld, ed., *Exile in Great Britain: Refugees from Hitler's Germany* (Leamington Spa, 1984).

11. A. Hearnden, *The British in Germany: Educational Reconstruction after 1945* (London, 1978)

'foreign history'. In the 1970s and 1980s it could be said that the age of 'nationalist historiography' was at an end in Western Europe.[12] Those of us who have been brought up since 1945 cannot imagine, and certainly not desire, any other climate in which to work. Even so, it may be premature to suppose that the problem has entirely disappeared.

On the other hand, this short sketch of the framework within which the British historical profession has worked has shown us how difficult it is for any historian truly to approach 'foreign' history without bias of one kind or another. Is it not just as misleading to believe that the ultimate goal of European history is its 'unification' as it is for our professional ancestors to have supported and justified one particular national hegemony? When we consider 'foreigners' and our 'image' of them, we cannot altogether escape from the historiographical tradition in which we have been reared. I start from the proposition that a key element in the identification of the foreigner is self-perception, either national or individual. If a person or group feels dubious about identity it is likely that 'the foreigner' will not loom so large in consciousness. The significance of boundaries can become blurred. In many parts of Europe — taking only the 200 or so years with which I am concerned — individuals and groups have been pulled this way and that, from Iceland to Macedonia. 'Foreigners' have become 'compatriots' and then 'foreigners' again in the shifting sands of war and politics. At one moment, 'Yugoslavs' together meet 'foreigners'; at another, they are foreigners to each other. There is, therefore, nothing permanent in the condition of 'foreignness'. Insofar as the term 'foreigner' is a legal concept and refers to a person from another state, it has involved, and can involve, the possibility that some portion of the inhabitants of one state may not regard some or all of the inhabitants of a neighbouring state as 'foreigners' in anything other than a formal sense.[13] Even in the present, we can all think of contexts in Europe where the inhabitants of one state have insisted on interesting themselves in the welfare of 'their own people' in neighbouring states. Such external support has taken a variety of forms in the past and has often, in appropriate circumstances, expressed itself in a demand for *Anschluss* or for a formal constitutional right of involvement, to some degree, in the internal affairs of a foreign state. Conversely, insofar as the term 'foreigner' refers to a person from another nation, such persons may in fact be members of the same state and subject to its laws and jurisdiction in precisely the same way. 'Staatsangehörigkeit' and 'Nationalität' are not the same.

British experience therefore connects with the experience of many mainland European countries but it does not exactly parallel it.

If we approach matters linguistically, the English language has not had to invent a word in common use to stand alongside 'nationality', in the way that

---

12. P.M. Kennedy, 'The Decline of Nationalistic History in the West, 1900–1970' in W. Laqueur and G.L. Mosse, ed., *Historians in Politics* (London, 1974), pp. 329–52.

13. G. Livet and F. Ropp, ed., *Histoire de Strasbourg des origines à nos jours iv De 1815 à nos jours xixe et xxe siècles* (Strasbourg, n.d.?1980)

the German language has. Calais and Dunkirk as English/British possessions, have faded into the past. In recent centuries there has been no English outpost on the mainland — if we omit consideration of Gibraltar. Although for long periods earlier the English state embraced substantial parts of 'France', the frontiers of England itself have scarcely shifted since the consolidation of the Norman conquest. The continuity of 'England' as a community is almost without parallel in Europe over such a long period. Medieval historians of England differ among themselves on the extent to which it is possible to talk about the existence of a sense of English nationality from a comparably early stage.[14] Without wishing to elaborate, we may suggest that there was some such consciousness, notwithstanding the reality of linguistic pluralism and a still incomplete fusion of Anglo-Saxon, Norman, Breton, Danish and Celtic elements. We may suggest that this early construction of the English state has helped to create an English nationality which has possessed a robust, not to say arrogant, self-confidence. It has not doubted its own identity, at least not until very recently. It has had a clear notion of the existence of 'foreigners' but, speaking generally, has not lived under the shadow of assimilation into or absorption by 'foreigners'.

Looked at from a geographical standpoint, it scarcely needs to be said that England is part of a complex of islands off the north-west coast of Europe. It is right to stress the insularity of the national experience. The strip of water which has separated southern England from France has had profound psychological and strategic significance, and arguably, the imminent Channel Tunnel notwithstanding, still has the former. Throughout the nineteenth century and down to the very recent past the Channel has been a very conspicuous and, as late as the Second World War, very effective means of distinguishing between 'home' and 'abroad', between fellow-countrymen and 'foreigners'. It offered a natural means of regulating movement, if a government were so inclined. This power is not something which the British government is very loathe to lose, even in the European Community of the Single Market. We may conclude that there seems to be something peculiar, for good or ill, about Churchill's 'island race'.[15]

Strategically, it has meant that the paramount concern of an insular government has been with the defence of the island. Naval supremacy was vital in order to keep the foreigner out. It might occasionally be necessary, against Napoleon or in 1914, to become involved in land warfare on the mainland and, temporarily, create armies comparable in size to those maintained by the major European states, but such expeditions were only undertaken reluctantly. For most of the interwar period it was the prevailing military orthodoxy, supported by governments, that there would never again be the need to

14. M. Clanchy, *England and its Rulers, 1066–1272: Foreign Lordship and National Identity* (London and Oxford, 1983)

15. It is significant, too, that Churchill should embark on writing a history of the English-speaking peoples.

despatch a comparable force to fight on the mainland.[16] It was only late in the day that this policy was changed. We all know what happened in 1940.

Over the two centuries we have largely been considering, therefore, whether by luck, resource or good judgement, this fundamental strategic disposition succeeded in rendering the island inviolate. There has been no conquest. No foreign forces have appeared on British soil in the guise of conquerors. That experience is unique in Europe, with only small exceptions. The contrast with the battlegrounds of the mainland remains striking. The English experience of 'the foreigner' has not been the experience of being a subject. On their own home ground, they have not had either to acquiesce in or resist the commands of the conqueror. They have not had the experience of defeat or liberation in their own country. It follows that, with the exception of such foreigners who came to this country, whom I shall consider subsequently, the only mass experience of 'the foreigner' was that possessed during time of war by those who went abroad to fight. It was warfare in foreign fields that was endured. It was foreign death to which the war memorials referred. European foreigners were encountered in what was expected to be a temporary stay until hostilities ceased. Other foreigners were also encountered by the military in wars of conquest across the globe in pursuit of an occupation which was supposedly going to be permanent.

As far as the European mainland was concerned, it was only in the aftermath of the Second World War that a substantial change occurred. British forces remained in Germany in the British zone of occupation and successive British governments have maintained the British Army on the Rhine under NATO auspices. That has meant that since 1945 'military families' have had a unique experience of living among 'foreigners' in a relationship which evolved to one of partnership from one of conquest.

In military/strategic terms the Second World War also ushered in what has proved to be an enduring British experience of foreigners — but this time on their own soil. The massing of American forces in preparation for the Normandy landings was the largest concentration of aliens encountered in modern Britain. Of course, the GIs were not there as conquerors.[17] They were also people who spoke the English language — in their own fashion. In varying capacities and at varying levels, American forces have been present in the United Kingdom ever since. Of course, they have been foreigners who could communicate with the natives without difficulty, though they have naturally remained under military discipline as a distinct 'foreign' entity within the population.

There is another major aspect of this relative detachment. Insularity, seapower and a position on the periphery of Europe made possible the incredible

---

16. B. Bond, 'The Continental Commitment in British Strategy in the 1930s', in W.J. Mommsen and L. Kettenacker, ed., *The Fascist Challenge and the Policy of Appeasement* (London, 1983), pp. 197–203.

17. N. Longmate, *The G.I.s: The Americans in Britain, 1942–1945* (London, 1975).

expansion of the British Empire through the nineteenth century. It is not my purpose here to elaborate on the mechanisms employed nor to discuss its morality. Suffice it to say that its existence, in all its manifold variety in practically every quarter of the globe amongst nearly all the races of mankind, was central to the British understanding of the 'foreigner'. At a certain level, more first-hand and practical knowledge of the diversity of mankind was contained within the British Isles than in any other country in the world.

It was inevitable that this contact would provoke debate and discussion, in an imperial context, about the significance of foreigners. Conquest in itself suggested that those subdued were in some sense inferior. But what did 'inferiority' mean? Was it general or only specific in certain respects? Was it endemic or merely the product of particular circumstances which could change? Such speculation, particularly post-Darwinian speculation, gave rise to a host of theories which we should now describe as racist.[18] Was there not a hierarchy of races? Were not some peoples inexorably 'dying' whilst others were vigorous and expanding? Was it possible to be 'scientific' in these matters? It seemed to imperialists, whether reluctant or enthusiastic, that in the kind of world in which they lived, shall we say from the mid century onwards, that there was a kind of British burden. Foreigners required tutelage. How far that in practice meant that they should cease to be 'foreigners' or could cease to be 'foreigners' was a vexed question.

It had naturally occurred earliest in the British experience of administration and then government in India. Should the English language be the medium of communication? Should Indians, or some of them, be turned into dark brown Englishmen, perfectly familiar with English modes and manners, mentally at home in the world of John Stuart Mill? Or was there an unbridgeable divide, however caused or explained, which prevented Indians from ever ceasing to be 'foreigners'. Whether to encourage 'assimilation' was at the heart of the imperial dilemma. It was the central issue wherever the British ruled although, given the lack of uniformity in its administration, there was no simple or single British imperial solution. The other side of the assimilationist imperative was a deep respect, at least in India, for the best features of Indian civilization in all its diversity. The Indian 'foreigner' could not be allowed to continue with certain customs deemed to be barbaric, but there was a profundity and a mystery about India which was to be admired even if it seemed impenetrably 'foreign'. Hence, as time passed, and as the British presence became more solid, the deep complexities of the British *Raj* developed.[19] Indians were foreigners but they could understand the charms of cricket in a way no mainland European could. An 'Anglo-Indian' society emerged and there was a limited amount of intermarriage. However, the impact of India on Britain

18. H.A. MacDougall, *Racial Myth in English History* (Montreal, 1982).
19. J. Brown, *Modern India: The Origins of an Asian Democracy* (Oxford, 1985); E. Stokes, *The English Utilitarians and India* (Oxford, 1959); K. Ingham, *Reformers in India, 1793–1833* (Cambridge, 1956).

domestically was not as great as one might suppose. British people in India tended to be there in families over generations, whether in the army or in civilian capacities. They too became, in a sense, 'foreigners' who were not in the main stream of Victorian life. Naturally, the Indian Mutiny (1857) excited much interest in the British press at the time and there was also some enthusiasm created when Queen Victoria became Empress of India or when King George V visited the country.[20] But India was a long way away and one suspects that the nature of its foreign character eluded the bulk of the British population. Some Indians came to Britain to study and they would not have been totally unfamiliar sights in major cities but there was no major settlement.[21]. It was possible, however, for an Indian to be elected to the House of Commons by a London constituency which was 'British', though he probably obtained a good many 'Irish' votes.[22]

India was arguably always a rather special case. British attitudes to the inhabitants of the African continent were, on the whole, less favourable. There was the fact of slavery at the beginning of the nineteenth century and all that implied. The abolition of slavery throughout the British Empire was not accompanied by a total transformation of assumptions about Africans. A mid Victorian *cause celèbre* was provided by the way in which Governor Eyre suppressed a rebellion in Jamaica in 1863.[23] To put matters in this blunt way is not to suggest that there was no respect for African civilizations and cultures, but I would suggest that there was less disposition to accord them the respect given to the Indian sub-continent.

These comments, however, are necessarily tentative and preliminary. There is a need to develop systematic studies of the British perception of the other major peoples in the world with whom they came into contact — Chinese, Japanese, Arabs among them. No doubt it will be possible to establish some kind of 'hierarchy of foreigners' in the experience of the British as imperialists.[24]

Empire presented the British people as imperialists with another problem of identity, at least in the longer term. The emigration of millions of British people to distant parts of the empire — chiefly to Canada, South Africa, Australia and New Zealand, as, for the sake of simplicity, we shall call these territories, was conceived in many quarters as the expansion of an imperial race: Greater Britain. From the outset, however, all of these territories possessed some

---

20. T.R. Metcalf, *The Aftermath of Revolt: India, 1857–1870* (Princeton, 1964).

21. K. Vadgama, *Indians in Britain* (London, 1984).

22. R.P. Masani, *Dadabhai Naoroji* (London, 1939).

23. B. Semmel, *The Governor Eyre Controversy* (London, 1962).

24. C. Holmes, *John Bull's Island: Immigration and British Society, 1871–1971* (London, 1988) is the fullest general survey. See also V.G. Kiernan, *The Lords of Human Kind: European Attitudes towards the Outside World in the Age of Imperialism* (London, 1969). It is not surprising that many colonial administrators had classical analogies in their minds. In his capacity as President of the Classical Association in 1909–10, Lord Cromer reflected on *Ancient and Modern Imperialism* (London, 1910). See M. Chamberlain, 'Lord Cromer's *Ancient and Modern Imperialism:* A Proconsular View of Empire', *Journal of British Studies* xii (1972), pp. 61–85.

institutions of self-government under the Crown. The Colonial Laws Validity Act of 1865 still ensured the British government a certain paramountcy, but the scope for colonial freedom was very large. In the latter decades of the nineteenth century there was talk in Britain of creating formal institutions to consolidate an Imperial Federation but, despite the activities of some enthusiasts, neither the Imperial Government (as it was frequently called) in London nor the colonial governments were anxious to follow this path, even supposing it was a feasible proposition. The participation of volunteers from elsewhere than Britain in the Sough African War of 1899 was seized on as a demonstration of the extent to which the British Empire evoked solidarity amongst the British people worldwide. Yet it was also apparent that there was a nascent sense of individual identity — as New Zealanders or Canadians or Australians. The issue of the twentieth century was how far the emergence of distinct senses of nationhood in the British 'Dominions' — as they came technically to be called — was compatible with a continuing sense of Britishness. Of course, in Canada and in South Africa there were French-speakers and Afrikaans-speakers who had never been anxious to be thought British anyway.

It would be tedious of me to chart this process of change in detail. By implication, it has been written about quite extensively by historians of the British Empire, its successor the British Commonwealth of Nations and its present successor the Commonwealth of Nations, but not, I think, specifically from the perspective of tracing the emergence of 'foreignness' in the context of a general enquiry into British attitudes towards 'the foreigner'. We may, briefly, outline some of the relevant stages:

During the First World War, technically, when Britain went to war, the self-governing Dominions went to war too. However, it soon emerged in the course of the conflict that their governments were not satisfied with the subordinate role, in terms of command, which they believed themselves to be called upon to play by the London government. The experience in battle — notably on the part of the Australians and New Zealanders at Gallipoli confirmed and strengthened a sense of national identity which would endure. There were pressing problems to be resolved in the area of defence, foreign policy and constitutional relationships. The periodic meetings of Prime Ministers of self-governing territories in London were for deliberative purposes only. There was no imperial executive. Ministers and their advisers wrestled with the issue alluded to above in the early post-war conferences. In 1926 a formula was found — codified in the Statute of Westminster (1931) passed in the British Parliament — confirming that the self-governing countries were not subordinate to Britain in any formal sense, even though it still remained the case that in practice Britain was the most powerful single country in the Empire/Commonwealth (terminology, at this stage, was deliberately fuzzy and both words were used). Words like 'nationality' were deliberately avoided and we find the use of a looser term 'community' rather than 'state'. The *modus vivendi* that had apparently been reached appeared to satisfy the politicians concerned (and not all the Dominions shared the same view as to their ultimate destiny). The position still seemed obscure, to Europeans or Americans who wanted to know clearly whether, from a British perspective, Canadians or South Africans were 'foreigners'.

The response by the Empire/Commonwealth in 1939 (which was no longer automatic) showed that, whatever might have been their attitude to European affairs earlier, the Dominions in general did not see themselves as 'foreigners'. Yet there was no desire for subordination and awkward occasions arose during the course of the conflict when (for example in the case of Australian reactions to the fall of Singapore in 1942) an individual interest pointed in one direction and such common imperial interest as existed pointed in another.

After the end of the Second World War, the question of 'identity' also had to be addressed as regards the 'non-British' part of the Empire. The Labour Government took steps to end the British *Raj* in 1947 but, as recent research has made very clear, it was also very anxious that both of the successor states, India and Pakistan, should remain within a Commonwealth. Britain would still play the major part in the association but, gently, it would be appropriate to drop the use of the word 'British' as a prefix. Such a body, which would be voluntary, would be capable, in theory at least, of infinite expansion on the assumption that decolonization would continue, at whatever rate. However, the idea of expanding the pre-1945 British Commonwealth in this way was not without its critics. It was argued that only those self-governing countries with substantial British-descended populations could really share a British understanding of democracy and possess sufficient continuing shared assumptions and values to make a meaningful association in terms of international politics. This view did not succeed.

The Commonwealth of Nations has, however, survived down to the present. Not all ex-colonies have joined, though the great majority have. Some members have since left — Pakistan and South Africa, and Pakistan has returned. It has developed its own secretariat and its meetings are no longer automatically held in London. In this context it is not for us to pass comment on its general significance and viability. It has meant, however, that one might still speak of 'degrees of foreignness' in the British perception of the outside world. Initially, in the post-war world, in terms of British government machinery, relations with the Commonwealth were dealt with by the Commonwealth Office and the rest of the world was handled by the Foreign Office. The absurdity of this arrangement, in practical terms, finally became apparent in 1968 when the Foreign Office and the Commonwealth Office merged.[25] Even so, the representatives of all Commonwealth governments in London have the title High Commissioner rather than Ambassador. However, such

---

25. J. Garner, *The Commonwealth Office, 1925–68* (London, 1978). The author, a former Permanent Under-Secretary in the Office, noted that at the time of its demise there was very little controversy. However, Patrick Gordon Walker, who served as both a Commonwealth Secretary and, briefly, as a Foreign Secretary, took the view that 'Britain's relations with other Commonwealth countries depend upon treating them as non-foreign . . .', p. 421.

vestigial signs of a former era do not detract from the fact that the three 'Old Dominions' have asserted their own national identity in all spheres in recent decades. In Australia, in particular, changes in immigration policy have resulted in non-European settlement and a European settlement (for example, from Greece and Yugoslavia) which had never had any sentimental links with Great Britain. Thus the 'Old Dominions' have in practice become more 'foreign' and emblems and signs of 'Britishness' are disappearing.

The constitutional development of the British Empire in the nineteenth century was in large measure guided by a desire to avoid the explicit and direct rupture of the late eighteenth century on the part of the American colonies. There could, of course, be no doubt from the achievement of American independence onwards that, for Britain, the United States was a foreign country. Moreover, it was a country with which Britain was at war again in 1812. Yet it was a land which could not be conceived to be totally alien. It received more immigrants from Britain than settled in any part of the British Empire. Culturally and linguistically, the English language facilitated the maintenance of contacts and the establishment of new relationships. The Atlantic Ocean constituted a bridge rather than a barrier. It is not surprising that the nature of the Anglo-American 'special relationship' has received a good deal of attention from both British and American historians, an interest which has extended to much discussion of its present condition. It is not possible to develop that examination further here, but the foreign/not-foreign elements need further investigation.[26]

Notwithstanding, the peculiarities produced by Britain's 'offshore' and 'global' roles, the relationships between Britain and other European nations are of great significance. Not unexpectedly, most of the extant literature on bilateral relationships has been written from the standpoint of diplomatic history. Innumerable books and articles have been written on particular aspects of British foreign policy in the nineteenth and twentieth centuries. To some extent such studies have concerned themselves with the underlying assumptions of diplomats in their dealings with foreign countries, but often they have done so only incidentally. Books which purport to deal with 'Franco-British relations' are normally only concerned with the content of official exchanges. Studies of the cultural contacts between the two countries are equally self-contained and rarely seek to place such links in a broader context. There is, therefore, plenty of scope for further work which seeks to bring out systematically the connexion between perception on the one hand and policy on the other. The only problem is that this is difficult to do — which explains in part why historians have been reluctant to tackle it.

26. D.C. Watt, *Succeeding John Bull: America in Britain's Place, 1900–1975* (Cambridge, 1984); J. Baylis, *Anglo-American Defence Relations, 1939–1984; The Special Relationship* (London, 1984; R. Edmonds, *Setting the Mould: The United States and Britain, 1945–1950* (Oxford, 1986). The literature on this topic is very large.

Certainly, in the nineteenth century at any rate, the Diplomatic Service was very important in conveying impressions of Europeans to the British political elite at home. Of course, in forming those impressions in the first place, diplomats did not start with a *tabula rasa*. Nevertheless, at the level of high politics, the official channels were very important in creating a picture of 'the foreigner' as encountered in particular postings. Yet, as has often been noted, there is always the possibility that diplomats will become too attracted to 'the foreigner' and convey an impression which is too favourable, or at any rate minimize the differences between 'abroad' and 'home'. 'Going native' was an occupational hazard and was best guarded against by insisting upon frequent rotation of postings. We must keep these points in mind when we consider the role of the Foreign Office and Diplomatic Service.[27]

If we continue for the moment to restrict ourselves to the political elite and the nineteenth century, individual impressions of 'the foreigner' were from two basic sources: personal travel and press reports. I am not aware that it has been done systematically, but it would not be difficult to compile a list of the frequency and scale of foreign travel engaged in by whatever one defines as the political elite. We could work out and evaluate the extent of foreign contact and correspondence built up by, say, William Gladstone, Richard Cobden, Richard Haldane or Sir Henry Campbell-Bannerman. The difficulty comes in relating the impressions they formed of foreigners to their political careers. Some prominent figures certainly formed clear personal preferences for one set of foreigners as opposed to another. In the case of Haldane, for example, his partiality for German *Kultur* was to cost him dear. But by no means all prominent British politicians travelled on the continent and came to a view about 'foreigners' in their native habitats.[28] Sir Edward Grey, British Foreign Secretary from 1905 to 1916, was notably (or notoriously) insular. The continent was a closed book as far as he personally was concerned and neither before nor after coming into office had he troubled to make himself familiar with its people at first hand.[29] It has often been suggested that a greater personal awareness of the *mores* of foreigners would have helped him in the supreme crisis of 1914. Grey's defence was that in his eyes all foreigners were equal. His policy judgements were made from his judgement of the national interest rather than from any taint of personal preference for Germans as opposed to Frenchmen, or whatever.

Those who did not travel and those who were not in receipt of official information had to rely on the press for such detailed impressions of 'foreigners' as they wished to obtain — though of course travellers and those with privileged sources also read newspapers. We shall therefore need to look

27. R. Jones, *The Nineteenth-Century Foreign Office* (London, 1971); *The British Diplomatic Service, 1815–1914* (Gerrard's Cross, 1983).

28. Sir Henry Campbell-Bannerman was the only British Prime Minister to have regularly visited Marienbad every year for more than thirty years. J. Wilson, *C–B: The life of Sir Henry Campbell-Bannerman* (London, 1973) pp. 137–46.

29. K.G. Robbins, *Sir Edward Grey* (London, 1971), pp. 283–84.

at the world of the foreign correspondent and the role of the news-gathering agencies.[30] As always, such men frequently only saw what they were looking for in their impression of foreigners. Equally, they did not start with completely blank minds. An aspect of our concern will therefore be to seek to establish the primary stereotypes which often informed assessments and accounts of 'foreigners'. Obviously, this is where the word 'image' comes in. It is a topic which has begun to excite a number of British historians. There has indeed been a recent publication, largely dealing with the eighteenth century, which has precisely been concerned with images of the foreigner as conveyed through caricatures and cartoons. Here was a tradition which blossomed and flourished in the nineteenth century, and beyond, in the columns of *Punch* and other magazines. 'John Bull', appropriately dressed, engaged in visual contests with 'Marianne' and other personified nations. The animal kingdom was also brought into play — Russian bears and Gallic cocks were deployed to make points about foreigners and their curious ways. Here is a rich field of signs and signals, only very partially investigated.[31]

In the twentieth century the proliferation of media has made the task of locating and evaluating images infinitely more complex. The output of radio, film and television, in ever-increasing volume has powerfully reinforced or exploded particular images of the foreigner. Here is a vast field, only imperfectly and tentatively explored at present.

The other major development of the middle and late twentieth century, in the British experience, has been the arrival of mass travel on the one hand and immigration into Britain on the other. Before 1914, and indeed before 1939, the British foreign traveller/holiday maker was a relatively rare and privileged species. The attraction of Southern Europe, and Italy, in particular has recently been discussed in relation to the Edwardian period in an interesting book.[32] We are here only dealing with an aristocratic and upper middle-class section of society. The currency restrictions and general condition of Europe in the decade after 1945 curtailed even this established custom. Yet when travel resumed, it began to escalate in a spectacular and unparalleled way. Charter flights and 'package holidays' brought European holidays for millions who had never before experienced them. I do not think that this seasonal migration has yet been historically evaluated. How enlightening and mind-broadening these sojourns in the sun have been is only a matter of conjecture at this stage. The

30. See the chapter 'Foreign News' in L. Brown, *Victorian News and Newspapers* (Oxford, 1985). The author notes that foreign correspondents, unlike other journalists, tended to remain in the same place for many years, if not for life. She adds that 'foreign news was primarily of diplomatic moves and reactions, and particularly concentrated on Continental Europe ... in general the reader learnt a great deal about foreign policy and little about foreign places and people ...', p. 242. See also P. Knightley, *The First Casualty* (London, 1975) for a comprehensive discussion of the 'war correspondent'.

31. M. Duffy, *The Englishman and the Foreigner* (Cambridge, 1986). This is a volume in a series on *The English Satirical Print, 1600–1832* of which Duffy is the general editor.

32. J. Pemble, *The Mediterranean Passion: Victorians and Edwardians in the South* (Oxford, 1987).

scale of holiday-making has of course meant that the British have tended to move about in packs of their own kind. They have been in a foreign land but have had little direct contact with foreigners.

Alongside holiday-making we must also place the proliferation of conferences, sporting contests and cultural exchanges which have become a commonplace in contemporary Europe (and, of course, in the world at large). There was also the very deliberate post-1945 policy in many European countries of 'twinning' particular towns and cities with the deliberate intention of creating bilateral links on a scale never hitherto attempted. There has been one history of this movement, but further investigation could be made. A visit from the European mainland has long-ceased to be an exotic happening, particularly since the foreigner is usually willing to talk English.

The vast scale of this temporary traffic has also been accompanied post-1945 by the arrival of 'foreigners' in Britain on a scale which would have been dismissed as late as 1939 as quite inconceivable.[33] Notwithstanding my initial remarks about the early consolidation of English identity, there had been pockets of 'foreign' settlement as a constant feature in society. There was scarcely a European nationality which did not have some kind of presence and maintain some kind of 'dual allegiance' to the country of origin and the country of settlement. We may think, for example, of Germans in Bradford and other northern cities; of Italians in Glasgow and elsewhere. The other significant addition to the 'foreign' presence in Britain was the growth of the Jewish community in the wake of events in Eastern Europe. Studies of all these settlements exist. There has also been some investigation of the non-Europeans living and working in Britain before 1914 — chiefly in seaports and coming from West Africa, the West Indies and the Near East. Reception of 'refugees' raised questions which were both legal and social. Indeed the influx of settlers prompted the passage of the Aliens Act (1905) designed to restrict immigration. Twentieth-century European developments brought new foreigners to Britain. After both world wars, many temporary exiles simply returned whence they had come, but not all did. Most Poles, for example, chose to remain, as did a number of German Prisoners of War. Particularly during the Second World War, the presence of governments-in-exile from various European countries created an unusual degree of public awareness of 'foreigners'. It was the case that the British government did not find it easy to establish a *modus vivendi* with alien leaders in their midst — I think particularly of Charles de Gaulle, but he was not unique in his awkwardness, as the British conceived it.

The 'foreigners in the midst' who arrived because of persecution or war were followed in increasing numbers in the post-war period by immigrants

33. The legal aspects of 'British nationality' are discussed in I. Macdonald and N. Blake, *The New Nationality Law* (London, 1982) and C. Holmes, *Immigrants and Minorities in British Society* (London, 1978). The same author's *John Bull's Island* contains a wealth of additional references.

from what was then termed the 'New' Commonwealth — chiefly from the Indian sub-continent and the West Indies. The political, cultural and social consequences of this population movement have naturally been subjected to considerable scrutiny by sociologists. It will be possible to draw upon this very large literature for whatever purposes we desire. The issues posed by this major change remain with us and are of such a complex character that they cannot be developed here. Individuals will have their own preferences and views on the balance to be struck between 'assimilation' and 'pluralism' and the processes by which and the extent to which the 'foreigner' should become a 'native'.

The issues raised over recent decades in Britain are not peculiar to Britain. It is possible to argue that the distinction between the 'foreigner' and the 'native', which could still be made in the early nineteenth century, is no longer an option in the late twentieth century. The world is still a long way away from containing one human society but 'home' and 'abroad' have arguably become relative concepts. We are still unable to see a clear solution to the tension between multi-ethnicity and an apparent need for identity. For it is my final reflection in this essay that there can be no image of the foreigner without a self-image to which it corresponds. Decolonization was accompanied by and, in the eyes of some commentators, caused a kind of British identity crisis. There has been a reassertion of both Scottish and Welsh identity either envisaged as coexisting with a 'British' identity or conceived as the antithesis of this identity. There are both 'strangers' and 'brothers' within these islands. If we add the intractable Irish question which hinges upon this very issue of identity it becomes difficult, perhaps impossible, to envisage a single homogeneous British identity against which what is foreign can be measured.[34] World and insular developments in the second half of the twentieth century have combined to transform the question in a manner which those English patriots who fashioned the image of 'John Bull' in the late eighteenth century would not be able to grasp.[35]

34. K.G. Robbins, *Nineteenth-Century Britain: Integration and Diversity* (Oxford, 1988).

35. Relevant theoretical and methodological issues are raised in R. Jervis, *Perception and Misperception in International Politics* (Princeton, 1976); W. Buchanan and H. Cantil, *How Nations See Each Other* (Urbana, IL, 1953); Caroline Bray, 'National Images, the Media and Public Opinion', in R. Morgan and C. Bray, ed., *Partners and Rivals in Western Europe: Britain, France and Germany* (Aldershot, 1986), pp. 54–77.

6

Institutions and Illusions: The Dilemma of the Modern Ecclesiastical Historian

The modern ecclesiastical historian is an uncertain and hesitant creature; an acute case, it may be thought, of status deprivation. He looks with envy at his august and serene colleagues who have the history of the medieval church as their field of study. He knows that they are in process of uncovering the different layers of belief in medieval or early modern society. It is, no doubt, an illusion to suppose that an 'age of faith' ever existed. Nevertheless, at all levels of society, the church seems to be central to the life of the time. If we consider the Reformation or Counter-Reformation periods, church questions seem to be in the forefront. The 'Wars of Religion' may not be at bottom about religion, but we cannot avoid some consideration of religious issues.

The ecclesiastical historian of these centuries can, I imagine, carry out his work in the knowledge that the main political and intellectual developments cannot be understood without reference to the position of the church or the churches. Granted such a presupposition, even undergraduates are prepared to wrestle seriously with theological ideas and ecclesiastical structures. Doubtless, pervaded by the prevailing secular ideas, the churches were not always as coherent and powerful as they seemed. Yet, whatever the precise relations between church and state, ecclesiastical claims could not be ignored. In this situation, presumably, no ecclesiastical historian feels inhibited and apologetic. He is, after all, dealing with a major aspect of the life of a period. A special subject in an undergraduate history course on the Elizabethan church or the Reformation in Germany and Switzerland seems entirely appropriate and will cause few raised eyebrows in the common room. Since their labour is worthy of their hire, such ecclesiastical historians can even indulge in the luxury of research without feeling they ought to be doing something else.

If we may take the French Revolution as the beginning of modern history, then these years also saw the first systematic attempt to replace organized Christianity. As we all know, the endeavour failed. Catholic Christianity was eventually restored but, in one sense of that much-discussed term, the era of 'secularization' had set in. Whether we regard subsequent developments in Europe as a blessed release from the trammels of power or as manifest decline, there can be no doubt that the modern ecclesiastical historian has few defined landmarks within which to work. He is a diffident fellow, to be nurtured and treated with care lest his light goes out. For the most part, indeed, we hide our lights under more popular bushels. We define our interests as political, social or diplomatic or whatever, adding quickly, as though in penitent afterthought, 'and ecclesiastical'. Publishers or selection committees nod knowingly. Everybody has to have some eccentricity but luckily, where it really matters, the fellow seems pretty sound. So long, therefore, as we have other strings to our bow, we are safe. Woe betide the modern historian who ventures out with an ecclesiastical ticket alone. The dilemmas of the modern historian of the church are acute for the scope and nature of his subject are uncertain. Accordingly, the 'sources, materials and methods' of modern ecclesiastical history will vary with our conception of its purpose and significance.

The theme of this essay is that there are, broadly speaking, two main approaches to the writing of church history. I use the word 'approaches' rather than 'schools' since I do not wish to suggest tight-knit or antithetical groups of historians. Certain people may feel that they adopt both approaches, or do not recognize themselves in the description of either. Equally, although I think the division applies with most force in the modern period, it is not confined to it.

The distinction can perhaps be most simply conveyed by referring to 'church historians' on the one hand and 'historians of the church' or 'historians of religion and society' on the other. Unfortunately, the former is considerably more concise than the latter. Inevitably at issue is the prefixing of 'church' or (worse) 'ecclesiastical' to 'history'. The point is at once trivial and profound. It will not surprise you to learn that there are those for whom 'ecclesiastical history' is too redolent of the Trollopean universe and too defiantly archaic to warrant serious attention. It is not that the idea of a sub-discipline offends such critics, for many of them are busily creating one of their own. It is very largely a reaction triggered off by prejudices and feelings connected with the word 'church'.

To consider the problems of 'church history' first. It is undeniable that the history of the Christian churches is a rich field and offers scope for very different types of historical investigation. Many notable ecclesiastical histories have been written; many still will be. We can all think of 'church historians' who excite our admiration and respect, yet there seem to be a number of reasons why they themselves and their genre have contemporary difficulties.

The linked questions of the appropriate stance towards the churches and the commitment to their beliefs immediately spring to mind. Historically, of course, the history of the churches has been primarily a study for churchmen. It has been studied by historians, both clerical and lay, who have been drawn to it by their own Christian beliefs. In large measure, they have accepted the Christian understanding of the nature and mission of the church. 'Church historians' have accepted the existence of God and have not been inclined to suppose that the worshipping life of the churches is an illusion. It is not surprising, therefore, that 'church history' has been most commonly taught in an ecclesiastical context. Where specific provision for it exists in British universities, the historians concerned have usually had closer connexions with a department of theology than with a department of history. Many students of ecclesiastical history have been ordinands not disposed to challenge a Christian understanding of the church.

At a different level, church history has been frequently studied from a denominational standpoint. In the past, history has been the arena for contests between spokesmen of different churches. Each church has found in the past confirmation of its present peculiarities and claims. However diminished at the moment is the fervour of these claims, the imprint of the denominational basis of 'church history' can still clearly be seen. It has meant that histories have been written on a denominational basis. It has been customary for them to be written by historians who are themselves members. The advantages of this situation are obvious. There is perhaps no substitute for personal knowledge when writing the history of any institution and churches are no exception. The disadvantages are equally plain.

It should also be stated that some 'anti-church history' has also been written by agnostics or atheists who have been equally committed in their writing. They have been anxious primarily to expose the fraudulent or inadequate bases of Christian belief and to reveal the shortcomings of ecclesiastical practice in their lurid detail.

A commitment of some kind has therefore seemed a prerequisite for a 'church historian'. The rules seem to have been laid down in advance. The question of whether detached yet sympathetic writing on recent ecclesiastical history is possible is one which remains open and unresolved.

The second aspect of 'church history' is more closely related to methodology. The 'church historian', at whatever point he chooses to make his particular investigations, cannot escape either the past or the ongoing life of the institution. The ubiquity of the church and its activities at very different social levels make it peculiarly difficult to study extensively through history. Put another way, the continuity of the church defeats our contemporary professional historical world. Few of us are capable of mastering church history in its chronological entirety. Even if we do gain a comprehensive knowledge we can probably only do so with a patchy and superficial understanding of the changing intellectual and political situations in which the church has had to exist through the centuries. It is perhaps the feeling that the 'church historian' simply does not know enough general history which causes many to have reservations about the validity of 'church history'.

This dilemma is, of course, an old one, though that does not make it any easier to solve. The modern 'church historian' has very often come to this study from an interest in earlier periods. If not formally trained in theology, he is at least well acquainted with the history of theological ideas. Committed or uncommitted, the focus of his interest lies in the church itself. He understands, for example, the complex historical inheritance of the European churches in 1800. With care and skill he traces the way in which the churches react to the pressures of a revolutionary age. It would be an error to suppose that he sees nothing new under the sun, but he is sceptical of glib generalisations about the decline of the church. He knows well that the churches have endured the heat and burden of the day in past centuries. While acknowledging that all ecclesiastical institutions cannot be isolated from the world, he stresses that they have a self-consciousness and resilience which enable them to withstand fads and fashions.

In such a perspective, the task of the 'church historian' is resolutely, even defiantly, to continue to write the history of the churches as discrete phenomena. He can write a history of the Church of England, the Methodist church, the Church of Scotland, the French Reformed Church or whatever, within such chronological limits as he sets himself. His sources and materials are largely determined by such an objective. He tries to get inside the life of the institution he is studying. We are shown how it is organized and governed, what its beliefs and practices are, and its success or failure in propagating or maintaining them.

If we take the question of government and ecclesiastical authority it of course figures prominently in accounts of any nineteenth century church, both internally and in its relations with state authority. The story generally is one of separation and schism. English Methodism was repeatedly disrupted; Baptists and Congregationalists found themselves troubled by the tension between independency and the pressures towards centralization; Scotland provided a classic case of disruption, paralleled in Switzerland; the Oxford Movement, in one aspect, was a reassertion of the autonomous life of the church — and so on in a comprehensive list. The material for the study of these questions is abundant. The nineteenth-century 'church historian' is troubled by the richness of relevant sources — printed debates, broadsheets, periodical literature, printed books, memoirs and biographies. There is also an abundance of manuscript material which is far from fully exploited.

We can all think of successful history written on such foundations. The sources allow the writer to produce a broad account of developments and at the same time grapple with the details. When one moves into the twentieth century, however, the situation is more disturbing. The private papers of an alarmingly high number of ecclesiastical figures have disappeared, presumed destroyed. In the nineteenth century, it would be virtually possible to write a corporate biography of the Society of Friends. It would be much more difficult in the twentieth. On reflexion, as one currently engaged in a life of John Bright and finding no scarcity of primary sources, perhaps the decline in output is not such a disaster. Lucky the contemporary bishop, however, who can confidently expect a biography by virtue of his office! Rare the publisher who seeks a volume of decanal memoirs! The decline in the number of ecclesiastical periodicals has gone on at a rapid pace. Not, of course, that the paucity of such sources is a problem simply for the 'church historian'. The contemporary historian in general knows that his enemies are telephones and television.

In any case, it might be argued that 'church history' written from the traditional medley of sources is no longer adequate, at least by itself. The view from the metropolitan denominational headquarters looks very different from a west-country chapel pew. The scene surveyed from an episcopal bench looks very different from the church choir. Perhaps too much 'church history' has been from the standpoint of the shepherds and too little from that of the flock. Church historians therefore need to shift their studies from clergy to laity and, at the same time, from the national to the local level.[1] There is, of course, a great deal of work being done on local ecclesiastical history and even more is needed. Information is emerging about the levels of church attendance and membership in different parts of the British Isles. We can begin to assess the causes of these variations and assess their significance.

In consequence, modern 'church history' which has been written from a demographic standpoint can look very different from one which is based on literary or biographical sources. On the one hand, we are often presented with a forest of maps and statistical tables. They are highly informative, but also somewhat indigestible. On the other, we are fortunate in having a number of recent 'church histories' notable for their literary skill and elegant presentation. The difficulty is to marry the two approaches in such a way that the virtues and insights of both are preserved.

It would be presumptuous to suggest how this should be done, but the challenge it presents cannot be ignored. It is, after all, commonplace that statistical accounts do not tell us many of the things we wish to know about the significance of church membership and attendance. Unless we know what importance various churches attach to regularity of attendance or what they understand by membership, the mere compilation of lists and league tables is pointless. It is also the case that local studies, by themselves, bewilder as much as they illuminate. It is a favourite trick for historians to produce an impeccable and meticulous article on church life in a specific locality and to demonstrate how, in almost every particular, it contradicts what is widely held to be the 'national picture'. This happens so frequently, and of course not only in respect of 'church history' that it is often tempting to believe that there is no national picture at all. Indeed, we are never sure whether the research in question is meant to lead us to this conclusion or to the view that it constituted a most exceptional case proving some general rule. Clearly, a balance between differing approaches has to be struck somewhere, but it is perhaps too early to try to strike it.

A similar kind of problem exists in the world of ideas. It would be a poor kind of 'church history' which was concerned simply with the organization and distribution of churches. The traditional answer has been to produce histories of theological thought, or to insert chapters on 'thought' within general histories. These insertions have not infrequently been distillations of these larger works. While again, not minimizing the difficulties of the enterprise, such treatment is surely inadequate. Karl Barth's *Protestant Theology in the*

---

1. Dr Kitson Clark's interesting *Churchmen and the Condition of England, 1832–1885* (London, 1973) for example, largely equates churchmen with the clergy of the established church.

Nineteenth Century is a very brilliant work. Besides telling us a great deal about Barth himself, we are given a provocative treatment of those theologians Barth considers we ought to be bothered with. Some years ago the former archbishop of Canterbury gave us *From Gore to Temple* and more recently Reardon has taken course *From Coleridge to Gore*. As surveys of certain theological developments they are excellent in themselves, even if the thinkers chosen for discussion are rather predictable. Professor Welch's first volume of his *Protestant Thought in the Nineteenth Century* is more ambitious than the other volumes. He tries to look at Protestant thought in the United States, Britain and on the Continent and to trace connexions and common themes. Once again, however, the gallery is a theologian's gallery of theologians.[2]

If we take the history of theology to be a branch of the history of ideas, than perhaps there is little cause for alarm at this state of affairs. If we consider it to be a branch of 'church history' there is cause for concern. We need to be sensitive to a whole range of beliefs and not simply consider the writings of those thinkers whom we consider to be the most profound or stimulating. Arguably the 'best' theologians had the least impact on the mass of church goers. A history of thought which contained no reference to Kierkegaard would seem odd; to include him as 'typical' or 'representative' wold be even odder. The Scottish theologian James Denney was reading him long before he is generally supposed to have been discovered in Britain, but any impact was obviously on a later age than his own. If we wish to know what the average man in the pulpit was preaching we start with his sermons and we go to the obscure and unknown preachers as much as to the great and famous. In the nineteenth century, being obscure and unknown was, fortunately, not an insuperable obstacle to publication. The themes and arguments to emerge from even the most rudimentary content analysis of the vast volume of published sermons would, in all probability, present a striking contrast to the 'History of Theology' as it is generally conceived. As yet, the use of sermons, tracts, hymns in a systematic way with this end in view has hardly begun. The thought of any age is not monolithic and we have to recognize the different audiences and constituencies for which writers and preachers prepared. We must have room for British Israelitism, for millennarianism and for Bishop Gore. The tendency of writers to plump for one kind of belief rather than the other only produces distortion. Why should not J.H. Newman and J.N. Darby appear in the same volume?

These methodological differences appear within 'church history'. They become even greater when we consider the attitudes of the historian of 'religion and society'. There is, of course, a very considerable overlap in the use of sources

---

2. K. Barth, *Protestant Theology in the Nineteenth Century; Its Background and History* (London, 1972): A.M. Ramsey, *From Gore To Temple* (London, 1960); B.M.G. Reardon, *From Coleridge to Gore* (London, 1972); C. Welch, *Protestant Thought in the Nineteenth Century, i, 1799–1870* (New Haven, 1972).

and materials between the two sets of practitioners. In part, too, the distinction is merely verbal. Many of us have probably had the experience of offering a lecture course which, as 'religion and society' attracted twice the audience drawn by 'church and state'. 'Religion', it would appear, is popular whereas 'church' is not. However, a preference for 'religion and society' is not simply a slavish following of contemporary fashion. It appears to give the historian a freedom and a scope which 'church history' does not allow.

In the first place, although one might suppose there is something rather odd about the joining of 'religion and society' as if religion could exist apart from society, the emphasis is not institutional. Inevitably, a great deal of attention is given to the history of the churches, but 'religion' may exist outside the forms of the churches. Considerable impetus to such an approach comes from contemporary sociology of religion. If we leave aside some of the more wearisome 'Prolegomena towards a medium-term definition of a Church-Sect typology', which we have all encountered, it would be idle to deny the enormous benefit which can be gained from sociology. Our categories are challenged, our simplicities exposed and our awareness deepened. We may feel resilient under criticism, lost in some of the higher criticism or indignant at opaque and pretentious language but, after a prolonged exposure, we cannot return to our old ways.

A concentration upon the history of religion, however we define it, paradoxically allows us to be more clear-sighted, perhaps, about the churches themselves. The circumstances in which 'church history' has been written have tended to reinforce stereotypes. Denominational historians, whether consciously or unconsciously, have often brought back their denominations to the intentions of their founders when they have erred and strayed. In addition, they have exaggerated the differences between denominations, though this is not to say that the student or religion sees uniformity in either belief or practice. However, particularly if he has an adequate knowledge of different countries and societies, he may be more struck by the similarities of ethos and outlook between denominations within one society in contrast to another. He may also be able to deal more adequately with those whose religious beliefs are firm but whose ecclesiastical allegiance is accidental and unimportant, depending on a host of factors which can include such things as family and geographical convenience. As far as I know, no systematic work has been done on the problem, but analyses of the number of 'conversions' or, less dramatically, 'transfers' from one church to another must have been considerable. Consideration of the traffic-flow may tell one more about the central religious issues of an age than the assumption that one or other church adequately catered for the needs of individuals. Of course, it is possible for such an approach to descend to a primitive anti-institutionalism — but perhaps there are worse faults. John Bright, no friend of the clergy or of the established church frequently expressed the opinion that Christianity would not come into its own until 'Churchianity' was brought low. He was not alone in this opinion in his own age and it is not unknown for such sentiments to be uttered today. Such convictions show how dangerous it is to equate the 'decline of the churches' with the 'decline of religion'.

'Society' receives as much attention as 'religion' in this alternative approach. It is vital for the historian to know as much, if not more, about the context in which religion operates than about the 'religion' itself. He will be conscious of parallels and movements in the wider society which, perhaps, the church historian is apt to feel are peculiar to the churches. This is not the place to embark on a detailed consideration of causation, but it often becomes difficult to determine in any particular set of circumstances whether 'religious' attitudes determine 'secular' values, whether 'secular' attitudes determine 'religious' values, or whether both have their origin in the psychological make-up of individuals or the economic structure. If false consciousness abounds, which consciousness is false? I wrote a thesis on conscientious objection in the First World War in Great Britain. One set of objectors were labelled 'religious' and another 'political'. What was apparent was that both groups, though not without their differences, had more in common with each other than they did with their confrères in religious or political bodies who were not conscientious objectors. Alternatively, we may look at the political and religious history of modern Ireland. In Northern Ireland, is the conflict 'about' religion as one might assume from the use of the terms 'Catholic' and 'Protestant' by the BBC, or is it 'political', between 'Republican' and 'anti-Republican' factions, or is it 'national' between 'Irish' and 'Scots-Irish', or is it a confused mixture of all three? No doubt we all have our own views, but it would seem unduly naive to suppose that we could write just a 'church history' of Ireland. Nothing less than a total history of Ireland can make sense of its ecclesiastical institutions.[3] The sources and materials which are relevant to the task take on a new order of complexity.

It is not my purpose to argue that one approach is wrong and the other right. In any case to attempt to distinguish two such categories may well smack too much of sociological 'ideal types' to be convincing. What matters is not the label but that the interpenetration of the church and the world, of religion and society, should be treated seriously and fully to the benefit of historiography as a whole. At the moment, unfortunately, far too many examples of partial history exist for one to feel at all complacent. 'Church historians' writing modern church history need to be warned against exaggerating the significance of the churches and perhaps underwriting the illusions of churchmen. General historians need to be warned against writing off the churches prematurely and subscribing to facile notions of secularization too early. The 'church historian' needs to examine sources and materials far beyond those which are narrowly concerned with the life of the institution if he is to gain an adequate perspective. The general historian in turn must take church materials seriously. We must not feel inhibited if a colleague, busy on his social history of the football pools, feels that an interest in modern papal history is very

3. J.H. Whyte, *Church and State in Modern Ireland* (Dublin, 1971).

outré. Some brief illustrations, touching on my own personal interests, may serve to make the point more sharply.

Not surprisingly, a good deal of international history concerning Anglo-German relations has been written, yet very little on the close ecclesiastical and theological connexions between England, Scotland and Germany. International history is ceasing to be narrowly diplomatic in emphasis but the study of international Christianity is only now getting under way in the modern period. It is obvious that eighteenth century 'Pietism', the nineteenth-century *'réveil'* or Roman Catholic modernism can only be comprehended in an international context. On the other hand, it is important not to accept the overestimation by contemporary church leaders of their own importance and standing. It is salutary to read the proceedings of the 1941 Malvern conference, or books like *Towards a Christian Order* or *Christian Counter-Attack,* and set them alongside the section on religious broadcasting during the Second World War in Briggs' history of broadcasting. In turn, there is little point in supposing that the theological and ecclesiastical wrangles which were a feature of the German church struggle form 1933–45 can be waved away and the contestants cast in convenient political roles. Yet the theological battles must not be taken too seriously; theologians even more than politicians have their own inimitable controversial manners.

My final example is a case where one-sided use of sources by different groups of historians has produced an inadequate understanding of a complex figure. I refer to the Reverend R.J. Campbell, Congregationalist minister of the City Temple in London from 1903 to 1915. He was a popular preacher of considerable renown, with many published volumes of sermons, although D.H. Lawrence, after listening to him, modestly thought that he could do as well. He suddenly became a public figure with the publication of his controversial *The New Theology* in 1907. With the perhaps characteristic exception of Dr Vidler, it has since been treated by most historians of theology as a piece of immanentist detritus, hardly worth reading. Yet, while not claiming that the book is 'original', working out the influences and sources upon which Campbell based his writing is a fascinating exercise. His real significance, however, lies as a broker of ideas, and the reverberations of *The New Theology* and the sermons, from West Wales to Durham and Northumberland need to be studied. On the other hand, labour historians have noted his *Christianity and the Social Order* and his sudden and fleeting involvement in the labour movement, but they take little cognizance of his 'religious' activities. By referring only to a narrow range of sources and materials, historians of theology, ecclesiastical historians and labour historians find themselves in some instances making the most jejune comments about the general significance of Campbell's career.[4] In the process of compartmentalisation, the many-sided impact he made on Edwardian England is lost.

4. R.J. Campbell, *The New Theology* (London, 1907); R.J. Campbell, *Christianity and the Social Order* (London, 1907); J.T. Boulton, *Lawrence in Love* (Nottingham, 1968) p. 140; A.R. Vidler, *Twentieth Century Defenders of the Faith* (London, 1965) pp. 26–28; P. Thompson, *Socialists, Liberals and Labour* (London, 1967) pp. 23–24. See below, chapter 10, pp. 133–48.

7

Religion and Identity in Modern British History

'The Church of England' declared a leading article in *The Times* on 8 July 1980 'is the British national church.' Such a novel declaration is liable to produce apoplexy outside England. My topic is an impossibly wide one, only tackled previously, in his distinctive fashion, by Dr Daniel Jenkins.[1] I cannot hope to cover every aspect of it. That apparently innocent sentence in the newspaper does, however, provide me with my text. Its context was an article concerning itself with the possibility that the Prince of Wales might marry a Roman Catholic. Concluding, perhaps not surprisingly, that it would seem intolerable to the 'broad public' that the heir to the throne should be excluded because of his wife's religion it added that 'any sensible person' would hope that the matter would not be raised. There were still what it called 'anti-Catholic prejudices' among a relatively small minority in England and Wales, a rather larger minority in Scotland and a considerable proportion of the Protestant community in Northern Ireland. A constitutional issue 'which would bring all these birds flapping down out of the rafters' was not desirable.[2]

Whatever view we take of the leader and the language it employed, modern British history, perhaps more than the history of any other European state, discloses a complex interrelationship between political attitudes, ecclesiastical allegiances and cultural traditions. The Christian religion in the British Isles, in its divided condition, has in turn been deeply involved in the cultural and political divisions of modern Britain and Ireland. Churches have been, in some instances and at some periods vehicles for the cultivation of a 'British' identity corresponding to the political framework of Great Britain and Ireland. They have also been instrumental, in part at least, in perpetuating and recreating an English, Irish, Scottish or Welsh identity distinct from and perhaps in conflict with 'British' identity, both culturally and politically. Sometimes this role has been quite unconscious, but in other instances it has been explicit and deliberate.

We must, I suppose, linger a little on the term 'national identity'. To tackle it comprehensively would take an essay in itself. Nations may be defined by a supposed common ethnic origin, by use of a particular language, by a shared literary inheritance, by reference to a well-defined geographical region — and so on — but few nations have all of these characteristics and some have none.

1. D.T. Jenkins, *The British: Their Identity and their Religion* (London, 1975).
2. *The Times*, 8 July 1980.

Indeed, prolonged immersion in the literature written by nationalists and in the writings of scholars primarily concerned with nationalism speedily leads to the conclusion that the nation is a very subjective concept.[3] Some nations have had a long history of statehood, some a short, and some have never achieved it at all. To reverse the order, some states have, in time, become consolidated into nations, whereas others have continued to contain distinct nations, living in harmony or conflict as the case may be. Given the frequent pattern of conquest, migration or dynastic merger, national identity has rarely been fixed and constant through time.[4] Some historians would argue that we cannot helpfully talk about national identity until, say, the end of the eighteenth century; others find such a sharp break untenable. The churches have played an ambiguous and contradictory part in the preservation or stimulation of national consciousness.

In such a context, it is not a straightforward matter to characterize British national identity or, to put it another way, how many national identities there are in the British Isles. The United Kingdom of Great Britain and Ireland of 1800 had been achieved through a centuries-long process of coercion and consent. I do not need here to discuss it in detail or to assess the degree of coercion and the extent of consent as regards each component part. It could appear that a British state would emerge — North, West and South Britain — which would transcend and perhaps submerge, in time, the nations — if that is what they were — of England, Ireland, Scotland and Wales. In this arrangement, there was no disputing that the English were the strongest (by almost any indicator one chooses) and arguably the most coherent. The terms 'Britain' and 'England' could seem virtually synonymous, particularly given the tendency of Europeans to refer simply to England. It therefore seemed in the logic of events that the consolidation of Britain should entail some degree of 'Anglicization'. Not wishing to imply a systematic policy to this end, I deliberately use a vague expression. 'Anglicization', however, although frequently criticized by its opponents, is not an easy term to use. At its simplest, it means only that, by one means or another, knowledge of the English language should become universal in Ireland, Scotland and Wales. This was judged to be necessary not only for administrative convenience but also in the interests of 'improvement'. To become fluent in English was to enter the commercial, intellectual and industrial world of the nineteenth century. 'Anglicization', however, involved more than language; it meant a subtle process of assimilation and acculturation. English methods and *mores* would tend to become the norm beyond the boundaries of England. Not that the exchange was all in one direction; over the period under consideration, travel and migration was to bring about an increase in the non-English population of England on a scale never before achieved. Although in this sense England

3. For example, A.D.S. Smith, *Theories of Nationalism* (London, 1971).
4. H. Seton-Watson, *Nations and States* (London, 1976).

became Britain in microcosm it was an open question how far immigrants would seek to maintain any kind of separate identity.

My suggestion is that the churches of the British Isles were inescapably caught up in this process of linguistic and cultural adaptation. The central problem was this: the main confessional families — Roman Catholic, Episcopalian, Presbyterian, Methodist, Baptist/Congregationalist, not to mention smaller groups — had all, by the nineteenth century, spread to all parts of the United Kingdom. In this sense, the British Isles could be thought of as one entity from an ecclesiastical standpoint. However, although all denominations could be found in all countries they did not, of course, exist in the same proportions in all countries. And, throughout the nineteenth century and into the twentieth there were to be significant shifts in those proportions within England, Ireland and Scotland in particular. This concentration within diffusion ensured that during our period no British church — of any confessional family — emerged. The Roman Catholic Church was unique insofar as the seat of its authority existed beyond the boundaries of the state but within the state it too organized itself on a basis which accepted Ireland and Scotland as distinct units, though England and Wales were taken as one single unit.

At the beginning of the nineteenth century, constitutionally and formally, the United Kingdom could be characterized as a Protestant state. By the close of the First World War, again in constitutional terms, this was only partially the case. The most striking changes were the disestablishment of the Church of England in Ireland and in Wales.[5] These two measures constituted a recognition of the fact that the ecclesiastical situation in these two countries was distinctive. The Church of England remained the established church in England and the Church of Scotland in Scotland. The United Kingdom therefore remains unique among unitary states in operating three different relationships with the churches in different parts of its territory. I say three deliberately, since the nature of the establishment in Scotland, both before and after 1929, is different from that in England and, of course, involves churches belonging to different confessional families. In the absence of devolved government, the churches have come to be perhaps the most significant institutional embodiments of regional or national identity.

In England, the Church of England rarely hesitated to claim that it embodied the Englishness of English religion. Its spokesmen, clerical and lay, often referred to it with approval as 'Our National Church'.[6] That claim rested upon the intertwining of church and state at many levels, consolidated over centuries. Its ethos was the essence of the English ethos. It was comprehensive and dogmatically generous, with an apparently instinctive capacity for compromise and conciliation. The English church suited the English character and the English

5. P.M.H. Bell, *Disestablishment in Wales and Ireland* (London, 1969)

6. Some other material on this theme can be found in R.H. Malden, *The English Church and Nation* (London, 1952), and C.H.E. Smyth, *The Church and the Nation: Six Studies in the Anglican Tradition* (London, 1962).

character had made the English church. It was the corporate expression of the Englishman's kind of Christianity. Anglican headmasters and bishops were not loathe to talk about 'the English people' and 'the English character'. At its best, of course, they embodied true Englishness themselves. A wide variety of illustration would be possible and I only put forward a few examples. Thomas Arnold, not unexpectedly, declared that he could 'understand no perfect Church, or perfect State, without their blending into one in this ultimate form'. His conviction of the importance of the royal supremacy — 'the assertion of the supremacy of the Church or Christian society over the clergy' made him 'equally opposed to popery, High Churchism, and the claims of the Scotch Presbyteries, on the one hand; and to all the Independents . . . on the other'.[7] To achieve the Christian England of his dreams he wished to make the Church of England even more comprehensive and draw in dissenters — although Roman Catholics, Unitarians and Quakers would be unlikely to join.[8] He noted in 1834 the 'tremendous influx of Irish labourers into Lancashire and the west of Scotland' which was 'tainting the whole population with a worse than barbarians element'. It was not surprising that 'the Roman Catholics are increasing fast amongst us'.[9] Believing that the thorough English gentleman — Christian, manly, and enlightened — was 'a finer specimen of human nature' than any other country could furnish, it was the duty of the Church of England to protect this paragon from the assaults of his enemies.[10] Whether the dissenters could really assist was doubtful because, for all their admirable qualities they also exhibited the characteristic faults of the English mind — narrowness of view, a want of learning and a sound critical spirit.

In the same decade, in *The Kingdom of Christ* F.D. Maurice wrestled with the problem of universality and national identity. 'We count it a great happiness,' he wrote,

> if we can discover forms of worship which have stood the test of ages; because the feelings that we most express in worship, are our deep, primary, human, universal feelings, not those which belong to our condition, as living in one period, or under one condition of circumstances. But though this be the case, here, too, the difference of language and manners must intrude itself. Our worship will not be true, will not really belong to us, if, starting from that deep and general foundation, it does not adapt itself to our own peculiar position, and avail itself of our native forms of expression.[11]

A proper stress upon the national identity of the Church of England did not compromise its catholicity. The nation was the appropriate unit of ecclesiastical

7. A.P. Stanley, *The Life and Correspondence of Thomas Arnold*, 2 vols (London, 1845), ii, pp. 190–91.

8. Thomas Arnold, *Principles of Church Reform*, ed. M.J. Jackson and J. Rogan (London, 1962)

9. Stanley, *Arnold*, i, p. 397.

10. Ibid., i, p. 391.

11. F.D. Maurice, *The Kingdom of Christ*, 3 vols (London, 1838), iii, pp. 356–57.

organization because the nation too embodied God's purpose. Although later in the century Charles Kingsley was to express his profound regret that Germans were not members of the Church of England, Maurice thought that even to talk of converting continental peoples to be members of the English church was 'a solecism in thought and language, of which I trust no reader can suspect me of being guilty'. The task of a patriot was 'to seize, confirm, and magnify all those principles and institutions of his Church, which belong not to one country but to all'. And, in the subordinate and ceremonial parts, to 'give effect and expression to that which is peculiar in the character and feeling of his own country'.[12] If asked why there should not be a Church of London or of Liverpool Maurice replied that

> we wish to adapt ourselves to God's methods, and not to man's. If he sees it good that the people of London should talk one language and the people of Liverpool another, that the people of London shall have one king and the people of Liverpool another, *then* must we also shape ourselves according to His designs, and submit to those differences which He has made necessary.[13]

Maurice does not seem to have considered the possibility that the people of London and Liverpool did talk different languages.

At the end of the century, Mandell Creighton as Bishop of London was writing that 'the English Church must be the religious organ of the English people. The people need not agree about details, but the general trend of the Church must be regulated by their wishes. The Church cannot go too far from the main ideas of the people.' The nation, he argued 'exists by virtue of a particular type of character. Character is largely founded on religion. There is in some quarters an attempt to bring back religious observances of an exotic kind which do menace English character'. The function of the Church of England was to be the church of free men. The Church of Rome was 'the Church of decadent peoples: it lives only on its past, and has no future . . . The Church of England has before it the conquest of the world . . . The question of the future of the world is the existence of Anglo-Saxon civilisation on a religious basis. The Church of England means a great and growing power in America and in the Colonies.'[14] J.N. Figgis in his *Hopes for English Religion* (1919) stressed 'the extraordinary power of the English character to stand by the old while assimilating the new, which has been her greatest political strength in the past, and is likely to be her greatest contribution to the future'.[15] So it was with the future of the English church. Nothing would be gained by members of the English church looking across the water and wishing that they were there. The path of what he called 'English Catholicism'

12. Ibid., iii, pp. 368–69.
13. Ibid., iii, p. 358.
14. L. Creighton, *Life and Letters of Mandell Creighton*, 2 vols in 1 (London, 1913), ii, pp. 301–2.
15. J.N. Figgis, *Hopes for English Religion* (London, 1919) p. 101.

was to be quite distinctive. Hensley Henson saw 'the best hope' for English religion in the effective union of the evangelical and liberal elements. Such an union could not be restricted to the Church of England, but would draw together men of goodwill in all the Churches of English speech.'[16] To take the Church of England off in any other direction would be to forfeit its place in the consciousness of the nation. The love affair of bishops with the English people continued unabated. Luke Paget, for example, was described as seeing in them 'a patience and good-humour, a soundness of judgement and readiness to forgive, a fairness and tolerance and, above all, a strange, tenacious, inarticulate recognition of Almighty God'. He hoped that 'the reserve, freedom and balance of English Churchmanship had contributed to this desirable amalgam'.[17]

This constant harping upon English attributes and virtues seems largely to have been passed from generation to generation. A common core of Englishness was self-evident; to have attempted to define it would have been un-English. 'Those, who have never left their own country', wrote R.W. Jelf in 1835 in a preface to sermons he had preached in Berlin, 'and who continue in the bosom of the Church, should learn to value their English blessings, and to thank God for their own exemption from danger'. He continued that 'the number of persons annually exposed to the immorality and unbelief of France, to the rationalism of Germany, to the _sensual_ devotions of the Church of Rome, and to the religious neutrality engendered by a cursory view of many modes of worship in succession, cannot be contemplated without alarm . . .' English parents who were settling abroad for the purpose of educating their children should realise that 'foreign accomplishments can be too dearly bought at the experience of those homebred qualities, which, with all the faults of our nation, do still distinguish the genuine _English_ character'.[18] Some Germans, as F.W. Robertson noted, wished to be delivered from 'the affliction of that horrid nation passing through our towns and besetting us like a plague of flies in our diligences, hotels, walks, with their stupid faces, their vulgarity, their everlasting inquisitiveness about hotels and sight-seeing, and utter inability to appreciate anything higher'. Robertson himself found that there was more scope for soul-searching of a high order in Heidelberg than in Cheltenham.[19]

This equation of the national ethos with the Church of England posed problems for dissenters both Protestant and Roman Catholic. Protestant dissenters pressed, with varying degrees of persistence and enthusiasm for the disestablishment of the Church of England. They sought no recognition from the state for themselves. They played no official part in the ceremonial life of the state. Their role in the nineteenth-century armed services, for example,

16. H. Hensley Henson, _In Defence of the English Church_ (London, n.d.), p. 43.
17. E.K. Paget, _Henry Luke Paget_ (London, 1939) p. 21.
18. R.W. Jelf, _Sermons, Doctrinal and Practical, Preached Abroad_ (London, 1835), pp. vii, xi–xii.
19. S.A. Brooke, _Life and Letters of F.W. Robertson_ (London, 1868), p. 99.

was slight.[20] Yet that expanded role in Parliament and public life actively sought and in large measure gained necessarily weakened their own internal coherence and sense of being, to an extent, a 'nation within a nation'. Independents, for whom 'the church' might be the church at Pembroke Place, Liverpool, were in process of forming and expanding the role of national unions — in both the Baptist and Congregational traditions. English nonconformists, who were, for the most part, English did not disavow their national identity or cease to feel as Englishmen felt. English preachers, like Newman Hall, could be recognized even on the summit of Snowdon and be compelled to preach a sermon. Two years later, in the same region, a man driving a cart containing a live pig gave him a lift and told him that his words had resulted in the conversion of fifty people. He added that 'as they only spoke Welsh they did not understand a word you said'. Hall reflected that he 'greatly admired the religious zeal of the Welsh, and their diligent attendance at public worship' but felt their denominationalism to be 'excessive' and to result in 'too great multiplication of churches'.[21] His extensive preaching in Wales made him aware that he was English. It made him, and other dissenters of his generation vulnerable to appeals to English history like that in a letter from Dean Farrar. Farrar wanted to see cordiality established between the national church and all branches of Christian Nonconformists. Religion as a whole would suffer by 'the nation's disavowing all connexion with the creed which it has held for 1,500 years . . .' Nonconformists would suffer 'as heavily as we, the *nation*, would suffer. The gain would be to Romanism and to secularism; the loss would be to the cause of Christ'.[22] Archbishop Magee, too, knew that the Englishman was almost as susceptible as the Irishman to the appeal of the past as a reason for maintaining the establishment. There was, he argued, still in the heart of the nation 'some reverence for the past, some love of old ways and institutions, not merely because they are old but because their very age proves their strength and worth . . .'[23] This desire not to be thought a race apart accelerated in the twentieth century.

Comparable problems existed for Roman Catholics. The particular quality of English Roman Catholicism was threatened from two sources during our period. Large-scale Irish immigration naturally posed great personal and organizational problems. The small English Catholic community, largely socially distant from the immigrants, struggled between a not inconsiderable dislike of the habits and outlook of the Irish and their obligation to assist their co-religionists. Should English Catholics seek to assist the Irish in becoming English and thus give Roman Catholicism in England a thoroughly English face or should they accept and perpetuate the Irish dimension thus perpetuating the

20. H.J. Hanham, 'Religion and Nationality in the Mid-Victorian Army', *War and Society*, ed. M.R.D. Foot (London, 1973).

21. Newman Hall, *An Autobiography* (London, 1898), pp. 158–60.

22. Ibid., pp. 356–57.

23. W.C. Magee, *Speeches and Addresses*, ed. C.S. Magee (London, 1893), p. 56.

notion that Roman Catholicism was un-English? The short answer would be to say that the outcome lay beyond the capacity of the English community to control. It was a matter which gave rise to considerable difficulty and tension, particularly where Irish priests in England in many instances frequently believed that the only way of maintaining a high level of practice in English conditions was to replicate, as far as possible, at the parochial level a pattern of activities comparable to life at home. This in turn by no means pleased their English parishioners and could result in a situation where some churches were de facto Irish. Their task was made easier by the fact that Irish immigration to England tended to be proportionately higher from the least Anglicized parts of Ireland, both before and after independence. The second problem stemmed from the flow of English conversions to Roman Catholicism.[24] It was not infrequently the case that acceptance of the authority of Rome was accompanied by a glorying in practices, devotional and otherwise, most calculated to shock and startle their fellow-countrymen or former associates. It was all part of the complete sea-change required to purge away all elements of Protestantism. To adapt a phrase, the Italianate Englishman became the epitome of sanctity. It may even be suspected that conversion allowed a small minority of Englishmen who have always wished they had been born Italian to become Italian relatively painlessly. Yet it was not necessary to become 'more Roman than the Romans'. An English attitude of mind and manner of worship was quite compatible with the acceptance of the claims of the Roman Church. To fashion such a spirituality required a degree of self-confidence not frequently found.

Creighton's conquest of the world by the Church of England had to suffer the no doubt temporary loss of Wales and Ireland. In both instances, the position of the Church of England was made untenable as the established church by its numerical strength and, ultimately, by its image on those sensitive issues of nationhood. In Wales, in the early nineteenth century, prominent figures in the episcopate either came from outside the principality or were not Welsh-speaking. The attitude of a Copleston of Llandaff towards the relatively limited amount of Welsh used in his diocese was frankly contemptuous. There could be no higher calling than to extend the work of the Church of England in Wales through the English language. It was not difficult, in those areas of Wales where Welsh predominated to see the church as an anglicizing force.[25] Its opponents frequently referred to it as the 'English church' though visitors from England tended not to have a high opinion of it. John Keble, on a visit to Snowdonia in 1840, was appalled at the dirty and disrespectful condition of the parish church at Llanberis in which he sought to worship. Everything, from the tottering three-legged communion table to the tumbled frill of the

24. J. Derek Holmes, *More Roman than Rome: English Catholicism in the Nineteenth Century* (London, 1978).
25. *A History of the Church in Wales*, ed. D.G. Walker (Cardiff, 1976).

clerical surplice showed a consistent dislike of soap and ecclesiastical decency.[26] W.E. Gladstone, somewhat later, found the amount of noise and chatter which went on during a Welsh service somewhat below his exacting standards. Welsh clergy, particularly Welsh-speaking clergy, increasingly found themselves in a dilemma. The young generation of the 1840s felt a need to stress that the Church of England in Wales was a Welsh institution. Young Rowland Williams, oppidan of Eton and Fellow of King's, but Welsh-speaking son of a Welsh-speaking vicarage, attended the first St David's day dinner held in Cambridge in March 1839.[27] The following year, he was at the eisteddfod held in Liverpool and there spoke against objections to *eisteddfodau* as tending to separate nations united by one crown. Excellence in music and literature elevated character which in turn lessened national animosities. His lines, *The Tears of Cambria or The Ancient Church of West Britain against the Tyranny and Usurpation of the Ecclesiastical Commission* were composed in protest against the proposal to unite the sees of St Asaph and Bangor in the interests of Manchester. Looking across the Irish Sea in 1845 he commented that 'The mere Protestants in Ireland are not a national Church, but an overbearing sect of foreigners. My whole sympathies are with the Celts, who are both abstractedly the injured party, and are my kinsmen, rather than the mere English.'[28] He did not feel his own church to be composed of an overbearing sect of foreigners.

Even the foreigners were not invariably overbearing. The very English Connop Thirlwall, Bishop of St David's, soon developed a fluency in Welsh. Such gestures, however, could not alter the strength of Welsh dissent or the vehemence of its opposition to establishment. H.T. Edwards, Dean of Bangor, claimed in a letter to Gladstone that the alienation of the church from the affection of the people was to be found 'in the violation of their national sympathies'. The influence of the higher classes would not avail and the efforts of the church to regain the attachment of 'the religious Cymric masses' would depend upon the efforts of a 'native' clergy and episcopate.[29] As the campaign for disestablishment gathered momentum, apologists for the church increasingly stressed that it was not a mere English importation.[30] The Celtic church became the subject of an intense scholarly scrutiny unrelated to immediate concerns. One writer in 1912, for example, did not believe that there was any other institution in Wales which could compare 'in the prestige of its hoary antiquity, with the national Church of the Cymry'.[31] One figure, not without some disciples, expressed himself even more forcefully.

26. J.T. Coleridge, *A Memoir of the Rev. John Keble* (Oxford and London, 1869), p. 348.

27. G. Williams, *Religion, Language and Nationality in Wales* (Cardiff, 1979), pp. 121–22.

28. *Life and Letters of Rowland Williams*, edited by his wife, 2 vols (London, 1874) i, pp. 51, 101, 116.

29. H.T. Edwards, *A Letter to W.E. Gladstone* (London, 1870), p. 49.

30. K.O. Morgan, *Freedom or Sacrilege? A History of the Campaign for Welsh Disestablishment* (Penarth, 1966).

31. J.E. de Hirsch-Davies, *A Popular History of the Church in Wales* (London, 1912), pp. 334–35.

'Dominant alienism, the real mischief, must be removed once and for all', wrote Wade-Evans: 'The Church of England in Wales must cease, and what is left in the Establishment of the national church, the Ecclesia Wallicana, must be given opportunity to recover'.[32] Disestablishment was not averted but the linguistic and cultural orientation of the Church in Wales (as it was significantly called) have remained. While some writers have taken the view that 'the Church of Christ attaches no importance to nationality or language', others have argued that the Church in Wales does have a special responsibility to the Welsh language.[33] Although it cannot claim to be the national church it remains a church committed to a nation. Conspicuous efforts have been made to remove the taint of being the 'English church'. In recent decades prominent members of the Church in Wales, both clerical and lay, have identified themselves with political nationalism to some degree or other. During the campaign before the referendum on devolution in Wales, the archbishop of Wales took a prominent part in favour of the proposals. The outcome may show how complex is the question of a Welsh nation.

Despite the controversial reorientation of the church in Wales, a reorientation by no means complete throughout Wales, recent studies have confirmed that in contemporary Wales there is a high correlation between regular attendance at a Welsh-speaking non-Church in Wales place of worship, membership of Welsh-medium cultural societies, self-definition as Welsh rather than British and intention to vote for Plaid Cymru.[34] It is a testimony to the enduring strength of the Free Churches in nineteenth-century Wales and the extent to which language, cultural and, to an extent, political identity became fused. All the important denominations — Baptists, Independents and the relatively small number of Wesleyans — operated virtually separately according to the use of Welsh or English. Immigration into industrial South Wales and the requirements of holiday-makers and settlers in North Wales accelerated the building of new churches for English-language services. Throughout Wales, in the nineteenth century, small towns or villages went through the agony of trying to determine the language for worship. For example a correspondent writing to Jabez Bunting from Llanidloes in mid Wales in 1836 reported that

the circuit town prefers at present an equal division of Welsh and English. The English congregation here is the largest most respectable, and the most liberal; beside the English is the prevailing language in the town. Landinam, 6 miles east of Llanidloes where we have a Society of 50 members, and 2 other places contiguous to this give the decided preference to the English language . . . There are 9 other Small places connected with the Llanidloes end that decidedly prefer the Welsh.[35]

32. A.W. Wade-Evans, *Papers for Thinking Welshmen* (London, 1907), p. 59.
33. D. Ambrose Jones, *History of the Church in Wales* (Carmarthen, 1926), p. 269.
34. C.J. Thomas and C.H. Williams, 'Language and Nationalism in Wales: A Case Study', *Ethnic and Racial Studies*, 1 (2 April 1978)
35. John Simon to Jabez Bunting, 27 July 1836, Bunting MS. I owe this letter and the following one to the kindness of Professor W.R. Ward.

Two years later, also speaking of Llanidloes, another correspondent reported that 'language is a perpetual subject of contention'. Nothing but a separate English cause seemed likely to settle the matter.[36] Similar problems attended the establishment of English-language Baptist churches along the North Wales coast from the 1860s onwards.[37] When a new Baptist chapel was opened in Bangor in 1865 the then minister of what was a Welsh-speaking congregation was prepared to introduce certain English services, though no English-speaking church was in contemplation. It was partly because the Welsh-speaking did not look with favour upon their minister's ventures into English-language services that a distinct English Baptist congregation emerged in 1872.[38] However, the language issue caused most controversy amongst the Welsh Calvinistic Methodists — considerably more numerous in Wales than Weslyean Methodists and, arguably the 'national' church of Wales insofar as is had emerged in peculiarly Welsh circumstances. Although it was to style itself the Presbyterian Church of Wales in the twentieth century, it was a somewhat distinctive addition to the reformed family even so. Whether there were to be English-speaking congregations and what degree of organization they were to be permitted was a source of lengthy controversy in the late nineteenth century.[39] The Union of Welsh Independents maintained uneasy relations with the Congregational Union of England and Wales. Inevitably, too, Welsh Nonconformists joined in the general pursuit of the Celtic church as a volume by the Rev. J. Johns, *The Ancient British Church and the Welsh Baptists* testifies.[40] 'It is not by its own strength that Nonconformity succeeds', one English writer argued, 'it is simply because it is the one means that enables the Welsh to resist the revived sacerdotalism that eager ecclesiastics are trying to force upon them. Nonconformity comes far nearer the old tribal idea of Celtic Christianity than anything else.' It is not surprising to find two of the most ardent nineteenth-century exponents of a political nationalism — Michael D. Jones and 'Emrys ap Iwan' — drawn from the ranks of the Independents and Presbyterians. Nor is it surprising to find contemporary political spokesmen in Wales drawn from the same denominations.[41]

Between the two world wars, a new element entered into the picture. The conversion of Saunders Lewis, foremost Welsh critic and playwright of his generation, to Roman Catholicism introduced a fresh emphasis. Brought up among the Welsh diaspora of the Wirral, he was the son, grandson and great-grandson of Calvinistic Methodist ministers. He became the president of the Welsh Nationalist party and his views reverberate through Wales to the

---

36. W. Drewett to Jabez Bunting, 9 April 1838.

37. W.T. Whitley, *Baptists of North-West England, 1649–1913* (London and Preston, 1913).

38. G. Roberts, *History of the English Baptist Church, Bangor* (Bangor, 1905)

39. R. Buick Knox, *Voices from the Past: A History of the English Conference of the Presbyterian Church of Wales, 1889–1939* (Llandyssul, 1969).

40. J. Johns, *The Ancient British Church and the Welsh Baptists* (Carmarthen, 1889).

41. J.W. Willis Bund, *The Celtic Church of Wales* (London, 1897), p. 510.

42. R.T. Jones, *The Desire of Nations* (Llandybie, 1974).

present day. The return to Rome enabled a certain coterie of intellectuals to by-pass oppressive English Protestantism.[43] One convert stressed how 'deeply instinctive' was the Welsh feeling for Rome and how, under Rome the Welsh first grew to nationhood.[44] But, in 'returning to the generative source of their own national body' the same writer recognized that in practice to become a Roman Catholic could seem to Nonconformists 'nothing less than an act of desertion in the thick of the battle'.[45] On the other side, to the urban Catholics of the south, largely of Irish descent, such concern with providing a Roman pedigree for Welsh identity seemed of little interest. Recent surveys suggest that pupils of English-medium Roman Catholic schools in Wales have little inclination to involve themselves in Welsh cultural life.

The position of the Church of England in Ireland showed obvious parallels with its position in Wales. Whatever its actual membership and composition it too was easily labelled the English church. During the period of its establishment it suited not only Roman Catholics but also Presbyterians to so regard it. Neither Presbyterianism nor Roman Catholicism was strong in England. It could therefore serve to stress both that Catholicism was indistinguishable from Irishness and that Presbyterianism was the authentic voice of the north east. Yet, although Mrs Alexander, hymn-writing wife of the Archbishop of Armagh struck what seemed to her the right note in her lines on disestablishment

> Dimly dawns the New Year on a churchless nation
> Ammon and Amalek tread our borders down

others refused to accept that their church was doomed to be regarded as simply 'Made in England'.[46] Lord Plunket, who followed the two Englishmen, Whately and Chenevix Trench, as Archbishop of Dublin wished to banish the word 'Anglicanism'. It has been noted how in mid century the improved character of early Irish ecclesiastical studies was very largely due to what, pace Lord Plunket, we must call 'Anglican' scholarship.[47] Leading scholars talked of setting aside all their spare time to learn the Irish language. Some of the leading figures in the renaissance of the 'New Ireland' were Protestants, Douglas Hyde being the most conspicuous example. Yet they remained exceptions. Those who talked of the need to roll back the tide of Anglicization normally assumed that Protestantism would be rolled back too. Not all the Irish-language plays written by the Protestant Sixth Earl of Longford could diminish this impression and the Irish-language services in the Protestant cathedrals in Dublin were not excessively well-patronized. Even so, there was a minority at the special synod

---

43. *Presenting Saunders Lewis*, ed. A.R. Jones and G. Thomas (Cardiff, 1973), pp. 62–63.
44. Catherine Daniel, 'Wales: Catholic and Nonconformist', *Blackfriars* (March, 1957).
45. Eadem 'Catholic Converts in Wales', *The Furrow* (April, 1956), pp. 212–13; D. Attwater, *The Catholic Church in Modern Wales* (London, 1935).
46. Cited in *Irish Anglicanism, 1869–1969*, ed. M. Hurley (Dublin, 1970).
47. Ibid., p. 36.

of the Church of Ireland in 1912 which argued that just as, so it seemed, opposition to disestablishment could now appear mistaken it was unwise to oppose Home Rule. However, the northern bishops of the Church of Ireland signed the Ulster covenant.[48] Their drift in this direction was a corollary of the apparent consolidation of the language movement and Catholicism into one concept of integral nationalism. Yet, insofar as opposition to Home Rule stiffened in the north it created greater difficulties for the Church of Ireland than for either Presbyterians or Methodists. The Church of Ireland had greater strength in the south, particularly in Leinster, than they did.[49] Insofar as emotion centred around 'Ulster', even though Sir Edward Carson was a Dublin Protestant, the crisis in the north aroused ambiguous feelings amongst southern members of the Church of Ireland. The 'two-nation' theory of Ireland's identity had little appeal in the Church of Ireland, certainly not in the south. If 'West British' values could not prevail, then it might be better simply to settle for a minority status within a partitioned Ireland. It is possible, too, to argue that the Irish Catholic hierarchy came steadily to accept the view that a partitioned Ireland would in fact permit the Catholic nation to become, substantially, a reality.[50] 'Since the coming of St Patrick, fifteen hundred years ago', Mr de Valera declared in a St Patrick's Day broadcast to the United States in 1935, 'Ireland has been a Christian and a Catholic nation. All the ruthless attempts made down the centuries to force her from this allegiance have not shaken her faith. She remains a Catholic nation.'[51] The corollary of this view, inevitably, was that, after partition, Northern Ireland, in the eyes of its political masters, if not constitutionally, was a 'Protestant state'. Yet, in fact, before the First World War, opposition to Home Rule among Presbyterians and Methodists was by no means solid. One Irish Methodist writer suggests that only some 2 per cent of Irish Methodists actually desired Home Rule, but a number of Methodist ministers and laymen felt that it could not be opposed with a policy of 'blank resistance' and he admits that, 'For a time it seemed as if the Church might be rent asunder'.[52] At the Irish Methodist Conference of 1914 'a resolution pledging continued opposition to Home Rule had 188 votes in favour but as many as sixty-one votes were cast against'.[53] There were similar cross-currents among the numerically more significant Presbyterian community. After the establishment of the government of Northern Ireland these hesitations and doubts were substantially submerged.

48. Ibid., pp. 86–87

49. R.B. McDowell, *The Church of Ireland, 1869–1969* (London, 1975): D.H. Akenson, *The Church of Ireland* (New Haven and London, 1971).

50. D.W. Miller, *Church, State and Nation in Ireland, 1898–1921* (Dublin, 1973) and also E. Larkin, 'Church, State and Nation in Modern Ireland', *American Historical Review* 80 (1975), pp. 1244–76.

51. Cited in J.H. Whyte, *Church and State in Modern Ireland, 1923–1970* (Dublin, 1971).

52. *Irish Methodism in the Twentieth Century*, ed. A. McCrea (Belfast, 1931), p. 18. See also F. Jeffrey, *Irish Methodism: An Historical Account of its Traditions, Theology and Influence* (Belfast, 1964).

53. Hurley, *Irish Anglicanism*, pp. 86–87.

The paradox remained that, notwithstanding the fact that it was the religious expression of a 'national' conflict that had produced partition, all the major churches maintained ecclesiastical organizations and structures as though partition had never happened. Whether there was, and is, an Ulster identity which is not simply the wish to be British in an Irish way admits of many answers, particularly at a time when the multi-dimensional nature of Irish identity is being explored by Irish historians, but it cannot be properly considered without a consideration of the final element in the British puzzle: Scotland.[54]

'The reunited Kirk is a national symbol', wrote one author in 1960. 'One may even doubt whether there could be a Scotland without it. Certainly there could be no Church of Scotland without a living Scotland.'[55] Professor Donaldson, writing at the same time, stressed that the insistence on a national church stemmed from the feeling 'not entirely without justification' that the English subversion of Scottish nationality in the cultural sphere would also be willingly completed in the ecclesiastical.[56] Such an assessment needs to be completed by two further observations. In the first place, Scottish nationality is itself a complex phenomenon and as a national church the Church of Scotland has had to accommodate Highlander and Lowlander, English-speaker and Gaelic-speaker and antipathy between these groups was not unknown. For example, when the Duke of Argyll appointed a Highlander to the Lowland congregation in mid eighteenth-century Campbelltown the Lowlanders left the church in a body, collected a substantial sum and erected a building to seat 1600 worshippers in eighteen months.[57] The propagation of Evangelical doctrine in the Highlands was also an assault on a whole way of life which many Lowlanders found repugnant. In 1790 one preacher described their object as

The rescuing of the remoter parts of the Kingdom and its adjacent islands from barbarism, disaffection, and Popery, by infusing into the minds of the inhabitants . . . the excellence of our civil constitution and the principles of our Protestant Reformed religion, that in process of time, Britons from North and South may speak the same language, live united and loyal under the same sovereign, and worship, agreeably to Scripture and conscience, the same God.[58]

54. 'The descendants of Scottish settlers under the Stuarts and Cromwells, I have always considered as Englishmen born in Ireland, and the northern counties as a Scotch colony. And yet I am told that this is not the true state of things', wrote a bewildered Crabb Robinson in 1826: *Diary, Reminiscences and Correspondence of Henry Crabb Robinson*, ed. T. Sadler, 2 vols (London, 1872) ii, p. 38.

55. J.M. Reid, *Kirk and Nation* (London, 1960), p. 173.

56. G. Donaldson, *Scotland, Church and Nation through Six Centuries* (Edinburgh, 1960).

57. J. MacInnes, *The Evangelical Movement in the Highlands of Scotland, 1688 to 1800* (Aberdeen, 1951), p. 98: Cf.D. Bowen, *The Protestant Crusade in Ireland, 1800–1870* (Dublin, 1978): Manx impressions are recorded in *Hugh Stowell Brown*, ed. W.S. Caine (London, 1887), pp. 12–13.

58. MacInnes, *The Evangelical Movement*, pp. 244–45.

The historian of the movement comments that 'a further important by-product of the Evangelical message was the fostering of a British, rather than of a local or even Scottish loyalty'. Scotland too contained at least two civilizations, though the success of evangelical missions in the Highlands, using Gaelic, meant that there was to be no simple equation between Gaelic culture and Roman Catholicism on the one hand and Scots/English and Protestantism on the other. Nevertheless, the regional pattern of distribution of the major Presbyterian churches was marked. The United Presbyterians were scarcely known in the Highlands, Highland suspicion among members of the Free Church delayed the formation of the United Free Church of Scotland.[60]

The second observation is that the Scottish scene was transformed by the large immigration of Irish Roman Catholics into the Glasgow area, south-west Scotland and, to an extent, to Dundee.[61] This influx has meant that in the view of one Church of Scotland writer 'the Church of Rome in modern Scotland is met, technically as a "foreign church", and bears the character of an Irish intrusion into Scottish life and tradition'.[62] Mid century journals like *The Scottish Protestant* naturally devoted themselves to criticizing the 'Irish Catholic'. A committee of the Church of Scotland considered Irish immigration just after the First World War and did not mince matters in its conclusions. The commissioners attempted to make clear that their criticisms did not apply to Scottish Roman Catholics who had 'a right to call Scotland their country' or to Orangemen who were 'of the same race as ourselves and of the same Faith, and are readily assimilable'. The advent of the Irish and the consequential expansion of the Roman Catholic Church was destroying 'the unity and homogeneity' of the Scottish people. Irish economic pressure was compelling the flower of Scottish youth to leave their country. It suggested that 'the great plain of Scotland stretching from Glasgow in the west to Dundee and Edinburgh in the east will soon be dominated by the Irish race.' The Scottish sabbath was already wilting under the impact. If such comment was thought unseemly, the report had no doubt that the Irish race and the Church of Rome would not welcome the incursion of half a million Scottish Protestants into the counties around Dublin. There was no mention of a population which had, in previous centuries, moved the other way. 'God' the commissioners concluded 'placed the people of this world in families, and history which is the narrative of His providence, tells us that when kingdoms are divided against themselves they cannot stand. Those nations which were homogeneous in race were the most prosperous

59. Ibid., p. 3.
60. O. Blundell, *The Catholic Highlands of Scotland* (Edinburgh, 1900). The small contemporary Free Presbyterian Church of Scotland is a highland church, apart from a few congregations in the major cities. See *The Free Presbyterian Church of Scotland* (Inverness, 1965).
61. J.E. Handley, *The Irish in Scotland* (Glasgow, 1964).
62. R.S. Louden, *The True Face of the Kirk: An Examination of the Ethos and Tradition of the Church of Scotland* (London, 1963), pp. 98–99.

and were entrusted by the Almighty with the highest tasks.'[63] Such comments give an idea of the strength of feeling. Not that relations between the Irish and the small indigenous Scottish Roman Catholic community were at all straightforward. The 1978 issue of the *Innes Review*, later published in book form, brings to light some bitter arguments which were directly related to the national issue.[64] Whether the thistle or the shamrock or both should be sculptured on a font or altar could give rise to the most spectacular quarrels. For some 150 years, the Irish Catholic community in Scotland was served by Irish-born secular priests, many of whom took a cultural political view of their pastoral work. They also identified themselves frequently with what their historian calls 'Irish causes' — the Gaelic League, the Irish language and games (the pioneers of hurling at Maynooth were active in Glasgow) and other specifically political organizations. To a certain Father Lynch, for instance, president of the Springburn (Glasgow) branch of the Gaelic League, goes the honour of being one of the first priests to preach in Irish in Glasgow during the St Patrick's Day celebrations. The lines of division were firmly drawn and neither side anticipated substantial conversion. It needs scarcely to be added that they have not disappeared.[65]

The Scottish Episcopal Church forms a third element which also touches the national nerve.[66] While its indigenous origins are indisputable it too became vulnerable to the charge during the nineteenth century that it was the 'English' church in Scotland. As late as 1950, John Highet, in his first book on the Scottish churches, felt obliged to pursue the extent to which the Scottish Episcopal Church recruited Scotsmen to its ministry — Scottish Baptist ministerial names were also subjected to similar scrutiny.[67] However, what differentiates the Episcopal Church in Scotland last century is that the 'Anglicizing' tendencies took place from within. On the episcopal level, Englishmen could only be invited to Scotland not imposed, as they could be in Ireland and Wales prior to disestablishment. The expansion of the Episcopal Church, outside its traditional position in the north east lay chiefly among the middle classes (particularly of Edinburgh) who were themselves attracted to English ways. Thus, in the adoption of the Thirty-Nine Articles as the doctrinal standard in 1804, the use of the English term 'rector' and the depression of the Scottish communion office in favour of the English, it did seem bent on becoming English in ethos. These steps, together with the rapid development of

63. Report of a Committee to consider Overtures from the Presbytery of Glasgow and from the Synod of Glasgow and Ayr on 'Irish Immigration' and the 'Education (Scotland) Act 1918' (Edinburgh, 1923).

64. *Modern Scottish Catholicism, 1878–1978*, ed. David McRoberts (Glasgow, 1979). See also P.F. Anson, *The Catholic Church in Modern Scotland* (London, 1937).

65. B.J. Canning, *Irish-Born Secular Priests in Scotland, 1829–1979* (n.p., 1979), pp. 394, 419.

66. I.B. Cowan and S. Ervin, *The Scottish Episcopal Church* (Ambler, PA, 1966); A.L. Drummond and J. Bulloch, *The Church in Victorian Scotland, 1843–1874* (Edinburgh, 1975); W. Perry, *The Oxford Movement in Scotland* (Cambridge, 1933).

67. J. Highet, *The Churches in Scotland To-day* (Glasgow, 1950), pp. 65–66.

'ritual' widened the gap between Episcopalians and Presbyterians. By statutes of 1840 and 1864 Scottish Episcopalian orders received full recognition in England. At the end of the century, Englishman followed Englishman as Bishop of St Andrews. 'I would *far* sooner have a good Englishman than a less good Scotchman', was the comment of a reputedly 'very extreme' Scotch bishop on the appointment of Wilkinson in 1892.[68] It was not easy for a former bishop in England (even one who had laboured among the Celtic Cornish, heavily protected against an English bishop by Methodism and male voice choirs) to accept the minor position in Scottish life occupied by the Episcopal Church.[69] In his first charge, Wilkinson expressed a yearning 'in our inmost heart to have a more living place in the national life of Scotland', though it would be wrong to seek that at the expense of quenching the hope of reunion with other branches of the Catholic church.[70] It also rankled that members of the Church of England, accustomed to worshipping in the national church, often joined the Church of Scotland on going north of the border. Episcopalian hopes of 'damming this avoidable and unnecessary leakage' remained constant.[71] The stance to be adopted towards the Church of Scotland by members of the Church of England had varied. In 1798, for example, Charles Simeon recorded of a tour in Scotland that, except when he preached in episcopal chapels, he had 'officiated precisely as they do in the Kirk of Scotland: and I did so upon this principle; Presbyterianism is as much the established religion in North Britain, as Episcopacy is in the South: there being no difference between them, except in church-government.'[72] Fifty years later, after visiting St Giles' in Edinburgh, H.P. Liddon came to a very different conclusion: 'I left the church feeling a deep and unutterable aversion for a system whose outward manifestations are so hatefully repulsive. I thank God the Church of England *is* very different from the Kirk of Scotland.'[73] In between these two reactions stand a wide variety of opinions. The late Ian Henderson's *Power without Glory*, which suggested, with no great delicacy, that what passed as ecumenicity in English-speaking countries was very largely Anglican imperialism, is recent exposition of a view from the other side which does not lack nineteenth-century precedent.[74] James Cooper, in an earlier generation, took a very different approach. He had advocated *A United Church for the British Empire* in 1900 and in a sermon delivered in St Paul's Cathedral in 1918 he argued strongly against the scandal of ecclesiastical disunity. The war itself was a preacher of the obligation that the two national churches should agree. It would 'seal and consecrate the union of

68. A.J. Mason, *Memoir of George Howard Wilkinson* (London, 1910), p. 305.

69. T. Shaw, *A History of Cornish Methodism,* (Truro, 1967): J.C.C. Probert, *The Sociology of Cornish Methodism,* Cornish Methodist Historical Association, Occasional Publication, 8 (Bodmin, 1964).

70. Mason, *Wilkinson*, p. 305.

71. Cited in Highet, *The Churches in Scotland*, p. 30.

72. *Memoirs of the Life of the Rev. Charles Simeon*, ed. W. Carus (London and Cambridge, 1847), p. 113.

73. J.O. Johnson, *Life and Letters of H.P. Liddon* (London, 1904), p. 15.

74. I. Henderson, *Power without Glory* (London, 1967), p. 42.

the British Empire' and hold out an olive branch to the rest of Christendom.[75] The British Empire is no more but the trends in churchmanship which these writers represent and their attitudes to England and the Church of England have their contemporary successors. Kirk and nation do indeed remain in close relationship, but not without some difficulties, since ecumenical involvement and a revived nationalism have sometimes pointed the leaders of the church in different directions.[76] In the immediate past, many moderators and statements of the Kirk have favoured political devolution for Scotland. During its period of growth, evidence seemed to suggest that the Scottish National Party drew more strongly from voters who described themselves as Presbyterians than from any other religious body. The difficulties experienced by the Labour Party in Scotland in making up its mind about devolution in part stemmed from the nature of its Irish-descended support in the west of Scotland. Devolution failed. Perhaps, paradoxically, if it had succeeded it is arguable that, in time, an assembly in Scotland would have deprived the General Assembly of the Kirk of that still significant place as a forum for the discussion of national issues which it possesses in its absence.

In the last decade or so, prompted in large measure by events in Northern Ireland, the relationship between churches and nations within the British Isles has been subjected to fresh and largely hostile scrutiny. However admirable the comments of theologians and sociologists, pleas for the prising apart of religion and national identity will only be superficial so long as the full complexity of that relationship within the British Isles is ignored.[77] This essay has attempted to draw attention to some of them, though its focus has meant that the contribution made to the ecclesiastical life of England by Irishmen, Scotsmen and Welshmen has been insufficiently stressed. The partiality of Scotsmen, from Tait to Runcie, for the see of Canterbury is a subject in itself and there was a period when Congregational thought in England seemed exclusively in Scottish hands. A critical scrutiny of the career of the Wesleyan Hugh Price Hughes which makes no mention of his Welshness neglects a complete dimension.[78] Lines addressed (in Welsh) by Saunders Lewis to the Rev. Dr J.D. Jones, C.H. (late of Bournemouth) give some indication of the tensions involved:

75. James Cooper, *A United Church for the British Empire* (1902); *The Church Catholic and National* (Glasgow, 1898); *Reunion: A Voice from Scotland* (London, 1918).

76. M. Small, *Growing Together: Some Aspects of the Ecumenical Movement in Scotland, 1924–1964* (Edinburgh, 1975).

77. A.E.C.W. Spencer, 'Christian Proposals for the Irish Churches' *The Month* (January, 1973); S.G. Mackie, *Ireland's Conflict Diminishes Me* (London, 1974).

78. J.H.S. Kent 'Hugh Price Hughes and the Nonconformist Conscience', *Essays in Modern English Church History*, ed. G.V. Bennett and J.D. Walsh (London, 1966). For a Welsh contemporary he was 'Un o Gymry enwocaf yr Oes' (one of the most celebrated Welshmen of his time), J. Price Roberts, *Hugh Price Hughes, Ei Fywyd a'i Lafur* (Bangor 1903). See H. Scott Holland, *A Bundle of Memories* (London, n.d.), p. 153.

From your feathered pulpit your tallow sermon
Dropped upon the gluttons
The lard-droppings of your greasy English
Was a service for the guzzlers.
Now your return to the land of the poor
That's sore under the thumb of the blusterer,
With your harsh ranting to a fragile nation
To bend to the yoke and the cord.[79]

'The concept of united national and regional churches goes back', concludes a Scotsman at Oxford, 'to the days of homogeneous societies geographically demarcated and, even so, represents a tradition that has proved itself hostile to freedom and openness.'[80]

79. Translation by Gwyn Thomas in Jones and Thomas, *Saunders Lewis*, p. 181.
80. J. Macquarrie, *Christian Unity and Christian Diversity* (London, 1975), pp. 12–13.

8

On Prophecy and Politics: Some Pragmatic Reflexions

Prophecy is inescapably controversial; tension is always in the air. Prophetic utterance, no doubt properly, is apt to make many historians irritable and uncomfortable. Preoccupied with the past, the last thing they want to be saddled with is any responsibility for discerning the future or even seeking to make sense of the present. When Hugh Trevor-Roper, as he then was, attacked the writings of Arnold Toynbee in a savage article in *Encounter* in 1957, the gravamen of his charge was that Toynbee was not a historian at all, but a prophet, and, for good measure, a false one at that. Decent historians should not bother with the ten volumes of *A Study of History* because they were not history.[1] The charges, in detail, may well have been justified, but the asperity went deeper. The caste of mind of historians, if they were truly professional, should make 'prophetic history' an impossibility. Prophets were indifferent to 'facts', or cavalier in their treatment of them, in pursuit of a grand vision. Historians, on the other hand, were obsessively fussy about details and were relatively unconcerned about grand theory. Indeed, historiography had 'come of age' precisely to the extent that it emancipated itself from prophecy.

The writings of Paul Tillich, widely thought in some circles to be a 'prophet', have likewise been subjected to fierce criticism by historians. Professor W.R. Ward, for example, is undoubtedly glad to have found a kindred spirit in a contemporary of Tillich who, in 1924, accused his friend of succumbing to the 'demonism of concepts'. Tillich's *Grundlinien des religiösen Sozialismus* (1923) endeavoured to move beyond both the sacramental-historically unconscious and the rational-historically critical attitudes to life in a spirit of prophecy. 'The sacramental and the critical attitude', wrote Tillich, 'unite in the consciousness of the *Kairos*, in the spirit of prophecy.' However, as Ward's exposition of Tillich's thought proceeds, he is unable to detect what the German theologian-philosopher otherwise dismisses as the empty precisely is the new content which Tillich seeks to insert in what the abstractions of freedom and equality. Ward speculates on whether the call for the application of a 'universal religious Eros' to the rational economy amounted to anything more than a

---

1. W.H. McNeill, 'Toynbee and the Historical Profession', in J.K. Burton, ed., *Essays in European History* (New York and London, 1989), pp. 77–84; H.R. Trevor-Roper, 'The Prophet', *New York Review of Books*, 12 Oct. 1989. Trevor-Roper was reviewing McNeill's biography of Toynbee.

routine call for 'a new spirit in industry'. By the mid twenties he believes that even Tillich was coming to recognize that history was not going the way his grandiose concepts suggested it should.

Tillich's response was not in any way to study history, but to adapt the concepts. Thus, he wrote that to observe a period as *Kairos* meant 'to observe it in the sense of inescapable decision, unavoidable responsibility, to observe it in the spirit of prophecy'. All of this did not have much connection with day-to-day politics: 'a venture into the ultimate depth and the whole breadth of what is human is to be the socialism we serve'. Tillich believed that historical periods were categorized by content and form. The modern era was bourgeois-capitalist and its form was democracy. He was not moved to defend democracy. Ward is scathing about the language of a man 'blinded by concepts to the facts of life'. Tillich had embarked upon an 'openness to culture' in 1919, but had merely 'ended in insulation from political existence'. After the Second World War, Tillich continued to assert that if the prophetic message was true, there could be nothing 'beyond religious socialism', though it was not applicable in the foreseeable future. One had to endure a period of living in a vacuum which might be deepened into a 'sacred void' of waiting. Ward comments tartly that a 'sacred void' is not a luxury available to a practising politician — and passes on to a consideration of marginally more congenial thinkers.[2]

The encounter between Tillich and Ward can be considered at various levels. We see on the one hand an Oxford-trained historian, who spent most of his professional working life in the robust atmosphere of northern English universities, and on the other hand a philosopher/theologian of a very different stamp and cultural ambience. We have a problem of language, though Ward readily concedes that the 'dismally unfruitful character' of the Protestant-social enterprise, as he calls it, cannot be ascribed to the peculiar seductions of the German language.

More fundamentally, however, there is the problem of 'prophecy' itself in the modern era. What is the historian to say about utterances 'in the spirit of prophecy', whether in German or any other language? What is meant by the attribution of 'prophetic insight' or a claim to 'prophetic status'? What is the relationship between 'prophecy' and the political process? Can 'prophet' and 'democrat' be reconciled? If God had formerly spoken through the prophets, did he come to favour the secret ballot in the nineteenth century? Do 'prophetic statements' come into the category of the 'great texts' of political or social philosophy whose interpreters have been excoriated by Quentin Skinner? Skinner argues that we should not regard the 'classical works' as attempts to set down universal propositions of perennial importance. Perhaps, therefore, we have to recognize that even a 'prophetic' statement 'is inescapably the embodiment of a particular intention, on a particular occasion, addressed to

2. W.R. Ward, *Theology, Sociology and Politics: the German Protestant Social Conscience, 1890–1933* (Bern, 1979), pp.208–16.

the solution of a particular problem, and thus specific to its situation in a way that it can only be naive to try to transcend'.[3] Yet, of course, throughout its history the church has resisted any such rigid contextualization. Plausibly or not, in particular instances, theologians have constantly engaged in what might be described as 'creative transcription'.[4] These are difficult questions which cannot be resolved in one essay, but they permeate all that follows.

The church historian will be well aware of the fact that 'prophecy' poses problems not only for the historian, but also for the church. The tension between 'prophet' and 'priest' is a perennial aspect of ecclesiastical history. In his study of Lamennais, for example, Alec Vidler directly reflected on this relationship. The encounter between Lamennais and Gregory XVI was not between a good 'prophet' and a bad 'priest' but between a good 'prophet' and a good 'priest', both of whom displayed the characteristic shortcomings of 'priest' and 'prophet' respectively. Gregory had a responsibility to maintain the ecclesiastical system intact and was not disposed to allow a 'prophet' an area of autonomy. Lamennais, however, believed that he was more accurately reading the signs of the times. He made no allowance for the church as a social institution. The compromises and intrigues of papal diplomacy were odious to him. The mission of the church was to return — immediately — to its pristine poverty. The priest, Vidler argues, drawing upon Congar, is primarily concerned with the maintenance of traditional doctrine and discipline in the church, and its hierarchical structure and cultus. The prophet, on the other hand, has a sense of being directly charged by God with a mission to declare the divine judgement on ecclesiastical or worldly corruption or to urge the church into new paths in changing circumstances.[5]

As in this instance, the relations between priest and prophet may become particularly acute in the Roman Catholic church because of the nature of its discipline and its centralized authority. It would not be difficult to give many more examples of Roman Catholic prophets. However, it would be quite misleading to suppose that 'prophecy' has posed no problems in the world of Protestant Evangelicalism. It is a question of balance and emphasis. In most instances within Roman Catholicism the priestly conception has been paramount, whereas within Protestant Evangelicalism there has been a reluctance, in many cases, to employ the term 'priest' at all. The 'sacerdotal spirit' has been looked upon with extreme suspicion, because all too often it had issued in 'priestly despotism'.[6] It is the 'prophetic mode' that has been

3. Q. Skinner, 'Meaning and Understanding in the History of Ideas', *History and Theory*, 8 (1969), and the debate and discussion in J. Tully, ed., *Meaning and Context: Quentin Skinner and his Critics* (Cambridge, 1988).

4. J. Barton, *People of the Book? The Authority of the Bible in Christianity* (London, 1988), pp. 12–23, 76–78; R. Morgan and J. Barton, *Biblical Interpretation* (Oxford, 1988).

5. A.R. Vidler, *Prophecy and Papacy: A Study of Lamennais, the Church and the Revolution* (London, 1954), pp. 275–78.

6. J.P. Parry, *Democracy and Religion: Gladstone and the Liberal Party, 1867–1875* (Cambridge, 1986), p. 205.

most appealing and normative. Nevertheless, whatever precise nomenclature has been employed within the diversity of Protestant Evangelicalism, an ordained 'ministry' has remained with a major responsibility for cult. Hence a tension between minister/pastor and prophet has been present, too, on the Protestant side, if not in such an acute form, and it has been demonstrated on innumerable occasions in the life of Christian congregations. A 'prophet' who has moved too far away from the views of his congregation has been apt to find himself out of a job; a 'pastor' who has merely pandered to its prejudices has been apt to sink into sterility.

Given an emphasis upon the 'centrality of the Word', therefore, it is not surprising that Protestant Evangelicalism has conceived itself to be in a constant and creative relationship with the prophet tradition of the Old Testament. In successive generations, preachers have uttered 'prophetic' words against the self-image of the age. Recent works have given us a fresh understanding of the importance of prophecy in the first half of the nineteenth century in Britain.[7] It engaged the sustained and systematic attention of minds as diverse as James Hatley Frere and John Henry Newman, amongst many others.[8] There remained a confidence in prophecy as prediction. Post-millennialists and pre-millennialists eagerly canvassed their views and found support for their particular interpretations in varied parts of Scripture. At Albury Park, his Surrey country estate, the banker Henry Drummond had a series of prophetic conferences in the late 1820s, not entirely to the liking of Charles Simeon.[9] The date of the millennium itself was naturally a source of continuing interest. Living in what he called the age of expediency and prudence, Edward Irving attempted not only 'prophecy', but stimulated 'prophesying', with unsatisfactory results. The Prophecy Investigation Society began its work in 1842. E.B. Elliott, a Fellow of Trinity College, Cambridge, produced four volumes of *Horae Apocalypticae* in 1844. These scholarly prophetic studies pointed to the arrival of the millennium two-thirds of the way through the nineteenth century. However, when it failed to arrive, good scholarly reasons were found why a later date should be preferred. This was the kind of world in which the Earl of Shaftesbury felt at home.[10] Every political crisis could be illumined precisely by prophetic interpretation — for example, *The Eastern Question. Turkey, its Mission and Doom: A Prophetical Instruction* (1876).[11] Similarly, I possess a pamphlet which is able to explain the Kaiser's behaviour in 1914 with the help of 'prophecy'.

7. W.H. Oliver, *Prophets and Milennialists: The Uses of Biblical Prophecy in England from the 1790s to the 1840s* (Auckland, 1978); P.J. Korshin, *Typologies in England, 1650–1820* (Princeton, 1982), particularly 'Typology and Prophecy', pp. 328–68.

8. S. Gilley, 'Newman and Prophecy, Evangelical and Catholic', *Journal of the United Reformed Church History Society*, 3, 5 (March 1985), pp. 160–88.

9. D. Rosman, *Evangelicals and Culture* (London, 1984), pp. 24–26; D.W. Bebbington, *Evangelicalism in Modern Britain* (London, 1989), pp. 85–86.

10. G.B.A.M. Finlayson, *The Seventh Earl of Shatfesbury, 1801–1885* (London, 1981), esp. chapter 7, 'Prophecy and Protestantism, 1841–1846'.

11. R.T. Shannon, *Gladstone and the Bulgarian Agitation, 1876* (London, 1963), pp. 161–62.

John Harrison has tried to distinguish between 'respectable millennialists' and 'popular millenarians', though he admits that the dichotomy cannot be applied rigidly. Anglican parsons and Dissenting ministers who possessed a penchant for prophecy were not in the same camp as Joanna Southcott, either in their own estimation or in that of the society in which they moved. His work, and that of other scholars, discloses a millennial world of great diversity, populated both by 'prophets' and 'madmen'. He admits that there are 'no neat conclusions to be drawn, only the record of an exploration into largely unknown territory' in seeking to describe and explain strange people with strange ideas.[12]

Thomas Arnold did not think himself a strange person. He addressed himself to the interpretation of prophecy in two sermons in 1839. Prophecy, he believed, should not be confused with history. Prophecy was 'God's voice, speaking to us respecting the issue in all time of that great struggle which is the real interest of human life, the struggle between good and evil'. Prophecy did not 'forecast' the coming of Jesus, and if He fulfilled prophecies it was because in Him the struggle between good and evil (the heart of all prophecy) was perfectly exemplified. Arnold knew some German scholarship, and there are some emphases in his writing which are similar to German writers. For Bunsen, for example, 'Prediction was the least important aspect of prophecy. What mattered more was the ability to see behind the outward course of events that divine government of the world that had the unity of mankind and the recognition of God as its goal'.[13] For many writers in the world of biblical scholarship, in Britain and Germany, it was 'the religion of the prophets' which achieved the greatest insights and, in the eyes of Wellhausen and his immediate successors, enabled Israel to rise above its surroundings. Prophets, it was supposed, stood apart from, and were often antagonistic to, cultic acts and ritual worship. The crime of Caiaphas, in the eyes of Dean Stanley, was 'the last culminating proof that the opposition of the Prophets to the growth of the Priestly and Sacrificial system was based on an eternal principle, which carries with a rebuke to the office which bears the name of Priesthood throughout the world'.[14]

It is not surprising, therefore, that Evangelical scholars were particularly attracted to the investigation of the world of the prophets and an exposition of their message. The major and minor prophets were subjected to intense scrutiny. The young Robertson Smith, who was later to write so brilliantly on Israelite prophecy, wrote in 1868 that

in Prophecy there was provided a certain supernatural *matter* of thought in vision, etc., probably by supernatural action on the nervous system. This

---

12. J.F.C. Harrison, *The Second Coming: Popular Millenarianism, 1789–1850* (London, 1979), p. 230.

13. Cited in J.W. Rogerson, *Old Testament Criticism in the Nineteenth Century: England and Germany* (London, 1984), p. 127.

14. Cited in Rogerson, *Old Testament Criticism*, p. 241.

fitted into the natural matter present to the prophet's mind, and the two thus combined were moulded into a thought by the action of the Prophet's mental powers guided by the formative influence of the Divine Spirit. The double divine action below and above the Prophet's own activity sufficed perfectly to control the result without interfering in a magical manner with the laws of human thought.[15]

Robertson Smith wrote the *Encyclopaedia Britannica* article on 'Prophet'. Prophets were very remarkable people, but for him no purely naturalistic explanation of their message was acceptable.[16]

It scarcely needs to be said that these issues were intensely controversial for Protestant Evangelicals. There were general problems associated with critical scholarship *per se* and particular problems relating to the structures and meanings of individual prophetic books.[17] Once a critical methodology had been accepted, British Nonconformists were poised to make a contribution to Old Testament scholarship on a far greater scale than would be suggested by their numerical strength. In successive generations, for example, Baptists were to produce such scholars as Wheeler Robinson, H.H. Rowley, and D.S. Russell.

These developments in scholarship, and their reception in the churches, have been placed in historical context in several recent studies, but no attempt seems to have been made to assess the relationship between the changing understandings of the prophetic on the one hand and broader political developments on the other.[18] We now pass on to consider this third area of tension.

Prophets remained sources of inspiration for Protestant Evangelicals, perhaps all the more so as emphasis shifted to an understanding of prophecy as judgement on the present rather than prediction of the future. 'New-style' prophecy is a neglected element in the crystallization of the 'Nonconformist

15. J.S. Black and G.W. Chrystal, eds, *The Life of William Robertson Smith* (London, 1917), pp. 96–97; William Robertson Smith, *The Prophets of Israel and their Place in History to the Close of the Eight Century BC* (London, 1882); R.A. Riesen, *Criticism and Faith in Late Victorian Scotland* (London, 1985).

16. Of course, prophecy came to be seen in many quarters as capable of purely 'secular' interpretation, and there were many contemporary Victorians who were anxious to be regarded, or were regarded, as 'prophets'. Froude described Carlyle as 'a prophet, in the Jewish sense of the word' and Matthew Arnold, in his introduction to *Culture and Anarchy* did not like to be referred to as an 'elegant Jeremiah'. Ruskin similarly springs to mind. See G. Landow, *Elegant Jeremiahs: The Sage from Carlyle to Mailer* (Ithaca, 1986), and his *Victorian types, Victorian Shadows: Biblical Typology in Victorian Literature, Art and Thought* (Boston and London, 1980); P. Keating, *The Victorian Prophets* (London, 1981).

17. W.B. Glover, *Evangelical Nonconformity and Higher Criticism in the Nineteenth Century* (London, 1954).

18. N.M. de S. Cameron, *Biblical and Higher Criticism and the Defense of Infallibilism in Nineteenth Century Britain* (Lewiston, NY 1987); D.C. Smith, *Passive Obedience and Prophetic Protest: Social Criticism in the Scottish Church, 1830–1945* (New York, 1987), pp. 254–55, explicitly suggests that the greatest contributions of Old Testament criticism was to awaken the church to the 'central message of the great prophets'.

Conscience' in the 1870s and 1880s. The belief that there was no valid or meaningful distinction between the spheres of 'religion' and 'politics' was itself presented as 'prophetic'. Prophets thought that attempts to delineate the sacred and the secular were fundamentally misconceived. If Amos had been alive in the last decades of the century he would have been a Nonconformist standing for the House of Commons — or he might have been Mr Gladstone.

In February 1877 Gladstone was informed by Newman Hall that a fellow Nonconformist described him in these terms: 'How grandly Gladstone carried himself last night. He becomes more & more a prophet of the most high God. We ought to be devoutly thankful to God for having called to the side of truth, righteousness and humanity, the most splendidly gifted man in Europe.'[19] Perhaps, indeed, 'prophecy' is a vital clue to understanding the liaison between Gladstone and the Nonconformists. They both believed, in Parry's words, that God spoke with equal force to all mankind, rather than primarily to the 'thinking classes'. Gladstonians saw the purpose of the politician was 'not to direct but to inspire. If he succeeded in maintaining the public mind in a state of alertness against manifestations of evil, those manifestations might be checked: if not, prospects were dark.' In effect, the politician was prophet. It was James Bryce who invited Gladstone to dinner on 12 July 1878 to meet Robertson Smith, and it is perhaps no surprise to find Gladstone reading Leathes on *Old Testament Prophecy* on 12 June 1880.[20] It was because he believed that the people could be infused with a thirst for righteousness that the Liberal leader could approve of the proverb *Vox populi vox Dei*.

The political mobilization of Nonconformity, largely in the form of Gladstonian Liberalism, was at once a crusade against certain specific 'evils' and the expression of the particular sense of injustice felt by a variegated but substantial section of the Anglo-Welsh population. Successive extensions of the franchise in the nineteenth century meant that this segment could now participate in the political process to a degree that had not been possible before. Deep-seated suspicions of the world of politics were replaced by a desire to participate. The 'democratization' of politics in nineteenth-century Britain, in so far as it had occurred, was put forward as a good in itself. Baptists and Congregationalists, in particular, were apt to see in their own ecclesiastical polity a model of democratic government. It was prophetic to be a Liberal.

But there was a problem. Nonconformists had been accustomed to see themselves as 'outsiders', yet they now appeared to be seeking to become 'insiders'. They could only enter Parliament by taking part in elections as members of a political party. The proportion of Nonconformist MPs could

---

19. Shannon, *Gladstone and the Bulgarian Agitation*, p. 163.
20. Parry, *Religion and Democracy*, p. 451; H.C.G. Matthew, ed., *The Gladstone Diaries, ix, 1875–1880* (Oxford, 1986), pp. 330, 539. Boyd Hilton, 'Gladstone's Theological Politics', in M. Bentley and J. Stevenson, ed., *High and Low Politics in Modern Britain* (Oxford, 1983), p. 53, speaks of Gladstone's 'prophetic admonitions'.

steadily mount, but Nonconformists were not a majority in the electorate pre-1918. At the heart of the evolving system of British government was the majority principle. Governments were made possible by winning a majority in a General Election, and then proceeded on the basis of majority support in Parliament. Old Testament prophets, on the other hand, appealed particularly to Nonconformist communities which felt themselves excluded, in a certain sense, from society. The notion of a 'remnant' — a group by definition minoritarian and 'against the stream' — had a haunting biblical basis. It was difficult, however, to sustain such a conviction when majorities were now sought and required as 'democracy' expanded.

The problem could only be 'solved' on the comforting assumption that the majority in an electorate could be brought to support or accept the policies and programmes which flowed from the prophetic insights which Nonconformists believed they brought to late Victorian politics. The career of John Bright was an initial illustration that this assumption was not well founded. His convictions on many public issues reflected his own understanding of the biblical message, but he had to face the fact that his opposition to the Crimean War had brought him a certain respect in some quarters but had no political consequence. He was emphatically in a minority and was seen by his admirers to be a voice in the wilderness. His admirers in Manchester diminished and he lost his seat there at the next General Election. It was possible to draw the conclusion that the role of prophet and the role of parliamentarian were incompatible, and indeed Bright was at times almost persuaded of that himself. When he did return to the Commons, as MP for Birmingham, he deliberately distanced himself from Birmingham Quakers who wanted him to espouse policies, on war and peace in particular, which he deemed unacceptable to his electorate. Compromises with conscience, Bright seems to have concluded, were incumbent on parliamentary prophets, although he would not have expressed himself as bluntly as Lord John Russell did in the 1841 debate on whether Jews could be admitted to municipal office. Prophecy, he had then declared, was of doubtful interpretation, and legislative deliberations could not take cognizance of prophetic Scriptures.[21]

Bright was not a democrat in the sense of believing in one man, one vote, and he vehemently opposed the notion of female suffrage. He had played a major part in winning the Second Reform Act, but he thought universal suffrage a dangerous concept. He supposed that to empower 'the poor' or 'the residue' by giving them the franchise could be disastrous, not merely for his own bourgeois prosperity, but for the progress of society as a whole. He seems to have believed that 'the residue' were xenophobic and warlike. Peace, but perhaps not justice, required their exclusion from power.

That was not a conclusion which would have commended itself to the generation after the turn of the century which saw fresh opportunities

21. K.G. Robbins, *John Bright* (London, 1979) and 'John Bright — Quaker Politician: A Centenary Appreciation', *Journal of the Friends' Historical Society*, 55 (1989), pp. 238–49.

for 'prophetic action'. Silvester Horne can serve as an example of this new confidence. A Congregational minister, he successfully stood for the Commons in the January 1910 election. He interpreted the result as a victory for 'the people' against 'the peers' and saw no conflict between his two roles as minister and politician. The Congregational way was itself democratic, and he certainly did not see himself as a priest living apart from the world. To campaign against poverty, cruelty, and disease was a Christian duty and authentically prophetic.[22] Horne's theme was echoed in many Nonconformist pulpits during this decade. Texts from Isaiah and Jermiah were pressed into service to urge righteousness and justice and to castigate corruption and conspicuous consumption. Yet Horne's own parliamentary career, brief though it was because of his early death, was not a 'success'. What made a big impression in Whitefield's Tabernacle did not go down so well at Westminster. Perhaps it was true, as the *Methodist Recorder* suggested on Horne's election, that a man could not do everything. There was a tendency for ministers to speak words of much heat and little judgement. They should learn that there was a time to keep silence.[23]

The intense politicization of Nonconformity provoked a modest backlash in some quarters. The anonymous author of *Nonconformity and Politics* (1909) was one of a number of voices to protest about the extent to which it appeared that all Nonconformist meetings were being given up to political discussion. Ministers were ready to produce *ex cathedra* pronouncements on any and every political argument of the day. This political activity was in turn held to explain the decline in Nonconformist denominational membership which was becoming apparent. Such claims, however, were vigorously contested by proponents of the 'social Gospel'. It was argued that the working classes were indifferent to the churches, because the churches were indifferent to social justice. It was also suggested that if denominational membership was indeed falling, because certain people could no longer tolerate the political messages to which they were subjected from the pulpit, that was even a cause for satisfaction. What was such a trivial thing as membership statistics as compared with the salvation of the world?

The coming of war in 1914 raised the old issue in a new form. Somewhat optimistically, John Clifford's new year message of 1914 proclaimed that militarism belonged to the Dark Ages and had to go. In August, however, he had to say something specific. This time the prophet had a new song to sing. He diagnosed a struggle between the forces of freedom and the forces of slavery. 'We believe', declared the Baptist Union Council in September, 'the call of God has come to Britain to spare neither blood nor treasure in the struggle to shatter a great anti-Christian attempt to destroy the fabric of Christian civilization.'[24]

22. D.W. Bebbington, *The Nonconformist Conscience: Chapel and Politics, 1870–1914* (London, 1975), p. 107.

23. S.E. Koss, *Nonconformity in Modern British Politics* (London, 1975), p. 107.

24. Cited in A. Wilkinson, *Dissent or Conform? War, Peace and the English Churches, 1900–1945* (London, 1986), p. 24.

Prophecy in the pulpit came to have a certain similarity of sentiment and expression. The President of the Primitive Methodist Conference, 1916–17, who declared that he was born to declaim, was able to preach to the text, 'And David went on, and grew great, and the Lord God of Hosts was with him' (II Smauel 5: 10), in politically suitable circumstances.[25] George Adam Smith, author of *Modern Criticism and the Preaching of the Old Testament* (1901) and many other books on the prophets, and at the time Principal of Aberdeen University, saw it his prophetic duty to go on a speaking tour of the United States to proclaim the justice of the British cause there.[26] Perhaps *Vox populi vox Dei* as conceived by the Gladstonians was perfectly exemplified?

There were, however, smaller voices who were apt to believe that such men did not have a monopoly of prophecy; indeed, in all likelihood they were false prophets. Turning swords into ploughshares was a task for Christians in time of war, even if it should result in unpopularity and criticism. Pulpit prophets of 1914–18 were telling the people what they wanted to hear, whereas the prophetic message of pacifists was of such a challenging character that its veracity was almost established by its rejection. Yet there was no doubting that the war was popular, even if the moral claims made for it were rejected as ill founded. That could mean that *vox populi* was at loggerheads with *vox Dei*. God was more likely to speak through a 'remnant' than through a parliamentary majority at Westminster. Prophecy and democracy pointed in different directions.

The post-war climate was suspicious of prophecy, whatever its precise content. The nature of the war, as it had turned out, seemed to make a mockery of the claims which had been made concerning its ultimate significance. Indeed, it was becoming increasingly difficult to find space for 'the prophetic'. Pragmatic politicians, often of Nonconformist stock, became somewhat ashamed of the rhetoric they had employed and confined themselves to less ambitious statements about their behaviour and objectives. Pulpit prophets also in some cases came to regret their own language and the uncomplicated way in which they had applied their understanding of the Old Testament to Europe at war.

In this respect, the First World War is perhaps a watershed. The surfeit of supposedly prophetic utterance left many contemporaries after 1914 wondering whether the term 'prophetic' was useful or even meaningful any longer. It is a problem which remains in the present. The use and abuse of prophecy raised fundamental issues of hermeneutics. In what way, if at all, was it possible to 'apply' the insights of the Old Testament prophets to the political and economic structures of a very of a very different mid twentieth-century world? The difficulty and even the absurdity of a simple-minded 'translation' from the one to the other had become apparent. After 1918, the further extension

25. Wilkinson, *Dissent or Conform*, p. 30.
26. S. Wallace, *War and the Image of Germany: British Academics, 1914–1918* (Edinburgh, 1988), pp. 172–73; L. Adam Smith, *George Adam Smith* (London, 1943), pp. 169–76.

of the franchise, and the subsequent extension to all women, confronted Nonconformists in particular with the political reality of a democracy which they had latterly pressed for, but whose consequence was to deprive them, over time, of the political influence they had managed to achieve under Liberal auspices before 1914.

The disintegration of the Liberal Party led to a three-way distribution of the Nonconformist vote and its collapse as a coherent entity. A symbol of this dissolution was that it was a Conservative Prime Minister, Stanley Baldwin, who addressed a National Free Church conference in March 1925 on the theme of 'Christian Ideals'. He treated his audience to seasoned reflections on the respective responsibilities, and spheres of operation, of the politician and the churches. It was quite right for politicians to be told, and to be told emphatically, that the Christian churches should give themselves to helping in the elevation of the social condition of the country. Yet, in moving to this objective, he pointed out that the politician had to deal with the mass of the people as they were. Parliament represented all the citizens in a way that religious bodies could not.[27] Neither in this address nor in others to similar gatherings did he make reference to Old Testament prophets. Parliamentary democracy, he implied, required a restraint and mutual respect if it was to function effectively as a system of government. The inspiration to which prophets laid claim could issue in tyranny and an insensitivity to the opinion of others.

Within a few years it had become apparent in Europe just how difficult it was to make a democratic system of government function effectively. It was against the background of Hitler's advent to power in 1933 that A.D. Lindsay addressed himself to *The Churches and Democracy* in lectures before a Methodist audience in 1934. Was Christianity specifically concerned with any particular system of government? He noted that Barthians did not appear to concern themselves with this form of government rather than that. It was as wrong, apparently, on their analysis, to identify the church with Liberalism as it was to identify it with National Socialism. Lindsay himself, however, went on to analyze contemporary trends and concluded (p. 38) that if the 'economic mass forces win the day and democracy, as we have known it, disappears, the Churches will disappear along with it'. It was therefore right for Free Churchmen to play their full part in a democracy and, by implication, to be prepared to defend it by force if need be against the threat of external aggression. Of course, democracy had its limitations, and there was always room for improvement, but as a system for Protestant Evangelicals it could not be bettered.[28] It could be further argued, though Lindsay did not specifically make the point, that Hitler, as a kind of prophet, was not the model to follow.

---

27. S. Baldwin, *On England* (Harmondsworth, 1937), pp. 208-9.
28. A.D. Lindsay, *The Churches and Democracy* (London, 1934).

Over the next few years, however, as the European crisis deepened, the tension between the claims of 'prophecy' and 'democracy' became more acute. Many 'prophets' in the churches renounced war and would not support another. The Peace Pledge Union attracted many into its ranks who were convinced that they were prophets for their times. It comes as no surprise, for example, to find Charles Raven described as 'an electrifying and prophetic preacher'. It has rightly been noted that 'Christians on the left charged those on the right with wilfully neglecting the Old Testament prophets and their passionate denunciations of the rich and social injustice'.[29] It remained the case that the prophets were attractive models for various types of Dissenter. It was still the case that biblical scholarship, in general, saw the prophets as individuals who were in rebellion against the cultic and social establishment.

The prophetic message of peace was attractive in many quarters in the 1930s. It could indeed be said for a time that 'prophecy' and 'democracy' walked hand in hand. but was 'democracy' asleep? There was a 'voice in the wilderness', but one 'the people' did not wish to hear. Churchill's 'prophecy', however, was secular. It did not root itself in biblical insights. Its specific content, indeed, appeared to be the direct antithesis of what was being offered as 'prophecy' within the churches. Churchill and some of his associates were denounced in various ecclesiastical gatherings as 'warmongers'. Church leaders signed their peace pledges and sought, with some success, to influence opinion against rearmament. Baldwin would have risked electoral defeat in 1935 if he had openly campaigned for rearmament.[30] By 1939, however, the tide of opinion had turned. 'Democracy' was prepared to support another war. There were many people who believed that it was a struggle for 'Christian civilization'.[31] In the reaction against 'appeasement', there was strong criticism of those pacifists who had allegedly placed 'democracy' in danger by a supposedly prophetic obsession with 'peace' to the exclusion of almost all other political and ethical considerations. From this perspective, prophets were not merely tiresome, they were anachronistically dangerous. They threatened the 'democracy' they professed to admire. This was the kind of paradox that appealed to Reinhold Niebuhr, whose stock as a 'true prophet' accordingly rose.

In the post-war world in Britain, discourse about prophecy and its alleged relevance continued to be heard, but the cultural climate in which it was uttered became ever more agnostic. The steady decline in basic biblical knowledge in society at large meant that references to the word of the prophets evoked less and less resonance with each succeeding decade. The growth of religious pluralism made it increasingly unlikely that politicians in a democracy, whatever their own personal beliefs and desires, could allow the 'prophetic' voice, as perceived by a minority, to be a major determinant of

29. Wilkinson, *Dissent or Conform?*, p. 127.
30. K.G. Robbins, *Appeasement* (Oxford, 1988).
31. See below, pp. 195–214.

policy. Even so, there has been a continuing concern within the churches for what is considered to be a 'prophetic' witness.[32]

It has become increasingly difficult, however, to suppose that there is a sufficiently coherent, single prophetical tradition in the Old Testament from which even to make a start in 'applying' the message. The thrust of biblical scholarship has been to draw out the diversity and complexity of the prophetic world.[33] It has also largely discounted the polarity between 'the prophet' and 'the priest' so dear to Protestant Evangelicalism.[34] It is a moral theologian who writes that, 'The Old Testament prophets provide dangerous models of black and white denunciation which can hinder Christians from perceiving the ambiguities and ambivalences involved in moral discernment in relation to detailed situations and policies.'[35] It is a contemporary Archbishop of York who has written of the way in which close contact with decision-makers and the complex problems they face can have 'a devastating effect on prophetic certainties. And actually to share responsibility is even more devastating'.[36] At the same time, there has been a fresh emphasis on the extraordinary subtlety of the language and imagination of 'the prophets' in the Old Testament.[37] Their insights were by no means as 'black and white' as some latter-day prophets presuming to interpret them, have supposed.

Biblical scholarship, on the one hand, and the exigencies of the conduct of democratic politics, on the other, have therefore combined to render 'the prophetic' problematic in twentieth-century Britain. Dr Carroll argues that since it is impossible objectively to differentiate between prophets 'mediated truth will not be apparent to people outside the discipleship of a particular prophet'. Yet it would be misleading to suppose that this is an entirely new situation. He himself suggests that the vexed question of who was a 'true' and who was a 'false' prophet was never resolved in biblical times and is most unlikely to be settled in a modern secular society.[38]

Naturally, the framework of democracy, as understood in twentieth-century Britain, was not present in the Old Testament, but the tension between statecraft and prophecy was endemic in the history of Israel. It was and is ultimately a debate about the nature of power and our apprehensions of the working of God in the world. It is often suggested that the relationship

---

32. R. Gill, *Prophecy and Praxis* (London, 1981); R. Ambler and D. Haslam, ed., *Agenda for Prophets* (London, 1980).

33. J. Bowden, *What about the Old Testament?* (London, 1964), pp. 86–90; J.F.A. Sawyer, *New Perspectives in Old Testament Study* (London, 1977); G. Newlands, 'The Old Testament and Christian Doctrine', *The Modern Churchman* (1973), pp. 238–44.

34. T. Ling, *Prophetic Religion* (London, 1966).

35. R.H. Preston, *Church and Society in the Late Twentieth Century: The Economic and Political Task* (London, 1983), p. 107.

36. J. Habgood, *Church and Nation in a Secular Age* (London, 1983), p. 105.

37. J. Davis McCaughey, 'Imagination in the Understanding of the Prophets', in J.P. Mackey, ed., *Religious Imagination* (Edinburgh, 1986), pp. 161–73.

38. R.P. Carroll, 'From Amos to Anderton: Reflections on Being a Prophet', *Theology* (July, 1987), pp. 256–63.

between 'the prophet' and 'the statesman' is one of simple incompatibility, whether we explain that incompatibility theologically or psychologically. It then appears to be a matter of taking sides with the prophets or the statesman.[39] A historian, however, brooding on the choice he is asked to make, may well conclude that the incompatibility is not simple but dialectical. And he may decline to make it.

39. W. McKane, *Prophets and Wise Men* (London, 1965), pp. 128–30.

9

The Churches in Edwardian Society

Historians rarely write or speak about Edwardian piety. It is assumed that whatever else Edwardian England was, it was not pious; it was a decade that cast aside the cramping conventions of the Victorian world. Certainly, at the highest level, King Edward did not appear to set a conspicuous example of holy living. As Prince of Wales, his Sunday luncheon parties at Marlborough House had already caused consternation, being considered an unbecoming way in which to pass the Sabbath. By the time he came to the throne one Liverpool minister even went so far as to accuse him publicly of licentiousness. The aged Archbishop of Canterbury, Frederick Temple, was more reticent but did not greatly care for Court goings-on. Having moved to Lambeth Palace at the age of seventy-six in 1896, he had to struggle through the coronation services with the aid of specially printed cards with large lettering, but even so, contrived to place Edward VII's crown on back to front.[1] In a new century, in which 'new' women smoked in public, it was easy to suggest that the churches would have little part to play in its life. The blind old man was leading the blind.

Even so, the coronation again confirmed the reciprocal relationship between crown and people, throne and altar, church and state. The Church of England remained the established church in England and Wales and seemed to have survived the periodic campaigns against its privileged status mounted in the previous century by Dissenters. The emotions and convictions which produced the separation of church and state in France in these years had only faint echoes in England. The Church was represented in the House of Lords by the two archbishops, the Bishops of London, Durham and Winchester and twenty-one diocesan bishops in order of seniority. Bishops were appointed by the Crown on the recommendation of the Prime Minister. The election which followed had no more significance than a plebiscite in a totalitarian state. Balfour, who had more interest and competence in metaphysics than most Prime Ministers, was not at all reticent in making his recommendations. 'I mean to propose your name to H.M. for Canterbury', he wrote to Randall Davidson on Temple's death in December 1902. 'From conversations I have had with him, I have no doubt that he will agreed.'[2] It was thus that Scotsmen dealt

---

1. D.L. Edwards, *Leaders of the Church of England, 1828–1944* (London, 1971), p. 296.
2. G.K.A. Bell, *Randall Davidson* (3rd edn, London, 1952), p. 384.

with the ecclesiastical affairs of England: Davidson had a sound Presbyterian background.

The Church of England did not govern itself. The clerical convocations of the provinces of Canterbury and York and the corresponding lay bodies did meet, but they were advisory bodies. The peripatetic annual church congresses were occasions for debate and discussion but they lacked any authority. Whether establishment was either necessary or desirable from the standpoint of the church itself was a contentious matter, though not acutely so. The Anglican Church in Ireland, disestablished in 1869, seemed to some observers healthier than formerly now that it had charge over its own affairs. In practice, of course, from the repeal of the Test and Corporation Acts in 1828 onwards, the privileged position of the Church of England in the eyes of the state had been steadily eroded. Creeping religious pluralism had reached the point at which Bishop Gore felt constrained to remark that the Church of England found itself disestablished almost everywhere except in the lunatic asylums. He was exaggerating, but the tendency seemed clear. It is not surprising that some prominent Anglicans pressed for more self-government, even if they still stopped short of formal disestablishment.

Such a separation would have caused acute embarrassment, to say the least. The bishops and clergy of the church were still closely linked to the public men of the time by ties of education and personal relationship. Mandell Creighton, historian and Bishop of London, was only one of those who stressed the importance of the Church of England as the expression of the religious consciousness of the English people. Church and state, he asserted, are the nation looked at from different points of view. In practice, as a diocesan, he found himself besieged by those who wanted certain ritualistic practices and those who wanted to prevent them. His own attitude — admittedly in an impatient moment — was 'If they want to make a smell, let them'.[3] He died, worn out, at the age of fifty-seven in 1901 unconvinced that the attempt (as he saw it) to make the English people adopt Italian practices would be successful. Other clergy, less articulate than Creighton, shared his sentiments. Hensley Henson spoke for some of them from the pulpit of St Margaret's, Westminster, and offered a vision of a great national church of the English people. It would, of course, be protestant. Gore, who became the first Anglican Bishop of Birmingham in 1905, attempted to prevent Henson from preaching at a famous Congregational church in the city. Davidson (who had taken a Third at Oxford) did not attempt to resolve these differences of outlook and doctrine at an intellectual level. The Church of England had always contained many mansions and it was his task to prevent the sinking of this particular bark of Christ by one faction or other. He was, on the whole, remarkably successful in a sober, uninspiring, way. Joined by Cosmo Gordon Lang at

---

3. W.G. Fallows, *Mandell Creighton and the English Church* (Oxford and London, 1964), p. 91.

the see of York in 1909, the two Scotsmen could reasonably claim that, in a constitutional sense, at least, they preserved for the Church of England a prominent place in English society.

On hearing of his appointment, Lord Curzon wrote to Lang that he took great pleasure, as the years advanced, in seeing his friends inhabiting 'spacious places'. No doubt writing as the humble son of a clerical father, Curzon's remark nevertheless reveals the problem confronting the church. Lang drew a very considerable salary at York and this Scottish minister's son half-revelled in the notion of being a prince-bishop. Behind him lay Balliol, All Souls and Magdalen — and Portsea and Stepney. The gap between Bishopthorpe and the East End was wide, too wide for Lang to bridge, but unless someone could cross it there was something specious about the talk of the Church of England as the national church of the English people.

Even bishops were having to accept that it was becoming more difficult to determine what the mass of Englishmen did in fact believe or what, in their inarticulate way, they expected of the churches. The crop of social investigations into the life of London and other cities produced fresh confirmation — it was hardly new information — that active participation in church affairs was a minority activity, though still a substantial one. A survey taken by R. Mudie-Smith for the *Daily News* in 1902–3 showed that in the London area only about two persons in eleven attended church or chapel.[4] Comparisons with earlier surveys suggested that it was Anglican attendances which had declined most markedly during the preceding twenty years. Of course, there was considerable variation from area to area, but there was no doubt about the general picture. In some provincial cities, church attendance was by no means derisory; but there was a general contention that the new 'city race', to use C.F.G. Masterman's phrase, did not find religion congenial. Religion was scarcely the opiate of the masses because the masses contrived to give it a wide berth. Some comfort could be drawn from the relatively stronger position (on the whole) of churches in rural areas, but that consolation might only be temporary.

To speak of the collapse of organized religion, however, would be an exaggeration. Statistics suggest, among Methodists for example, that although their membership as a percentage of the total English adult population was lower than it had been in the late nineteenth century, such membership was still growing. The same, broadly, was also true of the other major Free Churches. In fact, it was only in 1906 that some modest evidence of actual decline appeared. The roughly two and a quarter million Anglican Easter Day communicants in 1911 represented a higher density than at any decennial point since 1801.[5] It is not surprising, therefore, that reports from contemporary church congresses do not paint a picture of bleak gloom. The mood of the world-wide Anglican

4. R. Mudie-Smith, *The Religious Life of London* (London, 1904).
5. A.D. Gilbert, *Religion and Society in Industrial England* (London, 1976).

Communion which assembled in London in 1908 was quite buoyant. In the perilous world of statistics, the Roman Catholic Church, too, could point to a record of expansion. Differing criteria of membership make comparisons between churches notoriously hard, and contemporaries found the figures of adherence or allegiance puzzling. In 1911, for example, the Liverpool Free Churches organized a massive home visitation throughout the city involving the distribution of 190,000 record cards. Apparently, remarkably few of those interviewed expressed feelings definitely hostile to religion, only about fifty cards being marked specifically 'secularist' or 'atheist'. In a considerable number of cases, respondents who called themselves 'Church of England' helpfully added the rider that they did not attend anywhere, but did not want to be looked upon as heathens. If the figure of secularist support seems extraordinarily small, it does seem to be the case that as an active alternative to Christianity it made little progress. One clergyman grumbled to Charles Booth about the willingness of the working class to believe in a God to whom they ascribed their own vague humanitarian impulses and their own lax moral standards.

It was, therefore, clear that assumptions about the beliefs and practices of the next-door neighbour were increasingly difficult to make — in any social class. At parties at country houses proper provision for church attendance was still made, but abstention from worship on the part of guests was ceasing to require explanation. It was not at all clear what prominent men believed. Very little survived from even the Unitarianism of Joseph Chamberlain's youth. Balfour, on the other hand, although he could not make up his mind about tariff reform, was on balance a believer in the Trinity.[6] Asquith came from a firmly Congregational background, which was eroded by Balliol and his second wife, Margot; but it would be a mistake to think that its formative influence had been quite obliterated.[7] To dogmatize unduly about Lloyd George's mind would be rash, but his atheism does not seem to have prevented his becoming President of the Baptist Union of Wales and retaining a passion for Welsh hymns in a minor key. Despite his later role as the defender of Christendom, Churchill was more indebted to Winwood Reade's *The Martyrdom of Man* than to biblical theology. Bonar Law retained every outward appearance of being a son of the manse, but his inner convictions are more difficult to fathom. Such a cursory sampling does not pretend to resolve the question of what men believed, but it is enough to demonstrate the gap between the public impression and the private attitude.

Speaking more generally, one contemporary discussion of 'non-church-going' concluded that only in Scotland was a plausible excuse necessary.[8] It

---

6. In a letter in 1923 he rebutted the notion that he was an 'agnostic': '. . . I am not only a Theist, but a Christian'. A.J. Balfour to P. Gardiner, MS Eng. Lett., c.55. Bodleian Library.

7. Clyde Binfield, 'Asquith: The Formation of a Prime Minister', *Journal of the United Reformed Church History Society*, 2, no. 7, (1981).

8. W.F. Gray, *Non-Church Going* (Edinburgh, 1911).

was indeed the case that church attendance and membership were significantly higher in parts of the United Kingdom outside England. It is noticeable, too, that many influential figures in the religious press and pulpit in England were not Englishmen — from Robertson Nicoll of the *British Weekly,* through Hugh Price Hughes the Wesleyan, to George Tyrrell the Jesuit. To add a little *couleur locale* the same point can be made about prominent figures in the ecclesiastical life of Manchester. It is not necessary to take the view that 'Celts' had a greater sensitivity in religious matters to explain this phenomenon, but it was a feature of the Edwardian scene.

Some churchmen did not attempt to disguise the blurred pattern of allegiance emerging before them. Neville Figgis, Cambridge don and then Mirfield monk, pondered learnedly on the role of the churches in the modern state. The church, he argued, being a distinct and separate society, should have its own authentic life alongside other communities. All that was needed, it seems, was for the state to be comprehensively reorganized to permit a plurality of distinct communities to flourish. The church could then engage in an untrammelled assault on mammon.[9]

It was common ground among all the churches that mammon was rampant. They had little difficulty in detecting in contemporary life an unacceptable decadence. Giving the presidential address to the National Council of Evangelical Free Churches in 1906, the Wesleyan, Scott Lidgett, was sorely grieved by the evidence of vulgar materialism and, among certain classes, a love of luxury. There was, he thought, a fevered excitement and frivolity which manifested themselves in the manifold forms of intemperance, impurity, gambling and speculation which he witnessed.[10] If those words were a little too Puritan for Anglican tastes, clergy had little doubt that both in the domestic and public sphere standards of behaviour were deteriorating and parting company from Christian foundations. They all agreed that it was time, once again, to make known the great Christian affirmation as to the worth and responsibilities of human life. Scott Lidgett, indeed, professed to see many signs of revival on the horizon. Lifting his eyes to the hills, he took comfort from the remarkable activity in 1904–5 of the Welsh evangelist Evan Roberts. Thousands were converted and new life seemed to be flooding back into the chapels. 'The *Diwygiad* [Revival] is immense,' wrote Lloyd George in January 1905, 'I am quite its slave. Its effect in Caernarvonshire is unparalleled sobriety.'[11] Rugby players solemnly burned their shirts and enrolled in Sunday School classes.[12] Unashamedly imperialist, other contemporary pulpits made much of the threat to Empire if the excitement over football matches persisted. R.J. Campbell,

9. J.N. Figgis, *Civilisation at the Cross-Roads* (London, 1912).
10. J. Scott Lidgett, *Apostolic Ministry* (London, 1910).
11. J. Grigg, *Lloyd George: The People's Champion, 1902–11* (London, 1978), p. 49n.
12. D. Smith, 'People's Theatre: A Century of Welsh Rugby', *History Today*, (March, 1981), p. 32.

whose preaching attracted increasing attention, had an even more melancholy reflection on the state of the nation. He speculated that

> our best are parting from us, and it is a glorious thing if we are building up nations beyond the seas from our young manhood which will carry on the tradition of an England that was. But I am full of misgiving if our best leave us and our second best never try to rise.

He begged for a revival of the puritanism which, he claimed, was helping to make America great.[13]

T. Edmund Harvey, on the other hand, a Quaker and Liberal MP, warned his fellow Nonconformists against excessive devotion to negative prohibitions. Pleasure was desirable so long as it was shared. Joy was at the heart of Christian experience, and was to be welcomed, not avoided.[14] Ordinary church members threaded their way though these injunctions from their leaders with as much discernment as they could manage. Chapels did their best to provide joyful and not 'fevered' excitement. The most ambitious congregations laid on a thoroughly comprehensive range of activities on their sometimes spacious premises. Bible classes and prayer meetings mingled with choirs, literary circles and cycling clubs. This was no capitulation to the secular, supporters of these programmes argued, but a proper blending of the sacred and secular. In many towns and cities, Nonconformity offered a complete society within society which both insulated and sustained its members. In such circumstances, ministers of the Gospel could all too easily become superintending managers.

The busy organization of successive pleasant afternoons and evenings could sometimes lose its savour — even for Nonconformists. And, while the potency of great preaching could not be denied, perhaps the pull of the pulpit was at its zenith. The contemporary princes could still draw thousands to listen to them and queues could form outside particularly popular chapels, but there was more than a suspicion that these oratorical performances did not extend and deepen the spiritual life. Anglicans looked for modest stillness and tranquillity in a steadily ordered sacramental life and it was not only social pressure which caused Nonconformists to be drawn to Anglicanism.

The gulf between the Church of England and Nonconformity remained very apparent, though individuals looked at each other with slightly less suspicion and slightly more knowledge. Clergy and ministers were still drawn from substantially different social backgrounds, had different educational experience and enjoyed, or at least expected, a different social status. The 'clerical profession' had drawn substantially from the Victorian upper middle class and had thought of itself as on a par with other professions. The number of ordinands had ceased to keep pace with the rise in population in the 1890s and after the turn of the century the number of men coming forward began

13. R.J. Campbell, *Some Signs of the Times* (London, 1903).
14. C. Ensor Walters, ed., *The Social Mission of the Church* (London, 1906), pp. 72–73.

to fall.[15] There was also more than a suspicion that the most able were ceasing to offer themselves in such numbers — whether for intellectual or financial reasons. As far as the latter point is concerned, the 'pale curate', so frequently the butt of jokes, could be pale through undernourishment if he had a family and failed to obtain a living relatively quickly. The image of a clergyman and a gentleman, however, remained attractive and was still favourably contrasted with the 'peasant priesthoods' thought characteristic of Catholics and the uncultured roughness supposedly characteristic of the Nonconformist ministry. Aspiring to train ordinands 'with no half-baked gentility', both the Community of the Resurrection and the Society of the Sacred Mission offered free training, but many of their products were still thought more suitable for dioceses in the colonies. It was frequently suggested, though not proved, that differences of speech and manners inhibited the clergy in their evangelical and pastoral work.

In general, the fissiparous tendencies of the nineteenth century were being replaced by a disposition to cooperate, though not yet unite. The only reunions in the early twentieth century took place amongst some Methodists in England and some Presbyterians in Scotland. In neither instance did the union embrace denominations that had been long divided or which had previously differed deeply. However, both at a national and local level, quite successful attempts were made to strengthen and develop a new 'Free Church' consciousness — that is to say an attempt to emphasise a positive aspect rather than to stress the negative which the older terms of Dissent and Nonconformity implied. Acting in consort, Free Churchmen could wage more effective battle against the claims of the Church of England. The most contentious issue was education. The struggle against the 1902 Education Act, a measure which in Nonconformist eyes strengthened Anglicanism, was in some parts of the country fought with great bitterness. A Passive Resistance League attempted, unsuccessfully, to thwart this legislation, though some ministers did go to prison and others had their goods distrained when they refused to pay their rates. But if the issue seemed of vast importance, a number even of those who took part in the campaign were aware that there was no mass movement in the country as a whole.[16] They also encountered the view that this ecclesiastical squabble was standing in the way of a much-needed reform of the educational system. Supporters and opponents of the measure were in danger of over-playing their hand.

If differences between Anglicans and Free Churchmen were still extensive, there remained a strong sense in which the country continued to be Protestant in ethos and feeling. Roman Catholics were themselves uncertain of the recognition which they desired. The Irish issue complicated not only the internal life of that church but made it difficult for its leaders to take a

---

15. A. Russell, *The Clerical Profession* (London, 1980), pp. 242–43.
16. S. Koss, *Nonconformity in Modern British Politics* (London, 1975), pp. 50–60.

public position. Francis Bourne, Cardinal Archbishop of Westminster, was himself the son of an English father and an Irish mother.[17] He took advantage of visits from Catholic monarchs to bring the worship and life of Westminster Cathedral into the public eye. When Alfonso XIII stayed on to seek the hand of Victoria Eugénie, a granddaughter of Queen Victoria, he fiercely defended the conversion to his church that was a consequence of her acceptance. Archbishop Davidson was not at all pleased, nor was the *Daily Chronicle*. In 1908, the issue of the proposed Procession of the Blessed Sacrament through the streets of London in connexion with an Eucharistic Congress proved a *cause célèbre*. The Prime Minister in the end sent a telegram stating that the Government were of opinion that it would be better 'in the interests of order and good feeling' that the ceremonial 'the legality of which is open to question' should not take place. The Archbishop acquiesced. Sir Robert Perks, a Wesleyan MP, had claimed that if the Host had been carried, nothing but an army could have protected the procession from the wrath of Protestant England. Such feelings were frequently aired in Liverpool, where the Pope was regularly consigned to hell. Roman Catholic teaching on mixed marriages, particularly as embodied in the *Ne Temere* statement of 1907, aroused strong feelings amongst Protestants. Very serious rioting took place in Liverpool in 1909 of a clearly sectarian character. Houses were marked to make clear the religious allegiance of the inhabitants. Beatings and lootings were designed to ensure that particular districts were not polluted by the presence of people of a different faith.[18]

The interaction of religion and politics was peculiarly intimate in Liverpool but the specific issue of education played a significant part in the 1906 election campaign, in particular embarrassing Nonconformists who had begun to vote Tory. Education, however, was but one plank in the Nonconformist platform at this time. Silvester Horne, prominent preacher, writer and passive resister, preached a sermon on the eve of the poll calling for nothing less than 'Theocracy through Democracy', a goal which, he claimed, had been the ideal of English Free Churchmen for 300 years.[19] And, although there was some doubt about the precise allegiance of some of the newly-elected MPs in January 1906, the fact that there were over 200 Nonconformists among them seemed to give the Free Churches a quite new position of strength and influence. Yet, despite the ardour of the neo-Cromwellians, the years after 1906 were not to prove congenial to the simple revival of Commonwealth principles. Even on education, as a result of the obstruction in the House of Lords, the Liberal Government was by no means able to give satisfaction to its Nonconformist supporters. It was clearly not for nothing that the Bishop of Manchester filled thirty-two trains to take opponents of the Liberal bill to London to protest.

---

17. E. Oldmeadow, *Francis, Cardinal Bourne* (London, 1944).
18. P.J. Waller, *Democracy and Sectarianism* (Liverpool, 1981), p. 238–39.
19. Walters, *Social Mission*, pp. 116–24. See also C. Binfield, *So Down to Prayers: Studies in English Nonconformity* (London, 1977), on Horne.

Despite the apparent vitality of these entrenched positions and the excitement they generated, some church leaders were only confirmed in their view that ecclesiastical controversy of this order would only further alienate the masses and confirm the irrelevance of organized religion. It was admitted that 'social enthusiasm' was not a novelty but it was suggested that the churches needed to recover from the period when, allegedly, they had gloried in the Empire and overlooked the slums. That was the position of the contributors to *The Social Mission of the Church* (1906). Clergymen in slum parishes energetically promoted housing schemes. Unfortunately, advocates of the Kingdom of God on earth (in the form of a Socialist Commonwealth) proved singularly quarrelsome. Stewart Headlam had to dissolve the Guild of St Matthew in 1909 because of internal disputes — in which, it must be said, he himself had taken an energetic part. The Christian Social Union claimed 6,000 members at its peak in 1910 and included more bishops and professors in its ranks than 'real' workers. The Christian Social Union was too sedate for some ardent souls. Conrad Noel, who had been not infrequently inebriated as an undergraduate, denounced it as a 'mild and watery society' and helped to form the Church Socialist League in 1906. Amongst its early members was a subsequent clerical holder of the Stalin Peace Prize. Some churchmen joined the Fabian Society and others the Independent Labour Party. Socialism, generously interpreted, was preached from some influential pulpits. R.J. Campbell, now minister of the City Temple in London, talked of the need to hitch the 'waggon of Socialism' to the 'star of religious faith'.[20] Socialism was actually a swing back to the gospel of the Kingdom of God. John the Baptist, in his estimation, was exactly the kind of man who would have led the attack on the Bastille or addressed a Labour demonstration in Hyde Park. The Finsbury ILP, which Campbell joined, did not meet in an upper room but in a basement where portraits of Morris, Hyndman and Hardie covered the damp patches. A broad band of agreement seemed to be emerging both amongst Anglicans and Free Churchmen that a competitive system was unsatisfactory in practice and morally unacceptable in theory. Such doctrines, however, were largely clerical in inspiration and although such men as Keir Hardie, George Lansbury and Arthur Henderson were among the Labour politicians who shared such language and enthusiasms, neither the churches as a whole, nor the trade unions as a whole, were swept off their feet by the advocacy of the 'Social Gospel'.

At least at the level of the pew, there was a rather tenacious conservatism. Campbell, not surprisingly, was a passionate advocate of female suffrage. It was intolerable that men liked female subservience and dreaded female competition. That was the reason why the vote for women was opposed.[21] Yet in the structures and organizations of the churches themselves the position

---

20. R.J. Campbell, *Christianity and the Social Order* (London, 1907), p. 54.
21. Idem, *Women's Suffrage and the Social Evil* (London, 1907).

of men was strongly entrenched and there was little disposition to yield.[22] Clerical enthusiasts could not make much progress with many members of their congregation — particularly when the tables were turned and questions asked about the ministry or priesthood. 'Can we imagine the Blessed Virgin Mary wanting a vote in Parliament, or to harangue vulgar listeners?' was a telling question asked in the *Church Times*. Henry Scott Holland, an Oxford theologian, deplored the way in which elements in the religious press condoned and even encouraged the police treatment of demonstrators. 'A gentleman', he reminded the newspaper's editor, 'should remember that he is speaking of girls.'[23] It was not a matter of knocking rats on the head in the back yard. Of course, Christian women were themselves divided. Louise Creighton, for example, showed in all the manoeuvrings and changes of front on the suffrage issue that she would have made a more robust bishop than her late husband.[24] At a slightly later stage, militant suffragettes were determined to embarrass the episcopate. Mrs Pankhurst sent Annie Kenney to Lambeth Palace to 'demand sanctuary' until women won the vote. Mrs Davidson made it clear that she was not at all keen on her presence and Annie was arrested. Lacking a wife, the Bishop of London a little later declined to have Annie stay at Fulham Palace, on the perfectly proper ground that people might talk.[25]

The interaction between the churches and the political world was evident in other spheres. Campbell's statement that 'We are a great people and God has made use of us. He has granted to us certain powers which other races have not. Power brings responsibility, a responsibility we have no right to shirk' was not a personal quirk. The conviction that Britain occupied a position in the world 'from which she cannot recede if she would. Millions of swarthy subjects receive, or ought to receive, at her hands peace and good government . . . Here we are, and for the present it is our duty to stay' was general.[26] The British Empire facilitated the missionary work of the churches, though their activity was not restricted to its bound. Denominational societies were at work in all the important colonial territories and the plethora of medical and missionary auxiliaries brought an exotic touch to suburban church life. It is significant that Scott Lidgett's presidential address to the National Council of Evangelical Free Churches in Birmingham in March 1906 was on 'The World-Wide Mission of the Christian Church'. The marvellous progress of the modern world had transformed international relationships. Nations were linked together in ways which would have been undreamed of in previous centuries. No attempt

22. See B. Heeney, 'The Beginnings of Church Feminism: Women and the Councils of the Church of England, 1897–1919', *Journal of Ecclesiastical History* (1982).
23. Both quotations are cited in A. Marrin, *The Last Crusade: The Church of England in the First World War* (Durham, N.C., 1974), pp. 56–57.
24. B.H. Harrison, *Separate Spheres* (London, 1978), pp. 130–33.
25. Marrin, *Last Crusade*, p. 58.
26. Cited in A.H. Wilkerson, *The Rev. R.J. Campbell: The Man and his Message* (London, 1907), pp. 26–28.

to interfere with the spirit of international fellowship would be 'tolerated'. He noted that the rise of Japan was bringing the British churches into 'entirely new spiritual relations to the non-Christian world'. Praising the marvellous efficiency and splendid patriotism of the Japanese, he rejoiced in the cementing of the Anglo-Japanese alliance. But he also saw the possibility of a sympathetic interest in Christianity in the East and foresaw a time when those who had hitherto thought of themselves as Buddhists would be converted to Christianity. They would then 'make an invaluable contribution to the fuller realisation of Christianity as the manifestation of the grace, the condescension, and the gentleness of God'. If foreign missions were promoted 'on an entirely new scale' then 'the twentieth century will mark a turning to Christ throughout the world unequalled in the history of the Christian Church'.[27]

Such enthusiasm was one of the sources of the World Missionary Conference held four years later in Edinburgh. Missionary conferences had been held before, 'but Edinburgh was unique because of the carefully balanced representation of the different bodies, and the great influence and high positions of the participants'.[28] Even the Archbishop of Canterbury returned to his native city and, unlike his predecessor, thought that the trip north required something more than an address on the virtues of temperance. If the conference has perhaps been magnified in retrospect, the phrase associated with the American laymen, John R. Mott, 'The evangelization of the world in this generation' captures a mood and a confidence. In these years, the Student Christian Movement blossomed and flourished in universities. Clever young dons, like William Temple, even went to Australia to inform the inhabitants about the new trends in missionary thinking. This cooperative spirit, however, could lead to practical complications, placing church rules, particularly about admission to Holy Communion, under strain.

The missionary movement was not completely 'triumphalist' in spirit. Scott Lidgett, for example, was adamant that 'Christian nations must repent of such crimes against China as have disfigured our own history in the case of the opium traffic, and have marked the recent scramble to take advantage of her people, which came to so ignominious an end during the past year.'[29] Somehow or other, British imperial policy had to be made consonant with Christian feeling. It so happened that the new Liberal Foreign Secretary, Sir Edward Grey, had been 'shown how to work' in the drawing-room of a Northumberland vicarage by Mandell Creighton. Unfortunately no doubt, he showed no enthusiasm for it and the subsequent Bishop of London had little hold over the mind of the mature politician.[30] A Christian foreign policy is almost as difficult to define

27. Lidgett, *Apostolic Ministry*, pp. 256–59.
28. S.P. Mews, 'Kikuyu and Edinburgh: The Interaction of Attitudes to two Conferences' in D. Baker, ed., *Studies in Church History*, 7 (Cambridge, 1971), p. 346.
29. Lidgett, *Apostolic Ministry*, pp. 259–60.
30. K.G. Robbins, *Sir Edward Grey* (London, 1971), p. 15.

as a Socialist foreign policy — not that Grey made any attempt to operate at these elevated levels. The churches did make an effort to ease international tension on a modest basis. There was, for example, a British Council of Associated Churches for fostering Friendly Relations between the British and German peoples. Two Liberal MPs, J. Allen Baker, a Quaker, and Willoughby Dickinson, an Anglican, did a great deal of fostering and looked for the day when some great leader might arise, who 'with commanding eloquence and force will advocate a Christian method of settling international disputes'. For a time, it seemed to some of his admirers that the Kaiser might be the man. Bishop Boyd Carpenter, for example, declared him to be 'a lover of peace, earnestly desirous of promoting the welfare of mankind; they knew him to have a simple trust in Divine guidance'.[31] Even after the outbreak of war with Germany in 1914 the Archbishop of York told a public meeting of his 'sacred memory' of the mourning Kaiser at the funeral of his grandmother, Queen Victoria — whereupon the audience responded with a storm of abuse.

However, hope for future peace did not rest in the German Emperor alone. There was a confident assumption, particularly in Nonconformist circles, that the new government would pursue peace alongside retrenchment and reform. Campbell-Bannerman did indeed make a number of speeches in which he referred to the ruinous competition in armaments — at a meeting of the Inter-Parliamentary Union in London for example. The delegates were then trooped off to be shown Portsmouth dockyard. The next few years were to prove very disappointing for those who had anticipated disarmament. Even so, exchange visits between Britain and Germany took place in 1908 and 1909 organized by clergy and laymen in an apparent atmosphere of goodwill. In July 1908 a Universal Peace Congress was held in London, unfortunately overlapping with the conference of the Anglican Communion meeting at Lambeth. Addressing a Christian Peace Conference, the Prime Minister himself felt called upon to reproach the churches for their lack of activity on this matter. A few days later, Ben Tillett even claimed at a rally in Trafalgar Square that the churches were strong enough to prevent war if they chose. The problem was that they were supported by capitalists and warmongers. In 1910, however, the Church of England Peace League was formed — though it never became a major body. It was an indication, however, that concern for peace was not simply the preserve of the Society of Friends. In the event, of course, 'concern for peace' was one thing, agreement on how it was to be maintained, and at what cost, quite another. The Church of England, at any rate, was closely enmeshed in the existing social and political structure and its leaders, even if they had wanted to, could not have led the church as a body to take a stance on international issues which would have been at variance with the nation as a whole. There was, in these circumstances, no reason why the Archbishop of Canterbury's

31. Idem, *The Abolition of War* (Cardiff, 1976), pp. 17–18.

wife should not have been an entirely appropriate person to launch a battleship — as she did in 1911.

The charge of hypocrisy and insincerity was not infrequently made against the churches and it was extended to a renewed questioning of the essential nature and status of Christianity itself. T. Edmund Harvey sensed that Christian worship, hymns and prayers were full of 'unreality'. Too many men, he thought, persuaded themselves that they still believed in dogmas which had in fact ceased to have any influence upon their lives. What was needed was to find the truths that lay behind the old words and phrases. The outstanding work by contemporary British biblical scholars had to be absorbed and assimilated. The contemporary movements in philosophy and science had to be understood and their effect on Christian belief made plain. To speak of *Christianity and the Social Crisis* (1907), as did the influential American, Walter Rauschenbusch, was not enough. Christianity was itself in crisis. R.J. Campbell, minister of the City Temple, wrote *The New Theology* (1907), which became an immediate best-seller, turning its author into a major national figure.[32] There was nothing very new in what Campbell had to say but he succeeded in putting his views in a form that attracted wide attention. Even G.B. Shaw reputedly conceded that Campbell had put forward a view of Jesus Christ which a twentieth-century man could take seriously. Campbell argued that traditional beliefs in the Fall, the scriptural basis of revelation, the blood-atonement, salvation, the punishment of sin and heaven and hell were 'not only misleading but unethical'. He talked about the importance of immanence as opposed to transcendence and about the 'fundamental identity of God and Man'. He suggested that a major contribution to the advancement of the Kingdom of God would be the burning of theological colleges. Other contemporary theologians, in all denominations, and particularly those who worked in such colleges, were not very impressed by the arguments. P.T. Forsyth described Campbell as 'over-exposed and under-developed'. Bishop Gore wrote a vigorous defence of the 'old religion' in comparison with the 'new theology'.[33] G.K. Chesterton thought that the 'nigger-driver' would be delighted to hear that God was immanent in him.[34]

Doctrinal controversy, however, was not confined to writers of 'Liberal Protestant' persuasion. The 'Modernist' crisis was at its height within the Roman Catholic Church. Naturally enough, its focus was not in England, but there were indigenous manifestations. In February 1906, George Tyrrell was expelled from the Society of Jesus and in the same month said his last Mass. His posthumous *Christianity at the Cross-Roads* (1909) captured, at least in its title, the mood of many thinking men. Baron von Hügel agonized.[35] Tyrrell

32. R.J. Campbell, *A Spiritual Pilgrimage* (London, 1916) See below pp. 133–48.
33. C. Gore, *The New Theology and the Old Religion* (London, 1907).
34. M. Ward, *Gilbert Keith Chesterton* (London, 1944), pp. 170–71.
35. L.F. Barmann, *Baron Friedrich von Hügel and the Modernist Crisis in England* (Cambridge, 1972).

placed his hope for the future in 'the lay mind which will quietly impose a democratic growing inability to understand authority in any other way than as deriving from the whole community'. It was not, of course, a view which the hierarchy itself found congenial.[36]

Tyrrell's comment, even though it had a specifically ecclesiastical reference, has a more general application. It was not clear, in the struggle for authority in church and state, where the churches and their members stood, either intellectually or emotionally. Some were convinced that if the British Empire should fall, 'which God forbid!', it would be because of poverty, 'sweating', overcrowding, gambling, impurity and intemperance at its heart.[37] If these problems could be remedied the churches could both maintain their position in society and sustain a political order which had a providential purpose. Others began to suspect that perhaps the position of the churches in society had already reached its peak (and perhaps the British Empire likewise), and that what lay ahead might be a long and difficult struggle to 'hold the fort'.[38]

36. M.D. Petre, ed., *George Tyrrell's Letters* (London, 1920), p. 103.
37. Walters, *Social Mission*, p.v.
38. A.D. Gilbert, *The Making of Post-Christian Britain* (London, 1980).

10

The Spiritual Pilgrimage of the Rev. R.J. Campbell

The death of Canon R.J. Campbell on 1 March 1956 did not cause a national stir. There was an obituary the following day in *The Times* and some comment on subsequent days from friends and associates, but little to indicate that fifty years earlier he had been a substantial public figure. One obscure diarist, who had known Campbell as a young man, felt that 'the grudging admission ... of some academic distinction' was an inadequate summary of Campbell's life and work.[1] In part, of course, having outlived most of his contemporaries, Campbell was paying the penalty for his longevity. More important, however, was the fact that for decades he had consciously avoided the limelight. 'No man', he had written to the novelist Margaret Lane in December 1947, 'could more carefully avoid publicity than I have done for a generation.'[2] From 1930 to 1946 he had been a Residentiary Canon and then Chancellor of Chichester and before that served as vicar of Holy Trinity, Brighton for six years. It would appear that he possessed an eminently Anglican pedigree. In May 1903, however, a frail, ascetic-looking, prematurely white-haired Campbell had commenced his ministry at the City Temple, the leading Congregational church in London. W.T. Stead's *Review of Reviews* looked forward to the 'Renascence of Nonconformity' under the leadership of this thirty-five-year-old young man.[3] Over 7,000 people attended the services on his first Sunday. Picture postcards of Campbell were soon on sale and later admirers could purchase the *R.J. Campbell Birthday Book* containing his 'favourite poetical quotations, portrait and autograph'. There was even *A Rosary from the City Temple*, described as being threaded from the writings and sermons of R.J. Campbell. The publicity which attended his arrival in London rarely left him for the next dozen years. In September 1915, rumours of Campbell's intention to resign the pastorate and speculation about his subsequent course were thought of sufficient interest to reach the news columns of *The Times*. His resignation merited a leader in the newspaper and, following his reception into the Church of England in early October, the comments of prominent religious leaders were printed. In 1916 Campbell published *A Spiritual Pilgrimage*: a reconsideration of this volume throws interesting light on the cross-currents of Edwardian religious life.

1. Mr A. Sainsbury kindly communicated his diary entry for 3 March 1956 to the author.
2. *The Times*, 7 March 1956.
3. *Review of Reviews*, 15 May 1903.

133

It was inevitable that Campbell's departure from their ranks should occasion adverse comments from Free Churchmen. Speaking on 12 October 1915, the veteran Baptist, Dr John Clifford described the resignation as 'one of the heaviest blows that has come to me'. Such was the shock that he felt it necessary to reassure his brethren about his own position. 'For myself', he declared, 'the last thing upon this planet I should think about would be to join the Church of England.'[4] Some Nonconformists believed that Campbell's membership of the Church of England would only be temporary; he would eventually become a Roman Catholic. The shock in 1915 should not be underestimated, but for several years some of his erstwhile associates had been disappointed by what they considered to be his lack of leadership. A Free Christian minister, the Rev. J.M. Lloyd Thomas, for example, who had stood by Campbell when times were difficult for him, reported after a discussion with him that 'he had seen the colour of Campbell's bowels' — an expression which loses nothing when uttered, as it was, in Welsh.[5] 'Liberals', 'Progressives', 'Free Catholics' and others felt that Campbell's new enthusiasm for the obsolete clauses of the creeds was a shameful betrayal of all they had apparently been fighting for together. Even those Free Churchmen who had been critical of Campbell's theological liberalism were angry that his renunciation of his opinions was accompanied by a transition to Anglicanism. For them, he had been wrong before and he was now wrong again. Amid the Free Church criticism there is, indeed, more than a hint of relief that it would be for the Church of England to worry about Campbell in future.

The reception of distinguished converts is never easy and Campbell was not an exception. Initially, as vicar of Christ Church, Westminster from 1917, an attempt seems to have been made to turn Campbell into an Anglican preaching star, almost as though all that had happened was a move from one pulpit to another. He appears to have attracted some members of his previous City Temple congregation, but the idea of an Anglican preaching centre was not a success. Not even the award of an Oxford D.D. could prevent Campbell from becoming disconsolate in London and he began to look for a new role. Immediately, however, the conception of the Church of England which Campbell had embraced was not acceptable to all Anglicans. On reading *A Spiritual Pilgrimage* in October 1916, Hensley Henson wrote in his diary that he found the convert's acceptance of Gore's version of Anglicanism 'almost comically complete. Surely there never was a disciple more dog-like in his worship of the master of his choice'. Henson felt that the real problem which called for solution was not Campbell's Anglicanism but his former Nonconformity, commenting that 'It is obvious from the first that the man is temperamentally repugnant to Nonconformity . . .' Campbell's 'spiritual home' was surely the Church of Rome and he had only joined the

---

4. *The Times*, 13 October 1915.
5. The late Miss Muriel Lloyd Thomas kindly sent me this information.

Church of England because he had invested it with the Roman character. He had been 'hypnotized by the personal influence of Bishop Gore', and the Nonconformists had 'much to forgive'.[6]

Such reactions make it clear that Campbell's move from 'Nonconformity' to the 'Church of England' was not a straightforward exchange of allegiance. Although he did not take the path to Rome, apprehensions on this score are understandable. Campbell was by temperament impressionable and vacillating, subject, as will be seen, to conflicting pressures and experiences. These forces left their mark in the various illnesses and breakdowns which he suffered before he was fifty. Henson's remark that it was Campbell's Nonconformity that was the real problem, while characteristically shrewd, is not entirely satisfactory. It was hardly to be expected that an autobiography designed to describe and justify his movement towards the Church of England should dwell on the reasons why, earlier, he had found Nonconformity so attractive. Despite the concluding Irenicon towards Dissent in the autobiography (which Henson found most offensive) Campbell had contrived to scatter remarks throughout the book the cumulative effect of which is to give the impression that he had been an alien in the ranks of Nonconformity during his twenty years as a Congregational minister. There is no way in which the authenticity of some of these observations can be tested. It must be remembered, however, that while Campbell does not underestimate the complexity of his background, his perspective in 1916 dictated a certain shaping of the relative significance of elements in that background.

Campbell was born in 1867, the son of an Ulster Presbyterian who, rejecting the Westminster Confession, had come to England and had entered the United Methodist ministry.[7] He was not the first of his family to take such a course. One of Campbell's grandfathers had similarly come across the Irish Sea and entered the Congregational ministry in England. The ethos of Ulster Presbyterianism, if not the letter of Calvinist doctrine, remained strong in the family home. In addition, as a boy Campbell himself had spent several years in the Ulster countryside for the sake of his health. He was brought up there as a Presbyterian, although he records subsequently that his deepest desire then was to commune with nature. He was a 'strange, solitary boy' who, on returning to England to attend grammar school in Nottingham, did not find it easy to adjust to his new situation. He then worked as a student teacher in a number of elementary schools and studied at the new University College in Nottingham (a fact not mentioned in the autobiography).[8] Subsequently, he became a junior

6. Hensley Henson Diary, xx, p. 310 (Dean and Chapter Library, Durham). The entry is for 14 October 1916. I am grateful to Dr Brian Harrison for drawing my attention to this comment and to the Dean and Chapter of Durham Cathedral for permission to publish.

7. Unless otherwise stated, the personal information in what follows is derived from R.J. Campbell, *A Spiritual Pilgrimage* (London, 1916). Campbell's descendants have informed me that all his papers were destroyed on his death.

8. *Who was Who, 1951–1960* (London, 1961), p. 178.

master in a small high school in Cheshire. The tone of the school was Anglican and it was thought desirable that Campbell should be confirmed. He describes himself as taking this step wholeheartedly, though with little knowledge of what was really involved. In this rather casual fashion, Campbell first became an Anglican.

In Michaelmas term 1892 Campbell went up to Christ Church, Oxford, to read for a History degree, with the intention of taking orders and continuing as a schoolmaster. He was older than most of his contemporaries and already a married man (another fact not mentioned in the autobiography). The picture Campbell paints of himself as an undergraduate is that of a devout and enthusiastic Anglican. Guided by Dean Paget, he was attracted by the men and ideas of the *Lux Mundi* circle; in particular, he fell under the spell of Charles Gore, then at Pusey House. Yet, despite the predominantly High Church milieu in which he moved, Campbell records that he made contact with Oxford Nonconformists. His father had a friend who happened to be a United Methodist minister in Oxford and Campbell joined eagerly in the work of the Oxford YMCA, speaking and preaching for Oxford Nonconformists until Dean Paget urged him to desist. Campbell willingly obliged, yet he records that at this time he felt an increasing unease about the High Anglican position. On the one hand, the Presbyterian piety of his childhood still seemed as 'true and earnest' as anything within the Anglican system, while, on the other, the claim of Rome had to be faced. Did not the logic of Anglo-Catholicism really point towards Rome? But, while he did attend Mass at St Aloysius, he did not feel drawn to Roman Catholicism. Papal absolutism seemed to him a quite illicit development from apostolic Christianity. Perhaps, then, the Anglo-Catholic theory of churchmanship might itself be misconceived? Dean Paget could not answer these new doubts. Campbell states that he decided that he could not subscribe to the Prayer Book, or indeed to any formulary. He would join his grandfather's denomination, which required no formal doctrinal subscription. As Campbell recounts it, the decision was sudden, made with little grasp of Congregational principles, practice or history. Dean Paget told Campbell that he would soon realise what a mistake he was making.

Since the account of Campbell's Oxford days does not contain a single date, it is difficult to be sure of the exact sequence of events.[9] It seems clear that, despite ill-health, Campbell won for himself a prominent position at Christ Church, being president of the 'Cabinet Club'. a dining and discussion group which numbered presidents of the Oxford Union amongst its members. Although little independent evidence survives, Campbell's decision to leave the Church of England, probably made in the spring of 1895, caused a stir beyond undergraduate circles. Silvester Horne, minister of Kensington Chapel in London since 1889, noted in his diary in June 1895 the 'very remarkable

---

9. I am indebted to Mr H.J.R. Wing, the assistant librarian at Christ Church for confirmation of the details of Campbell's academic career.

story' of 'a Mr R.J. Campbell' whose influence over young men at Oxford was already being compared to that of Wesley. In Horne's version, Campbell was described as being of 'good family', sent to Christ Church to read for holy orders by his parents, who were 'furious' at Campbell's decision 'after two years or so' not to pursue this course. To put the situation in this form gave it additional dramatic quality.[10] Even if factually incorrect about Campbell's family background, Horne's entry reinforces the impression that there was nothing casual about this 'conversion'. Campbell's own account is so concerned to stress the ultimate accuracy of Paget's parting prophecy that he would return to the Church of England that he understates the determination he displayed in leaving it.

At this time of religious crisis, Campbell's health gave way when taking his History Schools in the summer of 1895. He apparently wrote but one answer, on the campaigns of Wallace — a subject which he confesses never to have touched at Oxford. He had hopes of a First but had to be content with a Second after a special viva. His tutor told him that he could contemplate a university appointment and later in the year an offer came his way. By that time, however, his career had taken a different course. He received an invitation to preach at Union Street Chapel, Brighton, and subsequently was offered the pastorate. Campbell records that he consulted Dr Fairbairn, Principal of Mansfield College, Oxford. Fairbairn, aware of Campbell's capacity to inspire young men, advised him to stay in Oxford and work among undergraduates. When a second invitation came from Brighton, however, the principal advised that it was a 'call of God'. It is somewhat surprising that Fairbairn should have encouraged acceptance, since Campbell had not received the theological and pastoral training for Congregational ministers which Mansfield was designed to supply. When Campbell was ordained in July 1895 there can rarely have been a Congregational minister with so little knowledge of the Congregational way.

Horne records that he was asked to take part in Campbell's ordination service, but had to decline because of absence from the country. The charge on this occasion was given by R.F. Horton, minister of Lyndhurst Road, Hampstead. It was, Campbell relates, the beginning of a personal friendship, 'the closest and most affectionate' that he ever had with a Free Church minister.[11] It is perhaps significant that when Campbell had first seen Horton, at Oxford in 1892, he had been instantly reminded of Charles Gore. It was with Gore (now at Westminster) that Campbell spent the last day before commencing his ministry at Brighton; an unusual preparation for the life of a Nonconformist minister. In his autobiography, Campbell claimed of Nonconformists that 'no one of their number has ever touched me at all from first to last'. This contrasts, however, with a later statement concerning Horton that, 'everything he said and did of public note had value for us;

10. W.B. Selbie, *The Life of Charles Silvester Horne* (London, 1920), p. 156.
11. A. Peel and J.A.R. Marriott, *Robert Forman Horton* (London, 1937), p. 310.

everything he wrote I read and kept on my bookshelves'.[12] Horton was indeed an unusual man, but Campbell's sweeping dismissal of all Nonconformists is unconvincing. On Horne's sudden early death in 1914, Campbell was much moved, praising him as 'a fearless defender of Free Church rights' and adding 'A more lovable man I never knew'.[13]

Campbell's ministry at Brighton was deemed a success, although ill-health prevented him from beginning work until 1896. A church membership of about sixty quadrupled in two years and continued to rise. Inevitably, a larger building was planned — drawings for an edifice costing £70,000 were exhibited at the Royal Academy in 1899, though subsequently withdrawn. Despite his youth and inexperience, Campbell soon became chairman of the Sussex County Association of Congregational Churches — an appointment which reads oddly alongside his claim that his ministerial colleagues disapproved of someone who had not been trained at a Congregational theological college. Privately, Campbell was undertaking an extensive reading programme to make good admitted deficiencies in formal training. He amassed a library of several thousand volumes, tackling, amongst others, the writings of Berkeley, Kant, William James, Edward Caird, J.H. Newman, Max Müller and Dean Inge. The devotional writings of Mother Julian of Norwich, St Francis of Assisi, St Francis of Sales and St John of the Cross had a special appeal. From this medley of influences emerged his first two volumes of published sermons — *The Making of an Apostle* and *The Restored Innocence* — both published in 1898. It was the theme of innocence which at this time preoccupied Campbell. Jesus Himself possessed this quality, and Campbell stressed that true innocence did not mean ignorance of sin but rather reflected an attitude of the soul towards it.[14] In an essay on the Atonement in a symposium, and in a series of sermons *A Faith for To-day*, published in 1900, Campbell argued that in the Incarnation 'The Divine Being laid aside His glory that a greater glory might be His. . . . Yet this one life was also the revelation of human nature to itself . . . To be true to our highest selves is to be like Him.'[15] The Brighton congregation, many of whom, according to Campbell, were Anglicans, found such general statements very acceptable and Campbell's reputation grew. His Oxford days, and what they had once signified, seemed to fade into the past. His congregation seemed attached to him and, although surprised by his request in 1900 to see the fighting in South Africa at first hand, it readily consented.

In *A Spiritual Pilgrimage*, Campbell was prepared to acknowledge that English Nonconformists, if they failed him in other respects, did give him

12. Ibid., p. 312.

13. *C. Silvester Horne: In Memoriam* (London, 1914), pp. 23–24.

14. Cited in C.T. Bateman, *R.J. Campbell, M.A., Pastor of the City Temple* (London, 1903), p. 57.

15. R.J. Campbell *The Atonement in Modern Religious Thought: A Theological Symposium* (London, 1900); idem, *A Faith for Today: Suggestions towards a System of Christian Belief* (London, 1900), p.3; for Unitarian criticism see R.A. Armstrong, *The Rev. R.J. Campbell on the Trinity* (London, 1900).

what he called 'a truer view of history and of the stern realities of modern life'. They had been responsible for instilling whatever democratic principle he possessed. If he had not come under the influence of Nonconformity he could not have 'escaped being more or less of an obscurantist in regard to public questions and social reform'. Even though this tribute is qualified by stating that Nonconformity erred on the side of individualism it remains conspicuous in a book more devoted to criticism. Campbell found it a relief, as he put it, to be released from the social snobbery and class consciousness of the Church of England. However, Campbell's political allegiance was as complex as his ecclesiastical. Once again, his family background provides a clue. His Ulster family was staunchly Unionist and hostile to Gladstone and Home Rule for Ireland. Campbell retained a firm admiration for Ulster life where the social hierarchy was not accompanied by English caste distinctions. There was, therefore, the paradox that this dislike of English social snobbery helped to drive him to a Nonconformity which was predominantly Liberal, admired Gladstone's career and largely, though not without distinguished exceptions, favoured Home Rule.

By the end of the century, Liberal politicians sojourning on the South Coast — Campbell-Bannerman, Birrell and Lloyd George among them — came to listen to this rising preacher. Herbert Gladstone, the Liberal Chief Whip, suggested that Campbell should become the Liberal parliamentary candidate for Brighton — an offer which was declined. Although active in Liberal politics, Campbell's sermons at this juncture were free of direct political or social reference; there is no hint of the 'Social Gospel'. However, his enthusiastic support of the imperial cause in South Africa caused unease in more than one section of the Liberal party. He left Cape Town in May 1900 but was smitten with enteric fever and it was December before he was able to preach again. During his convalescence, Campbell studied German writers such as Weiss, Beyschlag, Delitzsch and Pfleiderer. Gore was followed 'afar off', a comment which seems to indicate little personal contact, and other Anglican writers to impress were Illingworth on *Divine Immanence* and Moberly on *Atonement and Personality*. He was also influenced by the French Protestant writers Jean Réville and Auguste Sabatier. Campbell's reputation in Nonconformist circles steadily increased and he was frequently approached by politician and publisher alike. In 1901 he began a weekly column for Robertson Nicoll in the *British Weekly*. He was among the party of Nonconformist ministers invited by Campbell-Bannerman in March 1902 to discuss the condition of the Liberal party. While Campbell recalled that he was reluctant to give 'too much time and energy to purely political matters', he was willing to sit on the council of the 'Imperialist' Liberal League.[16] Campbell believed that God had

16. H.C.G. Matthew, *The Liberal Imperialists* (Oxford, 1973), p. 49. Matthew wrongly describes Campbell as a Methodist. Selbie (above n. 10), p. 127; R.J. Campbell to R.W. Perks, 10 July 1902 (Perks MS). I am indebted to Sir Malcolm Perks for access to these papers.

granted to the British people certain powers that other races did not possess. England occupied a position in the world 'from which she cannot recede if she would. Millions of swarthy subjects receive, or ought to receive, at her hands peace and good government . . .'[17] He saw no contradiction between Imperialism, progressive Liberalism and militant Nonconformity: a view not universally shared.

From October 1902 onwards, Campbell commuted to London to conduct the Thursday mid-day service at the City Temple. This service had been a feature of Dr Parker's ministry, but it was now proving too much of a burden. Although other names were mentioned, it was in this context that the deacons offered Campbell the pastorate on Parker's retirement. There was no bigger regular church congregation in London and it was hoped that his numinous personality would stem the tide of secularism and indifference. The influence the minister of the City Temple possessed could not be ignored and it was in the pulpit that Campbell was supreme. The journalist, A.G. Gardiner, was one who described the 'absolute self-surrender' of his preaching. There was 'no strain either of thought or diction, no effort after effect, no flowers of speech'.[18] There was certainly no 'tub-thumping' and, unlike his predecessor, Campbell does not appear to have required a hot bath, a cold shower, a spare meal and a cup of tea before he entered the pulpit to preach.[19] Campbell's biographer found that his eyes possessed 'a luminous attractive power, inspiring confidence and friendship'.[20] D.H. Lawrence, who paid one visit to the City Temple, felt that he could preach as well.[21] A Welsh visitor, D.R. Daniel, felt 'disappointed on the whole with preacher and sermon. I failed to discover the secret of his popularity . . .', but they were exceptional in their criticism. There were thousands who went away satisfied. Isaac Foot's comment that he and his friends had 'to fight and struggle like footballers' in order to attend an evening service, having failed to get in at the morning service, is testimony to Campbell's appeal, particularly to aspiring young men.[22] Ever since his Christ Church days, he felt that he had a special mission to 'young men'. He founded and edited, for a while, a periodical *The Young Man*. He joined the veteran John Brown Paton in enthusiastically promoting 'The Young Men's Brigade of Service', a body which emphasised duty to the community.[23]

In his first three years at the City Temple, Campbell's reputation steadily

17. Cited in A.H. Wilkinson, *Rev. R.J. Campbell: The Man and his Message* (London, 1907), pp. 26–8.

18. A.G. Gardiner, *Prophets, Priests and Kings* (London, 1914), p. 241.

19. J.F. Newton, *Preaching in London* (London, 1922), pp. 35–36.

20. Bateman (above n. 14), 94–95. The young W.R. Matthews was another listener to be greatly impressed by Campbell's sermons. W.R. Matthews, *Memories and Meanings* (London, 1969), p. 56.

21. J.T. Boulton, ed., *Lawrence in Love: Letters to Louise Burrows* (Nottingham, 1968), p. 140.

22. S. Koss, *Nonconformity in Modern British Politics* (London, 1975), p. 50.

23. J.L. Paton, *John Brown Paton* (London, 1914), p. 421.

increased. His sermons, which automatically appeared in *The Christian Commonwealth*, were subsequently published in collected editions by Hodder and Stoughton. Individual sermons were also sometimes published separately. The emphasis in *City Temple Sermons*, for example, was doctrinal. Campbell addressed himself to the central themes of Christian faith. He exhorted his listeners not to perplex themselves with questions about the Trinity. 'If God be like Jesus', he concluded, 'if Jesus can pledge God, humanity has nothing more to fear.'[24] In *Sermons Addressed to Individuals*, he talked about what he called the 'agnosticism' of Jesus. He did not know everything twentieth-century men knew. 'He could not be at once finite and infinite — Himself and somebody else. He was Jesus. He brought to us the manhood of God, and everyone of you who is trying to live the life of Jesus in the spirit and strength of Jesus is showing forth the same thing. For God is not something apart from humanity. He is humanity and infinitely more.'[25] He had little time for his contemporaries in London who worried about 'empty churches': 'Churches may die; Christ lives.'[26] As far as national life was concerned, he detected a certain deterioration in quality. The behaviour of the idle rich might ruin Imperial Britain as it had ruined Imperial Rome. The working class, he felt, was seeking to do as little work for as much pay as possible — without heed to the consequences for the country as a whole. He pleaded for 'a revival of Puritanism to remake England'.[27] In his fear that the 'craze for excitement' on the stage, football field and elsewhere might lead to the gambling-table and the drinking-hall unless kept in check, Campbell appeared to epitomise the 'Nonconformist conscience'.[28] The same was true of his position in the educational controversy of the early years of the century. He declared in May 1903 that it was wrong that 'We Nonconformists' should be compelled to pay directly for a form of religious belief 'against which our very existence as Nonconformists is a standing protest'.[29] It is true that Lloyd George, at one point, did suspect that Campbell, whom he described as 'a power, at all events at present', had 'completely gone over' to Joseph Chamberlain, but this suspicion was not well-founded.[30] On the other hand, there were some doubts about the integrity of Campbell's Nonconformity. Not everybody liked the fact that the choir at the City Temple was robed. Campbell also had the temerity, on one occasion, to feel that the language employed by Dr Clifford about the bench of bishops was unfortunate. And again, while himself a teetotaller, Campbell endorsed the provisions of the Tory Licensing Act which required compensation to be paid to licensees whose licences were

24. R.J. Campbell, *City Temple Sermons* (London, 1903), p. 11.
25. Idem, *Sermons addressed to Individuals* (London, 1904), p. 281.
26. Idem, *The Song of Ages* (London, 1905), p. 35.
27. Idem, *Some Signs of the Times* (London, 1903).
28. Idem, *City Temple Sermons*, pp. 157–59.
29. Idem, *Sermons on Passive Resistance* (London, 1903).
30. R.W. Perks to Lord Rosebery, 1 April and 13 April 1904, Rosebery MS., National Library of Scotland. I am indebted to the Rev. M. Edwards for this reference.

withdrawn.[31] Undoubtedly, Campbell felt the strain of this public role. 'Poor boy!', wrote Silvester Horne after visiting Campbell in April 1905, 'He has a lonely time of it, and with his somewhat morbid conscience and habit of introspection I am really sorry for him.'[32] The minister was beginning to feel that he could not go on publishing three sermons a week indefinitely. He needed more time for rest and reflection.

His appointment in 1906 as Chairman of the London Congregational Board of Ministers ensured that no such opportunity came his way. The controversy which was about to break out, however, was Campbell's own responsibility. He addressed the Board in September 1906 and his remarks on this occasion led to considerable private argument.[33] It became public when Campbell gave an interview to the *Daily Mail* in January 1907. The term 'New Theology', though not itself new, soon came into popular currency. It was loosely used to characterize a theological outlook which stressed the concept of divine immanence, the vital importance of the Holy Spirit within and the relevance of philosophical Idealism. It was generally supposed to involve a liberalism on all dogmatic matters.[34] Campbell's sudden importance lay in the fact that he stated boldly, even crudely, what more meticulous minds perhaps formulated more circumspectly. Describing the New Theology as the product of 'a spiritual awakening, a renewal of life and energy within various Christian communions and even beyond them', Campbell stressed that it represented 'an attitude and a spirit rather than a creed'. The barrier between Unitarians and Trinitarians seemed no longer relevant. Critics and supporters of what Campbell was alleged to stand for rushed eagerly into print. The *British Weekly* was especially pleased to report the resignation of one of the City Temple's deacons and of Miss Lucie Johnstone, the chief contralto soloist. Campbell's supporters formed a 'New Theology League' which later became the more elevated 'Society for the Encouragement of Progressive Religious Thought', only to re-emerge subsequently as the 'Progressive League'.

Campbell himself retreated to Cornwall and there, at great speed, produced his attempt to meet the request that 'the New Theology ought to be dealt with in some comprehensive and systematic way'.[35] Campbell argued that

31. 'I see our old friend Campbell has said this', wrote Perks to Rosebery on 22 April 1904, 'but it will make his congregation furious'. Rosebery MS.

32. Selbie, *Horne*, p. 192.

33. A. Porritt, *The Best I Remember* (London, 1922), p. 121.

34. *British Weekly*, 17 January 1907; H. Drummond, *The New Evangelism and other Papers*, (London, 1899). For a general discussion see H. Davies, *Worship and Theology in England: The Ecumenical Century, 1900–1965* (London, 1965), pp. 125–35; R.T. Jones, *Congregationalism in England, 1662–1962* (London, 1962), pp. 344–54; J.W. Grant, *Free Churchmanship in England, 1870–1940* (London, n.d.), pp. 132–42; J.S. Lawton, *Conflict in Christology: A Study of British and American Christology, 1889–1914* (London, 1947); E.A. George, *Seventeenth-Century Men of Latitude: Forerunners of the New Theology* (London, 1909), is an attempt to establish an intellectual pedigree for the movement.

35. R.J. Campbell, *The New Theology* (London, 1907), p. 5. A German translation, *Die neue Theologie*, was published in Jena in 1910.

traditional beliefs concerning the Fall, the scriptural basis of revelation, the blood-atonement, salvation, the punishment of sin, heaven and hell were 'not only misleading but unethical'.[36] In his view, where churches were vigorous 'it is not their doctrine but their non-theological human sympathy that is doing it'.[37] Campbell's book has an energy and personal commitment which makes it still readable, whatever may be thought of its arguments. He talked about 'the fundamental identity of God and Man' and urged his readers not to mind 'what the Bible says about this or that if you are in search for truth, but trust the voice of God within you'.[38] Having declared that a major contribution to the Kingdom of God would be the burning of theological colleges, he concluded that the business of Christians was 'to show that the religion of Jesus is primarily a gospel for this life and only secondarily for the life to come'.[39] In the autumn of 1906, with a sermon on 'Christianity and Collectivism', Campbell proclaimed himself a Socialist and deepened a personal friendship with Keir Hardie which had begun in his Brighton days. It was reported in July 1907 that Campbell was fulfilling the Labour leader's engagements in South Wales for him. Cardiff ILP approached Campbell with the request that he would be its parliamentary candidate. In these circumstances, though he declined the offer, Campbell hurriedly wrote a second book, *Christianity and the Social Order*. It was the product of his belief that 'the waggon of Socialism needs to be hitched to the star of religious faith'.[40]

'The objective of Socialism', he argued, 'is that with which Christianity began its history. Socialism is actually a swing back to the gospel of the Kingdom of God ... the traditional theology of the churches is a departure from it.'[41] He then moved on to discuss the concept of the Kingdom of God in Jewish history and in primitive Christianity. He described John the Baptist as 'exactly the kind of man who would have led the attack on the Bastille, or who would nowadays be found addressing a Labour demonstration in Hyde Park'.[42] As for Jesus, he admitted that it would be 'ridiculous to call Him a Socialist, in the ordinary everyday use of that word, for He had no economic theory whatever ...' and drafted no schemes of industrial organization or political constitutions. Nothing could be simpler yet more inchoate than his social ethics. Nevertheless, it was beyond question 'that Jesus preached an ideal social order on earth when he preached the Kingdom of God, and that He was driven to do so by His clear perception of the ills under which His countrymen suffered in a time when justice for the oppressed was seldom to be had'.[43] There could, therefore, be no individual salvation

36. Ibid., p. 9.
37. Ibid., p. 11.
38. Ibid., pp. 201–2.
39. Ibid., p. 256.
40. Ibid., p. 8.
41. Idem, *Christianity and the Social Order* (London, 1907), p. 19.
42. Ibid., p. 54.
43. Ibid., p. 85.

and Socialism provided the key to the future. Anything which stopped short of Socialism was a mere palliative. There would be no room for greed and fear in the coming social order. Socialism might be preached by Robert Blatchford of the *Clarion* or by Father James Adderley 'but in so far as their objective is what is here stated they are both Christian'.[44]

Campbell did not confine his zeal for Socialism to the printed page. Over the next couple of years he appeared on different platforms in support of the Labour movement — trade union parades, ILP meetings and Fabian debates. He joined the Finsbury branch of the ILP and was elected to the executive of the Fabian Society in 1908, though he was apparently too busy to attend a single committee meeting.[45] He shared the platform with Keir Hardie on several occasions, particularly at a great meeting in Liverpool during March 1907. He was also in contact with Ramsay MacDonald, writing in June 1907 that the achievements of the Liberal administration were very poor in comparison with the promises given at the general election. Old Age Pensions were postponed. The starving children and the unemployed were neglected. Women's suffrage was more unpopular on the Liberal than on the Tory benches. The Land Bill was quite inadequate. All of these shortcomings convinced him of the need to work for 'a Labour and Socialist party which in the end will be strong enough to produce a Socialist government'.[46]

For these reasons, Campbell was rarely out of the limelight. Theologians were, for the most part, critical of the *New Theology*, but he continued to advocate it without apology. He addressed conferences up and down the country, exciting considerable enthusiasm. It was difficult, however, to decide what to do next. Some of his followers urged him to sever his connexion with the churches completely, but in a public statement issued in March 1908 he advised against such a course.[47] Amongst those in touch with him at this juncture were W.E. Orchard who had been, he records, 'captivated by the charm and magnetism' of the City Temple pastor's personality.[48] Fenner Brockway, on the other hand was 'repulsed by the hero-worship — and his love of it'.[49] The temporary solution adopted by his followers was to establish a 'League of Progressive Thought and Social Service' with F.R. Swan, a Congregational Minister and ILP member, as organizing secretary. In his preface to the popular edition of the *New Theology*, written in February 1909, Campbell reported that the Progressive League could count between three and four thousand members in over a hundred branches.[50] In his presidential

44. Ibid., pp. 149–50.

45. P.d'A. Jones, *The Christian Socialist Revival, 1877–1914* (Princeton, 1968), p. 422n.

46. R.J. Campbell to J.R. MacDonald, 22 June 1907, Labour Party General Correspondence, 16/1, 77 (Transport House, Smith Square, London). I owe this reference to Dr K.O. Morgan.

47. *The Times*, 4 March 1908.

48. W.E. Orchard, *From Faith to Faith* (London, 1933), p. 87.

49. F. Brockway, *Inside the Left: Thirty Years of Platform, Press, Prison and Parliament* (London, 1947), p. 16.

50. R.J. Campbell, *The New Theology*, Preface to the Popular Edition (London, 1909), p. viii.

address to the League in October 1909 Campbell emphatically declared that 'the only sense in which Jesus died for sinners was that in which any Son of God or martyr for truth and righteousness had died for the sake of his mission'.[51] Later, he attended an international gathering of Liberal Christians at Montreux and sought a place for his movement in the world-wide protest against outmoded dogmatic Christianity.

Although the Progressive League continued its activities until 1911, it was probably already at its zenith in 1910. As the months passed, the alignments and attitudes of the early phase of the New Theology movement changed. The strain of his multifarious activities began to tell on the sensitive Campbell. While the City Temple congregation had, on the whole, stood by him during the period of the most acute controversy, the atmosphere of constant debate was taxing for all concerned. In various ways, therefore, whether consciously or unconsciously, Campbell began to withdraw from some of his public commitments, though he did take part in Keir Hardie's campaign at Merthyr Tydfil during the general election of January 1910. He was particularly disappointed by the failure of the New Theology movement to develop a close association with Roman Catholic Modernism.[52] Gradually, he began to renew his contacts with Congregational ministers from whom he had been estranged. The Senior Student at Mansfield College, the young C.H. Dodd, was able to persuade Fairbairn's successor to invite Campbell back to Oxford and discuss his views with students. 'This was no raging tearing revolutionary', Dodd was surprised to find 'but a quiet, friendly, essentially humble character, reasonable and moderate in discussion. I felt more than ever that he had misrepresented himself to the public.'[53] It was also the case, however, that Campbell's own views were quietly changing in emphasis. The centre of theological controversy shifted and Campbell surprised some of his radical admirers by declaring his disagreement with Arthur Drews and his British followers. Even P.T. Forsyth was prepared to accept that the Christological statements that Campbell was now beginning to make constituted evidence of a partial return to orthodoxy. At the autumn meetings of the Congregational Union in 1911, a well-rehearsed public reconciliation between the two men took place. On this note, Campbell sailed for the United States and did not resume his ministry at the City Temple until February 1912.

Although the American tour removed Campbell from controversy in Britain, it proved a different kind of strain. It was announced in *The Times* on 20 February 1912 that Campbell was suffering from nervous exhaustion and a grave heart weakness. In consequence, he had decided to resign his connexions with any organization outside the City Temple. It is also clear that there was a crisis in his relations with the church officers of the City Temple. Campbell

51. *The Times*, 12 October 1909.
52. G. Tyrrell to A.L. Lilley, May 1909, Lilley MS, Library of the University of St Andrews; M.D. Petre, *Autobiography and Life of George Tyrrell*, ii (London, 1912), pp. 398–99.
53. The late Professor C.H. Dodd to the author, 15 January 1971.

desired the appointment of a permanent ministerial assistant but the officers, conscious no doubt that a substantial proportion of the congregation came solely to hear Campbell, declined. According to the writer of Campbell's obituary in *The Times*, it was this friction with his office-bearers, which did not disappear, that played a large part in causing Campbell's return to the Church of England. Campbell himself, on the other hand, stresses the fact that he was beginning to disengage himself from some of the theological opinions he had earlier advanced. In his autobiography he states that it was the criticism of the *New Theology* made by Bishop Gore, in a series of lectures in Birmingham which were subsequently published, that had most impact on his thinking.[54] It is difficult to judge how much weight should be given to his personal situation and how much to his intellectual development. In any event, Campbell claims to have told the Bishop of London in January 1914 that he was thinking of returning to the Church of England.

When war broke out in 1914, Campbell was again indisposed, but he soon joined his erstwhile opponent, Robertson Nicoll, in rallying Free Church opinion in support of British intervention in the war. This action angered some of the young men, like Fenner Brockway and Reginald Sorensen, who had formerly been admirers and now felt that the logic of the New Theology pointed to pacifism. It was no accident that Lloyd George chose to make his first public statement on the war at the City Temple. At the public meeting on this occasion it was Campbell who proposed a motion pledging Nonconformity to the fight. In the summer of 1915, he decided that he had to go out to France to see the fighting at first hand. The world crisis and his personal crisis seemed suddenly to come together. In March 1915, he withdrew the *New Theology* and purchased the rights from the publisher to prevent future reissue. The Bishop of Birmingham, with whom he discussed his position before leaving for France, expressed his satisfaction at this step. Campbell, who had contracted to write a Life of Christ, foresaw the end of his days as a preacher at the City Temple, but his final decision had still not been made. Campbell deeply impressed the Deputy Organizing Secretary of the YMCA as 'quite outstanding' in the influence he exercized on the troops in France.[55] Campbell returned from the Western Front impressed by the practical collaboration among Christians that he had witnessed there and became convinced of the need for Christian unity. He also became certain, however, that he had to rejoin the Church of England. Rumours to this effect reached the press in mid September and shortly afterwards he announced his resignation at a church meeting at the City Temple. In his autobiography, Campbell states that he also announced his intention to seek orders in the Church of England. According to a report of the meeting which reached *The*

54. C. Gore, *The New Theology and the Old Religion* (London, 1907).
55. The late Sir Frank Willis to the author, 26 March 1971; R.J. Campbell, *With Our Troops in France* (London, 1916).

Times, however, Campbell simply stated that 'later on' he might change his church affiliation before returning to the pulpit.[56] His last service at the City Temple was on 10 October 1915; it came as a surprise when, five days later, Campbell drove to Oxford where, at Cuddesdon, Bishop Gore received him once more into the Church of England. Partly to avoid press interviews about his future intentions, Campbell again departed for France.

In practice, Campbell's decision did not bring the New Theology movement to an end — it had already died. The synthesis which Campbell had tried to uphold for a decade was already proving inadequate and many of his former associates were undertaking fresh spiritual pilgrimages of their own. Nevertheless, the power of Campbell's personality, his semi-mystical *attrait* and his charm should not be underestimated. The late Lord Sorensen is only one of many to testify to the fact that young men in the decade before the First World War were 'overawed by his presence'.[57] Yet Campbell's ill-health and emotional instability combined to prevent him giving the organizational direction which might have made the Progressive League a body of considerable political and intellectual significance. While Campbell did not renounce his Socialism, the alliance so optimistically envisaged between Progressive Christianity and the Labour movement did not materialise, at least not in the form he desired. There is an irony in the fact that while Campbell was stressing his support for the British war effort, his former partner and friend Keir Hardie died, distressed by a world which refused to conform to his ideals.[58]

In the perspective of theological thought, the war witnessed a renewed emphasis upon divine transcendence as opposed to divine immanence. Campbell's 'conversion' must be seen in this context, but at the same time the personal elements in his pilgrimage must be stressed. Despite the prominence that Campbell gives to them in his autobiography, Gore's criticisms of *The New Theology* do not appear to have had any immediate impact. It was only in 1913–15 that they came to carry weight. Only then, combined with the crisis of the war and his own sense of intellectual and physical weariness, did they apparently lead him to put aside the burden of the City Temple, reassert the link with his Oxford past and seek an obscurity and quietness which he had not known for a dozen years.

56. *The Times*, 24 September 1915.
57. The late Lord Sorensen to the author, 7 December 1970.
58. R.J. Campbell, *The War and the Soul* (London, 1916); idem, *Words of Comfort* (London, 1917); idem, *A Letter to an American Friend* (London, 1918).

11

Free Churchmen and the Twenty Years' Crisis

It was E.H. Carr who coined the term 'Twenty Years' Crisis' to describe the period between 1919 and 1939. The optimism of the 'war to end war' soon faded as Europe was wracked by new tensions and conflicts. If the Great War had witnessed the defeat of the German bid for European hegemony, it had left fresh problems in its wake. The new states of Europe wrestled with the problems of nation-building. After their success in the civil war, the Bolsheviks consolidated their position in the Soviet Union. In Italy, Mussolini came to power and a new ideology 'Fascism' had appeared. Despite the restrictions of the Treaty of Versailles, German aspirations remained uncertain. Britain and France were frequently at loggerheads on the question of reparations from Germany. The United States played little part in European affairs. British governments and people had to recognize that the absence of war did not mean tranquillity. The Irish Free State was established after a bitter struggle. The 1926 Imperial Conference recognized equality of status between Britain and the Dominions. Political activity in India began to gather pace. Japanese power in East Asia became steadily more apparent. Writing in 1918, J.H. Shakespeare dreaded lest 'the Free Churches should maintain automatic movements and cries while with brain and heart, and even conscience, asleep, they march on through the wonderful new world, missing its golden harvests and deaf to its significant calls'.[1] The golden harvests proved elusive, and Free Churchmen did not find the 'wonderful new world' greatly to their taste.

'They all shared a Nonconformist origin', wrote A.L. Rowse in *All Souls and Appeasement* concerning Chamberlain, Simon, Hoare, Runciman, Wood and Brown, 'and its characteristic self-righteousness — all the more intolerable in the palpably wrong'.[2] Since 1961, with the release of Cabinet and other official papers, historians have tended to take a more sympathetic, though by no means uncritical, view of 'appeasement'. It is less common now for writers to take the view that Chamberlain and his colleagues were 'palpably wrong'. Perhaps the single most important factor contributing to this revision has been the growing awareness of the multiplicity of challenges confronting the British Empire in the 1930s. The predominating military advice was that if Britain should find itself simultaneously at war with Germany, Italy and

---

1. J.H. Shakespeare, *The Churches at the Cross-Roads* (London, 1918), p. 211.
2. A.L. Rowse, *All Souls and Appeasement* (London, 1961), p. 19.

Japan, its chances of success were slim. Yet, while a great deal has been written about 'appeasement' over the last decade, the dyspeptic remarks quoted above have, on the whole, remained in lonely eminence, or been cited elsewhere as if they represented an accepted truth. I want to look a little more deeply into Free Church attitudes to international affairs between the wars, particularly as events moved to a climax and war seemed imminent.

The relative absence of critical discussion of these matters is not surprising. Historians of international relations have not generally been interested in ecclesiastical opinion. Church historians have often discussed the attitude of churches on international questions without troubling to ask how they were manufactured, or what their influence might be. There is a wider problem. Historians as a whole may be prepared to grant that the 'Free Church tradition' was still important in the life of England between the wars. It is not easy, however, to move from such an assertion to offering a judgment on how important that tradition was, particularly in the sphere of politics and public affairs. What generalizations can be made about Free Churchmen? There is the obvious point that while there were Free Churchmen there was no Free Church. There were Methodists (united after 1932), Baptists, Congregationalists, Quakers and Unitarians — all more or less content to be described as 'Free Churches', though with the relics of 'Nonconformity' still present. Superimposed on these denominational bodies stood the National Council of the Evangelical Free Churches, augmented after 1919 by the Federal Council of the Evangelical Free Churches. As Dr Jordan pointed out, it was a vexed question, at least in the eyes of Church and State, whether it was the President of the former body or the Moderator of the latter who should be taken to represent 'the Free Churches' on the occasions when it was necessary for this to happen.[3] The Presidency rotated around the denominations on an annual basis. Ministers filled the office (Quakers apart) as they did the Moderatorship, but the latter was held for two years. It would be a bold man, however, who asserted that either the President or the Moderator spoke invariably as the 'voice of the Free Churches'. While his name might appear alongside that of the Archbishop of Canterbury or Westminster, his status cannot be compared. While not discounting the level of 'Free Church' activity on a local basis, I would suggest that 'Free Church' opinion remained firmly denominational — if that is not a paradox. Denominational prominence led to Free Church eminence, not the other way round. When individuals combined roles — as for example M.E. Aubrey did between 1936 and 1938 when he was both Free Church Moderator and Secretary of the Baptist Union — their position was strengthened. During such a juncture, Baptists might be expected to have more than usual interest in 'Free Church' activity. It would be unwise to assume, however, that his standing among other denominations was particularly high. Even the most ardent enthusiasts for Free Church Union

3. E.K.H. Jordan, *Free Church Unity* (London, 1956), p. 223.

could not escape from a denominational label in Free Church Council circles. The officers were there because it was appropriate that their denomination should have its turn. This is not to suggest that divisions of opinion at the highest level on quasi-political questions in the Councils were denominational in character. It does mean, however, that while the Assembly meetings of the 'Free Churches' could attract a Prime Minister, the political effectiveness of any resolutions passed depended upon the denominational standing of those involved. It is in this sense that any attempt to equate the statements emanating from the National Council or its officers with the views of x number of Free Churchmen is misleading. It could be said, on the other hand, that there was in the *British Weekly* a supradenominational Free Church voice, but while that is true I suspect that its influence suffered because of its disembodied nature.

Some related points must also be made at a denominational level. I need hardly elaborate on the fact that the internal structures of the various Free Churches differed considerably, particularly between Methodists and Baptists/Congregationalists. The resolution of a Baptist Union Council is not quite the same as the resolution of a Methodist Conference. The President of the Baptist Union has not quite the same aura as a President of the Methodist Conference. When the historian seeks the 'representative' expression of opinion concerning international affairs on the part of denominational hierarchies, he must be aware of these subtleties. In addition, it would be rash to assume that resolutions and statements drafted and passed at national level, filtered down through editorials and articles in the denominational press, do in fact represent 'what Baptists think'. People who sit on committees, attend assemblies and write to or for newspapers are unusual though not necessarily odd people. The historian seeks out the articulate and the identifiable 'leader', but we ought to be rather more sceptical before we make assertions about the views of Free Churchmen as a whole.

There is one further point I should like to make before moving on to particular aspects. It would be unwise not to ponder on the relationship between minister and laity. If we go back only to the turn of the century, it is clear that many ministers felt an uncertainty about their role and status. There was an uneasy tension reflected in Silvester Horne's *Pulpit, Platform and Parliament*. If it was conceded that the Gospel could not be confined to a narrowly religious sphere but had relevance to social, political and economic questions, then how far could or should the minister confine himself to the sphere of chapel life? To take an active as opposed to an exhortatory role seemed to involve the clear declaration of party allegiance. Before 1914, by and large, such activity could be acceptable in the context of a politically homogeneous chapel community. In South Bristol, for example, when some Liberal Free Churchmen felt that the services of thanksgiving for the election victory of 1906 were excessive, they were reminded that the bells of the parish church of Bedminster had been rung to celebrate the result of 1900. Such clear-cut partisanship did not dissolve overnight, but the unexpected impact of the Great War on the structure of British party politics meant that the Liberal alignment was less automatic. While a clear correlation continued to exist, it was not so clear and not so complete. For 1906 Professor Koss gives a total of 223 FC candidates (185 elected) of whom 191 were Liberal (157 elected), 20 Labour or Liberal-Labour (20 elected), and 9 Conservative (6 elected). In 1935, there were 146 candidates (65 elected): 90 Liberals (9 elected), 21 Liberal National (16 elected), 69 Labour (29 elected), and 12 Conservative (10 elected). In other words, in the new, though arguably rather special circumstances of the later thirties, Free Church MPs were roughly divided between the government and the opposition.[4]

It is dangerous to draw too precise a conclusion from this situation. The actual distribution of MPs in this parliament may well not be a very accurate measure of how the political allegiances of Free Churchmen (and even more of Free Churchwomen) actually were distributed. It may well underestimate the voting support given from the Free Churches to the National governments both in 1931 and 1935. Why had this extraordinary shift in party allegiance, or at least voting behaviour, taken place? In the first place, the specific grievances and inferiorities of Free Churchmen as such had very largely disappeared. In the second, Free Church voters came increasingly to vote in the confused and muddled way most people vote, that is to say mingling their class identification, economic interest and estimate of the qualities of the competing politicians. In this context, the marginal social and economic status of many Free Church congregations split the voting within the same chapel in different directions. In short, the political/social/ecclesiastical amalgam of pre-1914 Nonconformity was fast dissolving. In one sense, this development could be interpreted as the secularization of the politics of Free Churchmen. Politics could perhaps be seen as an autonomous sphere of activity with its own norms, pressures and compromises. It became increasingly more important to oppose or support 'Socialism' than to show denominational solidarity at the polls. Given the requirements of party discipline, a political opponent was no less an opponent for being a member of the same denomination, or even of the same chapel. Alternatively, the process could be regarded as the depoliticization of religion. The tendency for many ministers to regard themselves as recruiting sergeants for a particular party and to conduct themselves as if they were politicians had certainly not been eliminated, but it was held in check. A situation was developing in which politicians could not mobilize a Free Church lobby behind a specific social and political programme nor could ministers manipulate a compact group of politicians for their objectives.[5]

Perhaps all this is only an elaborate way of saying that as a pressure group the Free Churches were losing political significance. Yet one is tempted

    4. S. Koss, *Nonconformity in Modern British Politics* (London, 1975), pp. 227–36. See also W.L. Miller, 'The Religious Alignment at English Elections between 1918 and 1970', *Political Studies*, xxv (1977), pp. 227–51.
    5. S. Koss, 'Lloyd George and Nonconformity: The Last Rally', *English Historical Review*, lxxxix (1974), pp. 77–108.

to ask whether, apart from the pursuit of specific objectives relevant to themselves as institutions, they had ever been politically as powerful as has often been supposed. The concept of a Free Church politician is not an easy one to define. It is used somewhat elastically to embrace men who were Free Churchmen by descent, by active conviction, by passive membership. A list which includes H.H. Asquith, Lloyd George, John Simon, Walter Runciman, Arthur Henderson, Kingsley Wood and Ernest Brown makes the point. It may be that they had in common Dr Rowse's sanctimonious self-righteousness, but this has not been frequently remarked on. Even within this small group the relationship between their 'Free Churchmanship' and their political convictions and behaviour is by no means easy to discern. Lloyd George was universally described as a Welsh Nonconformist and he certainly cultivated Nonconformists sedulously at various points in his career, but was he a Christian?[6] Asquith and Simon both had impeccable Independent ancestry, but their own beliefs must be a matter for speculation. It has been unkindly suggested that Simon's interest in his Welsh Nonconformist ancestors only developed when he had to make it clear, as Foreign Secretary, that he was not a Jew. Both Asquith and Simon had early moved academically out of the ambience of Nonconformity. Although Runciman had been educated at Cambridge, however, he retained his Free Church connexions and continued to be an active Methodist. The same was true, from rather different backgrounds, of Arthur Henderson and Kingsley Wood. Ernest Brown, likewise, was very well known in Baptist circles, and accepted official positions within the denomination and the Free Churches generally. It should not be supposed, however, that only those who accepted office within their denominations were 'active' The pressures of political life were such that many MPs who were Free Churchmen played little part in the national life of their denomination and attended public worship most irregularly.

Whatever conclusion we might come to about the ecclesiastical status and beliefs of the most well-known Free Churchmen of the interwar period, it is clear that because of their divided political allegiance they could not act together as Free Churchmen. They owed their loyalty to their Cabinet colleagues and to their parties. They accepted collective responsibility for Cabinet decisions. The relationship of these leading figures to the churches from which they had sprung was therefore necessarily complex. Just as there was a delay before the numerical strength of the Free Churches in the country was reflected in the House of Commons in the early twentieth century, so there was a delay before their numerical decline was reflected in the Commons, and Free Churchmen were perhaps overrepresented in Cabinets in the thirties. The political eminence of the men I have mentioned, however, was in their own right, not *qua* Free Churchmen. Their position in public life was a reflexion of

6. W.R.P. George, *The Making of Lloyd George* (London, 1976). M.G. Fry, *Lloyd George and Foreign Policy*, i (London, 1977), pp. 21–23.

pre-war rather than post-war realities. Even so, they were never in a majority in a Cabinet. The situation made them particularly powerless. Almost by definition, Dissenters had been outsiders, critical of 'the Establishment', using that term in its broadest sense. If we move back into the nineteenth century, the problem of the transition from 'outsider Dissenter' to 'insider Dissenter' can be seen dramatically in the cases of John Bright and Joseph Chamberlain. The former's final gesture of resignation from the Cabinet in protest against the bombardment of Alexandria in 1882 represented an acknowledgement of the fact that almost as the 'stage Dissenter' he could do nothing to reverse a decision upon which his colleagues had agreed. He reverted to a role of vocal powerlessness which was by no means uncongenial.[7] Chamberlain, on the other hand (admittedly not a Quaker), made his rather erratic transition to office by apparently accepting with relish the rules of *Realpolitik.*

In the inter-war period, the instinctive mood of most Free Churchmen was still ancestrally oppositional. Yet the Great War had been a vital watershed. Many Free Churchmen had wavered before supporting Britain's entry into the war in 1914. Once that support had been given, it could not be given half-heartedly. Mr Clements' excellent article has illuminated Baptist attitudes.[8] The demand was for parity of respect for Free Churchmen (and particularly their ministers) and an equal sharing of the burden. The nature of the war meant that to some extent common suffering bound together different ecclesiastical traditions. Free Churchmen demanded recognition of their contribution by adequate representation on great occasions of state. They were not now an excluded and inferior minority. But, as I have suggested, acceptance could not eradicate the instinct of criticism, the impulse to petition and protest and at times appear indifferent to the problems presented by power and responsibility. The prophetic tradition could not be restrained, particularly in a denomination noted for its Old Testament scholarship.

It is in this context that I want to consider Free Church attitudes to war and peace, since it seems to me that they can be clearly related to the changes and tensions that I have been describing. There had been a relatively small number of conscientious objectors in the First World War, and amongst those who had claimed to base their objection on religious convictions Nonconformists had been prominent.[9] I have discussed pacifism during the First World War at length elsewhere, and it would not be appropriate here to repeat my discussion in detail. However, by the end of the war it was possible for Free Churchmen, indeed all Christians, to come together in advocacy of a new international order. The balance of power would be destroyed, and a new League of Nations created. It would be wrong to suppose that Free Churchmen were the only

---

7. K.G. Robbins, *John Bright* (London, 1978), explores this tension.

8. K.W. Clements, 'Baptists and the Outbreak of the First World War', *Baptist Quarterly,* xxvi (1975), pp. 74–92.

9. K.G. Robbins, *The Abolition of War: The British Peace Movement, 1914–1919* (Cardiff, 1976).

prominent advocates of the League, but it was a cause — if not a crusade — which had a particular appeal, certainly in the twenties. The League of Nations Union, the main body which tried to influence public opinion in favour of the League, had the advantage of being, at least in theory, above party allegiance. The LNU deliberately cultivated church opinion with a special committee called the Christian Organization Committee.[10] At its meeting in April 1924, for example, attended by M.E. Aubrey, T.G. Dunning and J.H. Rushbrooke, it was reported that 2,151 church congregations held corporate membership (though it was regretted that 517 were in arrears). There were but 354 Anglican Churches and six Roman Catholic. There were 195 Baptist corporate members. Lord Robert Cecil, not a notable friend of Nonconformity, was lavish in his praise for the part the Free Churches played in its work.[11] The LNU issued a series of *Preachers' Notes* and, as Dr Waley comments in his book on British public opinion and the Abyssinian War, 1935–36: 'In general, the Union took it for granted, with success, that membership of a church or religious body was prima facie evidence of support for the League of Nations and for the ideas of disarmament and collective security, those uneasy twins.'[12] This enthusiasm was readily reciprocated. A work like *Christianity and the League of Nations* by the Methodist, A.W. Harrison, is a very typical example of writing which reflected the assumption that the League of Nations was necessarily a symbol of progress and a body to be supported.[13] It was also very generally assumed that disarmament and peace were inseparably connected. Arthur Henderson's efforts both as Foreign Secretary and then as President of the World Disarmament Conference were very widely admired in the Free Churches, certainly by many who would not have voted Labour.

The advent of Hitler in Germany produced a new situation. In Free Church circles it began to bring out into the open the disagreements which had been covered over by general support for the League. It took time for these to be fully articulated, and Free Churchmen must have voted heavily for the Peace Ballot organized under the auspices of the League of Nations Union.[14] The strongest support came from some of the most Nonconformist areas of Wales where the whole operation must have been carried out on a chapel basis. The success of the Peace Ballot was indeed a major achievement, however much intellectual confusion it showed. The 'betrayal' of the League by the Baldwin government and by Hoare in particular in the ensuing crisis was a bitter disappointment to most Free Churchmen. Geoffrey Shakespeare, for example, made known his intention of resigning his minor ministerial post

10. Minutes of the Christian Organization Committee in the Lothian MSS, Scottish Record Office, Edinburgh.

11. In an address to the National Free Church Council in 1924 cited in Jordan, *Free Church Unity*, p. 181.

12. D. Waley, *British Public Opinion and the Abyssinian War, 1935–1936* (London, 1975), p. 93.

13. A.W. Harrison, *Christianity and the League of Nations* (London, 1928).

14. Dame Adelaide Livingstone, *The Peace Ballot* (London, 1935), pp. 55–58.

if the terms of the Hoare-Laval pact were adopted.[15] The failure of Britain to 'take a lead' on this occasion was 'a staggering blow to the whole Peace system', as one of the publications of the Council of Action for Peace and Reconstruction subsequently put it.

Attention now naturally centred on Germany. It was perhaps amongst the Free Churches that the question of its future objectives and the appropriate response led to most soul-searching. It was to Germany that leading Free Church scholars had traditionally gone to complete their theological education. Some had formed life-long friendships arising out of their residence. It is not therefore surprising that in the middle thirties there was a widespread feeling that German grievances against the Treaty of Versailles were to some extent justified. When Dr F.W. Norwood, Baptist minister of the City Temple, rejoiced on hearing of the German militarization of the Rhineland in 1935, this was not a bizarre reaction.[16] It was a reflection of the view that there could be no lasting peace with Germany while she remained shackled to the terms of an unfair *Diktat*. Peace with Germany was still desirable and achievable. There was a willingness to make allowances for German conduct and to accept guilt for failure to disarm completely after 1918 or for taking German colonies. Phrases were not infrequently used which suggested that Hitler and his regime were the supreme creation of the Treaty of Versailles. A French Protestant correspondent wrote, on 10 December 1937, very critically of this tendency in British Free Church circles in particular. 'A great many sincere Christians,' he concluded, 'while they admit that the Treaty which ended such a tremendous war was still war-like, are not at all willing to consent to see Versailles described as "a terrific denial of Christian principles".'[17] His correspondent was Mrs Dorothy Buxton, who had become a Quaker and was deeply concerned about the plight of Christians under the Nazi regime.[18] Here was another dilemma. Insofar as adequate information was available on a confused and varied situation, Nazi policy was ominous and suggested to some that the regime was of such a character that talk of territorial revision in the interests of peace was quite misguided.

I have discussed the reactions of British Christians to the plight of Martin Niemöller elsewhere, but it may be of particular interest to bring to light some information on the attitude of M.E. Aubrey at this juncture.[19] Having consulted with Dr Rushbrooke, in March 1937 he wrote that he did not feel able to sign a letter to *The Times* drawing attention to the death of Dr Weissler. He considered that 'it might simply be an irritant to the persecuting party in Germany . . .' and might make things worse.[20] In a 'strictly confidential' letter

15. Waley, *British Public Opinion and the Abyssinian War, 1935–1936*, p. 64.
16. Koss, *Nonconformity in Modern British Politics*, p. 217.
17. A. Monod to D. Buxton, 10 December 1937 (in author's possession).
18. See below, pp. 183–94.
19. See below, pp. 161–82.
20. M.E. Aubrey to D. Buxton, 2 March 1937 (in author's possession).

later in the month he revealed that plans were afoot for a possible visit to Germany as Moderator 'to represent the interest of our Free Churches, and in that way to give some sort of encouragement to those who are putting up a fight for freedom'. Now of course — though this is by the way — many of the most distinguished leaders of the Confessing Church denied that they were doing anything of the kind. He continued that he was doubtful of the wisdom of a visit. 'It is rather difficult', he wrote

> to persuade Germans that as individuals we cherish friendly sentiments toward their nation while at the same time we are critical of the actions of rulers for whom they have a regard that is almost akin to admiration. Hitlerism at the moment seems to have a vogue in Germany that it is virtually a religion, and I do not want to do anything, even in my small way, which would stir up passion.[21]

In early April it was in fact decided not to make a visit. He decided instead to write to the German Ambassador 'expressing the friendship of our Free Churches to the German people, for we all are children of the Reformation that had its birth in Germany . . .' He intended to add that the treatment of certain sections of Christians in Germany 'not only means suffering to our brethren over there but is making more difficult the task of those of us who are working for peace and friendship . . .'[22] Later in the month, after reading an article by Barth published in the *British Weekly* which stated that 'freedom' was not the issue, he commented: 'Though I do not think he has the whole truth, because I am by no means a Barthian, I think there is some value in the reminder that freedom has come not by talking about it but through courageous advocacy and proclamation of Christian truth, and that it will be gained by men who wish to declare the Gospel rather than by those who simply want freedom'.[23] As the months passed, he became more alarmed and depressed. 'The Government there', he wrote early in July, 'at the moment seems to be in so strong a position that they can do what they like . . .'[24] He was quite clear that public opinion in Britain could do little.

There was, of course, a complication, particularly for Baptists and Methodists. Aubrey discussed it in a letter of 13 October 1937. Some of the protests of the Evangelical and the Confessional Church had a grave weakness. 'They never even suggest renouncing their position as a Church given a special status by the State or having taxes collected by the State on its behalf.' The situation was very unsatisfactory from a Free Church standpoint, but he and others were trying to minimize it by, 'concentrating upon the fact that all this business is due to a desire on the part of a large section of the Nazi

21. M.E. Aubrey to D. Buxton, 24 March 1937 (in author's possession).
22. M.E. Aubrey to D. Buxton, 5 April 1937 (in author's possession).
23. M.E. Aubrey to D. Buxton, 23 April 1937 (in author's possession).
24. M.E. Aubrey to D. Buxton, 2 July 1937 (in author's possession).

authorities to suppress the inconvenient beliefs and teaching of Christianity. In their Gospel we stand by them and shall continue to do so'.[25] By and large neither German Baptists nor Methodists found themselves in conflict with the State. Kingsley Lloyd, then a Methodist minister in New Southgate, complained a little later that

> The compromising attitude of the Free Churches in Germany has its baneful reaction on the opinion of many Free Church people here ... I am always coming across Baptists and Methodists who say their co-religionists 'are quite free to carry on their work' which I fear is only too true but does not reflect much credit on their conception of the work they are called to do.[26]

In one way, the struggle in Germany was quite encouraging. 'It is quite clear', Aubrey wrote in June 1938, 'that a rebirth of Christian faith and life is taking place in Germany, under all the clouds, and we shall see the fruit of this one day.' In a later passage in the same letter he wrote that the whole international situation was 'so difficult and perplexing, and it seems impossible to know what will come out of it. If only our country could get on better terms with Germany diplomatically, I think we should be able to bring real pressure to bear, but at the moment things are not promising.'[27] Here was the dilemma felt acutely by many Free Churchmen. It was wrong to believe that war with Germany was inevitable, but what were the grounds for supposing that Britain could 'get on better terms' — except by making dangerous concessions? Aubrey was writing some months after the Austrian Anschluss, and the problem was one which preoccupied the Cabinet. Chamberlain and his colleagues were not blind or indifferent to the fate of churchmen and others inside Germany. Aubrey and others certainly had private conversations with Eden while he was still Foreign Secretary. Yet the internal behaviour of the Nazis did not constitute grounds for refusing to negotiate with them. It was necessary to try to discover precisely what were German objectives. If there could be 'peaceful change' which brought about an European order which the Germans freely accepted then a real and lasting peace might be achieved. Chamberlain was a man of peace, but he was not a pacifist. Britain was not in a condition to fight, in any case, and it was hoped that the more time there was the greater would be the state of preparedness.

Although many Free Churchmen found it hard to forgive the Prime Minister's previous and present scepticism about the League of Nations, this policy of 'appeasement', so defined, was given broad support. The Free Church members of the Cabinet could see no alternative. As Secretary of State for Air after May 1938 the Methodist, Kingsley Wood, occupied a very crucial office. Ernest Brown, as Minister of Labour, did not dissent

25. M.E. Aubrey to D. Buxton, 13 October 1937 (in author's possession).
26. A.K. Lloyd to D. Buxton, 18 November 1938 (in author's possession).
27. M.E. Aubrey to D. Buxton, 13 June 1938 (in author's possession).

from government policy. Yet, as the prospect of war drew nearer, so the minority of absolute pacifists within each Free Church denomination grew more determined and more vocal. In addition to the interdenominational Fellowship of Reconciliation, each denomination had its own pacifist body. These varied in their activity. In January 1937 the Presbyterian Pacifist Group reported a membership of 131, and its chairman added, 'Most members of the Church, however, have never so much as heard of the Group owing largely to the modest reticence of pacifist ministers who keep it a secret even from their own congregations'. The Methodist Peace Fellowship and the Christian Pacifist Crusade (Congregational) were much more active. The secretary of the Baptist Pacifist Fellowship reported a very good year in January 1937 with the membership doubling.[28] At the time of the Baptist Union Assembly meetings held in Manchester in April, the total membership was nearly 500. Approximately 150 of these were ministers. The publication of the Report of the Special Committee Appointed by the Council of the Baptist Union to Consider the Attitude of the Denomination to War, was, however, a disappointment to them. The document recognized the integrity of the pacifist position, but it did not endorse it. The Secretary of the Baptist Pacifist Fellowship, the Rev. W.H. Haden, submitted the document to critical study in an article in *Reconciliation*, and there was considerable controversy in the denominational press.[29] In December 1937 it issued a reply so that Baptists were able to examine the arguments put forward by both sides. The debate continued until the outbreak of war — and beyond. In January 1939 it was reported that the membership had reached 1,024 and on the eve of war stood at 1,288.[30] This, of course, represented a small percentage of the total membership of the denomination, but I suspect that the proportion of ministerial pacifists in relation to the ministerial body was higher. The most well-known figure to espouse this cause was perhaps the Rev. H. Ingli James, then minister at Queen's Road, Coventry. However, the intellectual traffic was not all one way, Dr Hugh Martin, then at the S.C.M. Press, was one of those whose analysis of the issues at stake in a future conflict led them to abandon a former pacifism. The writings of Reinhold Niebuhr whom, with difficulty, Martin published, began to make an impact.

In his perhaps not altogether reliable recollection, Arthur Porritt of *The Christian World* records a meeting with T.R. Glover, J.C. Carlile and Ernest Brown at Folkestone at the height of the Munich crisis.[31] Glover, it seems, was most concerned about the British Empire and feared, with some justice, that if war should come, it might strain — even snap — relations with his beloved Canada. He did not see, however, why his sons 'should fight and die to keep

---

28. *Reconciliation*, January 1937.
29. Ibid., June 1937, 'Baptist Union and War'.
30. Ibid., January 1939.
31. A. Porritt, *More and More of Memories* (London, 1947), pp. 169–70. K.G. Robbins, *Munich 1938* (London, 1968).

three million Sudeten Germans under Czecho-Slovak rule'. Ernest Brown in Cabinet had been a firm supporter of the Prime Minister's decision to fly to Berchtesgaden, and subsequently upheld the Munich agreement. In the Cabinet meeting held on the critical afternoon of 25 September 1938, he gave his opinion that 'the time had not come to abandon efforts to obtain peace by negotiation'.[32] These comments reflect a different set of considerations from those we have just been discussing. The relief which attended the Munich agreement, at least initially, was widespread in the Free Churches. There were few who shared the reaction of Duff Cooper and Winston Churchill. It was, after all, a Methodist, Lord Runciman, who had been summoned by the Prime Minister to investigate the situation on the ground in Czechoslovakia. There was a gratitude for the apparent 'Peace in our Time' which could unite pacifists and non-pacifists. Yet, by early 1939 following Hitler's march into Prague, it seemed increasingly that war had been postponed not avoided. The majority of Free Churchmen now came to feel that Britain would be justified in going to war. They were prepared to accept conscription. Throughout the late spring and summer of 1939, however, most pacifists remained highly critical of any attempt to give British policy any semblance of moral authority. Accepting the influential 'have' and 'have-not' dichotomy, an editorial in *Reconciliation* in May 1939 declared 'Those who are holding on to empire by force must share the blame with those who are taking empire by the same method'.

An editorial in June was strongly critical of the guarantee to Poland and the moral bankruptcy that it represented. 'Leaders of the Opposition,' it commented sadly, 'as well as leaders of the Church and of the Free Churches (if there is any difference nowadays), seem to rival each other in giving the Government their unreserved support.' The remark made in parenthesis, though intended ironically, was substantially true. Most Free Churchmen saw no alternative but for the twenty years' crisis to end in another war.

32. Cabinet Minutes, 25 September 1938.

12

Martin Niemöller, the German Church Struggle and English Opinion

The Gestapo arrived at Martin Niemöller's rectory in Berlin-Dahlem on the morning of 1 July 1937.[1] He was taken away for questioning and remained a prisoner for nearly eight years. His detention came as no personal surprise since he had been aware of his perilous existence. Ever since Hitler's accession to power in January 1933, the uneasy relations between church and state had received a certain amount of attention abroad. The precise issues at stake were, however, difficult to grasp. This complexity remained, but as the struggle appeared to centre on the fate of one man — Niemöller — interest became more widespread. Many years later, in England, whenever the Church Struggle is mentioned, the name of Niemöller most readily comes to mind.

In 1937 it was easy to describe the scene in titanic terms: Niemöller, the man who defied Hitler. Foreign observers, looking anxiously for the leader of an 'opposition', believed that they had found one. But the myth and the reality need to be carefully distinguished. English reactions to the German Church Struggle throw some light upon that contest and form a strangely neglected aspect of British relations with Nazi Germany, for contemporary English opinion was divided in its view of Niemöller and the persecution of the churches. In the first place, it was difficult to build up an accurate picture of the internal developments in the struggle. Press reports were normally accurate as far as they went, but reporters could not be expected to understand the theological subtleties at stake. It was not even possible to arrive at a standard nomenclature. Was it, for example, the Confessing Church or the Confessional Church? In either case, the opportunity for misunderstanding was considerable.[2] Those observers who had personal contacts could rarely claim to possess a complete knowledge of the entire German scene. As recent research is making clear, the struggle varied in its intensity from area to area. There were, however, deeper obstacles to an agreed interpretation. Many, though not all, of the issues involved in the German struggle had their counterparts in England, acknowledged or unacknowledged. The churches in both countries were suffering from the impact of the First World War.

---

1. D. Schmidt, *Pastor Niemöller* (London 1959).

2. Equally, there were few who possessed an accurate knowledge of the administrative and financial structure of the various Landeskirchen. There was an almost complete lack of studies of nineteenth- and twentieth-century German Evangelical Church life by English writers.

In their relations with each other, in their attitudes towards the state, in their own beliefs, they were all groping for solutions to difficult problems.[3] It is hardly surprising, therefore, that English churchmen believed certain actions of German churchmen were wrong because they believed that such actions would have been wrong in England.

In addition, the figure of Luther himself continued to baffle English minds. No profound school of Luther scholarship existed in England. Luther's theology received little serious attention from Anglican or Free Church scholars.[4] The implications of his writings naturally spread into politics and church government. Once again, however, there was no exact correspondence with English conditions. As far as church government was concerned, many Anglicans were convinced that the German Lutherans, having forfeited the Apostolic Succession, were in a doubtful ecclesiastical condition. There was no question of intercommunion; the affair of the Jerusalem bishopric had left its mark.[5] Nor, as far as Free Churchmen were concerned, was it the case that Lutherans were their German equivalents. The nineteenth century saw the planting of Anglo-Saxon denominations on the Continent. German Baptists and Methodists looked to England for support and encouragement when their own freedom of activity was restricted by official Lutheran pressure.[6] Diverse opinions on church and state were only to be expected.

In pre-1933 Germany, orthodox Lutheran exegesis (however much it represented an ossification of the 'real' Luther) still operated within the framework of the doctrine of the Two Regiments.[7] Niemöller fully accepted this intellectual inheritance. Born in 1892, the son of a Westphalian pastor, he became a cadet in the Imperial German Navy in 1910. When war broke out in 1914, he had little doubt about the justice of his country's cause. By 1916 he was a U-boat commander. The Armistice of 1918 was as much a blow to Niemöller as to other conservative Germans. Even more disturbing was the social turmoil in the months after the end of the war. As a naval officer, he refused to tow two U-boats to Britain to be surrendered under the terms of the Armistice. That was the responsibility of those who had signed the agreement.[8] He left the service and, in 1920, was admitted as a theological student at Münster. He was not a speculative theologian or a searching thinker; the man of action took precedence over the man of reflexion. Together with other anti-republican students, he trained in readiness for the day when an

3. See G. Mehnert, *Evangelische Kirche und Politik, 1917–19* (Düsseldorf, 1959).

4. For a brief discussion see G. Rupp. *The Righteousness of God: Luther Studies* (London, 1953), pp. 49–55.

5. R.W. Greaves, 'The Jerusalem Bishopric, 1841', *English Historical Review*, lxiv (1949), pp. 328–52.

6. K.S. Latourette, *Christianity in a Revolutionary Age* (London, 1960) ii, p. 75.

7. For a useful discussion of various interpretations of Luther see T.G. Sanders, *Protestant Concepts of Church and State* (New York, 1964), pp. 23–75. See also W.D.J. Cargill Thompson, 'The "Two Kingdoms" and the "Two Regiments": Some Problems of Luther's *Zwei-Reiche-Lehre*', *Journal of Theological Studies*, n.s., xx (1969), pp. 164–85.

8. M. Niemöller, *From U-boat to Pulpit* (London, 1936), pp. 147–48.

armed rising would bring back the institutions and traditions which he valued. The failure of the Kapp *Putsch* was a grave disappointment. His plight in these years made him a keen critic of reparations and eager to detect any slight on German national honour.[9]

The dissolution of throne and altar had left Niemöller discontented and troubled. In England throne and altar had survived superficially unscathed. Victory and continuity spared the Church of England some of the questions which perplexed German pastors. During the war, ardent spirits clamoured for 'Life and Liberty' for the church, but Randall Davidson steered the church away from premature disestablishment.[10] Nevertheless, the Enabling Act of 1919 was a sign of the desire for greater freedom from the state. The Prayer Book controversy of 1928 showed, however, that the ultimate authority over the church rested with Parliament.[11] The House of Commons might well have been expressing the convictions of 'Christian Englishmen', but that only made the position of the church more embarrassing. If the House of Commons could still in some sense be regarded as the assembly of the laity, the proposers of the new Prayer Book were made to look like members of an *'ecclesiola in ecclesia'*. The episcopate had no wish to find itself in such a position. It was wrong to push matters to logical conclusions. The minority who pressed for disestablishment were ignored and everything was done to reduce the temperature for a few years.[12]

Relations between Anglicans and Free Churchmen before the First World War were not good. The 1902 Education Act had revived old antagonisms and the Liberal benches after 1906 were teeming with Free Churchmen.[13] These embattled positions, however, did not survive the First World War in the same form; suspicion remained, but the vigour had gone out of the contest. The solid front of political Dissent had splintered with the disruption of the Liberal Party. Leading Free Churchmen began to feel themselves at ease in Lambeth.[14] Disagreement remained, but hostility began to disappear — not that the prevailing Free Church mood was favourable to discussions on the doctrine of the church: there were more important social questions to attend to. The achievement of Methodist Union showed what could be done by negotiators who, on the whole, shared the conviction that the institutional church was a human structure. Jesus Christ was not concerned with structure and, naturally, the early church had devised a form of government in terms of the prevailing political and social patterns. On this argument, as has been observed, the institutional structure of the *ecclesia* could be changed to suit

9. M. Niemöller, *From U-boat to Pulpit*, pp. 160–5.

10. G.K.A. Bell, *Randall Davidson*, 3rd ed. (London, 1952), pp. 961–67.

11. See R. Currie, 'Power and Principle: The Anglican Prayer Book Controversy, 1927–30', *Church History*, xxxiii (1964), pp. 192–202.

12. For a useful discussion of the problems of church and state in the British context, see the introduction to D. Nicholls, *Church and State in Britain since 1820* (London, 1967).

13. E.K.H. Jordan, *Free Church Unity* (London, 1956), pp. 77–126.

14. Ibid., pp. 168–79.

the new political ideals of society without breaking any divine law. Methodists in the early 1920s believed that democracy and representation had a high moral value and it was natural to work out a church order in terms of these ideas.[15]

Most importantly, Anglicans and Free Churchmen were both aware, at least subconsciously, that as the tide of faith continued to ebb, they were being drawn together. The First World War was a revelation to the clergy of the real nature of English religion.[16] Christian orthodoxy made only a fleeting appearance. The simple faith in a benevolent Providence, which did duty for Christianity, collapsed when surrounded by seemingly meaningless slaughter. Church attendance continued to decline and some men vowed that they would never enter a church again. Social Christianity apparently left men quite unprepared for the reality of evil.[17]

Similarly in Germany. Pastors rooted in old conventions were bewildered when confronted by the rapid changes in post-war Germany. As an organizer for the Home-Mission in Westphalia throughout the twenties, Niemöller was keenly aware of social distress and ecclesiastical weakness. In 1931, he was called to a parish in 'Christian' Berlin. There, as in London, the masses sat loosely by church obligations and religious beliefs. They were not bound by the more intimate ties of sheltered communities, although, as in London, during the twenties a firm majority of children were given Christian baptism. But, until 1932, there were also disturbing figures of departures from the Evangelical Church. The picture appeared to be one of steady decline. It is also significant that when, in the census of 1935, 2.62 per cent of the population of the Reich declared themselves to be without religion, the figure for Berlin was 9.05 per cent. In 1933, the Evangelical Lutheran percentage of the population of Berlin fell to 71.05.[18] Even so, there were, nominally and legally, 3,000,000 Evangelical Lutherans in Berlin. But the number who could be described as 'church-centred' or even 'church-orientated' must have been far smaller. The rest could be sorted into a wide variety of half-believers according to taste. Nevertheless, such people were 'members of the church' since they had not exercized their right to leave. The range of theological opinion among those committed to the church was equally wide. Amongst ecclesiastical bureaucrats there existed differences of emphasis on matters of church administration. Amongst pastors and theologians the war of the generations was particularly fierce. The theological battles were fought with

15. J.H.S. Kent, *The Age of Disunity* (London, 1966), pp. 13–14. The importance of this analysis is that it became logically impossible for Free Churchmen of this persuasion to object to a structure of church government in Germany embodying the virtues of the *Führerprinzip*.

16. See, e.g. E.W. Kemp, *The Life and Letters of Kenneth Escott Kirk* (London, 1959), pp. 33–34.

17. Barth's reactions to the war can be seen in *Revolutionary Theology in the Making: Barth-Thurneysen Correspondence, 1914–25*, trans. by J.D. Smart (London, 1964).

18. F. Zipfel, *Kirchenkampf in Deutschland, 1933–1945* (Berlin, 1965), pp. 18–20.

a grim regard for truth and a singular lack of charity.[19] Professors issued challenges to rival commanders and demanded the unconditional loyalty of the troops. Young colonels, however, sometimes mysteriously appeared fighting for the other side with a devastating volley of pamphlets. The scope of these differences varied greatly from hair-splitting minutiae to fundamental questions of belief and unbelief.

The most serious problem were raised by the advance of the 'German Christians' in the wake of national revival. It is often stated that in the parochial elections of 1932, National Socialist candidates camouflaged themselves under misleading titles, such as 'Association for Positive Christianity and for the German People', and deceived the electorate.[20] Certainly, there was some conscious deception, but on the other hand there were candidates with a genuine belief that theirs was the only credible form of Christianity. For them, orthodox Christianity was bruised, battered and dying. There was much in it, however, that was true and beautiful, once stripped of needless accretions. Instead of the Old Testament, every nation should travel to the summit of Christian ideas by its own path, helped by its own history and mythology.[21] The notion that any institutional church was essential to religion was dismissed as absurd — a contention which did not grate on scholars who were hypersensitive to suggestions of *'früh-Katholizismus'*.[22] Troeltsch, for example, contending that henceforth religion would develop outside the churches and outside formal theology, had signified his agreement with such a development by moving from a chair of Theology to one of Philosophy. The 'German Christians' were determined that Germany needed a religion, but also that religion needed to be fully German. So, the 'Glaubensbewegung Deutscher Christen' developed, wrapped in a respectable coating by respectable scholars and brazenly accepted by less scrupulous men.[23] If the tares were growing among the wheat, the time had not come to separate them. Niemöller found that he had 'German Christians' on his own parish council but, since they had been duly elected by the Evangelical Lutherans of Dahlem, how could they be dismissed?

Such was the background to the Church Struggle. It is not possible here to give other than a brief sketch of the struggle. However, the title of a chapter, 'Pastor versus the State', in one of Niemöller's English biographies, begs the entire question.[24] Niemöller, like other Evangelical leaders, was no

---

19. S.W. Herman *It's Your Souls We Want* (London, 1943) reported that in his experience, in 1935 and 1936, the professors of theology at German universities were chiefly interested in mental gymnastics. The students who graduated were learned but ill-prepared for practical church-work and the problems of their parishioners.

20. B. Forell, 'National-Socialism and the Protestant Churches in Germany', *The Third Reich* (for UNESCO) (London, 1955), p. 816.

21. Paul de Lagarde can be seen as a forerunner of such notions in Germany: see F. Stern, *The Politics of Cultural Despair* (Berkeley, 1961).

22. S.C. Neill, *The Interpretation of the New Testament, 1861–1961* (London, 1964), p. 344.

23. K. Meier, *Die Deutsche Christen* (Göttingen, 1955).

24. D. Schmidt, *Pastor Niemöller*, pp. 83–101.

enthusiast for republicanism.[25] In 1933 he felt that Germany needed strong leadership to bring back self-respect and discipline. There was an infectious vitality about National Socialism. It was selfless, idealistic, healthy and 'moral' in its emphases. Moreover, in the professed attitude of the Party towards religious questions, one could not discover outright atheism or agnosticism. Indeed, Article 24 spoke reassuringly of fostering a 'positive Christianity'. Outright condemnation seemed out of the question and throughout these years Niemöller never became in principle anti-Nazi. His living principle was freedom for the church to be the church. As a nationally-minded German, he praised Hitler's achievements in foreign policy and congratulated him on Germany's withdrawal from the League of Nations.[26] In Berlin, where the legacy of Stoecker still had some influence, some discrimination against the position of the Jews did not seem altogether objectionable. Niemöller favoured the creation of one Evangelical Church for all Germany, assisting von Bodelschwingh during his short period as *Reichsbischof*. As the slogan had it, he was 'Against the German Christians, yet with Hitler'.

The attitude of Englishmen towards the religious question reflected that taken towards the Nazi revolution as a whole. *The Times*, in February 1933, believed that Hitler would have to realize that the hall-mark of statesmanship was the close relationship between word and act. The mere statement of contradictory or futile claims would not impress, once in office. But it would be well understood that the conversion from demagogy to responsibility could not happen overnight.[27] The decisive nature of the *Machtergreifung* could not, however, be disguised. *The Times*, in March 1933, believed that however much foreign friends of Germany might deplore the maltreatment of some German citizens, that was primarily a matter for Germany herself. Only if these methods were applied to foreign subjects or in the field of foreign affairs would they become a matter of concern to other countries.[28] The treatment of Christianity in Germany was, on this approach, equally a matter primarily for Germany herself. But, even within this framework, was there room for personal activity? Division on this matter was not surprising since a political slant inevitably crept in.

George Bell, Bishop of Chichester, took a keen interest in the German church question from the start, and was exceptionally well-informed. He did not believe it was wrong to express views on Nazi actions and he declared that in the matter of the *Reichsbischof* 'the supersession through political means, of the Primate whom the Church has chosen, by the nominee of an all-powerful party' would be very damaging.[29] He may have hoped that

25. See D.R. Borg, '*Volkskirche*, "Christian State", and the Weimar Republic', *Church History*, xxxv (1966), pp. 186–206.

26. J.S. Conway, *The Nazi Persecution of the Churches, 1933–45* (London, 1968), p. 52.

27. *The Times*, 17 February 1933.

28. Ibid., 23 February 1933.

29. Letter to *The Times*, 14 June 1933.

such a comment would ultimately come to the notice of Hitler — for it was widely assumed at this early stage, by commentators both within and without Germany, that Hitler was not fully aware of what was being done by extremists in his name. *The Times*, for example, in June 1933, reported a meeting held in Berlin university to support Müller's candidature. When a resolution was read out in his favour, the bulk of the students left the hall. They assembled in the square outside and raised three cheers for Hitler to show that their loyalty was not affected by their inability to support political agitation in a matter of faith. 'Authoritative persons' had apparently satisfied themselves that the Chancellor had not been told the whole truth. Hitler, *The Times* correspondent commented, was undoubtedly finding his way quicker to the hearts of the people than was his party.[30]

It seemed sensible, therefore, to fly to the fountain-head. Duncan-Jones, Dean of Chichester, did this in July 1933. In an interview, Hitler declared that he had no wish to interfere with the internal working of the church. He was a Catholic and was accustomed to dealing with one church. Twenty-eight separate provincial churches made for disunity and inefficiency and one *Reichskirche* was needed. The churches could settle their own faith and order since, if they abstained from politics, they would have complete freedom on religious matters. When Duncan-Jones communicated these assurances to the press, suspicions were quietened.[31] At least in the eyes of the German Foreign Office, English opinion on the Church Struggle was important. The German Ambassador reported that sentiment among the clergy was divided, but perhaps predominantly unfavourable. The Archbishop of Canterbury epitomized those who were by nature favourable to Germany, but who were distressed by violation of the principle of equality before the law which they believed they saw in Germany. They distrusted the German Christians but had a 'boundless admiration for the moral and ethical side of the National Socialist programme, its clear-cut stand for religion and Christianity . . .'[32] Certainly, in September 1933, A.C. Headlam, Bishop of Gloucester and chairman of the Church of England Council on Foreign Relations, believed that he could congratulate Reichsbischof Müller on 'the formation of a united German Church, free from State control' and he trusted that other sinister rumours were ill-founded.[33] Shortly afterwards he received a personal assurance from Joachim Hossenfelder, the German Christian leader in Berlin, that they had been unfairly judged. Headlam consequently pleaded for time, so that the whole situation could settle down. He was an acute New Testament scholar, and an eirenic theologian with a keen concern for the unity of the church. Politically he disliked the growth of Socialism, for it had an 'ultimately

30. *The Times*, 21 June 1933.
31. Letter to *The Times*, 7 July 1933; S.C. Carpenter, *Duncan-Jones of Chichester* (London, 1956), pp. 85–86.
32. *Documents on German Foreign Policy* (hereafter cited as *DGFP*), Ser. C., i. 753.
33. R.C.D. Jasper, *A.C. Headlam: Life and Letters of a Bishop* (London, 1960), p. 292.

disastrous' effect on the development of character. He did not greatly care for the pink tints of ecumenical social Christianity, preferring the doctrinal flexing of 'Faith and Order'. Like his caustic contemporary, Hensley Henson, he did not find William Temple's path towards a Christian social order very alluring. A great many clergymen shared this mistrust of their brethren who attained notoriety as 'political parsons'. He felt that the uproar following the notorious speech by Dr Krause at the German Christian gathering in Berlin in November showed that the extremists were discredited.[34]

These anxieties about the frontier between politics and religion were, in fact, somewhat misplaced as far as Germany was concerned.[35] The Confessional leaders in 1934 and 1935 were anxious not to be politically involved, for their struggle was one for the identity of the church. The Confessional movement, in the eyes of Niemöller, was not, and should not be, a political party. He only drew the line when the state (as in the Aryan clauses and in the formation of the *Reichskirche*) tried to dictate to the church.[36] Bonhoeffer, with whom Niemöller was associated in a declaration of September 1933 calling for the repeal of the Aryan Clauses, which separated 'the Evangelical Church of the Old Prussian Union from the Christian Church', put the matter bluntly. He was in much closer contact with the Anglo-Saxon world than Niemöller, but he insisted that the church had no right to expect that the policy of the state should be based on 'humanitarianism'. The ordinances of the state, good or bad, were based on 'the sustaining will of God amidst the chaotic godlessness of the world'. New methods of dealing with the Jewish question were justified, but unless Jew and German could stand together under the Word of God, the church was no longer the church. But Bonhoeffer entered one caveat of great potential significance. The *raison d'être* of the state was the enforcement of law and order. Therefore, if the state's actions led to lawlessness and disorder, it was not acting rightly. The church then had the duty of reminding the state of its true function and of helping victims of lawlessness. This did not mean that the church was against the state (or the pastor versus the state); rather than revive dangerous notions of Caesaropapism, it had to persuade the state to be a proper state.[37] The disruptions, personal quarrels and changes of front which are characteristic of these years are, in part, the result of the fact that although conceptually the struggle was seen as apolitical, it was necessarily full of political complications.

The German Foreign Office took the Church Struggle seriously, believing it likely to jeopardise the Reich's political and economic relations abroad. A memorandum of June 1934 noted such universal disapproval that one could speak of a consolidated front of World Protestantism against the

34. J.S. Conway, *Nazi Persecution of the Churches*, pp. 51–54.

35. For a discussion of the background see K.-W. Dahm, 'German Protestantism and Politics, 1918–39', *Journal of Contemporary History*, iii (1968), pp. 29–50.

36. D. Schmidt, *Pastor Niemöller*, pp. 89–90.

37. D. Bonhoeffer, *No Rusty Swords* (London, 1965), pp. 221–30.

Reich Church Administration.[38] Bell, as chairman of the Universal Christian Council for Life and Work, saw the German ambassador in London at the end of April and pointed out that the autocratic rule of the Head of the German Church was impeding relations between the Evangelical Churches abroad and the Reich Church to such a degree that they might actually be broken off.[39] The Wilhelmstrasse, concerned that foreign Protestants had previously shown themselves supporters of Germany on questions of war debts and disarmament, tried to intervene. Following another report from London in September 1934, the Foreign Minister, von Neurath, called the *Reichsbischof* to his room. He observed that the methods being used to bring about the unification, 'desired by us all', of the Evangelical Church in Germany were causing serious disquiet among Protestants in Britain, America and Scandinavia. The relations had worsened to such an extent that they were no longer reconcilable with German foreign policy. He claimed to be in a position to threaten Müller with the withdrawal of Hitler's support unless unity was achieved by peaceful means.[40] Von Neurath's anxiety is easily explained by a message from London affirming that the conflict with the Catholic church and the dissensions within the Evangelical church constituted 'the main bone of contention in German-British relations'. The matter was alienating those circles which would otherwise be likely to be sympathetic towards the claims of the New Germany.[41]

Bell was chiefly behind the agitation, although the German embassy also received protests from the Baptist World Alliance and the World's Evangelical Alliance.[42] In the press, in the summer of 1934, there was some bewilderment about developments. *The Times* felt that the chief hope of finding a compromise satisfactory to both sides resided with Hitler himself. He seemed to realize that in that sphere, at least, persuasion and conviction alone could make men work together.[43] Readers of the paper continued to find letters from titled Germans insisting that 'the Church is free and its confession of faith is not subject to interference'.[44] They must have been even more puzzled to be told that, in the last analysis the conflict had much more to do with theological controversy than ecclesiastical polity. It was a struggle between a theology of creation and a theology of redemption.[45] But the protests seemed to have little result, and in October, following measures against the 'intact' Lutheran churches

---

38. *DGFP*, ser. C., iii, pp. 39–42.

39. The international ecumenical conference at Fanö in Denmark was due to take place in the late summer.

40. *DGFP*, ser. C., iii, pp. 417–19.

41. Ibid., ser. C., iii, pp. 425–26.

42. Bismarck to Berlin, 8 and 23 October 1934: German Foreign Office Documents, Evangelical Affairs, serial no. L432, frames L124006 and 124044.

43. *The Times*, 8 June 1934.

44. From Baroness von der Goltz, *The Times*, 8 June 1934.

45. From Dr Adolf Keller, *The Times*, 20 June 1934. Keller was an ecumenical pioneer with wide European contacts: see his, *Church and State on the European Continent* (London, 1936).

of South Germany, Bell again called on the embassy. He complained that, despite repeated statements by leading members of the German Government to the contrary, he had definite information that Government authorities were supporting the Reichsbischof and his actions. Protestant opposition was not to unification as such but only to the speed and methods employed. Chichester reiterated the view of church circles abroad that Hitler was not adequately informed on the matter and the foreign repercussions. The *Chargé* reported that his attempted rebuttal had little effect since the bishop was most fully informed, 'down to the minutest detail'. The embassy believed that if Anglo-German relations were to be improved, the Evangelical Church dispute had to be settled.[46]

The Archbishop of Canterbury made the same point to the German Ambassador. Lang said that the Anglican Church had no objection to the unification of the German Evangelical Church. It only objected to coercion. Action of this kind, together with the resurgence of certain 'German Christian' doctrines and the old controversial question of the Aryan clauses might make cooperation between Christian churches abroad and the German Evangelical Church impossible. Could not the disciplinary measures against the southern bishops be rescinded, or could not Jäger be moved?[47] These two interviews led to considerable activity in Berlin. Jäger was dismissed — even a section of the German Christians had protested against his attack on the bishop of Württemberg. The Archbishop wrote gratefully that the removal of Dr Jäger would make a great difference. If the Chancellor would take matters into his own hands he would be able to achieve a more satisfactory way of uniting the Protestant Church of Germany.[48] Lang was impressed by the fact that his wish had apparently been granted, although, in fact, English protests were by no means the chief reason for Jäger's dismissal. His only concern, he explained, was with coercion, it was not for him 'to express any opinion about the internal affairs of the Evangelical Church in Germany'.[49] But this was a false dawn.

The situation in Germany in 1935 and 1936 did not improve, contrary to some English anticipations. There was vague talk of reconciliation and pacification, but no success. The Confessing Church had, for the moment, entrenched itself behind the declarations of Barmen and Dahlem. But it was proving increasingly difficult to maintain a solid front, despite the assertion by *The Times* that the stand of the Confessing Church had rallied to its support 'the great majority of German Protestants'.[50] The formation of the Ministry

46. *DGFP*, ser. C., iii, pp. 478–80.

47. Ibid., pp. 487–9.

48. Ibid., pp. 546–7.

49. Ibid., pp. 478–80.

50. *The Times*, 23 March 1935. For Barmen see E. Wolf, *Barmen: Kirche zwischen Versuchung und Glaube* (Munich, 1957). Some Englishmen shared the judgment of S.W. Herman that at this stage, 'with typical German thoroughness the Confessional leaders proceeded too fast and too far in their attitude of defiance to the touchy Nazi State. Although all of their contentions were correct, their contentious way of presenting them was indiscreet': Herman, *It's Your Souls*, p. 133.

for Church Affairs in July 1935 encouraged many 'neutrals' to believe that a satisfactory compromise could be reached with the German Christians, or at least those outside Thuringia. The neutral leaders were dismissed by Niemöller and his followers as spineless. They should be fighting rather than trying to appear as arbitrators.

The English reaction to the Church Struggle was greatly complicated at this time by the widely-prevalent feeling of guilt towards Germany. William Temple felt it laid upon him to demand the excision of the so-called 'War Guilt' clause of the Treaty of Versailles.[51] Writing to *The Times* in May 1935 on the question of co-operation with Germany, he felt strongly that if the Allied attitude of 1919 could conceivably have been justified, it certainly was no longer. The war sprang from the international anarchy in which all nations acquiesced.[52] Chichester and Durham were alarmed. Bell agreed that peace and friendship with Germany was desirable, but when there was such clear evidence of a war being waged on Christianity, what sort of Germany was it with which Britain was being asked to make friends?[53] Henson felt that the pastors could well be fighting 'our battle also'. Christianity, he declared, could not make terms with the totalitarian state, 'nor subject its catholic character and claim to merely national interests'. Temple hastily wrote to associate himself wholeheartedly with Bell. Nothing so greatly hindered a policy of co-operation as the continuance of racial and religious persecution in Germany.[54] All English churchmen who had participated in ecumenical gatherings were well aware that the 'war-guilt' question was likely to 'raise the roof-tops'.[55] Many agreed that National Socialism, and all the mean and cruel things it stood for, 'was a reaction in exasperation and despair at the failure of France and Great Britain to make a generous, or even righteous, response'.[56] These were the words of the theologian A.E. Garvie who, somewhat bizarrely for a Congregationalist, had been brought up in Poland by Scots parents and had a deep knowledge of German thought. It was a 'tragic irony of history' that the two countries with the greatest natural affinity should be in conflict. Feelings of this nature made churchmen (at least of the older generation) ambivalent about making public statements. They were reluctant to see the Church Struggle used as the starting point for a general and anti-German crusade. Hitlerism could not be identified with the real spirit of Germany. Other press opinions called for a 'suspension

51. Archbishop of York to Lord Robert Cecil, 5 January 1932: Cecil of Chelwood Papers, BL, Add. MS 51154.

52. *The Times*, 24 May 1935.

53. Bishop of Chichester to *The Times*, 3 June 1935.

54. Bishop of Durham to *The Times*, 4 June 1935; Archbishop of York to *The Times*, 4 June 1935.

55. The distinguished Swedish theologian, Anders Nygren, wrote in one of the first English accounts of the Church Struggle, 'The carbuncle of Versailles was never lanced; instead internal poisoning ensued'. Despair and an inferiority complex had given rise to a noisy demand for *Ehre und Gleichberechtigung*: A. Nygren, *The Church Controversy in Germany* (London, 1934), pp. 5–6.

56. A.E. Garvie, *Memories and Meanings of my Life* (London, 1938), p. 217.

of judgment' on other grounds. While deploring Nazi policy towards Jews and Protestants, Sir John Marriott believed that the censoriousness of foreigners was apt only to exasperate.[57] G.M. Young felt that certain German utterances about Aryans, Nords, Odin and Youth were a way of putting things 'natural to a people whose educated class has not, like ours, been bred and immersed in real affairs'. These sentiments did not import a concerted attack on Christianity.[58] Finally, running through much comment was a comparison with the Soviet Union. The situation in Germany was bad, but was it not worse in the Soviet Union?[59] If some episcopal voices had made as much comment about Russia as they had about Germany, it was implied that their criticisms would have sounded more impressive.

The refusal of the German government to give freedom to the churches was the main burden of resolutions and correspondence. It, therefore, came as a baffling and bewildering surprise to some to learn that some Confessional circles did not see this as the issue. How was one to cope with the sparkling, spikey brilliance of Karl Barth and theological existence today? The anxious questions in the press — Was the intervention of the Government 'legal'? Had a proper majority been obtained? Was it not shocking that *bishops* should have been subjected to indignity? — were these not the convenient questions of a lifeless church-politics? That train of thought, Barth barked, was all wrong. 'The liberty of preaching and of theology, which is now to be guarded, cannot consist primarily in making safe against the external, machine-like oppression by the "German Christians"', he wrote in 1933. The liberty which concerned him was the sovereignty of the Word of God in preaching and theology. In other words, the concern for freedom manifested abroad was potentially a dangerous irrelevance. Pressure-group tactics, church-political struggling might succeed in persuading the German Government to give 'freedom' to the churches. It was not merely a case of freedom for the German Christians. The freedom of which Barth spoke had, in his opinion, 'been *for a long while* and quite *generally* threatened'. Might not God have become tired of 'Churchianity' in Germany? Might there not be a very different battle from the one that was ostensibly joined — 'a conflict having nothing to do with pollings and placards and protests with mobilisations and "fronts": a battle not *about* but *within* the Church?'[60]

How was one to deal with these questions? If the profusion of pungent paradoxes was properly grasped, the whole basis of the relationship between England and the German struggle was perhaps undermined. Was it, after all, the case that English Christians had the freedom that mattered although they were not being persecuted? The interest of agnostics and Christian Scientists in the persecution of the church in Germany was estimable from

57. Letter to *The Times*, 10 June 1935.
58. Letter to *The Times*, 7 June 1935.
59. S.M. Dawkins to *The Times*, 7 June 1935.
60. K. Barth, *Theological Existence To-day* (London, 1933), pp. 72–74.

a humanitarian standpoint; but did this interest really advance the Gospel?[61]
Barthian conceptual categories were, indeed, alien to the prevailing Anglican
theological climate, whether Modernist, Low Church Evangelical or Anglo-
Catholic. As Clement Webb commented in 1923, 'from all . . . extravagances,
which tend to cut the Christian religion adrift both from natural religion and
from the historical process in which the Law was ordained to lead the Jew
and Philosophy the Greek to the school of Christ, Anglican theology has
been preserved by its Platonism'.[62] Barth and Anglican Platonism were not
very congenial bedfellows. An Anglican, Sir Edwyn Hoskyns, had translated
the *Römerbrief* and it was through this work that Barth's name was chiefly
known. But, although Hoskyns talked of the 'strange language' of the Bible
and the 'breaking-in of divine righteousness in a particular history in such a wise
that moral idealism was itself under judgment', he was not strictly a Barthian.[63]
The elaborate arguments about the relation of the Barmen Declaration to the
Reformation Confessions passed Anglicans by. It was only in November 1939
that William Temple could write that the Christian's task was not to explain
the world but to convert it. The shattering impact of the Son of God would
meet its needs, not the discovery of its own immanent principle manifested
through Jesus Christ. The movement of the Holy Spirit in England might
'produce sharper divisions as well as deeper unity'.[64]

Sharper divisions rather than deeper unity seemed to be the pattern in
Germany. By 1937, the cleavage in the Evangelical ranks was complete. The
boldness of the Barmen Declaration could not be sustained and the ecclesiastical
principles of the Dahlem Synod could not be upheld. At Oeynhausen, in
February 1936, the rift had appeared. The leaders of the 'intact' Lutheran
Landeskirchen withdrew from the provisional church government of the
Confessing Church and established their own Lutheran Council. They distrusted the vehemence and 'irresponsibility' of the leading Confessionals. They
disliked the levity with which the 'radicals' appeared to treat the traditional
theological issues which separated Lutherans from Reformed churchmen.
They disapproved of the influence of Barth who was both Reformed and
a Swiss. Bishop Marahrens of Hanover, and others, had not given up hope
of effecting a settlement. In the eyes of Niemöller and his circle, a settlement
was tantamount to a compromise and a compromise meant death for the
church. A new provisional church government was elected, dominated by

61. M. Gilbert, *Plough My Own Furrow* (London, 1965), pp. 365–66, for the views of
Lord Allen of Hurtwood and Lord Lothian.

62. C.C.J. Webb, *A Century of Anglican Theology* (Oxford, 1923), p. 10.

63. A.M. Ramsey, *From Gore to Temple* (London, 1960), p. 132.

64. Ramsey, *From Gore to Temple*, quoted at pp. 160–61. For a somewhat inadequate
assessment of Barth's impact on the English theological and ecclesiastical scene see A. Keller,
Karl Barth and Christian Unity (London, 1933), pp. 144–71. Very broadly, as far as the Free
Churches were concerned, it tended to be the case that the younger generation of theologians
were receptive, though not uncritical, whereas the older generation tended to see Barthianism
as 'reactionary'.

Berlin pastors. Three groups could now be broadly discerned. The German Christians (including some who were 'better' and some who were 'worse'), the Lutheran 'neutrals', and the Confessing radicals. In Niemöller's view, the Confessing Church was the only 'true church'. Bonhoeffer expounded *extra ecclesiam nulla salus* to mean 'whoever knowingly cuts himself off from the Confessing Church in Germany cuts himself off from salvation'. Moreover, the Confessing Church was not sectarian — it had not been 'founded' at Barmen. It was not in revolt against the Established Church for it was the Established Church. Church collections and church taxes should properly go to the Council of the Brethren. In a period of turmoil, only the Confessing Church was being normal. It appealed to Hitler to discourage the various forms of paganism which were appearing in Germany, and protested against encroachments on Christian education.[65]

For their part, the 'neutrals' continued to co-operate with the Reich Church Committee under Dr Zoellner, on which German Christians were also represented. Kerrl, the Reich Minister for Church Affairs, made provocative remarks about the divinity of Christ, although he generally tried to present the churches in a positive light. In this situation, Zoellner's hopes of agreement with the state were, to say the least, optimistic. In February 1937 Zoellner was prevented by the Gestapo from visiting Lübeck to see nine Confessing pastors who had been dismissed by the local German Christian bishop. The Committee resigned, disillusioned and dismayed. Then Hitler himself proposed church elections, although, in the event, these were never held. The Zoellner affair, coupled with the threat of elections, did, however, serve to induce the Lutherans and Confessionals to greater cooperation once more. The pressure on the Confessing Church tightened. In June 1937 all church finances throughout the Reich were placed under Kerrl and it became criminal to contribute to any church body not approved by him. Financial weapons could now be used to induce hesitating pastors to be less obstinate. In addition, there was constant surveillance of the Confessing leaders, continual harrassment of the Confessional theological institutions and sporadic arrests. Morale was sinking. Niemöller's arrest on 1 July together with that of many other Confessional pastors could only add to the despondency. His nominal offence was that he had read from the pulpit the names of those who had left the church.[66]

It is certainly true that Niemöller's arrest caused a tremendous stir, both inside and outside Germany. But this should not be taken to mean that the reaction was completely sympathetic. Developments in Germany in the first six months of 1937 had continued to cause some controversy in England. The Bishop of Gloucester reproached the leaders of the Confessional Church for, in his view, failing to give adequate support to Zoellner and the Church

65. D. Bonhoeffer, *No Rusty Swords*, pp. 282–84.
66. Conway, *Nazi Persecution*, pp. 204–9.

Committees.[67] Bell and the Rev. Dr A.J. Macdonald both visited Berlin early in the year and came back to present the Archbishop of Canterbury with very different impressions.[68] Headlam and Macdonald both vigorously disputed that the Confessing Church had a monopoly of true religion. The great majority of German pastors were living peacefully in their own parishes and were doing very good work. The attacks on traditional dogmatic Christianity were not peculiar to Germany. The reformulation of the Faith was bound to be difficult and there was undoubtedly crude thinking in Germany. But Headlam asked, 'Do most of us really think that an exaggerated emphasis on the Confessions of the Reformation is the best way of meeting the demands of the twentieth century?' He also believed that one should be careful about the political aspect of the Church Struggle. He had no doubt that when members of the Nazi Party were themselves judges of what constituted 'political action' they were not always sympathetic. But, if there were political parsons who mixed up their religion and politics 'in an indescribable confusion', prosecution could only indirectly be called religious persecution. Englishmen did not like National Socialism any more than they liked Communism, but there was wide evidence that the regime in Germany had accomplished for the country what the liberal regime failed to do. 'We have no justification for imposing the political and social ideals of this country on the rest of the world.' Bell and Duncan-Jones vigorously contested this view. Wherever churchmen were restricted in any way in their freedom to preach the Gospel then persecution existed. Headlam seemed to ignore the increasing number of arrests and restrictions.[69] The Bishop of Gloucester was unmoved. There was no demand of conscience that the pastors should disobey the Government edict forbidding them to read out from the pulpit the names of those who had left the church. The pastors, he wrote a few days before Niemöller's arrest, 'are deliberately irritating the Government, and they cannot complain if as a result of that they are arrested; and it seems to me very foolish on our part to encourage them in these pin pricks. They are exactly what a good Christian clergyman ought not to indulge in.'[70]

After the arrest of Niemöller, Bell wrote to *The Times*. The announcement of his arrest suggested that he was an agitator against the state. 'The truth is

67. Letter to *The Times*, 24 February 1937.

68. R.C.D. Jasper, *George Bell, Bishop of Chichester* (London, 1967), pp. 219–20; Church of England Council on Foreign Relations, *Fourth Survey on the Affairs of the Continental Churches (German Evangelical Church), April 1936 to April 1937*, preface by the Bishop of Gloucester. Bishop Heckel, Head of the Evangelical Church's Foreign Relations Department, was 'particularly grateful for the preface . . . as an attempt to depart from an originally one-sided view': Heckel to the General Secretary of the Council, 2 July 1937 (seen by courtesy of the late Mrs Caroline Duncan-Jones).

69. *Proceedings of the Church Assembly*, xviii, pp. 274–89. Duncan-Jones had shifted from his earlier standpoint.

70. A.C. Headlam to Mrs D.F. Buxton, 29 June 1937: Buxton Papers, Lambeth Palace Library, London. For fuller details of Mrs Buxton's prominent role in giving publicity to events in Germany see below, pp. 183–94.

that he is a preacher of the gospel of God, and that he preaches the Gospel without flinching . . .' The question was not merely the fate of one man, but of the whole attitude of the Germans to Christianity and Christian ethics.[71] Macdonald also wrote to the same newspaper. He had the very greatest respect for Niemöller as a Christian minister and spiritual teacher. But he became 'fanatical' on the question of church and state. 'If he had contravened the regulation of the German "Home Office" we can only expect that he will be dealt with as other such offenders . . . We in this country have also to obey police instructions of this kind.'[72] Other letters mainly took the view that Niemöller was not fighting the state; he was merely defending the rights of the church 'against unwarranted and unjustified interference by the State'. In this exchange of views, both Bell and his opponents skirted the issue. Perhaps deliberately, no serious attempt was made to define a 'political act'. Bell attempted to deny that Niemöller might be described as an agitator against the state by saying that the truth was that he was an unflinching preacher of the Gospel. But it is, of course, both logically and empirically possible to be both a preacher and an agitator against the state. Bell's critics were right to observe that refusal to obey an edict of the state was in fact a political act. But whether it was a desirable, justifiable or, indeed, feeble act of defiance was not discussed. Bell had to rest content with an assurance from Hess that, like any other citizen, Niemöller would have to be subject to the law.[73]

There were also reservations among some leaders of the English Free Churches about the stance of Niemöller and the Confessing Church, notwithstanding their admiration for his personal courage. In view of their own traditions, Free Church leaders were less worried about the fact that Niemöller had been arrested on what could be deemed a quasi-political charge. They were still extremely sensitive about any semblance of state interference in their own affairs. Their difficulty with Niemöller and his followers was rather that they seemed to want the best of both worlds. Speaking at a National Free Church Assembly in April 1935, Dr J.H. Rushbrooke, the Baptist leader most in touch with events in Germany, had lamented Germany's lack of a historic dissent, but he rejoiced that the Confessing Church now seemed to be filling that role.[74] But if it was filling that role, it was doing so in a somewhat selective way. This view was cogently expressed in a letter by the Moderator of the Free Church Federal Council. The protests of the Evangelical and Confessing Churches had a grave element of weakness. 'They never even suggest renouncing their position as a Church given a special status by the State or having taxes collected by the State on its behalf. The idea that they should accept a position of dependence upon

71. Letter to *The Times*, 3 July 1937.
72. Letter to *The Times*, 7 July 1937.
73. Jasper, *Bell*, p. 223.
74. Reported in *Manchester Guardian Weekly*, 12 April 1935. See also E.A. Payne, *James Henry Rushbrooke* (London, 1954), p. 60. There is disappointingly little information in this short biography on Rushbrooke's many connexions with Germany.

the State and at the same time demand to be wholly free from State control is one that is completely foreign to our Free Church way of thinking. If the State is asked to maintain a Church in a position of special privilege, it obviously has the right to say what sort of Church it will maintain.' The Moderator emphasized that when Christianity itself was being fundamentally attacked by the Nazis the question was 'relatively unimportant'.[75] Nevertheless, at certain points, the matter could not be ignored. For example, when the salaries of Confessional pastors were withdrawn, Free Churchmen symphasized with the plight of the pastors and their families; nevertheless, they could not refrain from observing that, as a matter of principle, English Free Church congregations held themselves responsible for the support of their ministers.

The problem for the Confessing Church, as a German exile explained to Micklem, was whether to seek a *Volkskirche* or a *Freiwilligkeitskirche*. The average Confessional leader maintained that some 60 per cent of the German population was Protestant and that Germany was, thus, a Protestant country. He did not conceive the Protestant section of the population as a small minority (some 3 per cent of the entire German population) gathered around the centres of church resistance to National Socialist ideology. In educational matters, for instance, the Confessional Church still purported to act on behalf of two-thirds of the population, yet it protested vehemently when Hitler led the 95 per cent German Protestants of the periphery into voting at church elections, thereby exercizing rights given them by the church constitutions. 'The church opposition claims the advantages of both *Volkskirche* and free church and it denies the responsibilities and burdens attached to the *Volkskirche*.'[76] It was, of course, true that some Germans made precisely the same kind of point about the Church of England: Was it not basically a *Volkskirche*? English bishops made loud complaints about state interference in the affairs of German Evangelical Churches, but, in a curious way, they seemed to be able to maintain their offices in a church whose revised Prayer Book had been rejected by the state. Certainly, no one could deny that there was a very deep division in the Church of England between those who saw it primarily as a part of the Church Catholic independent of the state and those who believed it to be primarily a national institution more or less under the control of the state.[77] These problems were

75. Rev. M.E. Aubrey, C.H. (General Secretary of the Baptist Union) to Mrs D.F. Buxton, 13 October 1937: Buxton Papers in the possession of the author. See his views in the *Report of the Archbishops' Commission on the Relations between Church and State, 1935* (London, 1935), pp. 244–48.

76. H.W. Liepmann to N. Micklem, 24 September 1937: Buxton Papers, Lambeth. Micklem, Principal of Mansfield College, Oxford, and the author of *National Socialism and the Roman Catholic Church*, played a leading part on the Free Church side in maintaining contacts with the Confessing Church. See his *The Box and the Puppets* (London, 1957), pp. 104–13. Micklem's ecclesiastical and theological sympathies, however, somewhat estranged him from other leading figures in the Congregational Union.

77. The Archbishop of York expressed himself in these terms to Lord Robert Cecil, 21 July 1932: BL, Add. MS 51154.

the staple of the Oxford Conference on Church, Community and State held in July 1937.[78]

Niemöller had originally intended to be present at this conference, but then came his arrest. Indeed, after prolonged negotiation, no delegation from the Evangelical Church arrived, but two German Free Church delegates came, Otto Melle, Bishop of the German Methodist Episcopal Church, and Paul Schmidt of the Federation of German Baptists. Their presence at the conference caused difficulties when it was proposed to send a message of sympathy with the Evangelical Church and the Roman Catholic Church in their struggles, without directly criticizing the German Government. Although they had previously given their agreement, on further consideration they declared that they were unable to approve the message. Both men explained that they had full liberty to preach the Gospel and implied that the Evangelical and Roman Catholic Churches had only themselves to blame. Melle later spoke of German gratitude to God for sending to Germany a leader who had banished Bolshevism and given new purpose to the nation.[79] In an interview in the *Methodist Recorder*, Bishop Melle declared his belief that the German army was simply intended for defence.[80] These statements led to considerable unpleasantness at the conference, but the message was sent to Germany notwithstanding. Dr Aubrey, as Secretary of the Baptist Union, noted that Baptists in Germany had a tradition of piety and that they felt justified in keeping quiet as long as they were not hindered. But he was rather shocked that some were now actually coming out in praise of Hitler. They would have to understand that Baptists in Britain and the United States could not stand by them in these statements, 'for we have our tradition of protest against every form of tyranny'.[81] Yet this was not the only reaction. Amidst the welter of criticism, a writer recalled that the German Baptist movement was little more than a century old and had been persecuted by both the Evangelical Church and by the state in Germany until the 1870s. It was only recently that the ecclesiastical authorities had ceased to ostracize Baptists. The Nazi regime in Germany had given Baptists in Germany greater freedom of the kind they valued than ever before. The dispute within the Evangelical Church did not directly concern them — no British Baptist in the late eighteenth century would have rushed to help the Church of England in a quarrel between it and the state. Of course, the situation in Germany had other aspects, but other branches

---

78. See the volumes on *Church, Community and State* (London, 1938). W.M. Horton, *Contemporary Continental Theology* (London, 1938), elaborates on the theological gulf apparent at the ecumenical conferences of this year between the Continent and England/America.

79. Jasper, *Bell*, pp. 226–29. Conway *Nazi Persecution*, p. 200, is somewhat misleading in supposing that the disunity among the sects was demonstrated by allowing Melle to go to Oxford and counter the efforts being made on behalf of the Confessing Church. This does not follow at all. Of course, the German Free Churches were so small that Hitler could leave them in relative tranquillity.

80. *Methodist Recorder*, 5 August 1937.

81. *Baptist Times*, 29 July 1937.

of the Christian Church should not be too quick to rush to judgement.[82] Naturally, for their part, the German Evangelical leaders conveyed to Bell their dismay at the 'utter failure of the Free Churches at this possibly decisive juncture of German Church history . . .'[83]

Meanwhile, Niemöller was still in custody. Rumours of his impending trial circulated late in 1937, but it was still delayed. When Lord Halifax, a high Anglican, was having exploratory talks in Germany in November, he emphasized what a bad impression Nazi policy towards the churches was making.[84] A letter to *The Times* at the end of December, signed by a handful of bishops, drew attention to the plight of Christians in Germany. There were many pastors in prison, 'including Dr Niemöller, whose most pure and therefore also intrepid piety is known to the world. They have sacrificed themselves not only to the cause of religious freedom, but the cause of Christianity itself.'[85] But, having failed in its prosecution of Dibelius, the German Government was anxious to bring a convincing case against Niemöller, and to prevent a long trial in which world public opinion would be focused on Nazi dealings with the churches. The Propaganda Ministry accused Niemöller, amongst other things, of being a traitor to his country. It pointed to the volume of press protest abroad as evidence that Niemöller was looked upon as a leading opponent of the regime. When news came through that the trial was to take place in early February, Bell believed that 'we should be very slow to make an agitation now about the fact of a trial'. No statements should be made which might suggest 'that the Courts would be influenced either by British or Nazi political pressure'.[86]

The trial was announced for 7 February 1938 and the Dean of Chichester travelled to Berlin with Dr W.G. Moore, a Congregational layman, in the hope of witnessing the trial.[87] They were, in fact, refused admission to the court. Niemöller's defence emphasized that he was *ein Vaterlandstreuer Mann*, having served as a U-boat commander and in the *Freikorps*, having voted National Socialist since 1924, and having also supported the revolution of 1933. But, although Niemöller admitted to finding Jews unsympathetic and strange, God, nevertheless, was not to be conceived in an Aryan image. He had revealed himself in the Jew, Jesus Christ, though some might find this difficult to accept. After some wrangling, on 2 March the Court pronounced him guilty

82. Rev. E.A. Payne (later to be General Secretary of the Baptist Union and a leading figure in the World Council of Churches) to the *Baptist Times*, 29 July 1937.

83. Jasper, *Bell*, p. 233. Not, of course, that Confessing Church leaders refrained from expressing gratitude for Hitler's success in banishing Bolshevism and giving new purpose to the nation: see F. Baumgartel, *Wider die Kirchenkampflegenden* (Neuendettelsau, 1959).

84. *DGFP*, ser. D., i, p. 56.

85. *The Times*, 20 December 1937. The letter was in fact organized by Mrs D.F. Buxton.

86. Bishop of Chichester to Mrs D.F. Buxton, 24 January 1938: letter in the possession of Miss Eglantyne Buxton.

87. A.S. Duncan-Jones, *The Struggle for Religious Freedom in Germany* (London, 1938), pp. 149–54. I am indebted to Dr W.G. Moore, Fellow of St John's College, Oxford, for discussing his experience with me.

of violating the pulpit-clause and sentenced him to prison for seven months with additional fines. As he had already been in prison for longer than this period, the verdict was tantamount to an acquittal. Charges of offences against state and party were dismissed. Both within and outside Germany the verdict was interpreted as an affront by the court to the state. Rejoicing, however, was premature. On Hitler's orders, Niemöller was rearrested and sent to the concentration camp at Sachsenhausen, then to Dachau, where his conditions of restriction were much more severe than they had been previously. Some members of the Nazi hierarchy were uneasy about this flagrant act, and there were protests from both naval and army officers, as well as church circles, but all to no avail. Niemöller's active role in the German Church Struggle was now over. He never left prison until the end of the Second World War.[88]

The detention of Niemöller after his trial was a significant step both in the evolution of Nazi Germany and in the interpretation of the regime by foreign observers. Rosenberg, Bormann, Hess and Hitler himself now saw little future in attempts by Kerrl to mobilize the Evangelical Church behind the Nazi Party. It was not the business of the Party to determine which elements of the doctrinally divided churches would be useful. It should press ahead with the dissemination of Nazi philosophy and so create a Germany free from any kind of Christianity. In January 1939 Bormann privately declared that a great portion of the clergy of both churches were 'in concealed or open opposition to National Socialism and the State led by it'. In time of crisis, the churches would pass from concealed to open opposition and leave the state to its fate.[89] Of course, it took time for these plans to mature, but the detention of Niemöller, with its open contempt for legal processes, was an important turning point.

In England, the effect of Niemöller's detention was considerable. There had been very wide press coverage of the trial and, in view of the subsequent developments, the *Manchester Guardian* commented that Hitler's Germany could not hope to command the full respect and sympathy of the world so long as the persecution of the churches continued.[90] Letters of protest appeared in *The Times*, accompanied by a declaration by world church leaders. The Archbishop of Canterbury had been uncertain whether or not to sign, for, as he told Lord Robert Cecil, 'foreign countries have a way of regarding the Archbishop of Canterbury as in some way associated with the Government of the country', and he did not wish to embarrass the Foreign Secretary in his conversations with Ribbentrop.[91] Cecil hoped that supposed *raisons d'état* would not deter him — these were objectionable enough when they distorted the morals of statesmen and had to be even more carefully watched

88. W. Niemöller, *Macht geht vor Recht: der Prozess Martin Niemöllers* (Munich, 1953); Zipfel, *Kirchenkampf*, pp. 99–103.
89. Conway, *Nazi Persecution*, pp. 214–17.
90. *The Manchester Guardian*, 3 March 1938.
91. Archbishop of Canterbury to Lord Robert Cecil, 7 March 1938: BL, Add. MS 51154.

in the case of churchmen.[92] The Archbishop agreed. His primary motive in hesitating had been fear that such protests stiffened the obstinacy of the German Government, but, that fear notwithstanding, he now felt that he ought to sign in the name of the 'universal Christian conscience'.[93]

The Foreign Secretary raised this fear with the British ambassador in Berlin. Sir Nevile Henderson replied claiming that 'if we had not made such an outcry in England about Niemöller, he might never have been sent to a concentration camp at all'. Sad though it was to have to admit it, any attempt 'to express in public one's own feelings or to mobilize public opinion in England or in Germany against persecutions here of religion or of individuals merely recoils against the very causes which we are seeking to defend'.[94] Lord Robert Cecil replied that he felt that letters to *The Times* did little harm or good, but they did serve to keep the extent of Nazi tyranny before the public.[95] Lord Allen of Hurtwood recognized the dilemma, but felt that, in this instance, the Archbishop of Canterbury had been right. The ambassador seemed to have overlooked the fact that the 'outcry' was after and not before Niemöller had been sent to a concentration camp.[96] But he felt that an act of appeasement towards Germany was an essential accompanying gesture. In these circumstances, controversy about Niemöller continued. The Bishop of Gloucester stood by his view that nothing would be gained by hectoring Germany from the outside; an attitude of friendship might achieve more.[97] The Bishop of Durham argued that the cause of friendship between England and Germany was best served by demonstrating their agreement in the fundamentals of civilization, but 'the treatment of Pastor Niemöller involves precisely that rejection of the fundamentals . . .'[98] A group of English admirals deplored the continued detention of their fellow naval officer.[99] Articles appeared in various journals giving the latest available facts about Niemöller's condition.[100] From time to time, suggestions appeared in the press that Hitler would respond with sincere good-will if Niemöller would agree to avoid using his pulpit for political purposes.[101] Bell and others kept up contact with Frau Niemöller. On the anniversaries of Niemöller's arrest and detention, services of intercession were held on his behalf.

Throughout the war, therefore, a considerable number of Englishmen

---

92. Lord Robert Cecil to Archbishop of Canterbury, 8 March 1938: BL, Add. MS 51154.

93. Archbishop of Canterbury to Lord Robert Cecil, 9 March 1938: BL, Add. MS 51154.

94. A copy of the letter is in some Buxton papers in my possession. It was obviously widely circulated to those known to have an interest in German affairs.

95. Lord Robert Cecil to Lord Halifax, 12 March 1938: BL, Add. MS 51084.

96. Gilbert, *Plough My Own Furrow*, pp. 394–95.

97. Letter to *The Times*, 14 July 1938. For an explanation of Headlam's attitude see Jasper, *Headlam*, pp. 300–1.

98. Letter to *The Times*, 16 July 1938.

99. *The Times*, 28 July 1938. The letter was again organized by Mrs D.F. Buxton.

100. See articles by Mrs D.F. Buxton under pseudonyms in the *Spectator*, 1 July 1938, and *Time and Tide*, 5 March 1938.

101. Letter from Sir James Marchant, *The Times*, 22 July 1938.

continued to pay Niemöller the homage of their admiration; he was a symbol of the real Germany's plight. But the symbol was clearer than the reality to which it pointed. What precisely Niemöller was suffering for was, one suspects, left deliberately vague. Paradoxically, those who had most doubts about Niemöller's allegedly 'political' stance could hardly have believed him, if they had known more, to be a fundamental opponent of the Nazi state. His restatement of his strong Nazi sympathies at his trial in 1938 was, quite possibly, simply tactical. But, when war broke out in September 1939, he appealed to be allowed to serve in the German navy 'in any capacity', and this cannot be interpreted merely as a device to secure release. Equally strangely, those who defended Niemöller from the charge of political meddling were those whose own political sympathies would have inclined them in the direction of outright political opposition. Indeed, in private, they were somewhat puzzled by Niemöller's stance and were careful to keep public discussion off such matters. Fundamentally, neither Niemöller's supporters nor his opponents were able to make him match their own English standards either of political behaviour or of Christian conduct.[102]

102. The author wishes to thank the Rev. Professor W.O. Chadwick, D.D., F.B.A., for his comments on an earlier version of this article, although he is alone responsible for its final form.

13

Church and Politics: Dorothy Buxton and the German Church Struggle

The German church struggle in the 1930s inevitably involved Christians in Germany in a reconsideration of their attitudes towards politics, but its significance was not confined to Germany. The fate of Martin Niemöller, in particular, was a matter of lively concern in Britain.[1] Conway contends that 'the English-speaking public was all the more disposed to give every credit to the "Bekennende Kirche" because all the books published in English before the war were wholeheartedly on their side'. English-speaking authors, he adds, unanimously, if one-sidedly, saw the struggle as one of church versus state, good versus evil, and Confessing Church versus Nazi storm-troopers. A brief study of the activities of one of the writers mentioned by Conway, Mrs Dorothy Buxton, reveals that the 'English-speaking public' was not quite as unanimous in its interpretation of church and politics in Germany as the contemporary literary works might suggest.[2]

Mrs Buxton was no stranger to the techniques of political campaigning. Her husband, Charles Roden Buxton, was an active Liberal and then Labour politician all his life, though only for short periods was he a Member of Parliament. During the First World War he had been associated with the Union of Democratic Control and had campaigned for peace by negotiation. He believed that the Treaty of Versailles was a disgrace which would have evil consequences. His wife, a niece of Sir Richard Jebb, the Cambridge classical scholar, largely shared his views on these matters. During the war, she had compiled for the *Cambridge Magazine* items from the foreign press and was able to demonstrate to her own satisfaction that not all Germans shared a desire for extravagant war-aims. After the war, they both continued to maintain their interest in international affairs. Buxton was active as chairman of the Labour Party Advisory Committee on Foreign Affairs. Mrs Buxton gained a considerable knowledge of social conditions in Europe — her sister pioneered the Save the Children Fund.[3]

The rise of the Nazis in Germany worried the Buxtons, though it did not greatly surprise them. They did not sympathize with the methods and ideals of

1. See above, pp. 161–82.
2. J.S. Conway, *The Nazi Persecution of the Churches, 1933–45* (London, 1968), pp. xvii–iii.
3. F. Wilson, *Rebel Daughter of a Country House* (London, 1967).

the Nazis, but for years they had argued that the Allied treatment of Germany would lead to such a reaction. After 1933, therefore, they were torn in different directions believing that British guilt required some expiation but also realising that the Nazis might well destroy those liberal Christian values to which they were committed. As the years passed, their reactions differed: Charles, with his eyes on the disaster of another war, grew more and more determined to fight a lonely struggle to avoid it, at almost any cost;[4] Dorothy, as she learnt more of the Nazi treatment of Christians in Germany, felt that if war did come British intervention could be justified.

Dorothy Buxton's knowledge of Germany was not superficial, nor was her interest merely passing. She devoted a great deal of time and money to gaining information from Germany and drawing the attention of British people to the situation. There were, however, considerable problems because some of the information was confidential and might cause harm to people in Germany if it were made generally available. There was also the constant danger that protests from Britain would make it easy for the Nazis to brand Christians in Germany as traitors. Initially, she was herself prepared to admit that, however disturbing, events in Germany admitted of more than one explanation. It might be reasonable to wait and see. It was possible that extravagant things were being said and done in the first flush of the revolution and they would later be regretted and abandoned. In 1935, she determined to go to Germany herself and investigate the position of the churches. Dr Bell, Bishop of Chichester, whom she consulted, warned her that people would be unwilling to give information — 'the externals and the internals are so often different, and people are very, very reserved.'[5] She also wanted to find out about concentration camps. J.H. Oldham, whom she asked, shared her anxiety on this score but doubted whether the problems of the Confessing Church 'should be complicated by the introduction of the other question, in spite of the fact that it is one in regard to which the Christian Church ought in normal times to take vigorous action'.[6] Not for the last time, Oldham's reservation raised the problem of 'politics'. In the event, Dorothy did go to Germany, reporting on her return that everyone she had talked to 'seemed oppressed and bound with the apparent necessity of extreme caution'.[7]

By 1936, the following year, however, she did not believe that judgement could any longer be suspended. From this point on, she tried in a variety of ways to make the English Christian public aware of what was happening in Germany. She was not a theologian and made no attempt to write a theological

---

4. V. de Bunsen, *Charles Roden Buxton* (London, 1948).

5. R.C.D. Jasper, *George Bell, Bishop of Chichester* (London, 1967). G. Bell to D. Buxton, 4 February 1935. A letter in the possession of Miss Eglantyne Buxton. Any letters in her possession are hereafter referred to as Buxton Papers (A).

6. J.H. Oldham to D. Buxton, 1 February 1935, Buxton Papers (A). Oldham was a leading figure in the developing ecumenical movement. See his *Church, Community and State* (London, 1935).

7. Jasper, *Bell*, p. 205.

guide to the complexities of the conflict. Nevertheless, although like her husband she had joined the Society of Friends, she was in general sympathy with the Confessing standpoint. Inevitably, therefore, she came into conflict with the Bishop of Gloucester. Arthur Headlam was the leading English exponent of the view that Christianity in Germany could not be identified simply with the Confessing Church. He urged sympathy and understanding rather than condemnation, though he was himself critical of certain aspects of the new Germany.[8] In February 1935, for example, he wrote to Rosenberg that he was much disturbed by accounts of the existence of concentration camps and of restrictions on pastors. The secular power was interfering in matters which were strictly religious.

The anti-semitism of Streicher and his paper was deplorable and only alienated British public opinion.[9] In October 1935, he was hopeful that the German government would make a new start and allow the German church to work out its own salvation.[10] Throughout 1936, while deploring particular episodes, he remained optimistic. Mrs Buxton, however, by the end of the year, became more dispirited. Dr Micklem, Principal of Mansfield College, Oxford, who was also deeply interested in the German question, agreed that from a worldly point of view, the prospects of the Confessing Church were gloomy, but he doubted whether the church in Germany had been as alive and as Christian as it now was at any time since the Reformation. It was a difficult task to keep public opinion informed of German developments, but he hoped that she would continue her 'quite invaluable work'.[11]

The Bishop of Chichester visited Germany from 28 January to 1 February 1937 and had a long round of talks with various church leaders, including Lilje, Niemöller and Dibelius. Bell learnt of the increasing tension between Zoellner and Kerrl, and the German conviction that 'the future of the Evangelical Church must depend on public opinion in England'. Public opinion in England, however, did not speak with one voice. Just before Bell's visit, the Rev. Dr A.J. Macdonald, at the Bishop of Gloucester's request, also met church leaders and produced a different interpretation of the situation. In acknowledging Bell's report and covering letter, the Archbishop of Canterbury related that Macdonald was critical of 'the more decisive attitudes of people like Niemöller' and was even prepared to recognize some merit in many 'German Christians'. Macdonald thought that the attitude of some of the leaders of the Confessing Church towards the 'Church Committees' had hindered a

8. R.C.D. Jasper, *A.C. Headlam: Life and Letters of a Bishop* (London, 1960), pp. 292–93.

9. Headlam to Rosenberg, 25 February 1935 quoted in Jasper, *Headlam*, p. 295. See also *Das politische Tagebuch Alfred Rosenbergs, 1934/35 und 1939/40*, ed. H.-G. Seraphim (Munich, 1964), p. 65.

10. Headlam to Miss P.L. Wingfield, 28 October 1935, Jasper, *Headlam*, p. 296.

11. N. Micklem to D. Buxton, 3 January 1937. A letter in the possession of the author. Letters in his possession are hereafter referred to as Buxton Papers (B). N. Micklem, *The Box and the Puppets* (London, 1957).

reasonable reconciliation between church and state.[12] The disagreement was acute because at this juncture Zoellner resigned. In a letter to *The Times* on 24 February 1937, Headlam also lamented what he regarded as the failure of the Confessing Church leaders to give Zoellner adequate support. Hitler had offered new church elections and he believed it was unwise to assume that this was only a clever device to injure the church further. 'We have no reason', he concluded, 'for thinking that the Chancellor's action is not a wise and honest attempt at a settlement.'[13] Mrs Buxton refused to accept this interpretation. She wrote to Headlam that she did not believe his claim that police interference had diminished after Zoellner's appointment. Indeed, his resignation had been basically because he had been refused permission to go to Lübeck where some Confessing pastors had been dismissed by a local German Christian bishop.[14] In other words, no great opportunity had been lost.

Mrs Buxton's scepticism about the regime's intentions was increased in these months because she was horrified by the fate of Dr Weissler, former head of the secretariat of the Confessing Church. After the 1936 Olympic Games were safely over, he was arrested, presumably for his part in drawing up a protest memorandum submitted to Hitler by the Confessing Church in May 1936.[15] A few months after his arrest it was announced that he had committed suicide. Mrs Buxton tried to obtain signatures for a letter to *The Times* implying scepticism about the suicide and deploring the fact that he should have been imprisoned simply because he had allegedly given a copy of the memorandum to the foreign press. She told those she approached that she had come to the conclusion that letters of this kind were an important means of expressing solidarity with the Confessing Church. The replies she received reveal that not all her correspondents were so certain.

The Moderator of the Free Church Federal Council, the reverend M.E. Aubrey, a Baptist, replied that Dr Hans Bohm of Berlin had urged that the British Free Churches refrain from any public action unless they received some indication from Berlin. Aubrey feared that signing the letter 'might simply be an irritant to the persecuting party in Germany'.[16] Hensley Henson, bishop of Durham, shared the consternation of 'all who care for the future of religion in Germany and the possibility of any honest & lasting co-operation with her'. Yet he feared that any comment he made would be discounted 'as coming from a known opponent of the Hitler regime'.[17] The Bishop of Croydon agreed to sign the

---

12. Jasper, *Bell*, pp. 217–20. See also the article by Macdonald in *The Nineteenth Century*, March 1937.

13. *The Times*, 24 February 1937.

14. D. Buxton to A.C. Headlam, 17 June 1937. In an unsorted collection of Buxton Papers in Lambeth Palace Library, London, hereafter referred to as Buxton Papers (C), 5a.

15. Conway, *Nazi Persecution of the Churches*, p. 164.

16. M.E. Aubrey to D.F. Buxton, 2 March 1937, Buxton Papers (B). Aubrey was general secretary of the Baptist Union.

17. H.H. Henson to D.F. Buxton, 2 March 1937, Buxton Papers (B). For Henson see H.H. Henson, *Retrospect of an Unimportant Life*, ii (London, 1943) and E. F. Braley, *Letters of Herbert Hensley Henson* (London, 1950).

proposed letter, though he feared that it might do more harm than good.[18] Lord Hugh Cecil declined, believing that an imputation of murder needed more than suspicion to justify it. Furthermore, he believed that there was always a danger that tyrants would finish off those captives whose sufferings excited foreign sympathy. In his view, there were signs that Hitler did not possess that absolute control exercized by Mussolini and, quite possibly, 'was told nothing about the crimes'. Except for callous indifference, therefore, he had no responsibility.[19] The Bishop of Fulham (the Anglican bishop for north and central Europe) also declined, explaining that if he took a public stand he would probably be refused entry into Germany. He had seen Niemöller and all the leaders of the different sides in December and feared that a letter would not bring peace, but more persecution.[20] In reply, Mrs Buxton acknowledged Fulham's misgivings, but argued that 'on the whole it must surely be harmful that the authorities in Germany should be able to count on the ignornace of the British public. If they feel they are being watched, and that some of the terrible happenings are realised over here, it must surely exercise some restraining influence.'[21] The Bishop of Gloucester replied that he would write to Bishop Heckel in Berlin, telling him what a very bad impression these 'strange events' created in England. He added his thanks for some translations of German neo-paganistic literature Mrs Buxton had enclosed, but felt that she exaggerated 'the extent to which the Germans are prepared to listen to Rosenberg, and so on'.[22] The Bishop of Birmingham, Dr Barnes, added another twist in his reply. He wished to go on record as an admirer of the 'Christianity and heroism' of the Confessional leaders rather than of their theology. The murder of Weissler was a grave scandal. It was almost incredible that 'the Nazi tyranny in Germany should be a development of the twentieth century'.[23]

When the letter did appear in *The Times* on 11 March 1937, Aubrey wrote approving of it. He also sought some political advice. Should he go over to Germany in his capacity as Moderator? Would not those who were unfriendly towards the Confessional Church consider such a step foreign interference in the concerns of the German people? He felt that it was 'rather difficult to persuade Germans that as individuals we cherish friendly sentiments towards their nation while at the same time we are critical of the actions of rulers for whom they have a regard that is almost akin to adoration'.[24] Mrs Buxton advised him to go. She believed that there were many among the persecuted Christians of Germany who longed for any sign of sympathy

18. Bishop of Croydon to D.F. Buxton, 3 March 1937, Buxton Papers (B).
19. Lord Hugh Cecil to D.F. Buxton, 10 March 1937, ibid.
20. Bishop of Fulham to D.F. Buxton, 2 March 1937, ibid.
21. D.F. Buxton to Bishop of Fulham, 9 March 1937, ibid
22. A.C. Headlam to D. Buxton, 4 March 1937 and 10 March 1937, ibid.
23. Bishop of Birmingham to D.F. Buxton, 8 March 1937, ibid.
24. *The Times*, 11 March 1937; M.E. Aubrey to D.F. Buxton, 24 March 1937, Buxton Papers (B).

from English Christians.[25] In the event, the Moderator decided not to go but to seek an interview with the German ambassador in order to express his disquiet. Karl Barth, however, questioned the value of demands in the liberal tradition for 'freedom of expression' for the Confessing Church. Aubrey, who described himself as 'by no means a Barthian' felt there was some value in the reminder that real freedom would be gained by men who wished to 'declare the Gospel rather than by those who simply want freedom'.[26] Mrs Buxton was not sure that Barth was right. If he was, why had Confessional Church leaders recently pressed for a visit to Germany? Was he right to be so certain that representations to Germany never had any effect, particularly since the German government was apparently anxious to be on good terms with Britain? Finally, she wondered whether Barth represented the views of the Confessional Church as a whole.[27]

In this month, April 1937, Micklem was in Germany, first in the Rhineland and then in Berlin. One of the problems discussed was the question of German participation in the Oxford conference on church, community and state, scheduled for later in the year. Mrs Buxton was most anxious for a fully representative delegation from Germany to appear so that full publicity could be given to the German situation. On his return, Micklem reported to Mrs Buxton that the Confessing Church delegation would be prevented from attending.[28] He agreed that the whole situation was extremely confusing. What was really needed was an 'oecumenical bureau of information'.[29] British efforts to help in Germany were hindered by 'lamentable disorganization'. Of course, disorganization was not the only problem, for there was continuing disagreement about the 'facts'. At the spring meeting of the Church of England Council on Foreign Relations, for example, Bell and the Dean of Chichester, Duncan-Jones, had successfully opposed the incorporation of MacDonald's report into the council's official survey. Nevertheless, Headlam insisted on a preface emphasizing the difficulties of forming a judgement on the realities of the situation. Much of the difficulty, he held, sprang from the inability of the German mind to compromise. Tension was increased because each group held to its opinion without any willingness to see the other point of view. In the second place, he distrusted the tendency of English opinion to become 'furiously partisan' about events in foreign countries when it could not possibly comprehend the full context. The Confessing Church did not have the monopoly of true religion. Citing figures, he held that by the end of 1936 'the great majority of the German pastors were living peacefully in their own parishes and were doing very good work'. He criticised anti-semitic propaganda and crude neo-paganism, but thought it wrong to judge National

25. D.F. Buxton to M.E. Aubrey, 29 March 1937, ibid.
26. M.E. Aubrey to D.F. Buxton, 23 April 1937, ibid.
27. D.F. Buxton to M.E. Aubrey, 27 April 1937, ibid.
28. N. Micklem to D.F. Buxton, 7 May 1937, ibid.
29. N. Micklem to D.F. Buxton, 13 May 1937, ibid.

Socialism by the foolish utterances of the more extreme members of the party. It was better to ascribe to Hitler good intentions rather than treat him as if he were a criminal. Finally, he urged all Christians in Germany to recognize the need for unity to help the nation in a crisis of its history. It was wiser for the Confessional churchmen to join with all the other 'Orthodox Lutherans' rather than to stand in isolation.[30]

When the *Survey* was presented to the Church Assembly on 22 June 1937, Bell vigorously contested these views and the Archbishop of Canterbury insisted that they were in no way official but simply Headlam's own. Mrs Buxton also challenged Headlam.[31] The bishop replied that persecution was too emotive a term to describe the situation in Germany, 'though there may be very stupid interference'. A recent set of arrests, he contended, arose because certain German pastors deliberately banded themselves together to disobey an edict of the government which forbade the reading out during a service of the names of those who had left the church.

If the Government feel it wise to forbid it,' he wrote, 'I do not think we can complain very much, but, at any rate, there can be no demand of conscience that the Pastors should disobey it. They are deliberately irritating the Government, and they cannot complain if as a result of that they are arrested; and it seems to me very foolish on our part to encourage them in these principles. They are exactly what a good Christian clergyman ought not to indulge in.[32]

Mrs Buxton was not convinced, agreeing with Aubrey that it was an 'appalling utterance'.[33]

At this time, the summer of 1937, she was deeply immersed in the final stages of her pamphlet, *The Church Struggle in Germany* which was published early in July by the *Kulturkampf* association.[34] This association is somewhat shrouded in mystery. A report on church matters in the Third Reich, *Kulturkampf*, had appeared in French and German from 1936, and then in English from early in 1937. It had a circulation of some 2,500 copies and Mrs Buxton ardently sent it to editors of various journals in the hope that information it contained would appear in their own columns.[35] In her own pamphlet, Mrs Buxton gave a brief survey of the outstanding events in the church struggle from March 1933. She accepted that the full story might

---

30. *Fourth Survey on the Affairs of the Continental Churches (German Evangelical Church), April 1936 to April 1937* (London, June 1937). Preface by the Bishop of Gloucester.

31. D.F. Buxton to A.C. Headlam, 17 June 1937, Buxton Papers (C), 5a.

32. A.C. Headlam to D. Buxton, 29 June 1937, ibid.

33. M.E. Aubrey to D.F. Buxton, 2 July 1937, ibid.

34. In order to protect her informants she simply described herself as 'An English Protestant'. *The Church Struggle in Germany: A Survey of Four Years, March 1933–July 1937* (London, 1937).

35. See A. Wiener's article 'Untersuchungen zum Widerhall des deutschen Kirchenkampfes in England, 1933–38', *On the Track of Tyranny; Essays Presented by the Wiener Library to Leonard G. Montefiore*, ed. M. Beloff (London, 1961).

seem incredible to some readers, but believed her facts were correct. She had no doubt, however, that 'Hitler and his regime are the supreme creation of the Treaty of Versailles'. The peace treaty, 'a terrific denial of Christianity', prepared the way for the religion of race. Hitler wanted to see a fusion of politics and religion, but his religion was one of hate, not love. Therefore, Christians in England, who shared responsibility for his rise to power, could not turn a deaf ear to cries from Germany. 'If many Germans to-day deny Christ', she concluded, 'and His supreme law of universal love, let us not forget that we of the Allies denied Him first'.[36]

The booklet was well-received. Hensley Henson felt that it was a powerful statement and the facts it contained should not be swept away by the 'intense desire to get into friendly relations with Hitlerite Germany'. We are confronted, he added, 'by a frantic nation, obsessed by a false idea'. He thought the condemnation of Versailles was somewhat severe, wondering what would have happened if the boot had been on the other foot.[37] William Temple, however, found her conclusion most impressive, and Bell found nothing to take exception to in her judgement.[38] Other reviewers tended to ignore the section on Versailles, though the editor of the Anglican paper, the *Guardian* agreed that the church struggle and the consequences of the treaty could not be separated.[39] The booklet quickly went into a second edition, but Mrs Buxton was rather at a loss to know what to do next. With the arrest of Niemöller the situation seemed to be deteriorating in Germany. As Micklem had forecast, there were endless difficulties concerning the German delegation to the Oxford conference. The Bishop of Chichester was also depressed at this time, worried by what he believed to be the decreasing attention given to the German church struggle in Britain.[40] The Anglo-German political situation was very delicate. Lord Halifax was about to visit Germany and prominent people approached by Bell were unwilling to write letters to *The Times* about the German church lest they be accused, one way or the other, of trying to influence the politicians.

To counteract this apparent malaise, Mrs Buxton drafted another letter which she hoped to see published with an impressive list of signatories. The letter mentioned that it was difficult to see how a Christian church in Germany could survive as an outward organization. It outlined recent speeches by Herr Kerrl and concluded that the culminating blows could be expected shortly. Niemöller and his fellow-pastors in prison had sacrificed themselves, not only to the cause of religious freedom, but also to the cause of Christianity. However, it did indeed prove difficult to obtain signatures. A number of bishops, understandably, were unwilling to commit their names to collective

36. *Church Struggle*, pp. 23–4.
37. H.H. Henson to D.F. Buxton, 14 July 1937.
38. W. Temple to D.F. Buxton, 14 July 1937; G. Bell to D.F. Buxton, 13 August 1937, Buxton Papers (B).
39. G. Mayfield to D.F. Buxton, 20 August 1937, ibid.
40. Jasper, *Bell*, p. 235.

letters when they could not check some of the statements that were made. Many others felt that a letter would not do any good, and might even lead to harm. Hensley Henson was prepared to write simply on his own behalf. It was paradoxical to him that at the very juncture that serious politicians were casting about for some reconciliation with Germany, Germany was embarking on an anti-Christian policy which made it difficult to regard any approaches to her 'without something like moral repugnance'.[41] The Bishop of London, on the other hand, although sympathetic, felt that he was working to the same end by personal influence through the ambassador. 'My policy', he wrote, 'is to make friends with Germany, and thus acquire an influence over her, which we have not got at present'.[42] The Bishop of Ripon agreed with the proposed letter, but wrote that he had decided not to put his name in print 'with regard to affairs which are outside my proper diocesan job . . .'[43] The dean of St Paul's confessed that he was simply perplexed about the situation. He had been in Hesse during the summer and 'at the time I could find no evidence of religious persecution, and nobody complained to me about it'.[44]

Another large group of episcopal correspondents indicated that they would do whatever the Bishop of Chichester recommended. Bell was not in fact very enthusiastic about Mrs Buxton's idea. People would rightly comment that all the bishops who might sign did not really know the facts of the situation. He did not want to sign himself because of several impending meetings, but suggested that Mrs Buxton might send the letter under her own name. 'Why should not', he added, 'a Church survive as an outward organisation even if it is persecuted to the very depths?'[45] When the letter finally appeared in *The Times* on 20 December 1937, with a small number of episcopal signatures, Bell felt even more strongly that it was a wrong move. The notion of 'culminating blows' in the destruction of the church would be regarded by some of the most stalwart members of the German evangelical church 'as almost surrender'.[46] Micklem, on the other hand, felt that it was a 'most admirable' letter. He thought 'you are much more likely to be accurate on some of these points than is the Bishop'.[47]

Meanwhile, Mrs Buxton kept a vigilant eye on the press. Whenever correspondents to any newspaper wrote arguing that the Third Reich had taken a strictly impartial stand on religious questions in return for ecclesiastical abstention from politics, she sent a letter denying the claim. In an article in the *Spectator* in February 1938, she traced the evolution of the new concepts of

---

41. H. Henson to D.F. Buxton, 7 December 1937, Buxton Papers (C).

42. Bishop of London to D.F. Buxton, 14 December 1937, ibid.

43. Bishop of Ripon to D.F. Buxton, 28 December 1937, ibid.

44. W.R. Matthews to D.F. Buxton, 8 December 1937, ibid.

45. G. Bell to D.F. Buxton, 7 December 1937, 13 December 1937, 16 December 1937, Buxton Papers (B). See also Jasper, *Bell*, p. 235.

46. G. Bell to D.F. Buxton, 20 December 1937, Buxton Papers (B).

47. N. Micklem to D.F. Buxton, 21 December 1937, 13 January 1938, 21 January 1938, ibid.

justice in Germany, concluding that in essence 'all crimes are reduced to an act of treason against the National Socialist State'.[48] She conceded that there were some 'undisturbed areas' in the German church, but this was 'in so far as the officials of the Church are willing to accept the persecution of Jews and refrain from befriending victims of the Secret Police, or fellow-Christians with some degree of Jewish blood'. Niemöller was being detained, despite being found not guilty on all points of substance, because he was 'incapable of juggling, either with his conscience or with his mind'.[49] Impressed by Karl Barth's lecture, 'Trouble and Promise in the Struggle of the Church in Germany', delivered in Oxford on 4 March 1938, she at once took steps to see whether it could be printed in a cheap edition for wide circulation.[50] She acted as hostess for Barth so that he could meet a group of some thirty leading church people. All the while, she continued her regular work of circulating translations of statements by Nazi leaders and details concerning the plight of individual pastors. On receiving one such collection of testimonies by imprisoned pastors, Aubrey wrote that it was quite clear that a rebirth of Christian faith and life was taking place in Germany. Prayer apart, however, what could be done to help? The international situation was perplexing, he wrote in May 1938, and concluded, 'If only our country could get on better terms with Germany diplomatically ... we should be able to bring real pressure to bear'.[51] Mrs Buxton had become more sceptical.

On the anniversary of Niemöller's arrest, she described his dilemma in an anonymous article in the *Spectator*. She dismissed the contention that Hitler was not deeply implicated in the church struggle. It would be an insult to his intelligence to suppose that the campaign had escaped his attention or did not represent his own wishes.[52] Besides this article, she gathered together a group of admirals to write to *The Times* about the former German naval officer. They recorded their respect for a former valiant foe now suffering for no less a cause than that of common Christian faith.[53]

Mrs Buxton next found herself in a fresh public controversy with the Bishop of Gloucester. Headlam had paid a further visit to Germany, but did not change his views as a result. He admitted that a section, but only a section, of those in authority in Germany was antagonistic to Christianity but still believed that the best way of meeting this antagonism was that adopted by 'five-sixths' of German pastors rather than that advocated by the Confessional Church. The paramount need was for a united church, but the Confessing leaders prevented this and in doing so irritated the authorities against the church.[54]

48. A special correspondent, 'Justice in Germany', *Spectator*, 18 February 1938.
49. Q.R.S. (D.F. Buxton), 'Dr Niemoller and the Confessional Church', *Time and Tide*, 5 March 1938.
50. K. Barth to D.F. Buxton, 28 May 1938, Buxton Papers (B).
51. M.E. Aubrey to D.F. Buxton, 13 May 1938, ibid.
52. A special correspondent, 'Dr Niemöller's ordeal', *Spectator*, 1 July 1938.
53. *The Times*, 28 July 1938.
54. Ibid., 20 July 1938

Mrs Buxton felt that the bishop had been misled by 'official' Germany. There was another Germany where to speak the truth might land the speaker in a concentration camp.[55] Headlam reiterated that all sections of the German church were anxious to be friendly with the Church of England and resented the way in which British interest was lavished on the Confessing Church. 'The theology of the German Christians', he wrote, 'is much more in accordance with our ideas than those of the Confessional Church.' The Confessing Church was largely under reformed influence and the theology of Karl Barth, and there was a considerable opposition to episcopacy.[56] Mrs Buxton, however, had now completed arrangements for the publication of Barth's Oxford lecture and now asked the Swiss theologian for an introduction, telling him that the majority of her fellow-countrymen were in 'deplorable ignorance' on the subject.[57] Barth obliged with a fierce introduction declaring that British Christians would be forced to see in the cause of the Confessional Church their own cause as well.'[58]

Besides the Barth lecture, Mrs Buxton was also responsible for the English edition of letters from imprisoned German pastors.[59] It was well received and sold well. Nevertheless, in the late summer of 1938 events, both ecclesiastically and politically, seemed to be moving to a crisis. The Munich crisis produced strains on all sides. Charles Roden Buxton and his brother Lord Noel-Buxton were both keen advocates of appeasement but Dorothy was acutely conscious of the consequences for Christians of an international settlement which avoided war but perpetuated Nazi rule.[60] In Germany, a service of intercession drawn up by a small group of Confessing leaders at the height of the Sudeten crisis was denounced by the Nazi hierarchy as high treason and the Lutheran provincial bishops dissociated themselves from it.[61] To complicate matters further, Barth wrote to the Czech theologian Hromadka declaring that every Czech soldier who fought Nazism did so in the cause of Christ. In the end, Mrs Buxton was reasonably satisfied with the settlement, yet did not have much confidence that it would be permanent.

In any case, it did not result in any improvement in the situation of the Confessing Church. She therefore continued her watch on the press.[62] Early in February 1939, for example, the *Church of England Newspaper* published an article from an Englishwoman who had long been resident in Germany. She claimed that if one defined Christianity as the acceptance of the spiritual

55. Ibid., 10 August 1938.

56. Bishop of Gloucester, 'The German Church', *Guardian*, 2 September 1938.

57. D.F. Buxton to K. Barth, 20 September 1938, Buxton Papers (B).

58. K. Barth, *The German Church Struggle; Tribulation and Promise* (London, 1938), Foreword.

59. *I Was In Prison*, ed.D.F. Buxton (London, 1938).

60. K.G. Robbins, *Munich 1938* (London 1968). D.C. Watt, 'Christian Essay in Appeasement: Lord Lothian and his Quaker Friends', *Wiener Library Bulletin*, 14, 2 (London 1960).

61. Mrs Buxton was responsible for the fact that the service was reproduced in *British Weekly*, 1 December 1938.

62. See, for example, an exchange of letters in the *Scotsman*, 6–26 January 1939.

meaning of Christ's teaching, with a sincere effort to apply it to everyday life, 'one may discern Christianity as the "Leitmotiv" of the National Socialist philosophy in Germany'.[63] In a long letter to the editor Mrs Buxton pointed to Nazi racial theory and treatment of Jews, but he declined to publish it arguing that it would only inflame passions still further at a time when so many were trying to get a better understanding and closer co-operation with Germany. He added that he had heard that after Hitler came to power some of the church began to act politically.[64] Naturally, if the church was paid by the state a dictator would say that it ought not to carry on propaganda against the state. In a further letter, Mrs Buxton expressed surprise and shock, stating that she had tried in vain to get information from the Bishop of Gloucester and others about the precise 'political propaganda' in which the Confessing Church had indulged.[65] In the end, after a further contribution from the Bishop of Gloucester, the editor finally allowed Mrs Buxton space to express her own views.[66]

While challenging the editor about the 'political' Confessing Church, Mrs Buxton added that, personally, she would not mind if such information was discovered, being convinced that 'until Christians do "interfere" more in politics our world will go from bad to worse'. She never claimed that her own role was a major one. She never possessed political power nor aspired directly to possess it. Her work was rather in the field of propaganda and personal relations, creating a network of contacts and information. Her own position, however, revealed how double-edged was her injunction to Christians to 'interfere' more in politics. It is at least arguable that the two causes most dear to the heart of the Buxtons, international appeasement of Germany and support for the oppressed Christians of Germany, were incompatible. In the end, in 1939, a choice had to be made between the horrors of war and the horrors of Nazism. Dorothy tended to go one way and Charles the other. Interference in politics was, after all, a choice of evils.

63. *The Church of England Newspaper*, 10 February 1939.

64. D.F. Buxton to the editor, *Church of England Newspaper*, 13 February 1939; editor, *Church of England Newspaper*, 21 February 1939, Buxton Papers (B).

65. D.F. Buxton to the editor, *Church of England Newspaper*, 23 February 1939, ibid.

66. Articles in the *Church of England Newspaper*, 17 March 1939 and 31 March 1939; editor, *Church of England Newspaper* to D.F. Buxton, 3 April 1939; D.F. Buxton in the *Church of England Newspaper*, 6 April 1939.

14

Britain, 1940 and 'Christian Civilization'

Spring in Cambridge in May 1940 was poignantly beautiful. It was noted that the rich promise of the blossom contrasted strikingly with the destructive activities of men.[1] Some dons sought relief from exposed East Anglia in the land of Lyonesse and asked themselves whether they should send their children to Canada.[2] All over the country, indeed, questions of life and death became urgent. Harold Nicolson advised his wife to flee to the security of his brother's Dartmoor farm. He sent his own will westwards as a precaution. It was indeed late, 'late in the afternoon of the city', but if invasion and conquest should come, was it the end of 'Christian Civilization' or was such a concept merely a lingering piece of exhausted rhetoric? This essay explores meanings and mentalities in various segments of English society at a time when national survival seemed at least in jeopardy. Kenneth Clark, future guide to *Civilisation* who was, at his end, to receive the sacraments of the Roman Catholic Church, directed the pictures from the National Gallery into a vast and disused slate cavern near Blaenau Ffestiniog in North Wales. It was known locally as 'the Cathedral'. It might be an unanticipated symbol.[3]

There was no especially Christian aura to be associated with Churchill's incoming government. However, the Prime Minister found it appropriate, on occasion, to use language which had religious connotations. There were references, allusive to be sure, to the defence of home and altar. 'The Battle of Britain', he declared in June 1940, 'is about to begin. Upon this battle depends the survival of Christian civilization.'[4] Such dogmatic language, however, came from an undogmatic mind. It was no part of his purpose to define the term at such a juncture or to express a personal conviction. He stood in relation to the Church of England as a flying buttress — supporting, but external. Archbishop Lang was not for him the epitome of Christian civilization and these public sentiments did not presage an intimacy with the episcopate. It was Destiny that he was content to walk with. Some of his closest associates

---

1. A.S.F. Gow, *Letters from Cambridge, 1939–1944* (London, 1945), p. 41.
2. B. Willey, *Cambridge and Other Memoirs* (London, 1968), pp. 100–1.
3. K. Clark, *The Other Half* (London, 1977), pp. 4–5.
4. Robert Rhodes James, ed. *W.S. Churchill: Complete Speeches, 1897–1963* (New York, 1974), p. 6238. It should be noted that the remit of the Religious Division of the Ministry of Information was to impart 'a real conviction of the Christian contribution to our civilization and of the essential anti-Christian character of Nazism'. Cited in I. McLaine, *Ministry of Morale* (London, 1979), p. 151.

were not even sure that all their past lives had been but a preparation for the present. Anthony Eden allowed references to *Pilgrim's Progress* and McNeile Dixon's Gifford Lectures on *The Human Condition* to give an elevated tone to some of his speeches and even referred, in August 1940, to a belief that Britain would achieve the kind of peace she believed in 'by God's help', but he was not explicit about Christian civilization.[5] Although Nelly Cecil was later to describe Attlee as 'the most Christian-living P.M. in our time', he himself had no religious experience and disliked 'mumbo-jumbo'. He did not know whether he was an agnostic.[6] About the ailing Neville Chamberlain there remained only vestigial traces of ancestral Unitarianism. Ernest Bevin could only bring the spiritual dowry of a long-lapsed Baptist. Lord Beaverbrook was at best a devious propagandist, though there was more life in the Presbyterian pedigree of Sir John Anderson. Lurking in the distance was Lloyd George who seems sometimes to have thought that a last stand against the Teutons might be made in *Festung* Gwynedd. Meanwhile, he sought solace in the unlikely combination of William Carey's *Missionary Sermons* and Boccaccio's *Decameron*. He also strengthened the defences of Bron-y-de.[7]

As a body, the Cabinet did not trouble itself with Christian civilization, apart from discussing the propriety of ringing church bells should a victory occur. The diaries of Sir Alexander Cadogan, Permanent Under-Secretary at the Foreign Office, do not disclose any change of atmosphere after the advent, a little later, of William Temple to Canterbury. The Archbishop is recorded as 'bleating' rather than 'talking'. On Easter Saturday 1943 Cadogan conceded that religion no longer played the part in society that it had once had. Moral atrophy, he thought, might be avoided 'by setting ourselves to some form of common endeavour, some kind of sacrifice — our duty to our neighbour, to the State, to the world'.[8] This objective smacked of the burning faith in the high ideals of the British people which Eden sought to kindle, since he apparently believed it was 'not enough merely to preserve Christian civilization, now in such deadly peril . . .' While the Prime Minister's immediate reaction to Temple's death — 'There's a total abstainer died of gout. How right we all are' — cannot be taken as a rounded appreciation, it betrays a determination to keep the church in its place.[9]

There were, however, other currents. The news of the Fall of France reached Lord and Lady Halifax when they were walking in the Yorkshire Wolds near

5. A. Eden *Freedom and Order: Selected Speeches, 1939–1946* (London, 1947), pp. 18, 81.

6. K. Rose, *The Later Cecils* (London, 1975), p. 181. Attlee came from an active Anglican household and had siblings who remained committed Christians. He believed in 'the ethics of Christianity'. K. Harris, *Clement Attlee* (London, 1982), p. 218.

7. C. Cross, ed., *Life with Lloyd George: The Diary of A.J. Sylvester, 1931–1945* (London, 1975), pp. 269, 274.

8. D. Dilks, ed., *The Diaries of Sir Alexander Cadogan* (London, 1971), p. 523.

9. Dilks, *Cadogan Diaries*, p. 675. Although Temple was a supporter of the Labour Party, Churchill told Attlee that he had recommended his appointment to Canterbury because 'he was the only half-a-crown article in a sixpenny bazaar'. Harris, *Attlee*, p. 218. See also M. Cowling, *Religion and Public Doctrine in Modern England* (Cambridge, 1980), pp. 284–312.

their home. Gazing at the Vale of York, they thought it sad to contemplate that the 'Prussian jackboot' might force its way into this true fragment of 'the undying England'. They thought of the villages where, for generations, men and woman had knelt in worship and prayer.[10] From his lofty standpoint, Halifax had made no secret of his Christian belief and had made a number of public statements. Broadcasting on the Christian attitude to war in July 1937 he had spoken of the danger that in every war the original motives became overlaid with others less worthy. It could be the duty of the Christian man 'constantly to be searching the possibilities of concluding a righteous peace'. The true model of international peace ought to be a relationship between nations comparable to that which 'ought to obtain between Christian individuals as members of Christ's body'.[11] In November 1939 he broadcast an address on *The Purpose of the Struggle* — his remarks owed little to Foreign Office advice — arguing that in the war 'as indeed in all life, it is finally the spiritual side that counts'. Physical force could not in itself destroy the evil which was the source of war but if 'we rest inert before action which we hold evil, we are surely surrendering to annihilation the expression of spiritual values which have inspired and guided all human progress'.[12] Speaking as its Chancellor, he told the University of Oxford in February 1940 that the wounds inflicted on 'our' civilization need not be mortal 'but I do think we are fighting for its life'. He was certain that there was 'an active force of evil which, unless we fight it, will rapidly reduce our civilization to a desert of the soul'. It rested with the 'British race', with all its faults, to wage that struggle.[13]

Such sentiments were close to those articulated by Lord Lloyd. He believed that the defence of 'Christian civilization' was an integral aspect of 'the British case'. Pre-war failings of policy had stemmed from a failure to bring before the British people the view that national endeavour should be 'shaped and determined by the requirements of Christian morality' since 'we are still, I believe, a Christian people'. He was distressed by signs of a reluctance 'to go on with the task of building up a Christian civilization in Africa and Asia, in our facile and foolish assumption that any other civilization is likely to be just as good'.[14] After 1939, he had no hesitation in claiming that the European conception of freedom derived directly from Christianity. Greece and Rome were slave civilizations whereas Man redeemed by Christ could never again be enslaved to man. Hitler's actions against Poland were 'not only an outrage against the public law of Europe, but an affront to every Christian conscience'. These were not merely the passing thoughts of an ex-Governor of Bombay. Lloyd played a vital role in the 'projection of Britain'. His own *The British*

10. Lord Birkenhead, *The Life of Lord Halifax* (London, 1965), pp. 457–58.
11. H.H.E. Craster, ed., *Viscount Halifax: Speeches on Foreign Policy* (London, 1940), pp. 102–3
12. Ibid., p. 334.
13. Ibid., pp. 362 and 368
14. Lord Lloyd, *Leadership in Democracy* (Oxford, 1939), pp. 16–17.

Case contained an introduction by Halifax himself.[15] He was nearer the centre of power, however, than old Lord Salisbury who could only take comfort in January 1940 from an Oxford Group conference in Bournemouth where it was revealed that, in Papua, Christian tribesmen covered their eyes with their hands as battle approached, whereupon their war-painted neighbours faded away.[16] Even so, Churchill took no risks with the Christian peers and knights. Sir Samuel Hoare, another prominent High Churchman, was banished to that recently reclaimed fortress of Christendom, Madrid. Lloyd died and Halifax went to Washington. In the United States, the new British Ambassador would be further away from Lord Baldwin and his visions. It was to Halifax that the former Prime Minister had communicated his experience of July 1940 when he had heard a voice speaking (and felt himself to see with extraordinary and vivid clarity). The purport of the message was, 'You have now one upon whom to lean and I have chosen you as my instrument to work with my will.' It was to be hoped that this could be interpreted to mean that England would survive.[17]

The defence of Christian civilization had been undertaken in the Washington Embassy even before Halifax's arrival. His predecessor, Philip Kerr, Marquis of Lothian, a Christian Scientist of Roman Catholic extraction, had stated, before sailing for the United States on the eve of the war, that the Christian tradition of praying for governments was more useful than criticizing them. He added that the only way that the reign of international morality might be secured was by 'Federal Union'. His capacity to pick up the latest contemporary fad and invest it with an intolerable significance was to be further demonstrated in public speeches during his short but critically important mission. 'At bottom,' he told the American Pilgrims in October 1939, 'we are fighting a defensive struggle. We are trying to prevent the hordes of paganism and barbarism from destroying what is left of civilized Europe.' A Swarthmore audience was told more explicitly in November that the war was becoming 'a struggle between the totalitarian and the democratic and Christian way of life'. The ultimate foundations of 'our civilization, were indisputably true', he claimed, but 'we' were in our present troubles 'because we have allowed religion to fall from its high estate, and allowed politics and economics to take its place'. His purpose, he said, was not to talk about theology, but he did so at some length. He also advocated 'a single constitution' for the world. It was the function of religion to change the hearts of men towards universal brotherhood and thus make possible such a political development. In April 1940, as the picture darkened, he told the St Louis Chamber of Commerce that 'a truce with Nazi Germany now would be the end of most of the civilized values which Christianity and

---

15. Idem., *The British Case* (London, 1939), pp. 14, 48. For Lord Lloyd's connection with the British Council see P.M. Taylor, *The Projection of Britain: British Overseas Publicity and Propaganda, 1919–1939* (Cambridge, 1981), pp. 283–84.

16. Rose, *Later Cecils*, p. 101.

17. K. Middlemas and J. Barnes, *Baldwin* (London, 1969), pp. 1058–59.

Western democracy have laboriously built up in recent centuries'. In what proved to be his last speech, in December 1940, he claimed that Britain was not in the least dismayed by her circumstances. She would win decisively, by 1942, if not before. That confidence had a spiritual basis since the core of Hitlerism was 'moral rottenness' and all history proved wrong the belief that ruthless power led to greatness. 'The Sermon on the Mount is in the long run much stronger than all Hitler's propaganda or Goering's guns and bombs.'[18] Lothian died before he was able to ascertain what might happen in the short run.

Lothian's language betrayed an association with Lionel Curtis. His *Civitas Dei: The Commonwealth of God*, a volume of nearly one thousand pages, had appeared in 1938, sections of it having already been published in 1934 and 1937. Embedded in his survey of man's development was his claim that 'Belief, in the true sense of the word, is not the assertion of knowledge, or dogma, but courage to act on the best hypothesis we are able to conceive. Unbelievers are those too timid or idle to guess at the truth and to act on the guess.' That was a message for 1940. Curtis could not think of a time which appeared 'so fraught with disaster to the human race as a whole as the present'. However, from the Christian story he drew the message that: 'From that moment of utter despair there sprang the movement which has gone some way to create, and in the ages before us will bring to fulfilment, the Kingdom of God upon earth, the Divine Commonwealth . . .' In his view, Our Lord 'was trying to convince the world that men can grow to perfection, but only in so far as they mould their relations one to another on the principle that each man owes an infinite duty to God, and therefore to all his fellows'. He wanted to discover the means of passing from the national to the international state. Here was a role for religion. He felt that once the Protestant churches came to regard the creation of a world commonwealth as an 'all-important' aspect of their work 'an international commonwealth in the English-speaking world would come into being in a few generations'.[19] The outbreak of the war neither served to modify his convictions in these matters nor to discipline his prose. The history of civilization was now seen as a war between freedom and despotism. Amidst no paucity of proposals for reconstructing the world came the cry: 'Who, indeed, would wish to have lived in the days of Agincourt or the Armada, or Trafalgar or Waterloo rather than here in England today with her ruined hearths and her broken shrines?'[20]

Arnold Toynbee noted that a cross dangled from Curtis's watchchain. He had no such emblem himself, but it was almost inevitable that when he came to Oxford in May 1940 to lecture in the Sheldonian it should be on *Christianity*

18. J.R.M. Butler, *Lord Lothian* (London, 1960), p. 256; *The American Speeches of Lord Lothian, July 1939 to December 1940* (London, 1941), pp. 10, 23, 34, 71, 139.

19. L. Curtis, *Civitas Dei. The Commonwealth of God* (London, 1938), pp. 288, 822–24, 953.

20. L. Curtis, *Decision* (London, 1941), pp. 75–76.

and Civilisation. His message was not straightforward. Christianity might be conceived historically as either the destroyer of civilization or the humble servant of civilization. If religion was a chariot, he suggested, 'it looks as if the wheels on which it moves towards Heaven may be the periodic downfalls of civilisations on Earth'. It was obvious that 'we' had been living, for a number of generations, on spiritual capital, clinging to Christian practice without possessing the Christian belief. Practice unsupported by belief was a 'wasting asset', as had been suddenly discovered 'to our dismay, in this generation'. He considered that 'if our secular Western civilisation perishes, Christianity may be expected not only to endure but to grow in wisdom and stature as a result of a fresh experience of secular catastrophe'.[21]

Brisker, less qualified, but doubtless more acceptable thoughts flowed from other pens for less refined audiences. Having once believed in *Peace with Honour*, A.A. Milne was now converted to war to end war. Seeking 'victory by any end and every means, victory regardless of any other consideration whatever', he concluded that: 'In fighting Hitler we are truly fighting the Devil, Anti-Christ, the negation of every spiritual value which separates mankind from the rest of creation.' The British people would have to be ready to suffer and to inflict death 'to bring salvation to the rest of humanity'.[22] This was no mere international conflict. It was a struggle between Good and Evil. Hitler was a crusader against God, 'just that'.[23] Addressing a wider audience than the readers of the *Children's Newspaper*, Arthur Mee shared this vision. He had little doubt that 1940 would be remembered in all history as 'our finest hour'. Disasters, betrayals, risks, burdens, humiliations and grief were all experienced but 'we carried on. Guided by the Hand of God and sustained by our own right arm, we came through the shadows of defeat into the sunlight of a nobler dawn'. It was this conviction that 'If for one day the common people of these islands lost their faith in God the cause of Freedom must perish.' Dunkirk was an indication that 'we are part of some sublime event to which the whole Creation moves'. He concluded that never in the history of civilization was the ordinary life of a man or woman of such solemn account. 'If we are generous, ardent, patient, believing, refusing to despair, confident in right, upholding truth and loving justice more than all, we are fighting for God's kingdom and the island in which He has set us.'[24] It was this spirit which Vincent Massey broadcast back to Canada on Dominion Day, 1 July 1940. The spectacle of Empire troops, together with other soldiers of freedom, French, Polish, Norwegian and Dutch, reminded him inescapably 'of the warfare against the infidel, when Christian men from every part of Europe were gathered together to fight for the deliverance of the Holy Sepulchre'.[25]

---

21. A.J. Toynbee, *Christianity and Civilisation* (London, 1940), pp. 22–27.
22. A.A. Milne, *War Aims Unlimited* (London, 1941), p. 31.
23. Idem., *War with Honour* (London, 1940), pp. 16–17.
24. A. Mee, *Nineteen-Forty: Our Finest Hour* (London, 1941), pp. vi, 27, 60, 118–19.
25. V. Massey, *The Sword of Lionheart* (London, 1943), p. 25.

The Times turned to 'Religion and National Life' in February 1940. Barrington-Ward, its new editor, had recorded in 1934 'a sense of liberation in worshipping Christ without miracles. His message is for us on earth and in our own day, to build or to build towards his earthly commonwealth . . .' Time would expose the emptiness of the Fascist and Nazi 'philosophies'. It was a comment which revealed that he had been reading Curtis's *Civitas Dei*.[26] Ten years later, he remained convinced that a moral purpose had to be rediscovered in the nation: 'To have any true vitality it must be rooted in religion, and our present-day religion lags behind the needs of the age, cluttered up with intellectual difficulties.' The problem was that the 'restatement' which might deal with such difficulties would shatter the churches as organizations.[27] However, in a leader of 17 February 1940, his newspaper was eloquent, declaring that it would be of little use to fight 'as we are fighting today, for the preservation of Christian principles if Christianity itself is to have no future, or at immense cost to safeguard religion against attack from without if we allow it to be starved by neglect from within'. It seemed odd that a country which was 'staking its all in defence of Christian principles' should have a national educational system 'which allows the citizens of the future to have a purely heathen upbringing'.

This comment sparked off a lengthy and vigorous correspondence. Writers concerned themselves with the paradox, not to say hypocrisy, of a situation in which it was claimed 'that we are fighting for a faith to which most of us appear to be completely indifferent'.[28] The Bishop of St Albans was quick to point out that both Stalin and Hitler ensured that "the faith" was properly taught. 'They take no chances; we do. They see to it that every generation as it comes along is taught "the faith" and converted to it (if possible) . . . When shall we learn?'[29] The Bishop of Southwark appealed for better instruction for he agreed that without better teaching of religion there would be 'an increasingly secularist outlook among our people, which will render them less and less capable of standing up to ideologies such as those which are enslaving the people of Russia and Germany'.[30] The Dean of Winchester added his support to the view that Scripture teaching in all schools should be inspected like other subjects. Such a step would show that 'the State was in earnest about the character of our country's civilization in the future'.[31] Writing as President of the Boys' Brigade, Lord Home declared that the European tragedy would not have been in vain 'if we are led as a nation to a new realization of the primary place which should be given to the Christian faith in the education of our young people'. It was vital to ensure that the next generation 'in this Christian country' was helped to grow in favour with God

26. D. McLachlan, *In the Chair: Barrington-Ward of The Times, 1927–1948* (London, 1971), p. 276.
27. Ibid., p. 243.
28. Sir Edward Cadogan in *The Times*, 20 February 1940.
29. The Bishop of St Albans in ibid., 21 February 1940.
30. The Bishop of Southwark in ibid., 23 February 1940.
31. The Dean of Winchester in ibid., 24 February 1940.

and man.[32] The pressure of correspondence was very heavy, drawing in the President of the Mother's Union, the British and Foreign Bible Society and a host of clergymen and laymen.

The Times itself returned to the subject in a leader on 9 March. It noted that its original comments, published in pamphlet form, had excited great interest. Nearly 400,000 copies of the leaflet had been sold in twelve days. It took this concern to be an indication that the question was not merely one for specialists in religious education. The topic was seen 'to affect the whole future of our national life'. In proportion as the spiritual principles at stake in the war were clearly discerned, 'the greater will seem the need not merely of defending but of developing those principles by a national system of education which is definitely Christian'. Recognizing that the role of the home would be central, it concluded: 'Almost the chief gain that will follow the reform of our national system of education will be its development of Christian children who in due course will become Christian parents. By this means the old order will be restored, when the task of the school will be to continue, instead of having to replace or even to combat, the teaching that has been begun in the home.' It would be difficult to envisage a more comprehensive endorsement of Christian civilization.

Confronted by such eminent wisdom from so many quarters, church leaders and committed Christians found themselves in an embarrassing position. The allegedly unreflective and strident patriotism of the churches during the First World War had been frequently criticized in the years that followed, not least, as George Orwell noted, by those who had no respect for the Christian principles which had supposedly been ignored. In part, the enthusiastic espousal of 'pacifism' by influential figures in the major denominations sprang from a determination that church and state should never again be so closely entangled.[33] Yet, by the late 1930s, it became increasingly evident that, if war should come, the issues at stake might entitle the government to wholehearted support. It would be a struggle for 'Christian civilization' in a deeper sense than had been true in 1914. The elderly Hensley Henson, writing in 1940, saw the struggle as '*au fond* a civil war fought out on the fundamental principles on which Christendom, in so far as it is an effective unity at all, must needs stand'. Secular politicians talked about a 'war of ideologies' but he was prepared to call it a Crusade which had to be 'fought out to the bitter

32. The (Thirteenth) Earl of Home in ibid., 28 February 1940.
33. M. Ceadel, *Pacifism in Britain, 1914–1945* (Oxford, 1980). In 1938, for example, Charles Raven argued that: 'The last war produced Communism and the Treaty of Versailles, Fascism and the new Paganism. The next will leave no victors, will inevitable destroy freedom and, as many think, the Church.' *War and the Christian* (London, 1938), p. 158. In 1940 he was still a pacifist and found himself at loggerheads with the B.B.C. on this account. F.W. Dillistone, *Charles Raven: Naturalist, Historian, Theologian* (London, 1975), pp. 343–47. Bishop Barnes of Birmingham found himself unable to support the war. J. Barnes, *Ahead of his Age* (London, 1979), pp. 361–63.

end. There can be no compromise or patched up peace'.[34] Significantly, it was in the Temple Church on 5 May 1940, on the 700th anniversary of its consecration, that he reflected on 'Christendom' and its implications. It was not unreal or extravagant to consider the Christian citizen of Great Britain as wrestling against the spiritual hosts of wickedness in the heavenly places. He believed that 'for us and for our Allies this war is *The Good Fight*'.[35] *May God Defend the Right* was also the plea of Nathaniel Micklem, Principal of Mansfield College, Oxford, though as a committed Liberal he might have chosen his title with more care. 'The reign of Christ in the hearts of men can never be furthered by the sword', he conceded, 'in that sense we hesitate to say we fight for Christ, for He needs none to fight for him with earthly weapons; but we believe ourselves to be fighting not merely for the decencies of international life but for Christian civilization on the Continent of Europe.' There was no peace for the world except in Christendom. By that phrase he did not mean a given state of human society pretending to be the Kingdom of God, nor a political order controlled by ecclesiastics, nor one composed of professing or practising Christians, but rather an order 'in which the living God is publicly acknowledged and his righteousness and justice are accepted as the ultimate ground and sanction of human law'.[36] It was because Europe had to so great an extent repudiated its Christian ancestry that civilization had come to disaster. Echoes of these sentiments could be heard from many contemporary pulpits, but there were other opinions.

'The devilry of Hitlerism', proclaimed A.R. Vidler in his editorial in the October 1939 issue of *Theology*, 'does not automatically transfer us into angels of light or prophets of the Lord.' He thought it right to draw attention to what he considered the shortcomings of French policy in the years after the Peace of Versailles. Such a robust utterance provoked rumblings. Following the events of May 1940, his publishers felt that the time was not ripe for such arguments. The journal might have to close. It was not right to publish material which could be interpreted as 'anti-British' propaganda or as 'tending to weaken the national will for victory . . .' Vidler stood his ground and the controversy died away.[37] It is interesting to note, in passing, that in July 1937 he had been lamenting that talk of war was preventing reflection on 'a menace that is more certain — namely, depopulation'. In a later editorial he stressed the distinction between fighting for Christian civilization or Christendom and fighting for Christianity. To talk of the former implied that, 'Christendom is

---

34. E.F. Braley, *Letters of Herbert Hensley Henson* (London, 1950), p. 123.

35. H. Hensley Henson, *Last Words in Westminster Abbey* (London, 1941), p. 82.

36. N. Micklem, *May God Defend the Right* (London, 1939), pp. 127, 139. In his autobiography, Micklem records a conversation at an Oxford High Table around this date where suicide seemed to those present an urgent problem. N. Micklem, *The Box and the Puppets* (London, 1947), p. 115.

37. A.R. Vidler, *Scenes from a Clerical Life* (London, 1977), pp. 114–15.

still a going concern which has to be defended instead of a kind of social order which has in future to be re-created'.[38]

Here was a note which many thought prophetic. It was scarcely conceivable in radical Christian quarters that the Britain of the summer of 1940 was a Christian civilization which merited conservation. The young Martin Wight, for example, declaring himself to be a conscientious objector, expressed the view that the war was 'the convulsion of a civilization that has forsaken its Christian origins'. It was a divine judgement on that civilization. To take part in the war would not solve the 'fundamental problem of spiritual apostasy'. The task, rather, was 'to prepare the foundations of a new civilization that will be less in conflict with the Kingdom of God'.[39] Others had also expended much energy in exposing its shortcomings and inner corruption. The young Donald Mackinnon pointed an accusing finger at the debilitating role played in this respect by *Songs of Praise*. The hymn book was an indication of spiritual sterility and determination to eliminate the message of redemption from the Christian Gospel. A generation had lent credence to the notion that Christ had come to reveal the perfectibility of man. It had neglected the awful truth that the restoration of the *natural* order demanded of God an intervention that was in every sense supernatural. 'In this present hour of judgement', he concluded, 'God is surely recalling us to a comprehension of the utterness of our dependence upon Him. He is revealing to us the bankruptcy of our achievement apart from the impact of His grace . . .'[40] Another fluent exponent of this perspective was Langmead Casserley, who did not believe that any Christian could desire the perpetuation of the existing industrialized imperialistic order of society. 'The West', though dear because it contained so many relics of the first Christendom, was not the Kingdom upon earth, nor even a very good basis from which to journey to that Kingdom. Between the West and the Kingdom there was no broad highway, only a wilderness upon whose verge men sat waiting for Moses.[41]

There were some who discerned 'Moses' in the conclusions of the Malvern conference on 'The Life of the Church and the Order of Society' held in January 1941. Anglicans, from Dorothy Sayers to T.S. Eliot, had a good deal to say there about civilization. There were pleas to think 'in terms of a wider perspective' and 'to see the divine purpose at work, even in the collapse of a civilization which has brought about its own destruction because it has been founded on the profit-motive and the artificial segregation of the human race into separatist national sovereignties, and privileged and non-privileged classes'. The coming civilization, Kenneth Ingram further indicated, would be based on planned production for communal use. The

---

38. *Theology*, October 1940.

39. Cited by Hedley Bull in his introduction to Martin Wight, *Systems of States* (Leicester, 1977), p. 4

40. D.M. Mackinnon, *God the Living and the True* (London, 1940), pp. 31, 87.

41. J.V. Langmead Casserley, *The Fate of Modern Culture* (London, 1940), and *Providence and History: A Tale of Two Cities* (London, 1940).

task of the church was to provide the nucleus of those who would 'lead the vanguard in the social-political-religious struggle'.[42] Middleton Murry declared that the church failed to provide leadership because it showed 'no sign of having known despair'.[43] Mackinnon's complex address, for whose obscurity he apologized, could not be criticized on such grounds. He stated that as members of the Established Church Anglicans had particularly allowed themselves to be blinded to the true condition of British society. They found it 'hard to admit the fundamental contradiction between the assumptions of our capitalist-industrialist civilization, and those of the faith to which as Christians we are pledged to bear witness'. The burden of his paper he summarized as being that there was a fundamental opposition between the church and the modern nation state. That was 'a fact underlying the whole conflict of our time'.[44] It was an assertion which did not easily marry with Britain as the ark of Christian civilization.

William Temple concluded that the Malvern conference had 'put the Church on the map'. Mervyn Stockwood, who was telling the inhabitants of a Bristol air-raid shelter that the Archbishop was 'running a show to put the world right', was equally pleased. Temple himself was prolific in speech and on paper, expounding the conviction that 'faith and freedom must stand or fall together; for it is only faith in God that can make the world safe for freedom or freedom safe for the world'.[45] He stressed, however, that he did not believe that 'we are fighting for Christianity'. Christianity could only be freely accepted and could not be served by physical force. But, while true of Christianity itself, it did not follow that it was also 'true of a civilization largely influenced by Christianity and threatened by one which has deliberately repudiated the fundamental elements in the Christian conception of life and the way to live'. In short, 'we are fighting to keep open the possibility of a still more truly Christian civilisation in the future'. Christianity would have more to say about the right ordering of life 'than had been heard for some centuries'.[46]

Attempts to give content to a 'still more truly Christian civilization' were not lacking. Sir Richard Acland launched *Our Struggle*. He urged that if all men could not be persuaded, at once, to accept 'our new morality' then 'at least we shall make sure that the destiny of our nation and of mankind is in the hands of those who do accept it'. To love your neighbour as yourself 'must be made an established fact'.[47] Sydney Dark believed that the church was being presented with a great chance, perhaps the last chance, to influence the evolution of society. 'Without the vision that the Christian religion can provide, the people perish, whether they live in a democracy or under a

42. *Malvern 1941: The Life of the Church and the Order of Society* (London, 1941), pp. 176–77.
43. Ibid., p. 197.
44. Ibid., pp. 107, 116.
45. W. Temple, *Thoughts in War-Time* (London, 1940), p. 130.
46. *Towards a Christian Order* (London, 1942), pp. 8–9
47. Sir R. Acland, *Our Struggle* (Australian edition, 1940), pp. 20–21.

Totalitarian tyranny.'[48] However, he wanted to crush capitalism with rather more verve than envisaged at Malvern. In the mind of Sir Stafford Cripps, *Towards a Christian Order* was the same as *Towards Christian Democracy*. He argued that the churches had 'condoned conditions which Christ would have stigmatised as intolerable, partly because they could see no way of improving matters, and partly because they had compromised with society as it existed'. It was the function of the church 'to create those moral standards compelling material changes . . .'[49] Sir Stafford saw his own career in the light of that injunction.

The simplicity of these visions stood in marked contrast to the intricate discussions associated with J.H. Oldham and the 'Moot', that group of intellectuals and professional people which had first met in April 1938. On the outbreak of war, T.S. Eliot (whose lectures on 'The Idea of a Christian Society' had been delivered six months earlier) wrote to Karl Mannheim suggesting that while many of their friends had been expecting war for some time, its arrival confused them. 'We are involved in an enormous catastrophe which includes a war', was how he put it.[50] The *Christian News-Letter* would attempt to bring enlightenment and would 'enter imaginatively into the ordeal through which the nation is passing'.[51] The *News-Letter*, however, was only a means to a 'greater end' — the growth of a body of people dedicated to the task of creating a new order of society. The choice before mankind, it suggested, lay between Communism, Fascism and something more difficult to define but offering 'for most of us' the only satisfactory alternative. The objective was 'a community of free persons united under the rule of law, directing its activities increasingly to Christian ends and leavened by Christian insight, values and standards'.[52] Here were the makings, almost, of a Christian conspiracy. In optimistic moments, it seemed to some members of the Moot that it might be the agency for mobilizing 'the intelligent people of good will in this country' who were invariably thought to be waiting for a lead. In gloomy moments, it was thought that the Moot might serve as a nucleus which might enable a Christian minority to survive the coming tyranny. Vidler, in particular, was impressed by the latter role. He was already sending out a confidential letter to friends and colleagues. In April 1940 there was a gathering of the 'St Deiniol's Koinonia' in Essex.[53] Its members were very conscious that they appeared to be

48. S. Dark, *The Church, Impotent or Triumphant?* (London, 1941), p. 8.
49. S. Cripps, *Towards Christian Democracy* (London, 1945), p. 33.
50. For Eliot's own views see R. Kojecký, *T.S. Eliot's Social Criticism* (London, 1971); A.D. Moody, *Thomas Stearns Eliot: Poet* (Cambridge, 1979) – especially Appendix C; A. Cunningham, 'Continuity and Coherence in Eliot's Religious Thought', in G. Martin, *Eliot in Perspective* (London, 1970); D.L. Edwards contributes a helpful introduction to the 1982 reprint of *The Idea of a Christian Society*.
51. *Christian News-Letter*, 18 October 1939.
52. Ibid., 22 November 1939.
53. Vidler, *Clerical Life*, p. 109. Paul Tillich commented during his European journey in 1936 that 'the idea of the religious order is encountered everywhere'. He added that nobody believed any longer 'that the masses can be directly re-educated. This is a retreat, to be sure. But it also makes it possible for the leading intellectual and religious forces to regroup and gather strength.' P. Tillich, *My Travel Diary: 1936* (London, 1970), p. 85.

witnessing the uprooting of the Christian tradition over large areas of Europe. Alike in the areas occupied by the Russians and the Germans, massacres and removals of population were accompanied by systematic attacks on cultural and religious life. The *Christian News-Letter* had no doubt that what was left of a 'Christian' civilization was now forced to contend against monstrous evils 'all of which, upon close analysis, reveal themselves to be fruits of its own vices, wrong answers to its own unanswered problems and accentuated forms of its own decay'.[54] There was no denying the gravity, complexity and urgency of the task of ensuring Christian survival.

Even so, members of the Moot could not agree on whether analysis or action was the first priority. Noting that Hitler started with six people, Mannheim in April 1940 wanted the Moot to ensure that a 'well-established programme' should be available in three months.[55] Three months, even bearing in mind the circumstances, seemed a decidedly short time to many hard-pressed university professors in which to agree on the nature of the ailments which afflicted civilization and to find a prescription for their remedy. It was already apparent that some deep philosophical chasms between members had to be bridged, not least between Thomas Torrance and H.A. Hodges in the matter of interpreting Dilthey.[56] In general, however, the basis of a Christian civilization was explored with exemplary thoroughness and immodest expertise. Hodges, a Professor of Philosophy, addressed the Malvern conference on what the church should say about the threat of a post-war slump, the revival of the rural community, the recasting of the monetary system and the subordination of mass production to human values. At least he had the good judgement to declare not only that his paper could not be published but that it could not be made suitable for publication.

Roman Catholics stood apart from these learned exchanges on the crisis of the times. In the summer of 1940 a certain delicacy attached to their position. The example of Vichy France was not, perhaps, without attraction in certain Roman Catholic quarters, or at least there were anxieties both within and without the church that this might be so. The *Clergy Review* published in June 1940 an article by Christopher Hollis on 'Catholics and the War'. He had evidently felt a need to convince his co-religionists that 'whatever the pressure against religion may be in England and France, it is as nothing to the pressure against it in Russia and Germany . . .' The article had, in fact, been written in April and Hollis added a note that: 'It was strange that two months ago any Catholic in any country could doubt that the cause of Catholicism required the defeat of Nazi Germany. It is incredible if any

54. *Christian News-Letter*, 14 February 1940.
55. Cited in Kojecký, *Eliot's Social Criticism*, p. 176.
56. Comments by T.F. Torrance on the paper by H.A. Hodges, 'Christian Thinking To-Day', can be found in a set of moot papers in the John Baillie collection, New College, Edinburgh.

who value Catholicism doubt today.'[57] Christopher Dawson, who took over the editorship of the *Dublin Review* in July, declared that: 'The Christian cause at the present time is also the common cause of all who are defending our civilization against the blind assault of mass despotism and the idolatry of power which has resulted in a new paganism that is destructive of all moral and intellectual values.' His own writings, so frequently referred to in contemporary discussion, made it clear that Christianity had long since ceased to dominate society and culture. However, the 'sublimated Christianity' of liberals and humanitarians was not to be despised, at least not in present circumstances. The 'working religion of Western democracy' was significant and could not be regarded with complacency or indifference: 'The cause of God and the cause of man are one.'[58]

John Baillie, the Scottish theologian and member of the Moot, had been in France and witnessed at first hand the collapse of the French army. This experience forced him to ask himself whether the Christian religion held out any hope in the triumph of justice in the present world.[59] Iulia de Beausobre, with the physical resilience which survived a Soviet labour camp and the spiritual patience which proved compatible with marriage to Lewis Namier, brooded on *The Tragedy of France and the Testing of England* in a meditation written in July 1940. 'In a moment of crisis such as this', she wrote, 'the grand abandonment which is the first stop towards transfiguration can only be achieved through a sustained readiness to be an instrument of God, and through a sustained effort in sincerity. We are hard pressed for time . . . And yet it is at once, now, that we must bring about the change in ourselves and in our country.' She claimed that: 'The transfiguration of England through the will of every citizen of the British Empire to make of himself an instrument of God is the crying need of the whole world.'[60] No outsider was more prolific and cogent in his comments on Britain's plight than Reinhold Niebuhr. 'In terms of the enemy which civilization is called upon to oppose', he wrote, 'history has never confronted decent men with a more sharply defined "evil"'. Yet moral and religious scruples should not be abandoned, even in the present crisis. Commenting on 'Europe's catastrophe', he argued that it was not in the providence of God 'that the destruction of civilisations should be complete, before a new civilisation arises . . . We have no right to capitulate to anarchy

57. *Clergy Review*, xviii (June 1940), no. 6. See also Michael J. Walsh, 'Ecumenism in War-Time Britain: The Sword of the Spirit and Religion and Life, 1940–1945', *Heythrop Journal*, xxiii (1982), and G. White, 'The Fall of France', *Studies in Church History*, xx (Oxford, 1983), pp. 431–41.

58. *Dublin Review*, no. 414 (July 1940). Dawson's best-known writings were *Christianity and the New Age* (London, 1931); *Religion and the Modern State* (London, 1935); *Progress and Religion* (London, 1937).

59. J. Baillie, 'Does God Defend the Right?', *Christian News-Letter*, 30 October 1940. Another scholar to wrestle with these issues was Edwyn Bevan, *Christians in a World at War* (London, 1940). Bevan's book was published in May.

60. I. de Beausobre, *The Tragedy of France and the Testing of England* (London, 1940), pp. 27, 31.

in a period of anarchy. It may be in God's providence that the island of sanity and order which we are able to preserve in a disintegrating civilisation shall become the basis of a new world.'[61] Perhaps the 'miracle of Dunkirk' meant that the reference to 'the island of sanity and order' was to be taken literally?

The *Christian News-Letter* noted that many of those who had taken part in the evacuation experienced it 'as a miraculous intervention of Providence'. Unexpected and inexplicable happenings awakened the minds of men to 'a sense of the mystery of existence'. Nevertheless, it cautioned against too naive an interpretation of the connection 'between our prayers and the deliverance granted to us'.[62] There were others who were less restrained in their acknowledgment of the hand of God — an acknowledgment which at least one foreigner in Britain found ludicrous.[63] Perhaps Stanley Baldwin had the right perspective. With many millions, as he supposed, he had prayed hard at the time of Dunkirk 'and never did prayer seem to be more speedily answered to the full', but there had also been prayers for France and the next day she surrendered. It was hard to say, 'Thy will be done'. It was apparent to him that mere 'mites' could never see God's plan, 'a plan on such a scale that it *must* be incomprehensible'.[64] The *Christian News-Letter* reiterated that it did not follow that, because the British Commonwealth seemed to embody a higher conception of life than the tyrannies it was fighting, God would grant victory. The religious mind knew that life did not offer such clear and simple solutions.[65]

The secular mind found much of the foregoing discussion either absurd or distasteful. The *Freethinker* was forthright. It took the gravest exception to any notion that the war was being 'fought for the preservation of Christianity'.[66] Beatrice Webb, who had latterly been expounding the succulent attractions of a new civilization elsewhere, reacted 'philosophically' to the plight of Britain in 1940, taking it as proof that '"Western Civilisation" is going, going, gone.'[67] The Dean of Canterbury was eager to agree. J.B. Priestley was prepared to admit that 'the decay of religious belief' was a hindrance to democracy, but in existing circumstances he had no desire to see packed churches and chapels, prayers at every hour and loud *Te Deums* and *Hallelujahs*. He himself had no wish to be converted and baptised. There was no need for an explicitly Christian basis for society. He much preferred to be a man of good will, 'determined

61. R. Niebuhr, *Europe's Catastrophe and the Christian Faith* (London, 1940), p. 24.
62. *Christian News-Letter*, 19 June 1940.
63. C. Ritchie, *The Siren Years: Undiplomatic Diaries, 1937–1945* (London, 1975), p.61.
64. Middlemas and Barnes, *Baldwin*.
65. *Christian News-Letter*, 3 July 1940.
66. Cited in J. Herrick, *Vision and Realism: A Hundred Years of 'The Freethinker'* (London, 1982), p. 84.
67. N. Mackenzie, ed., *The Letters of Sidney and Beatrice Webb, iii, 1912–1947* (London, 1978), p. 440.

that all that is best in our civilisation must be preserved'. The churches had all proved as faulty as the societies in which they were set. However, he was certain that 'the fundamental values of the new society must be spiritual and therefore religious values' — a claim whose meaning was apparently self-evident.[68] This advice was indeed matched by long-awaited comments from a newly Episcopalian poet in New York. In order to defend civilization, W.H. Auden told Stephen Spender, it was necessary to kill Germans and destroy German property while minimizing the loss of English lives and property. Further, it was necessary to create things from houses to poems that were worth preserving and to educate people to understand what civilization really meant.[69]

Learned men at Oxford and Cambridge who had spent a lifetime explaining what it really meant took fresh stock of their positions. Gilbert Murray, registering alarm at the waxing domestic power of his cook, still had sufficient liberty to make fundamental assertions. He was coming to the conclusion that he and his contemporaries belonged to a 'martyred' generation, but there was 'no warrant for any wholesale condemnation of modern civilization, no warrant for rejecting our own ideals of progress, humanity and justice'. There was no hint, here, of the good pagan's failure, though some fear that, the war apart, the march of progress was being hindered by the popularity of football pools.[70] The President of Corpus, Sir Richard Livingstone, another guardian of civilization, also felt that the legacy of Greece was being threatened by the insidious activities of Mr Moores of Liverpool. He remembered that Lord Bryce had replied to a questioner who had asked what would be the effect of the disappearance of religious education from schools by saying that the impact could not be judged until three generations had passed. Livingstone had no doubt that he was witnessing 'the weakening or dissolution of the traditions and beliefs which for many centuries have ruled Western civilisation and held it together'. Those who rejected Christian beliefs could not be surprised if Christian morals collapsed. Greek thought and Christianity, he supposed, had created 'the soul of Western Civilisation', formed its mind and were the vitamins of its life-blood. It was not too late to suggest that 'everyone' should have an idea of them.[71] Murray was less enthusiastic about the Christian contribution to this synthesis. Somewhat obsessed by his own kitchen arrangements at this time he was already moving to the view that the advent of 'real democracy', coinciding with two world wars, was cooking 'the goose of civilisation'.[72] The *Nordic Twilight* of 1940 worried E.M. Forster in Cambridge. Much as he longed for peace, he could not contemplate life

---

68. J.B. Priestley, *Out of the People* (London, 1941), p. 109.
69. H. Carpenter, *W.H. Auden. A Biography* (London, 1981), p. 309.
70. G. Murray, *A Conversation with Bryce* (Oxford, 1944), p. 30. In 1940, Murray had collected together lectures given over a quarter century on the theme 'Stoic, Christian and Humanist'. While it might be true that what was being endangered in Europe was 'the Christian spirit', it was a spirit as humanized and liberalized in the nineteenth century.
71. R. Livingstone, *Education for a World Adrift* (Cambridge, 1943), p. 96.
72. P. Clarke, *Liberals and Social Democrats* (Cambridge, 1981), pp. 284, 287.

under German domination, for 'if you make power and not understanding your god ... you atrophy the impulse to create. Creation is disinterested. Creation is passionate understanding. Creation lies at the heart of civilization like fire at the heart of the earth.' He took comfort from the knowledge that 'violence has so far never worked. Even when it conquers, it fails in the long run'. He permitted himself to say that this failure 'may be due to the Divine Will', though it might also be ascribed 'to the strange nature of Man, who refuses to live by bread alone, and alone among the animals has attempted to understand his surroundings'.[73] Elsewhere in Cambridge it was comforting to know that civilization was 'always recognisable'. These words were spoken by G.M. Trevelyan to Harold Nicolson as they surveyed Trinity College silver and port. The new Master was struggling to feel at home in the Lodge 'before the bomb comes'.[74]

G.D.H. Cole did not feel so comfortable in the civilization that surrounded him. He hated Nazism so deeply that there was nothing he wanted more than its overthrow. He desired 'our civilisation' to be saved but he did not trust the government (he was writing in November 1939) 'either to make this a war for democracy or to conduct either war or negotiations for peace by democratic methods'. He claimed that Mr Chamberlain was more shocked by Hitler's methods than by his ideas. Christianity was not, for Cole, a matter for serious consideration. Nevertheless, a little transcendental reference slipped into his language when considering Hitler. No doubt he was 'a much greater sinner than any of our statesmen, if you judge him by his deeds. But he has, and they have not, the excuse of being out of his mind. There can be no lasting peace with Hitler, because he thinks he is God, and above all human morality.' A little later, he added 'Hitler menaces us to-day, a demon of our own making, the Frankenstein monster of our own incompetence and folly.'[75] It was a little naughty of Cole to be talking about Gods and demons at all, though he clearly found difficulty in distinguishing between them. Clarification on this score might have come from C.S. Lewis. It was on 15 July 1940 that 'Screwtape' entered his mind.[76] His contribution to the Battle of Britain was to illumine the plausible wiles of the Devil — and the personification of Evil seemed not inappropriate to some disbelievers in the existence of God.

Harold Laski thought that for something like a century and a half it had been the 'central purpose of Western civilisation' to find the secret of combining individual freedom with social order. The Nazi system represented a challenge to that central purpose. He had two explanations for the contemptuous attitude of Nazi party leaders towards Christianity. They disliked 'its insistence of the

73. E.M. Forster, *Nordic Twilight* (London, 1940), pp. 31–2.

74. N. Nicolson, ed., *Harold Nicolson: Diaries and Letters, 1939–1945* (London, 1967), p. 140; M. Moorman, *George Macaulay Trevelyan* (London, 1980), p. 231.

75. G.D.H. Cole, *War Aims* (London, 1939), pp. 28–29 and 58.

76. Roger Lancelyn Green and Walter Hooper, *C.S. Lewis, a Biography* (London, 1974), p. 191.

universality of the rights of man' but, no doubt, they also coveted 'the immense property of the Churches as a fund through which to cope with their financial difficulties'. He suggested that 'the philosophies of Greece and Christianity' had discovered the infinite worth of the individual being and thus insisted that the justification of social institutions lay in their power to evoke that worth. This 'central tradition of Western civilisation' was one 'which all political parties have shared in common. Conservative and Socialist, Liberals and even Communist, Christian and Jew and Agnostic, may have differed about its realisation in method or in pace; about the validity of the large ends it has in view they have hardly differed at all.' In contrast, the Nazi leaders represented 'that ultimate corruption of the human spirit which pervades and infects every government which denies its responsibility to ordinary men. Like the Satan of Milton's great epic, they have identified good with evil.' It followed, therefore, that it was not Christian civilization as such which Laski wished to defend but he supposed that Christianity had a place in that Western civilization whose purpose it was 'To make the common man the master of his own destiny.'[77] On these grounds perhaps Christianity merited the two cheers that E.M. Forster was prepared to accord to democracy itself.

Invited to comment on certain propositions about the future ordering of society in *The Times* in December 1940 by representative churchmen, William Beveridge permitted himself the assertion that 'The sense of a Divine Vocation must be restored to a man's daily work.' He was finding the language of crusading infectious and it was to be summed up in his remark that 'A war of faith is what the world is waiting for .'[78] That 'faith', however, was apparently not Christian faith. Beveridge explained that he was not brought up in any religious faith and had never been a member of any religious community. He asserted that 'there should be something in the daily life of every man or woman which he or she does for no personal reward or gain, does ever more and more consciously as a mark of the brotherhood and sisterhood of all mankind'. Marking the brotherhood and sisterhood of man, he was willing to add, 'leads to the fatherhood of God'. It could be said that the Beveridge Report would not be undergirded by any elaborate theological foundation.[79]

By the end of 1940, when the immediate pressure on Britain had eased, the intense discussion of 'Christian civilization' declined, though it did not disappear. Later in the war, and immediately after it, theologians continued

---

77. H. Laski, *The Rights of Man* (London, 1940), pp. 15, 29–31.

78. W. Beveridge, *The Pillars of Security* (London, 1943), p. 32.

79. Ibid., pp. 38–39. José Harris points out in her biography that it was incorrect of Beveridge to claim that he had a 'wholly non-religious upbringing'. His father professed no religion, but his mother contrived to circumvent his wishes and the Beveridge children said daily prayers and attended Sunday School and divine service in Calcutta Cathedral. J. Harris, *William Beveridge* (Oxford, 1977), pp. 15–16.

to address the issue, but with less popular resonance.[80] The question Jacques Maritain had asked in 1939 was whether 'in the face of an unprecedented loosing of pagan violence and of all the means which draw strength from the degradation of the human being, we understand the need of going back to the first source of spiritual energies.[81] The circumstances of Britain in 1940 produced, at least briefly, a widespread willingness to *look* back at that first source; actually to *go* back was a journey which many could or would not make. 'We have got to be children of God' wrote George Orwell in April 1940, 'even though the God of the Prayer Book no longer exists.'[82]

80. For example, H.G. Wood, *Christianity and Civilisation* (Cambridge, 1942); J. Baillie, *What is Christian Civilization?* (London, 1945); E. Brunner, *Christianity and Civilisation* (London, 1948).

81. J. Maritain, *The Twilight of Civilization* (London, 1946), pp. 46–47

82. S. Orwell and I. Angus, ed., *The Collected Essays, Journalism and Letters of George Orwell*, ii (London, 1968), pp. 17–18.

15

Prime Ministers and Primates: Reflexions on their Twentieth-Century Relationship

So far as I am aware, there has been no systematic exploration of the twentieth-century relationship between Prime Ministers and Primates, though it seems to me not unworthy of serious attention. As in so many other areas in modern British history, the absence may be explained by the fact that political historians, generally speaking, have little interest in Primates and ecclesiastical historians, generally speaking, little interest in Prime Ministers.[1] I cannot hope to explore all areas of contact, connection and comparison between the holders of these two offices. I propose, however, to identify certain general issues relevant to this relationship and to consider some specific examples.

In the first place, it is worth remarking upon the extraordinary continuity of the two offices in twentieth-century Britain. There are very few other European countries where Prime Ministers have succeeded Prime Ministers, and Primates have succeeded Primates, without one or other, or both, experiencing exile, imprisonment or displacement arising from war, revolution or the formal consequence of the separation of church and state. Prime Ministers in England expect as a matter of course to have a Primate with whom they will form some kind of relationship, and vice versa. The antiquity of this expectation provides it with a shape and context, whatever the personalities involved. The significance of the relationship therefore hinges upon the interaction of these two elements: office and person. The former establishes certain expectations, duties and functions objectively, while the latter determines subjectively how they are executed. It would, however, be an excessive nominalism to suppose that the office of Prime Minister or the office of Primate has an unchanging character as decade succeeds decade. The mere fact of the continuity of these offices does not mean that the 'job-description' is unchanging. Both offices have been subjected to considerable pressures, some of which have been welcomed and others resisted. The pressures have sometimes coincided but on other occasions have been exerted in contrary directions. Nothing has been static.

It is the office of Prime Minister which, predictably, has been subjected to the greatest scrutiny. Most twentieth-century British Prime Ministers

---

1. I have given some attention in my *The Eclipse of a Great Power: Modern Britain, 1870–1975* (London, 1983) pp. 250–51, but that is not usual in a general text. There is no mention of Archbishops Fisher, Ramsey or Coggan, for example, in Kenneth O. Morgan, *The People's Peace: British History, 1945–1989* (Oxford, 1990). See G. Drewry and J. Brock, 'Prelates in Parliament', *Parliamentary Affairs*, 24 (1970–1), pp. 222–50

have had at least one biographer, and many of them have written their own autobiographies, or so they say. There have been, in addition, many studies of 'The Prime Ministers' as a group. Other writers have concentrated upon the evolution of British government, though there is only one book with the specific title *The Office of the Prime Minister* — written by an American.[2] Political scientists have tried to piece together information about the functioning of Cabinet government, particularly with a view to discovering whether or not Prime Ministers have gained more power over their colleagues. If there has been a growth of Prime Ministerial power it is not clear whether this has arisen from the inexorable pressure of business which afflicts all government, or from the style and inclinations of specific Prime Ministers. On all these matters, scholars continue to argue amongst themselves. It is right that the nature of the highest secular office in the land should come under such scrutiny. The Prime Minister undoubtedly does have power, however we seek to identify that elusive concept. In our system the way in which a Prime Minister uses that power is a key element in his or her survival. The power is considerable, yet it can disappear overnight either as the result of a General Election defeat or of party dissatisfaction. Prime Ministers are always alert to the necessity of survival and their power is circumscribed by their vulnerability to the vote.

The office of Archbishop of Canterbury, on the other hand, has received far less attention from political scientists or historians. It is not difficult to find reasons why this should be so. The Primate no longer holds formal power in society and to that degree is a 'marginal' figure. Primates, unlike Prime Ministers, do have tenure. Their position does not depend upon the fickle whims of the political world. We have biographies of all the archbishops of this century but the issue of their use of power is not central to any of them. Those aspects of the office of Primate which are most akin to the office of Prime Minister are normally of least interest to archiepiscopal biographers, whose concern is rather with the spirituality, the theology or the pastoral capacity of the Archbishop of Canterbury of the day. Even so, it is worth noting that at least two twentieth-century Archbishops were as undergraduates thought likely to have been possible Prime Ministers, or thought of themselves in this office.[3] In an earlier age, too, there were contemporaries who supposed Gladstone to have been a likely Archbishop of Canterbury and Manning a potential Prime Minister. Clearly, in earlier decades at least, the qualities judged to be suitable for the highest office in church and state cannot have been so very far apart. There was an assumption, too, at the beginning of the century, that both Prime Minister and Primate would be likely to emerge from a comparable social, educational and cultural background.

The continuity of their offices should not disguise the fact that incumbents have had to come to terms with substantial changes. The unwritten constitution

2. Byrum E. Carter, *The Office of Prime Minister* (London, 1956)
3. Lang and Ramsey.

of the United Kingdom gives the Prime Minister a formidable role. Insofar as the sphere of government has been substantially extended, at least until recently, the influence of the Prime Minister has been apparent in all walks of life. 'Prime Ministerial government' has been detected by many observers and has not been restricted to the last decade. It is equally the case, however, that the ever tighter sense of party loyalty can, on occasion, work against the Prime Minister. At least when things are going well, it can look as though a Prime Minister is in a position to put policy into effect without undue difficulty from an Opposition. There is a case, therefore, for arguing that Prime Ministers have more power and are more generally known now than was the case in 1901, 1931 or 1961. The advent of television has catapulted a Prime Minister into millions of homes. There is the illusion that the electorate knows the Prime Minister intimately and its assessment of his or her performance can make or break a government.

On the other hand, viewed from outside the United Kingdom, the office of Prime Minister may appear of less significance in each succeeding period of thirty years as external factors have buffeted the United Kingdom. We can note that a British Prime Minister is no longer responsible for a vast empire spanning the globe. The British Empire which Balfour knew as Prime Minister in 1902 was significantly changed as a result of the formula which he himself helped to devise at the 1926 Imperial Conference. The self-governing Dominions ceased to be subordinate. They were equal in status, though not in power. A British Prime Minister in 1939 could not behave as one had done in 1914 in dealings with the Empire. By the 1930s, the British Empire was becoming the British Commonwealth. India and Pakistan became self-governing in 1947. The British Commonwealth lost its adjectival prefix in 1952 and its organization and periodic conferences subsequently ceased to be in the hands of the British Government.

The United States was the superior partner in a 'special relationship' to which the British at least attached great significance. Decolonization has proceeded apace and direct Prime Ministerial responsibility for events in distant parts of the world has diminished. The United Kingdom remains a not inconsiderable middle-sized military power, but its position as a member of alliances is very different from the 'splendid isolation' so lauded at the beginning of this century. Prime Ministers are not insignificant but their importance is considerably less than it was. In this sense one might say that the office of Prime Minister has been devalued and is likely to become even more so as European integration proceeds.

The office of Primate has been subjected to changes which are naturally not the same but which are comparably profound. It was still possible at the beginning of the century to think of the Church of England as occupying a central place in the life of England, though the strength of Nonconformity was such that it was not reasonable to think of it as the religious expression of the English nation. The Roman Catholic Church had grown in numbers but still seemed of marginal significance in English life. Nearly a century later the picture is different. The Free Churches have declined and the Roman Catholic Church has grown. However, whatever the precise balance now between the three main traditions, all churches would acknowledge a loss of adherents as they have struggled to cope with 'secularization'. The effect would appear to be that, taken simply on a numerical basis, Primates have had increasing difficulty in 'speaking for England'. They may on occasion articulate the aspirations and views of many outside the Church of England but they must choose issues and occasions with care if they aspire to a wider national role. In addition, the growth of the ecumenical movement since 1945 has steadily introduced a new element into the picture. It would be too simple to suppose that ecumenism is merely a response to institutional decline but it would appear to be the case over recent decades that the expression of ecclesiastical opinion carries most weight in national politics insofar as it can be taken to represent the collective voice of all of the main religious traditions in the country — 'better together'. This means that the occasions when the Primate wishes to express a specifically Church of England view (and to take advantage of his privileged position for the purpose) have become more restricted, partly out of consideration for the views of other church leaders. Even so, it would be rash to assume that even when a collective Christian opinion can be mobilized, its political weight is such that any Prime Minister would feel obliged to defer to it, given the pluralism of contemporary society.[4]

There is, however, another side to the story which further complicates the position of the Primate. A British Prime Minister can no longer be described even as *primus inter pares* in the Commonwealth of Nations. Other Commonwealth Prime Ministers or Presidents do not feel themselves under an obligation to defer to the wishes of Downing Street. Since the difficult issues of decolonization, there have been occasions in which British Prime Ministers have found themselves in a minority and have asserted their right to conduct British policy in whatever manner they felt suitable, regardless of any Commonwealth consensus. The existence of a Commonwealth Secretariat and Secretary-General has meant for decades that the organization of the Commonwealth is not in the hands of the British government and the presumption that the Commonwealth Conference will automatically be held in London has also been abandoned. British Prime Ministers may continue to value the existence of the Commonwealth but they do not appear to believe that it is one of their primary responsibilities to 'keep the Commonwealth together'. They seem to accept that it is indeed a voluntary organization. Members come and go and sometimes come back.

It would be wrong, of course, to suppose that the Anglican Communion is exactly analogous to the Commonwealth, though it only exists in strength

---

4. Kenneth N. Medhurst and George H. Moyser touch on many of these issues in *Church and Politics in a Secular Age* (Oxford, 1988). I also consider the tension between 'prophecy' and 'democracy' above, pp. 105–18.

in countries either of erstwhile British settlement or British rule. It is my impression, however, that the role of the Archbishop of Canterbury in maintaining its loose cohesion has increased over approximately the same period that the role of the Prime Minister in 'keeping the Commonwealth together' has declined. I am not in a position to make a precise assessment, but I would suggest that the proportion of time recent Prime Ministers give to Commonwealth affairs has sharply diminished, while the contrary would be true in the case of the Archbishop and the affairs of the Anglican Communion. It seems, therefore, that the reconciliation of the role of an English Primate with the role of the Archbishop of Canterbury in the Anglican Communion has become, and will continue to be, one of the most difficult aspects of the office. It points to a disjuncture in the fields of vision of a Prime Minister and Primate which has become steadily more apparent since the days of Archbishop Fisher. Until the 1960s the mental map of the world of Prime Minister and Primate, of British Commonwealth and Anglican Communion — the United States apart — would have been very similar. That is now not the case.

I believe that there is an important corollary of this development in relation to Europe. No one can pretend that successive British Prime Ministers and the English people as a whole have found it easy to accommodate themselves to developments in Western Europe since 1945. It is obvious even now that considerable scepticism and hostility exists in certain quarters towards the further integration of the European Community. However, whether they have relished it or not, it has been within the context of Community politics that British Prime Ministers have increasingly had to work. European Prime Ministers talk to each other and meet each other with a frequency which would have surprised and alarmed a Lord Salisbury or a Stanley Baldwin. This almost constant contact has become central to the life of a British Prime Minister and seems largely to have replaced the Commonwealth connection as the 'first port of call'.

This transferred focus of attention places the Primate in a dual difficulty. The Church of England is *sui generis* in its claim to be both Catholic and Reformed, with whatever degree of emphasis upon the one or the other which individuals prefer. Its doctrinal, liturgical and constitutional position, however, only makes sense when seen in the context of the English history with which it is so closely interwoven. It has no exact counterpart on the European mainland. Where other 'national' churches exist, they belong clearly to a Lutheran or Orthodox family. In its self-perception as a *via media* it has been able, to an extent, to establish contacts both with the historic churches of the Reformation and, in recent decades, with the Church of Rome. Its 'bridge' role has been an advantage in a general ecumenical sense but, by the same token, it has not been able to 'integrate' anywhere.[5] Primates have found it difficult to relate to or understand the issues which have affected European

5. Some of these points are discussed in Grace Davie, '"An Ordinary God": The Paradox of Religion in Contemporary Britain', *British Journal of Sociology*, 11 no. 3 (September 1990)

churches in the twentieth-century for this reason. I instance, for example, Archbishop Lang's grapplings with the issues which afflicted the churches in Germany in the Nazi era.[6] Anglicanism does not easily 'export' to the European mainland despite the view, once expressed by Charles Kingsley and felt in every subsequent generation, that Europeans would be the better if they became Anglicans. Prime Ministers and, with them, the general structure of public affairs become willy-nilly more 'European' but the Primate can only with exceptional difficulty insert himself into Europe, sandwiched as he is between English insularity and an Anglicanism which is almost global and firmly anchored in the 'English-speaking world'.

Indeed, the dual aspect of the problem seems to be that there remain many of its members, and probably even more of its loose adherents, for whom the Church of England is an essential part of their self-identity as 'English'. Viewed from this perspective, whatever the Prime Minister may be up to in Europe, it is the duty of the Primate to remain as English as possible. The Church of England may be an odd institution, full of anomalies and absurdities, but we like it like that. That is what an English Church should be. I have heard it said in Canterbury itself, for example, that the town is being spoiled: during the summer months hardly a word of English is spoken because of the influx of 'continentals'! Such a remark points to the difficulty in reconciling the attraction of the Church of England as cultural landmark with a creative role within an ecclesiastically evolving Europe.[7]

In any event, for most of the twentieth century the literal territory of the Prime Minister and of the Primate has not coincided. It is only in England, within the United Kingdom, that a church of the Anglican Communion is established, although the London-based media do not seem to be invariably aware of this fact. The Prime Minister has responsibility in a country where another church is established in Scotland, though on a somewhat different basis, and where no church is established in Wales and Northern Ireland. There cannot, therefore, exist a one-to-one relationship in which Prime Minister and Primate look at precisely the same ground but respectively from a 'secular' and a 'religious' perspective. As things have worked out, in the first thirty-five years of the century, most Prime Ministers were not English — Balfour, Campbell-Bannerman, Lloyd George, Bonar Law and Ramsay MacDonald stand out. They could not but approach the Church of England as outsiders and were under no compunction to identify personally with its claims and aspirations. Neither did it mean, on the other hand, that they were absolved from their obligations in the matter of episcopal and archiepiscopal appointments. It was, of course, a situation which advocates of disestablishment within and without the Church of England, found anomalous

---

6. I have discussed the problem of interpreting events in Germany, above, pp. 161–82.
7. The integration of 'Englishness' and 'Catholicism' is explored in part in W.S.F Pickering, *Anglo-Catholicism: A Study in Religious Ambiguity* (London, 1989).

and unsatisfactory. How could any self-respecting church be beholden to such Prime Ministers?

I deliberately used the expression 'as things have worked out' to emphasize the random, though possibly providential, aspect of these relationships. In fact, since 1945 Prime Ministers can all be described as English — though Churchill, Macmillan and Callaghan have a 'mixed' ancestry — with the exception of Sir Alec Douglas-Home. Only Callaghan and Douglas-Home represented constituencies outside England. The reemergence of English Prime Ministers may argue, in a general way, for a closer correspondence between their perspectives and those of the Primate. But, if so, it is only in a general way, for many other factors are involved in the establishment of a relationship, most of which are fortuitous.

The nature of the party system as it has developed in twentieth-century Britain has avoided the division between 'clerical' and 'anti-clerical' factions which has been so characteristic of other European countries, even down to the present. No British party has called itself 'Christian'. It follows that Primates have never had to confront a Prime Minister heading a party with an explicitly anti-Christian outlook or been tempted to manoeuvre and meddle politically in order to prevent the emergence of an 'anti-Christian' Prime Minister. It is a peculiar aspect of British politics which is frequently overlooked. There is, however, another side to the coin. We may wish to applaud a situation in which members of the Church of England are active in all major political parties at all levels. Such participation may be more mature and beneficial than a political system in which 'Christian values' are believed to be particularly located in one political party. Nevertheless, such a Christian political diaspora precludes the possibility of an a priori assumption of a meeting of minds, on the basis of a shared faith, between Prime Minister and Primate. A Primate has no means of knowing where any particular Prime Minister might stand in matters of belief in the event of a particular party victory. He cannot tell either from the party label anything about the extent to which Prime Ministerial policies might reflect a personal concern to be, in some sense, Christian. All such relationships between the holders of the two offices, therefore, contain a strong element of uncertainty. A Primate has to make what he can of a Prime Minister who comes without benefit of an advertized label: Liberal, Conservative or Labour will offer few clues to the personal disposition of individuals. It would be difficult to think of any Prime Minister whose climb to the top of the pole has owed anything, positively or negatively, to membership of the Church of England.

The record is therefore both fascinating and unpredictable — because the unexpected does not only derive from the Prime Ministerial side. Between 1903 and 1942 there were only two Archbishops of Canterbury and they were both Scots and Presbyterian by upbringing. Of course, they became Anglicans and made their ecclesiastical careers in England, but their provenance remained unmistakable. It was on the advice of Balfour that his fellow-Scot, Randall Davidson, succeeded to Canterbury — and one might argue ironically that it was the Prime Minister who had the speculative philosophical and theological intelligence and Davidson the capacity for affairs. It probably helped this Primate initially, too, that it was a Scotsman, Campbell-Bannerman, who headed the flood of English Nonconformity into the House of Commons in 1906. Asquith, Sir Henry's successor, was not a good Church of England man but neither did he adhere firmly to his Nonconformist ancestry. In his relations with the Archbishop, the Prime Minister could not ignore the Nonconformists on the benches behind him, but he was no longer with them in spirit. In any case, as industrial, foreign and Irish issues mounted in the course of his premiership, he had other things on his mind than English disestablishment. Even so, despite a scepticism in religious matters which was apparently profound — like almost all the leading Liberals of that generation — Asquith was assiduous in his correspondence with the Primate and showed a concern for the welfare of the institutional church. Davidson, in turn, relished his membership of the House of Lords and played a not insignificant part in the passage of the Parliament Bill in 1911. The two men were much of an age — in their early sixties — but neither was likely to shift the other in their underlying convictions, or lack of them.

This was even more the case with Asquith's wartime successor, Lloyd George. The new Prime Minister was more problematic and unpredictable. Asquith could be fitted comfortably into the English elite but Lloyd George not only had not been to Balliol but was Welsh into the bargain. His Nonconformist identity was more explicit, at least as far as the singing of hymns was concerned. He was a less assiduous correspondent on church matters than Asquith, but he was simply a less assiduous correspondent in general. On the other hand, there was a war on — between them, a Welshman and a Scotsman would ensure that 'England' won the war. More fundamentally, however, the two men appeared to have little in common. Perhaps Lloyd George could never understand how a Scotsman could have come to identify himself with a church which he never ceased to find alien and oppressive.

In any case, by 1919, Davidson had reached the age of seventy and, while he remained mentally alert, found it difficult to adjust to the values and tempo of the post-war era. And in the early 1920s Prime Ministers came and went very swiftly — Lloyd George, Bonar Law and Ramsay MacDonald. The latter pair, though both Scots, were neither of them Edinburgh Scots nor members of the Church of England. It was only in his last years as Primate — he retired in 1928 — that Davidson had dealings with a Prime Minister who was an active English churchman, in the person of Stanley Baldwin. The crises of the early years of that premiership, however, showed that the mere conjuncture of a Church of England Prime Minister did not in itself produce a harmony of outlook or suggest an agreed formula for the resolution of industrial disputes or other social problems. It was evident that Baldwin did not favour the active intervention of Davidson in the General Strike.[8] That was not the business of a Primate.

8. Adrian Hastings, *A History of English Christianity, 1920–1985* (London, 1986), pp. 186–91.

There was little danger that Lang would follow a path of vigorous inter-vention in politics. He was the kind of Scot who very much enjoyed being English. He came to Lambeth from York where he had been appointed twenty years earlier. A few years older than Baldwin, their relationship was as close as that of any two Prime Ministers and Primates probably can be in the twentieth-century. It was interrupted only by the two years of Labour government. Lang was not without respect for the magnitude of MacDonald's rise from the obscurity of Lossiemouth, which exceeded his own from Glasgow, but there was little solid intercourse between the froth of MacDonald's evolutionary Socialism and the grand, if concerned, Anglicanism which Lang had forged for himself at Oxford. Lang and Baldwin, however, after Baldwin again became Prime Minister, could purvey a romantic decency with Christian conviction. Together they could deal with a new King who seemed indifferent to the private values which they both upheld. Lang could not sustain the same intimacy with the brisk, unromantic and Unitarian-descended Neville Chamberlain after 1937, but could understand, share and promote that concern to avoid war which preoccupied the Prime Minister during his short but dramatic tenure of power.[9] Yet from George Bell and other sources Lang had knowledge of the plight of 'Christian Europe' which could only be mitigated by the horror of war. It was a dilemma which the Primate shared most acutely with that other quondam Fellow of All Souls, the Foreign Secretary, Lord Halifax. It seems, however, that the Prime Minister was too much an old man in a hurry to take much note of what the even older man in Lambeth had to say.

As Prime Minister, Churchill, though apparently sceptical in matters of religion, took out proprietary rights over the defence of 'Christian civilization'.[10] He supported the appointment of William Temple as Archbishop of Canterbury when Lang finally stood down in 1942 at the age of seventy-seven.[11] He did so in the full knowledge that Temple's allegiance to the Labour Party was explicit and that Temple's zest for the propagation of his views in speech and on paper was in marked contrast to the reticence in the realm of ideas displayed by his predecessors. Churchill also knew that he did not find many of the ideas congenial or comprehensible. However, he is reputed to have recognized in Temple the only 'half a crown article in the sixpenny bazaar.' He got his own back, however, by being photographed with the new Archbishop with himself 'the Conservative' wearing a boiler suit and the Archbishop 'the Socialist', in

9. The first volume of David Dilks, *Neville Chamberlain* (Cambridge, 1984), which takes the story up to 1929, contains no reference to Davidson.

10. See above, pp. 195–214.

11. Hugh Dalton recounted in his diary in March 1942 the story of a Tory businessman who had told a Labour colleague. 'You Socialists are getting in everywhere, I must say I do admire you. One of you is deputy Prime Minister, and you have got control of the Navy and the Police and Scotland and all our Trade, and now you have worked in one of your members as Archbishop of Canterbury.' B. Pimlott, ed., *The Second World War Diary of Hugh Dalton, 1940–1945* (London, 1986), p. 391.

gaiters. We can only speculate, however, on how the relationship between two men of such dazzling difference could have developed — since Temple died in 1944. He was succeeded by a man of great ability but very different style in Geoffrey Fisher. In these appointments there was not only tragedy but irony. Churchill himself was defeated and was replaced as Prime Minister by Attlee, many of whose new Labour MPs had been much influenced by Temple's wartime writings. Attlee and Fisher were much of an age and shared an Anglican, public school, Oxford background but in fact were not close throughout the six years Attlee was Prime Minister. Attlee was a lapsed Anglican who left Christian Socialism to Sir Stafford Cripps. Fisher would have been happier with a Conservative government and was zealous in applying his formidable administrative capacity to the Church of England rather than playing his part in the creation of a 'New Jerusalem'. When Churchill returned in 1951 he showed no new disposition to seek to understand the Church of England, though he was content to be a 'flying buttress' and to play his part in the glorious Coronation of 1953 which showed the world that the English were still at heart a kind of Christian nation. Eden, too, in his relations with Fisher was correct but not intimate, though in his own complex and distressing agonies issues of faith were not absent. In the person of Eden's successors, however, the Church of England made an unexpected come-back. Macmillan was not only a Church of England man but allowed himself to say in public that belief in God was central both to individual and collective well-being. There were some who suspected that this was yet one more pose, but they were probably wrong. In the persons of Macmillan and Douglas-Home, Etonian Anglicanism enjoyed an Indian summer in Downing Street, but it did not prove to be a mixture of enduring appeal.[12]

The return of Labour in 1964 also produced a reversion, though not to the same type, in the person of Harold Wilson, a man with a northern Congregationalist/Baptist background and an Oxford career as distinguished as Asquith's. Despite all the social and ecclesiastical changes of the twentieth century, this Prime Minister seemed to show the enduring vitality of the Liberal/Labour/Chapel pedigree just as his two predecessors had shown the vitality of the Tory/Church pedigree. However, Michael Ramsey, who had been appointed under Macmillan, did not have the impeccable Anglican pedigree possessed by Temple and Fisher. Although he moved away from it, Ramsey never ceased to understand and respect the Congregationalism of his father, though the Congregationalism was that of a Cambridge don rather than of the small Yorkshire community from which the Prime Minister had made his way in the world. Ramsey, like Wilson, had been a university Liberal and a don. It was again as though, unwittingly, Macmillan had paved the way for a relationship which would be likely to be more intimate than his own had been with Ramsey in the brief period during which they had overlapped. In

12. Lord Home, *The Way the Wind Blows* (London, 1986), pp. 76–77.

practice, however, Ramsey and Wilson, despite these common elements which might have produced a close meeting of minds, did not see eye to eye. In the Rhodesian crisis, in particular, the perennial problems of principle and pragmatism reappeared to produce sharp confrontation between the two men. There was additional irony, however, in the fact that both Prime Minister and Primate had to devote an increasing amount of their time and energy to maintaining intact a Labour Party and a Church of England respectively which seemed in danger of succumbing to internal divisions.

I stated at the outset, perhaps to the disappointment of some, that I would exercise a self-denying ordinance and refrain from commenting about the particular relationships of the last twenty years, though I did refer earlier to certain general developments down to our own time. I am only too aware of the fact that in trying to provide a general sketch I have neglected many important aspects and been too superficial in others. Nevertheless, I hope I have said enough to convince you of the interest and the relevance of my theme. It admits of no simple conclusion because I have been at pains to stress that the relationships between Prime Ministers and Primates, whether close or distant, depend upon an unpredictable host of variables.[13] You will not be astonished to learn that the advent of a woman Prime Minister led to some fresh surprises and I am sure that, in the future, the advent of a woman Primate will add yet another twist to the story. You will understand, however, that I am an historian, not a prophet!

13. I did include all the Archbishops in Keith Robbins, ed., *The Blackwell Biographical Dictionary of 20th Century British Political Life*. (Oxford, 1990) but received a rebuke, in a review by Paul Johnson, for having done so on the grounds that they were not 'political'.

16

State and Nation in the United Kingdom since 1945

No one in London in 1945 would have supposed that the United Kingdom might be discussed nearly half a century later under the general title 'State and Nation'. The integrity of the United Kingdom did not then seem to be an issue. The British people had apparently just won the war and in these circumstances there was no incentive or desire to consider afresh the constitutional and administrative structure of the country. By comparison with the ethnic issues afflicting many states in Central Europe, the United Kingdom was stable and peaceful.

Indeed, the United Kingdom appeared more integrated than had even been the case in 1939, particularly as far as Northern Ireland was concerned. It was in 1921–22 that a new framework of Irish government had been settled. The 'Articles of Agreement for a Treaty' had provided for the establishment in the South of the 'Irish Free State' with a separate parliament in Dublin. Its powers were very considerable — the analogy was specifically made with the position of Canada within the British Empire. Even so, although defeated in the Civil War which had raged around the treaty terms, republican opinion wished to take every opportunity to erase the remaining British links. It was in this context, following a new constitution in 1937, that the Irish Free State stood aside from the Second World War. In Northern Ireland, however, a devolved Parliament in Belfast had been established within the United Kingdom with extensive domestic powers. The province continued, nevertheless, to send MPs to Westminster and to be bound by decisions of the United Kingdom government on questions of defence and foreign policy. It followed that Northern Ireland went to war in September 1939 and, as the war developed, particularly after the intervention of the United States, its geographical position was of considerable importance to the Allies. Northern Ireland's 'loyalty' contrasted strongly with the declared neutrality of Eire. There were rumours that a 'deal' was being contemplated in which Eire might come into the war on the promise that the question of the partition of Ireland would be reopened. In the event, however, by 1945 nothing had changed. In Britain there was considerable gratitude for the help provided by the majority of the people of Northern Ireland. The Prime Minister and the Parliament of Northern Ireland expected, in return, that the constitution of the province would be maintained. And so it proved.[1]

1. See J.T. Carroll, *Ireland in the War Years* (Newton Abbot, 1975); Kevin Nowlan and T. Desmond Williams, *Ireland in the War Years and After, 1939–1951* (Dublin, 1969); Robert Fisk, *In Time of War: Ireland, Ulster and the Price of Neutrality*, 1939–1945 (London, 1983).

In Britain itself, the heroic defiance displayed during the Second World War had served to strengthen a sense of 'British solidarity' against a common enemy. It had certainly not been necessary for Churchill's wartime government to take any special measures to strengthen the relationship between England, Scotland and Wales. The election of a Labour Government in 1945 with a substantial majority did not signal a new programme of constitutional reform. The leaders of the new administration believed that there were far more important matters to concentrate upon. Labour had a majority in English, Welsh and Scottish constituencies and the government believed that there was much more popular interest in the creation of the 'Welfare State' and in the nationalization of certain industries than there was in nationality issues. The Cabinet contained prominent figures from all parts of Britain who would work together to build Socialism irrespective of their national background. The Labour government correctly believed that there was massive support for the unity of Britain and therefore expressed its satisfaction with the existing structures of government and administration. 'State' and 'Nation' were in harmony. Given its strong 'Unionist' traditions, the Conservative opposition made no attempt to cause difficulties in this regard.

Even so, the United Kingdom was not a homogeneous 'nation-state' and its institutional structure was more complex than the description of it as a 'unitary state' might imply.[2] This remained most apparent in the case of Scotland, which retained a distinct legal, educational and ecclesiastical system after the 1707 Act of Union. Periodically, the Liberal Party in Scotland had pressed for 'Home Rule' during the years of the party's late nineteenth- and early twentieth-century strength — but without success. Scotland had, however, achieved distinctive territorial recognition within the British system in that the 'Secretary of State' for Scotland had a seat in the British Cabinet.[3] There was also a modest expansion of the civil service in Scotland — the Scottish Office. In the interwar period, however, various groups remained dissatisfied and sought new solutions, ranging from devolution within a federal United Kingdom to independence for a fully sovereign Scotland. The Scottish National Party operated from the mid-1930s but, apart from a brief by-election victory at the end of the Second World War (lost in the 1945 General Election), it made little impact on the general course of Scottish politics. It only had the resources and energy to contest a minority of seats in Scotland and polled poorly. Even so, there was a latent dissatisfaction with some aspects of Scotland's position within the United Kingdom expressed in the

2. Keith Robbins, *Modern Britain: The Eclipse of a Great Power, 1870–1975* (London, 1983); idem, *Nineteenth-Century Britain: Integration and Diversity* (Oxford, 1988); paperback as *Nineteenth-Century Britain: England, Scotland and Wales: The Making of a Nation* (Oxford, 1989).

3. G. Pottinger, *The Secretaries of State for Scotland, 1926–1976: Fifty Years of the Scottish Office* (Edinburgh, 1979); J.S. Gibson, *The Thistle and the Crown: A History of the Scottish Office* (Edinburgh, 1985).

first post-war decade in various petitions in favour of 'Home Rule', a phrase which is capable of being interpreted in very different fashions.[4]

In Wales, too, in the late nineteenth century there had been some desire for 'Home Rule' under Liberal auspices. The century had witnessed various manifestations of a national consciousness in the form of a national university and a national library. Certain pieces of British legislation specifically recognized the distinctiveness of Wales. However, as in Scotland, at the end of the period of Liberal strength — the First World War — Wales had not achieved 'Home Rule'. It was far from clear that most Welshmen really wanted it. Ambitious politicians chiefly wanted to operate on the more significant British political stage — Lloyd George, for example, became the first ever Welsh-speaking Welshman to become Prime Minister of the United Kingdom. Of course, unlike Scotland, Wales had never been a separate renaissance state with its own parliament and government. It did not have a distinct legal system. There was no Secretary of State for Wales and its separate 'image' within the British political system was weak. What it did have, however, was a distinctive Celtic language which was alive and vigorous, though not equally so throughout the principality. By the end of the nineteenth century there were more people able to speak Welsh than at its beginning, though the proportion of Welsh-speakers in the population had fallen. It is not surprising, therefore, that when a Welsh Party (*Plaid Cymru*) was formed in 1925 the main emphasis in its programme was cultural. Only if Wales gained its independence could its language be adequately safeguarded. It was already apparent that the Welsh language was under threat. However, although it attracted certain intellectuals and clergymen into its ranks, Plaid Cymru made little impact on the major centres of population in industrialised and largely anglicized areas of Wales.[5]

It can therefore be stated that for the two decades after 1945 the 'national factor' had scarcely any significance in United Kingdom politics. Both major political parties, the Conservatives and Labour, contested almost every seat throughout Great Britain – though neither party contested constituencies in Northern Ireland. There the seats at Westminster were divided between the majority Ulster Unionists (in loose alliance with the British Conservatives) and various anti-partition groupings. Neither Labour (1945–51) nor the Conservatives (1951–64) were under any pressure to embark on wide-ranging plans for constitutional reform in the United Kingdom. The status quo was only questioned by the small Liberal Party in the House of Commons but it was never in a position to make governments move in this direction. There was a British nation and there was a British state. Unionists dominated the

4. H.J. Hanham, *Scottish Nationalism* (London, 1969); K. Webb, *The Growth of Nationalism in Scotland* (Glasgow, 1977); Christopher Harvie, *Scotland and Nationalism: Scottish Society and Politics* (London, 1977); Michael Fry, *Patronage and Principle: A Political History of Modern Scotland* (Aberdeen, 1987).
5. K.O. Morgan, *Wales, 1880–1980: The Rebirth of a Nation* (Oxford and Cardiff, 1981); Alan Butt Philip, *The Welsh Question: Nationalism in Welsh Politics, 1945–1970* (Cardiff, 1975); D.H. Davies, *The Welsh Nationalist Party, 1925–1945: A Call to Nationhood* (Cardiff, 1983).

devolved parliament of Northern Ireland and at the same time firmly asserted their loyalty to the Crown and adherence to the United Kingdom.[6]

In retrospect, these two decades seem exceptional in their political 'Britishness'. They were, of course, decades in which vast changes took place in the place of the United Kingdom in world politics. They witnessed, substantially, the formal end of the British Empire; a process which began with independence for India and Pakistan in 1947. It was true that both countries — and the great majority of other colonies which subsequently gained independence — were willing to remain members of the British Commonwealth of Nations. However, it was not long before the prefix 'British' was dropped. It might be the case that the Commonwealth might still be a useful organization in world politics but, as the years passed, it became increasingly impossible to suppose that it could continue to act as a means of preserving British influence as a 'Great Power' in the world. Decolonization on this scale and at this speed was a disorientating experience for British governments and the British people, accustomed to a 'world role'. It has also to be seen in the context of increasing anxiety about the performance of the British economy. It has also to be related to the moves on mainland Western Europe to begin a process of economic integration which might have far-reaching political implications. It scarcely needs to be said that British governments found it very difficult to adjust to the new mood in Europe and have frequently been accused of 'missing the European bus'. In addition, despite emphasis on the Anglo-American 'special relationship', British policymakers had to endure the humiliation of Suez in 1956.[7]

Twenty years on, therefore, it was often supposed that the great victor of 1945 was now in serious crisis. What role was Britain supposed to play and on what stage? It was at this point asserted in some quarters that the *raison d'être* of the United Kingdom had also ceased to exist. 'Britain', it was suggested, was an imperial figment. It had served its purpose in the great days of the British Empire when all national groups within the British Isles had played a part — varying in degree — in its conquest, administration, conversion to Christianity and commercial development. Those days were now over. Just as the United Kingdom had to come to terms, in a difficult fashion, with the emergence of 'Europe' so its component parts had to work out a fresh relationship. That might even require the 'break-up' of Britain and the emergence of three or four independent states or some kind of explicit federalism. These ideas were aired in the press and in the eyes of some observers were far too extravagant ever to become serious political possibilities.[8]

6. P. Buckland, *A History of Northern Ireland* (Dublin, 1981); D.W. Harkness, *Northern Ireland since 1920*.

7. J. Darwin, *Britain and Decolonisation: The Retreat from Empire in the Post-War World* (London, 1988).

8. T. Nairn, *The Break-up of Britain: Crisis and Neo-Nationalism, 1965–1975* (London, 1977).

Yet this is just what happened. For approximately fifteen years, from 1964 to 1979 the issue of 'state' and 'nation' reached the forefront of United Kingdom politics. In the 1966 General Election, both the Scottish National Party (SNP) and Plaid Cymru (PC) sensed some possibility that they might at last be on the point of a breakthrough. In the event, neither party gained more than 5 per cent of the Scottish and Welsh electorate respectively, but in 1966/67 both parties gained a seat each in the House of Commons. It was the first ever victory for a PC candidate. In the 1970 General Election both parties greatly increased the number of their candidates and gained 11.5 per cent and 11.4 per cent of the Welsh and Scottish vote respectively, although only the SNP won a seat. In Wales, in the two General Elections held in 1974, PC gained just under 11 per cent of the total Welsh vote but in the October election it gained three parliamentary seats (a twelfth of the total number of Welsh seats at Westminster). It was in Scotland, however, that the electoral situation appeared to be changing very fast. The SNP gained seven seats in February 1974 and eleven seats (out of seventy-one) in October 1974. In the latter General Election it gained some 30 per cent of the total Scottish vote. Such a speedy expansion of support suddenly threatened the survival of the British state. If the SNP continued to grow at its recent rate then it might soon acquire a majority of the Scottish seats at Westminster and present a formal demand for independence.

In addition to the general background factors that have already been mentioned, there were certain other specific developments which help to explain the advance of the SNP. The most significant of these was the discovery and initial exploitation of substantial oilfields in the North Sea off the Scottish coast in the early 1970s. Here was 'Scotland's Oil' waiting to be developed in Scotland's specific interests rather than to disappear to the British Treasury. Between 1970 and 1974 it was also apparent that the Conservative government was in grave difficulty in both its industrial and economic policy. It was supposed in the press that Britain was 'the sick man of Europe' and no easy recovery could be anticipated. It was argued that Scotland could govern its own affairs better. A further new element in the picture derived from the eventual British membership of the European Economic Community. The SNP in fact opposed British membership but also suspected that, over time, a 'new Europe' would emerge. In such circumstances it would be best for Scotland to negotiate directly with Brussels and play its part in the European Parliament. It did not escape notice that the Republic of Ireland had an enhanced role in European politics but Scotland, as such, had no role at all.

It was the political scene in Scotland which caused the Labour government after 1974 most difficulty. There were divided opinions on how matters should best be handled and a variety of considerations applied. The 'break-up of Britain' was not something which the Labour government welcomed. Although there had been 'Home Rule' elements in its ranks throughout its history, the majority view had always favoured a 'united' Britain. That was how Socialism was going to be achieved. There was also a strong element of self-interest in resisting anything so complete as independence for Scotland. The possibility of a Labour government in the United Kingdom had latterly come to hinge upon electoral support from Scotland and Wales — where the Labour majority over the Conservatives was assured. Both countries, incidentally, were overrepresented in the House of Commons in London in proportion to their respective populations. A separatist solution appeared likely to make it impossible for there to be ever again a Labour government at Westminster, since the Conservative majority in England looked unassailable. To take no action, however, might only strengthen the appeal of the SNP. It was suspected that many Scottish voters who had voted SNP did not really want independence but merely a greater degree of Scottish control over decisions which had consequences in Scotland.[9]

In these circumstances, after the General Election of October 1974, the Labour government wrestled with some possible solutions. The Labour Party in Scotland itself was in a quandary and deeply divided between pro-devolutionists and anti-devolutionists. Eventually, however, it produced proposals for a Scottish Assembly with certain legislative powers (which did not include taxation). It pushed these proposals strongly in the House of Commons but had to abandon its precise initial proposition because of opposition from various quarters. Critics argued that Scottish voters should signify their approval of these proposals in a referendum (a very unusual device in British politics). Amendments ensured that the proposed change would not operate unless at least 40 per cent of the electorate registered affirmative votes. A vigorous and not very good-natured campaign then followed in Scotland in 1979 in which it emerged that 32.8 per cent of the electorate supported the proposals and 30.8 per cent opposed them. The remainder abstained. The proposal had therefore gained the support (narrowly) of those who voted but the supporters constituted less than a third of the total Scottish electorate. In these circumstances the proposal collapsed — and so did the Labour government. In the 1979 General Election that followed the SNP's share of the Scottish vote almost halved and its representation in the House of Commons fell from eleven to two MPs.

It had been the momentum in Scotland which had forced the Labour government to experiment with a proposal for a subordinate 'Assembly' there but, as always, it was felt that Wales had to be treated in somewhat similar fashion. Wales had 'copied' Scotland, as it were, for decades having at length achieved a capital city (Cardiff) and a Secretary of State who sat in the British Cabinet. Wales too, therefore, was to be offered some 'devolution' though its Assembly was not to have legislative powers. That proposal was also, eventually, put to the Welsh electorate and, despite the official endorsement by Labour (the majority party in Wales) the scheme was resoundingly defeated.

9. V. Bogdanor, *Devolution* (Oxford, 1979); H.M. Drucker, *The Politics of Nationalism and Devolution* (London, 1980).

Only 11.9 per cent of the Welsh electorate wanted the Welsh Assembly which the Labour government had initially wished to impose on the principality by legislation alone.

In the event, therefore, the plans for both Scotland and Wales failed completely. The technical problems of administering this quasi-federal scheme were formidable but the schemes would have to have been attempted if the electorate had wished. In the event, according to opinion, there was relief, bitterness and even a sense of farce. So much time had been spent in arguing and debating but in the end nothing had happened. Dedicated supporters of the SNP and PC could not altogether make up their minds whether what was on offer was a 'first step', which would lead inexorably to independence, or whether it was a 'half-way house' which would ensure that independence would never be achieved. Most voters endorsed the status quo despite the fact that prominent Welshmen and Scotsmen had been saying that the status quo was intolerable. In any event the verdict showed how divided were the Scottish and Welsh 'nations' and how complicated a matter 'Britishness' was. The non-Welsh-speaking majority of the Welsh electorate feared, whether rightly or wrongly, that an Assembly would lead to the domination of Welsh public life by a Welsh-speaking minority. And, although the SNP had made such an impact on Scottish politics as a whole it had failed to gain General Election seats in Glasgow and Edinburgh, the country's two major cities. There was at one time the spectacle of a country gaining independence in defiance of its major centres of population.[10]

The apparent growth of some kind of nationalism in Scotland and Wales in the late 1960s coincided with the descent of Northern Ireland into political turmoil and protracted violence.[11] The history of Northern Ireland since 1968 cannot be recounted in detail but some of the most significant events should be mentioned. The decision to send substantial British forces to the province, in the first instance as a protection for the minority community, has in turn led to further political changes. After a political experiment which had lasted for half a century, the British government decided in 1972 to suspend the Northern Ireland Parliament. The province is now governed by the Secretary of State for Northern Ireland (a new post), who is a member of the British Cabinet in London, supported by junior ministers. His position, however, is not altogether analogous to that of the Secretary of State for Scotland and the Secretary of State for Wales. These latter offices are filled (normally but not invariably) by prominent Scottish or Welsh MPs drawn from the ranks of whatever party is governing the United Kingdom. In the case of

10. W.L. Miller, *The End of British Politics? Scots and English Political Behaviour in the Seventies* (Oxford, 1981); J. Brand, *The National Movement in Scotland* (London, 1978); J.B. Jones, *The Welsh Veto: The Politics of the Devolution Campaign in Wales* (Glasgow, 1979); D. Foulkes, J.B. Jones and R. Wilford, *The Welsh Veto: The Wales Act 1978 and the Referendum.*
11. The literature on this question is enormous. One very recent survey, Thomas Wilson, *Ulster: Conflict and Consent* (Oxford, 1989), contains many references to relevant literature.

Northern Ireland, however, since 1972 the Secretary of State has not been an Ulsterman — since neither Labour nor the Conservatives contest Westminster seats in Northern Ireland. Attempts have been made periodically since 1972 to create some local instrument which would enable both communities to share in the government of the province but they have not endured. Once it became clear that the old Northern Ireland Parliament would not be restored, the parliamentary representation of Northern Ireland in London was increased, but Ulster MPs do not have formal links with the parties which contest elections in Britain.

Successive British governments, both Labour and Conservative, have tried simultaneously to control the level of violence, to meet legitimate grievances felt by the minority, to reassure the majority and also to involve the government of the Irish Republic in fighting terrorism. The most significant recent development has been the conclusion in 1985 of the Anglo-Irish agreement between the British and Irish governments. Like every other aspect of policy in Northern Ireland it has been contentious from the outset, it has been bitterly criticised by leaders of the Unionist majority — who had no part in its negotiation — on the grounds that the liaison body established under this agreement represents an improper intrusion into the affairs of Northern Ireland by a foreign government.

Above and beyond the merits or demerits of particular proposals for 'solving' the problem of Northern Ireland, however, lies the fundamental question of identity and allegiance. A majority in the province continues to assert that it is both Irish and British. A minority asserts that it is not British at all. Another section of the population believes that it is simply 'Ulster' and is almost equally suspicious of the English in London and the Irish in Dublin. It would be a considerable oversimplification to believe that all Ulster Roman Catholics wish to see the end of partition.

This issue of 'dual identity' embraces Ulster, Scotland and Wales with varying degrees of intensity. In each country, interviewers have identified three main categories of self-definition: 1. Ulster, Scottish, Welsh; 2. Ulster/Irish/British, Scottish/British, Welsh/British; 3. British *tout court*. In the long term, one suspects, the political configuration of the United Kingdom, perhaps of the British Isles as a whole (that is to say including the Irish Republic) will be determined by the sense of identity which triumphs. At the moment, it is impossible to predict with any certainty which it will be.

Superficially, it might seem that the 'national crisis' of the United Kingdom has been in its peripheral regions. Certainly, there has been no English National Party which has emerged as a serious electoral force. Yet one of the major problems in the governmental structure of the United Kingdom is England itself. That is to say, it is 'England' which historically has been the driving force which has created that kingdom by a mixture of coercion and consent over centuries. It is England that has been the dominant partner and which has had its remarkable institutional and territorial continuity. It is England that over the past century and a half has become more populous and more prosperous (in general) than the other constituent elements in the United Kingdom. It is arguable that a successful federal system requires its units to be of approximately equal weight. If so, England upsets the balance and its weight can only be reduced by a regionalization of the government of England. Proposals along these lines have been regularly made for over a century but have equally regularly been ignored. Why should England be 'de-nationalized' in order to permit the governments of Scotland and Wales to be 'national'?

It is not surprising that the attitude of English MPs over the period 1964–79 oscillated between indifference and hostility confronted by 'peripheral nationalism'. The Labour government after 1974 had no plans for an English Assembly or regional assemblies in England. Its proposals therefore meant that English domestic legislation would have to be passed through the House of Commons in which Scottish MPs would continue to sit, while English MPs would have no say on questions of Scottish domestic legislation which were to be devolved to the Scottish Assembly in Edinburgh. Here was a vital issue which had perplexed legislators a century earlier when Irish Home Rule legislation had been in contemplation. English MPs from both major parties began to feel increasing irritation that, at a time when there were many grave issues confronting the country, parliament and the government was spending so much time on constitutional issues which, it was argued, were of little benefit to the major country in the state, namely England.

The year 1979 marked a divide because the incoming Conservative government under Mrs Thatcher set its face firmly against any more discussion of 'devolution'. The referendum had settled 'state' and 'nation' in the United Kingdom for a considerable period. There would need to be massive evidence of an overwhelming desire on the part of Scotland and Wales to become 'self-governing' or 'independent' before a Conservative government would take any initiative in this matter whatsoever. Meanwhile, there were more important matters to be considered. Such a stance did not entail a disbelief in the reality of a sense of Scottish or Welsh nationhood or an unwillingness to support cultural diversity with central funds. It did mean a hostility to political separatism as a solution to the complex problems of identity within the United Kingdom.

This stance has been sustained throughout the 1980s and into the 1990s with great determination. However, difficulties have not disappeared and they again surface most strongly in relation to Scotland. The debacle of 1979 removed the impetus for a number of years only to revive, to some extent, in the later 1980s when it was again claimed by advocates of constitutional change that opinion in Scotland favoured it. Inevitably, however, the context was not what it had been precisely a decade earlier. Mrs Thatcher obtained three consecutive electoral victories in the United Kingdom and established a rare degree of authority over the politics of the decade. Yet the strength of the Conservative appeal in England was not repeated in either Scotland or Wales over the same elections. The authority of the Conservative Government in Scotland is challenged by those who point to the substantial Labour majority in Scotland over this period. It is supposed that a 'self-governing' or 'independent' Scotland (albeit a Scotland-in-Europe independence) would not have a Conservative government and could therefore follow social and economic policies markedly different from those followed in England. The same point applies, in general, in the case of Wales.

This delicate position poses problems for both major British parties, Labour and Conservative. The Labour Party in Scotland appears largely to have shaken off the opposition to devolution which complicated its response in the mid 1970s. It is not clear, however, just what kind of parliament it does want and how far it is prepared to collaborate with other parties in Scotland in order to obtain it. A self-styled 'Constitutional Convention' emerged to examine these issues, with the Labour Party the dominant element in its proceedings. Both the Conservative Party in Scotland and the SNP, for diametrically opposed reasons, have refused to take part in the deliberations of this body. It may be that the Labour Party in Scotland will commit itself to a structure which has more legislative and financial power than was envisaged in 1979. If so, it is likely that the excessive Scottish representation in the House of Commons will have to be reduced. But, if it is, and if something comparable happens in Wales, it will be Labour, the party of devolution, which will lose seats and so make its task of forming a British government even more difficult than it already is. Yet while such a scenario might make the Conservative Party happy, from one point of view, it would also cut clean contrary to its own image of itself as preeminently a Unionist party and not just a party which dominates England. On the other hand, if it does not make some concession to national sentiment in Scotland and Wales it may risk being branded the 'alien' party even more than it is already in the eyes of many Scotsmen and Welshmen.

In any case, at least from an English perspective, interrelationships between the four 'native' nations of the British Isles were kept in perspective by the major transformation in the ethnic composition of the United Kingdom brought about by immigration from the Commonwealth from the mid 1950s onwards.[12] There is no space in this essay to develop consideration of this issue at length. Immigrants from the Indian sub-continent, Africa, the West Indies and elsewhere have brought in considerable strength a diversity of languages, religions and cultures hitherto not known in the British Isles. The impact of this settlement has been considerable and permits no simple generalisations. Public debate, however, has revolved around issues of identity. How far should immigrants be required to 'assimilate' into whatever values and conventions are held to be 'British'? How far, on the contrary, should there be a public acceptance of 'multiculturalism' with little attempt to produce conformity through the education system or by any other means? The answers to these questions remain uncertain.

12. The literature on this topic is likewise vast. See J.L. Watson, ed., *Between Two Cultures: Migrants and Minorities in Britain* (Oxford, 1977); Paul Rich, *Race, Government and Politics in Britain* (Basingstoke, 1986).

'Nation' and 'State' in the United Kingdom since 1945 is therefore a story of surprises and paradoxes. It does not allow any clear-cut conclusion. The United Kingdom is an untidy state.[13] Its constitutional arrangements have evolved over a long time and do not depend upon the interpretation of a written constitution. It is not a unitary state, in the strict sense of the term, but neither is it federal. It is both 'national' and 'multinational'. Its inhabitants admit to various kinds of identity, most of which can be subsumed under the comprehensive formula 'Britishness'. But not all of them can. The United Kingdom of Great Britain and Ireland did not hold together. In a very different world it is not altogether fanciful to contemplate the 'Balkanisation of Britain', but the obstacles in the path of British national disintegration remain formidable, not least in the wishes of still a majority of the British people.

13. A.H. Birch, *Nationalism and National Integration* (London, 1989).

17

Core and Periphery in Modern British History

Throughout western Europe, recent decades have witnessed a great interest in local and regional history. Historians have stressed the distinctive aspects of particular localities in speech, land tenure, religious practice and much else. Archival research has been matched by psychological and anthropological insight. This zeal both reflected and fed a certain disenchantment with the contemporary centralized state. It seemed important to stress the vast diversity lurking behind Italian or German 'unification'. Even in the case of France, Baron Haussmann's claim that she was 'the most "one" in the world' seemed preposterous to Professor Weber as he explored, with the eyes of a foreigner, its regional characteristics. In discussing contrasting *mentalités*, he referred to the 'two nations' of Disraeli's *Sybil* and added that the author's concern with 'rich' and 'poor' stemmed in part from the fact that 'regional differences were of less account in England than in France'. There was nothing in England that approached the distance that separated the departments of Nord and Seine-Inférieure, say, from Lozère and Landes.[1]

In this country, however, local history was blossoming and new journals were devoted specifically to the north, the midlands and the south of England. The *Scottish Historical Review* found new life and was matched by the *Welsh History Review*. County record societies maintained their publications. The new urban historians ensured that no major city was left unstudied. Social historians stressed local custom and practice. Alongside this activity there developed an obsession with the small world of the political élite. Regional historians and the practitioners of 'high politics' seemingly had little to say to each other, but together they have combined, no doubt innocently, to exclude from serious consideration what might be termed the territorial dimension in modern British history. The interplay between the constituent elements of modern Britain has elicited, until recently, only casual comment.

Professor Weber himself casually assumes that it is the degree of diversity in *England* which has to be compared with France in discussing the two countries — and he is not using England as synonymous with Britain. A French sociologist, Gustave d'Eichthal, who did visit England *and* Scotland in 1828 could have given better advice. 'The character of the Scots', he wrote,

---

1. E. Weber, *Peasants into Frenchmen: The Modernization of Rural France, 1870–1914* (London, 1977), pp. 8–10.

'is quite different from that of the English. They are not at all starchy, formal, and fastidious like that of their neighbours, whose lack of free-and-easiness often makes them very tedious. Here you are allowed to have the knot of your tie awry.' Despite the 'auld alliance', however, he found it surprising how little even well-informed men in Edinburgh knew about France. The country might have been in the depths of Poland for all they knew or cared.[2]

It was common nineteenth-century practice, of course, to use 'England' and 'the English' to refer to all the inhabitants of Britain. Lord Randolph Churchill, for example, had no qualms about speaking in Edinburgh in 1882 on 'England and Egypt'.[3] This custom remains commonplace on the Continent. Domestically, however, a long, though not altogether effective, campaign has been waged against the habit. Lord Randolph's son disliked being told to say 'Britain' and complained plaintively: 'I like England.'[4] Historians in our own time have great difficulty in deciding what it is they are writing about. Some books which purport to be about Britain are in fact about England, while others which purport to be about England also talk about Britain.[5] Social historians are no more sensitive in these matters than are their political colleagues. Such rampant confusion, needless to say, is reflected at all levels in schools and universities in the United Kingdom.[6]

The historian must admit, however, that it is easier to be censorious or amused than to find a solution. 'Britain' and 'British' are difficult words to use and define. 'Britannia', concludes Peter Levi, 'has her toes in the surf of the cold sea and whatever the sea carries comes to her. Her past is terrifying . . .'[7] That may be poetic licence, but in his Wheeler Lecture Professor Alcock drew attention to the enigmatic processes whereby Celtic Britain became England, Scotland and Wales.[8] Equally complex forces were at work in the attempt to re-invent Britain in the sixteenth and seventeenth centuries. In the 1540s and 1580s abortive schemes for union were given enthusiastic support in the interests of 'the empire of great Briteigne'.[9] Lord

2. B.M. Ratcliffe and W.H. Chaloner, ed., *A French Sociologist Looks at Britain: Gustave d'Eichthal and British Society in 1828* (Manchester, 1977), pp. 76–77.

3. *Lord Randolph Churchill's Speeches*, i (London, 1889), 70–85.

4. James Stuart, Viscount Stuart of Findhorn, *Within the Fringe* (London, 1967), p. 99.

5. All the volumes in the Arnold *New History of England* covering the years since 1760 have the subtitle 'Britain'. The Fontana *History of England* is also taken to embrace Britain in its modern volumes. Two of the volumes in the Pelican *British Social History* have the subtitle 'England'.

6. Sir Keith Joseph, when Secretary of State for Education and Science, referred to his belief that 'national, that is, for me, British history must play a central part in the construction of any history syllabus in English schools'. (*The Times*, 24 August 1984.) He could not, of course, speak with authority about schools outside England, but whether 'British' history is thoroughly taught in any part of the United Kingdom may be doubted. See above, pp. 00–00.

7. P. Levi, *The Flutes of Autumn* (London, 1983), p. 184.

8. L. Alcock, 'Cadbury-Camelot: A Fifteen-year Perspective', *Proceedings of the British Academy*, lxviii (1982), p. 386.

9. A.H. Williamson, *Scottish National Consciousness in the Age of James VI* (Edinburgh, 1979), pp. 151–52.

Protector Somerset referred to Britain as 'the indifferent old name', though he did not originate it. Historians and writers of tracts produced remarkable descriptions of a common past, but enthusiasts had to wait until 1603 and the union of the crowns for their desires to be gratified. The role of North Britons in the invention of Great Britain was very considerable but a commitment to an imperial vision did not imply the erosion of Scottish identity.[10] There was an ambivalence from the outset, as events in the mid-seventeenth century were to demonstrate.[11]

The circumstances of full union in 1707 have been subjected to fresh scrutiny. The tendency has been to minimize the element of 'vision' and to stress the extent to which negotiators on both sides of the border were motivated by short-term considerations.[12] The creation of a new political entity was not accompanied by such an outpouring of poetic fervour as had accompanied the union of the crowns. Historians will naturally disagree on the extent to which the union was inevitable, as they will on whether or not it was desirable. It is generally agreed, however, that after the disappearance of the Scottish parliament the power of the magnates did not long survive exposure to British politics. Scotland, Dr Riley argues, became an 'additional buttress of court dominance'.[13] Of course, the events of 1715 and 1745 required exceptional and specific attention to Scotland at Westminster but, in general, the 'management' of Scotland did not pose undue difficulties. Recent studies have illuminated the mechanisms and personalities involved. By the middle of the century, the repeal of the union and the rejection of the Hanoverians disappeared as a serious possibility. The 1707 settlement, with its guarantees concerning the nature of the Church of Scotland, the universities, the legal system and courts, and the rights and privileges of the royal burghs, were as entrenched as a doctrine of parliamentary sovereignty could permit. It seemed appropriate to develop the notion of a 'North Britain' and a 'South Britain'. The former style was to have a useful life for some two hundred years, but then rapidly declined. 'South Britain', on the other hand, never seriously established itself as a conceivable alternative to 'England'.

Historians have dabbled from time to time in the language of core/periphery or centre/fringe but for the most part have left the concept in the realm of

---

10. Williamson, 'Scotland, Antichrist and the Invention of Great Britain', in J. Dwyer, R.A. Mason, and A. Murdoch, ed., *New Perspectives on the Politics and Culture of Early Modern Scotland* (Edinburgh, n.d.), p. 52; J. Wormald, 'James VI and I: Two Kings or One?', *History*, lxviii, no. 2 (June 1983), pp. 187–209.

11. See Roots's own essay in I. Roots, ed., *'Into Another Mould': Aspects of the Interregnum* (Exeter, 1981); D. Stevenson, *The Scottish Revolution, 1637–44* (Newton Abbot, 1973), and *Revolution and Counter-Revolution in Scotland, 1644–1651* (London, 1977).

12. W. Ferguson, *Scotland's Relations with England: a Survey to 1707* (Edinburgh, 1977); T.C. Smout, 'The Road to Union' in G.S. Holmes, ed., *Britain After the Glorious Revolution* (London, 1969); T.I. Rae, ed., *The Union of 1707: Its Impact on Scotland* (Glasgow, 1974).

13. P.W.J. Riley, *The Union of England and Scotland* (Manchester, 1978), pp. 312–13.

grand theory to be fought over by political economists or geographers.[14] Scholars in these disciplines have made interesting suggestions but have by no means agreed on what constitutes a 'core' and what a 'periphery'. Some have argued that the notion has 'an intuitive meaning', a conclusion which has in practice informed the writing of modern British history.[15] The general assumption is that, as Lord Beloff puts it, 'It is possible for the 1914–45 years to deal with politics nationally, that is inevitably London-based', though he concedes that 'a future historian' might well decide to allot more space to Scotland and Wales.[16] His statement finds a ready echo in practically every general history of Britain since 1707.

There is, indeed, little point in contesting the view that London was the core of national politics in the British state. It was in the forum of Westminster that the new Scottish MPs had to operate after 1707 and they did so with some relish. It has been calculated that of the 261 between 1707 and 1760 151 came from titled families. Sixteen Scottish peers, selected from their total number, sat in the House of Lords. The grander among them had no taste for a return to merely Scottish public life. It was the 'poor worms' who remained in North Britain. This exodus was not confined to the representative peers. A recent examination has concluded that there were only a dozen non-soldier representative peers who could have taken part in public work in Scotland for more than five consecutive years. One of them, the 4th Earl of Selkirk, was known to have lived 'in the most retired manner' in the University of Glasgow for a decade after 1742.[17] There was nothing retiring about the Duke of Argyll in England. In 1742 he became Commander-in-Chief of the British Army, in which post he was succeeded by another Scotsman, the 2nd Earl of Stair. It was the beginning of a notable Scottish role both in the command and composition of the British Army.[18] Scottish sailor peers, who had a markedly short life expectancy, also left Scotland and played no significant part in its affairs. The 'management' of Scotland rested in the hands of the Earl of Islay (who succeeded his brother to the dukedom of Argyll in 1743) from the mid-1720s until his death in 1761. His nephew, the 3rd Earl of Bute, with whom he was by no means invariably in accord on Scottish matters,

14. D. Sears, B. Schaffer, and M.-L. Kiljunen, ed., *Under-Developed Europe: Studies in Core-Periphery Relations* (Hassocks, 1979); J. Gottman, ed., *Centre and Periphery: Spatial Variations in Politics* (London, 1980).

15. J. Galtung, 'A Structural Theory of Imperialism', *Journal of Peace Research*, viii, part 2 (1971), pp 81–117, ad E.L. Gidengil, 'Centres and Peripheries: An Empirical Test of Galtung's Theory of Imperialism', ibid., xv, part 1 (1978), pp. 51–66.

16. M. Beloff, *Wars and Welfare: Britain, 1914–1945* (London, 1984), p. 8.

17. Sir James Fergusson, *The Sixteen Peers of Scotland* (Oxford, 1960); J.S. Shaw, *The Management of Scottish Society, 1707–1764: Power, Nobles, Lawyers, Edinburgh Agents and English Influences* (Edinburgh, 1983), pp. 5–9; A. Murdoch, *'The People Above': Politics and Administration in Mid-Eighteenth Century Scotland* (Edinburgh, 1980).

18. For the role of Scots in the Victorian Army see H.J. Hanham, 'Religion and Nationality in the Mid-Victorian Army', in M.R.D. Foot, ed., *War and Society: Essays in Honour and in Memory of J.R. Western* (London, 1973). For a comment on the twentieth century see J. Keegan, *Six Armies in Normandy* (Harmondsworth, 1983), pp. 166–70.

rose to spectacular heights, if briefly, to become Prime Minister in 1762. The prevalence of Scottish influences in the early years of George III, or so it was believed, led to various popular expressions of anti-Scottish sentiment, though Wilkes's use of 'North Briton' was supposedly an attack on the government in particular than on Scotsmen in general.[19] On his accession, George III had caused some surprise by his firm declaration that he gloried in the name of Briton — there is some suggestion that this was interpreted to mean that he was a Scot. If so, he did not require to explore his northern kingdom in person. That was left to the extravagant visit of George IV in 1822.[20]

In this transitional period of 'British' politics it is not easy to find the right terminology either for the state or the men who operated it. To confine ourselves to Bute and Islay, neither man could be said to be deeply Scottish. Islay had been born in Surrey and educated at Eton. He only came to live in Scotland at the age of seventeen to study at the University of Glasgow. He then went to Utrecht and returned to England in the year of the union. Bute was educated in England and at Leiden and did not actually live in Scotland before 1739 and did not return there after 1745. Are they early 'Anglo-Scots', 'Englishmen of Scottish extraction' or 'Scoto-Britons'? Did their careers confirm that at least in an age of aristocratic politics Scotsmen had no alternative but to come to Court and Parliament in London if they wished for power in a British context? Distance and the difficulties of travel ruled out the possibility of rapid movement between North and South Britain. And where did this leave Scotland itself? Historians, on the whole, speak of it as a 'province' — Lenman refers to it as the most subservient and undemanding — but to do so is not altogether satisfactory.[21] In England, by the end of the eighteenth century, the term 'the provinces' was coming into use to describe the regions beyond London but in such a context Scotland was emphatically different.[22]

Eighteenth-century Edinburgh in the heyday of the 'Scottish Enlightenment' would not have seen itself as 'provincial' and remained, in a sense, a capital. The scholarship devoted to the intellectual life of late eighteenth-century Scotland over recent decades makes it impertinent merely to offer a few remarks.[23] However, explanations for its brilliant flowering are still somewhat elusive. Paradoxically, an element in its vitality may be the removal of independent

19. G. Rudé, *Wilkes and Liberty* (London, 1962), pp. 13–14.

20. Its flavour is given in *A Historical Account of His Majesty's Visit to Scotland* (Edinburgh, 1822). D. Cannadine, 'The Context, Performance and Meaning of Ritual: The British Monarchy and the "Invention of Tradition", *c.* 1820–1977' in E. Hobsbawm and T. Ranger, ed., *The Invention of Tradition* (Cambridge, 1983), makes no mention of this event. Indeed, there is no mention at all of the not insignificant Scottish element in the British monarchy during this period.

21. B. Lenman, *Integration, Enlightenment and Industrialisation: Scotland, 1746–1832* (London, 1981), p. 42.

22. D. Read, *The English Provinces, c. 1760–1960* (London, 1964).

23. A.C. Chitnis, *The Scottish Enlightenment: A Social History* (London, 1976); N. Phillipson, 'The Scottish Enlightenment', in R. Porter and M. Teich, ed., *The Enlightenment in National Context* (Cambridge, 1981); R.H. Campbell and A.S. Skinner, ed., *The Origins and Nature of the Scottish Enlightenment* (Edinburgh, 1982).

political life. While it may be right to speak in a political sense of Scotland being 'ignored', this was not so either commercially or intellectually. The spectacular growth of the Glasgow tobacco trade in the 1760s and early 1770s had indeed been at the expense of the ports of the southwest of England and of London.[24] It was the very 'peripheral' position of Glasgow, in a British sense, which made it, for a time at least, pivotal in the wider British North Atlantic world. In that world 'Scotus Americanus' had an important part to play.[25] Intellectually and commercially, neither Glasgow nor Edinburgh was on the edge of that Britain which, sadly for them, was to be shattered by war and revolution in the American colonies.

It was a Scotland which could attract a clutch of young English aristocrats north of the border at the end of the century, though admittedly, if there had not been a continental war in progress, they might never have come. After Eton and Cambridge, William and Frederick Lamb came to Glasgow to sit at the feet of John Millar (and lodge in his house) in the last years of his life. It no doubt comes natural to Melbourne's biographer to characterize the inhabitants of the house as 'earnest, industrious and provincial'. Two of young Lamb's companions each thought himself as wise as Aristotle and Plato. Millar himself was pronounced 'a little jolly dog, and the sharpest fellow I ever met'. William reported to his mother that the Scotch universities were very much calculated 'to make a man vain, important and pedantic'. At least Melbourne contrived not to fall into the latter category himself.[26] A year later, the younger and less sophisticated Harry Temple set off for Edinburgh in mid September 1800 and arrived there a month later. His father took him *en route* to Glasgow, Loch Lomond, and an ironworks at Stirling — a fine estimate of what Scotland had to offer the southern visitor. The future Lord Palmerston lodged in the house of Dugald Stewart and was subjected to a rigorous diet of universal history, moral philosophy and languages. He also took Scottish dancing classes and, in the summer, failing to find sufficient Scottish cricketers, was forced to take up golf, a poor pursuit in comparison. He was deemed to be a 'Paddy' and invited to celebrate St Patrick's Day.[27] Lord John Russell had initially shown resistance to the idea of acquiring 'Scotch knowledge in a Scotch town'. Political economy might surely be studied in England and he hardly knew the meaning of the term 'metaphysics'. In the end he spent three years in Edinburgh.[28]

---

24. T.M. Devine, *The Tobacco Lords* (Edinburgh, 1975).

25. A. Hook, *Scotland and America: A Study of Cultural Relations, 1750–1835* (Glasgow, 1975); W.R. Brock, *Scotus Americanus: A Survey of the Sources for Links between Scotland and America in the 18th Century* (Edinburgh, 1982); J.M. Bumsted, *The People's Clearance* (Edinburgh, 1982).

26. Lord David Cecil, *The Young Melbourne* (London, 1954), pp. 54–56. Millar's most notable works were his *The Origins of the Distinction of Ranks* (London, 1779) and *An Historical View of the English Government* (London, 1787). See W.C. Lehmann, *John Millar of Glasgow* (Cambridge, 1960).

27. K. Bourne, *Palmerston: The Early Years, 1784–1841* (London, 1982), pp. 11–30.

28. J. Prest, *Lord John Russell* (London, 1972), p. 11.

The arrival of three English aristocrats in Scotland for part of their education was not a development which many would have envisaged a century earlier: even less that these three men should become Prime Ministers of Great Britain. Lord Lansdowne and Lord Dudley, two future Cabinet Ministers, were also in Edinburgh at this time. However, this conjuncture was not to set a pattern; indeed it was never to be repeated. With the conclusion of peace, the Continent again proved a more attractive alternative to men of standing seeking an occupation between school and university in England. In addition, the waning of the intellectual power of the 'Enlightenment' after the early decades of the nineteenth century was apparent, even south of the border. While all three men undoubtedly benefited from their experience of Scottish life and gained some insight into its character, it would be unwise, except perhaps in the case of Russell, to trace any very specific intellectual legacy.[29]

The general movement of population, however, was from north to south. In most professions and in commerce the financial rewards were, on the whole, greater in England than Scotland. Quite apart from overseas emigration, the Scottish element in the English population steadily increased so that we can perhaps speak of a million Scots who have been absorbed into the English population.[30] The Scottish-born inhabitants of London constituted just over 1 per cent of the total population in each decennial census from 1841 to 1891.[31] Quite apart from those who settled permanently, many others came for short periods. Clubs, societies and churches at least for a time preserved a Scottish past for those who wished to retain it, but it is a moot point whether it makes sense to speak of a Scottish 'minority'.[32] As is frequently the case, however, some groups of Scottish 'exiles' in London were more self-consciously Scots than those who stayed at home. There were, therefore, networks of communication between London and Scotland which ran alongside official political channels.

It is, however, rather too simple to speak in the nineteenth century of both 'England' and 'Scotland', since the pace of commercial and industrial development in both countries accentuated differences between region and

29. R. Pares, 'A Quarter of a Millenium of Anglo-Scottish Union', *History*, xxix (October 1954), pp. 233–48, has some general reflections. See also S. Collini, D. Winch and J. Burrow, *That Noble Science of Politics* (Cambridge, 1983), pp. 23–61.

30. M.W. Flinn, ed., *Scottish Population History from the Seventeenth Century to the 1930s* (Cambridge, 1977). Dame Flora Robson was only one of many Scots brought up in England to be treated as an alien in Scotland. 'I expected to feel at home in Scotland,' she wrote, 'but to my surprise I was treated as a Sassenach. It was a great shock to me.' K. Barrow, *Flora . . .* (London, 1981), p. 71. Earlier generations had comparable experiences.

31. H.A. Shannon, 'Migration and the Growth of London, 1841–1891', *Economic History Review*, v (1935), pp 81–83. The 'tramp' of a Scottish working man in search of work is described in D. Vincent, ed., *The Autobiography of a Beggar Boy* (London, 1978). In 1830, for example, he travelled 1,400 miles from Glasgow before finding work in Dorset.

32. Perhaps old memories died hard in Northumberland. In 1846, a revising barrister struck off the list of voters persons 'chiefly Scotchmen' in Alnwick. 'There now,' he remarked, 'we have repelled the invasion of the Scots.' J. Prest, *Politics in the Age of Cobden* (London, 1977), p. 95.

region and created a multiplicity of new cores and peripheries. As Professor
Smout points out: 'Scotland is a periphery to south-east England, but Shetland
a periphery to an Edinburgh–Glasgow core, and the outer isles of Shetland,
Whalsay and Unst, a periphery to its capital at Lerwick.'[33] Likewise in the
case of England. Population growth was steady in London and the southeast
of England in the mid and late nineteenth century but so was it in the north,
northwest, and northeast of England. Population declined in an area through
the north midlands to the southwest. It was southern England which appeared to
be peripheral at a time when the north seemed dynamic. Cobden, so widely taken
as the personification of 'Manchester man', had moved from Sussex. Writing
of the general conditions of the Labour market in the late nineteenth century
Dr Hunt concludes that what emerged prominently from his research was 'the
plight of the rural labourer of southern England and parts of Wales and northern
Scotland'.[34] It was easier, cheaper and faster to travel between different parts of
Great Britain than it had ever been in the past.[35] Scotland as a whole appeared to
be closing the gap in its per capita incomes as compared with England. Wages in
central Scotland were, in Hunt's words, 'characterized by long-term improvement
relative to other parts of Britain'. By the turn of the century it had become one
of the four highest out of thirteen wage regions in Britain. Clearly, mere distance
from London did not in itself make a region 'peripheral'.[36]

At the level of high politics, in the transitional decades from oligarchy
to democracy, the integration of English and Scottish politics appeared
to be increasingly a fact, at least in terms of individual careers. Of the
men who either reached Downing Street or came close to doing so, the
proportion of Scots is astonishingly high. We must consider Lord Aberdeen,
William Ewart Gladstone, Lord Rosebery, A.J. Balfour, Sir Henry Campbell-
Bannerman and Andrew Bonar Law in the period leading up to the First World
War. There are many nuances and subtleties in such a list. Aberdeen, as his
recent biographer makes clear, follows firmly in the steps of the eighteenth-
century aristocratic diaspora. Most of his time was spent in England, where
he had largely been brought up. He was educated at Eton and Cambridge.
Although he eventually succeeded in becoming an English peer, he had earlier
been closely involved in Scottish politics and he took a keen interest in his
estates in northeast Scotland. There were times, not very frequent, when he
felt particularly Scottish and spoke in Parliament on Scottish questions with

33. T.C. Smout, 'Centre and Periphery in History: With Some Thoughts on Scotland as a
Case Study', *Journal of Common Market Studies*, xviii (March 1980), p. 263.

34. E.H. Hunt, *Regional Wage Variations in Britain, 1850–1914* (Oxford, 1973), p. 356.

35. Before the advent of the railways, the number of coach passengers conveyed between
London and Edinburgh in the 1760s has been put at some twenty-five monthly rising to 4,000
monthly in the 1830s. By that date several steamships sailed weekly between the two capitals. It
is well known that the dying Sir Walter Scott, returning from the Continent, chose to sail from
London to Leith. A.M. Milne and J.C. Laight, *The Economics of Inland Transport* (London,
1963), p. 28, 645,000 passengers flew between London and Glasgow in 1972.

36. Hunt, *Regional Wage Variations*, p. 177; see also S. and O. Checkland, *Industry and
Ethos: Scotland, 1832–1914* (London, 1984), p. 13.

some authority. That apart, he seemed an English peer.[37] Gladstone was a rather different kind of Scot. When described as a Scotsman, he did not disclaim the honour — at least not in Scotland. He admitted in Dundee, for example, that 'not a drop of blood runs in my veins except what is derived from a Scottish ancestry'.[38] His father, John Gladstone, had moved from Leith to Liverpool and, like other Scotsmen, played a major part in its commercial affairs.[39] William, however, became an Anglican and an Englishman through the exertions of Eton and Christ Church. Father Gladstone returned to Scotland as a landed gentleman and William always felt himself to have a particularly close grasp of Scottish life, even if that life needed purifying by the instrument of Glenalmond. It was fitting that he should latterly campaign in Midlothian.[40] Lord Rosebery might at first sight appear the very epitome of an anglicized Scottish peer.[41] Yet he had a deep feeling for Scotland which must be balanced against Mentmore, the Derby and the London County Council. As a youthful Rector of the University of Aberdeen he strongly urged the merits of a Chair of Scottish History. He played an important part in the establishment of a Scottish Secretaryship.[42] In 1882 he threatened to blow up a Scottish prison as a means of drawing attention to the country's needs. He gloried in 'our Scottish nation' in speeches in Glasgow, particularly when he could claim that Scots believed in levelling up rather than down.

The Scottish occupation of Downing Street continued into the twentieth century. Campbell-Bannerman became the first Prime Minister of Britain to go to school in Scotland.[43] He always claimed to be most at ease in Scotland and represented a Scottish constituency. His correspondence with other Scotsmen betrays a belief that they understood each other — even Rosebery had urged Ronald Munro-Ferguson to remember that 'C-B' was a Scot — though that did not seem invariably the case.[44] Sir Henry took the notable step of substituting 'Scotland' for 'N.B.' on his headed notepaper. His national allegiance also expressed itself in a partiality for continental travel. Campbell-Bannerman's preference for his own countrymen did not extend to his predecessor as Prime Minister, A.J. Balfour.[45] Despite suggestions to the contrary, Balfour undoubtedly thought of himself as a Scot, at least when he

37. M.E. Chamberlain, *Lord Aberdeen* (London, 1983). Dr Chamberlain devotes one chapter specifically to Scotland. It is entitled, significantly, 'A Scottish Interlude'.

38. A.J. Hutton and H.J. Cohen, ed., *The Speeches of the Rt. Hon. W.E. Gladstone, on Home Rule, etc., 1888–1891* (London, 1902), pp. 288–89.

39. S.G. Checkland, *The Gladstones* (Cambridge, 1971).

40. R. Kelly, 'Midlothian: A Study in Politics and Ideas', *Victorian Studies*, iv (1960–1), pp. 119–40.

41. R. Rhodes James, *Lord Rosebery* (London, 1963), pp. 130, 465.

42. Lord Rosebery, *History and a Chair of History: A Rectorial Address Delivered before the Students of Aberdeen University* (Edinburgh, 1880).

43. J. Wilson, *The Life of Sir Henry Campbell-Bannerman* (London, 1973), pp. 154–57.

44. Rhodes James, *Lord Rosebery*, p. 420.

45. A.J. Balfour, 'Race and Nationality', *Transactions of the Honourable Society of Cymmrodorion* (session 1908–1909). On p. 238 Balfour argued that 'there is no such thing in these islands as a man of pure descent from any race whatever'.

was in Scotland. He took communion in both the Church of Scotland and the Church of England in royal fashion. His appointment as Chief Secretary for Ireland brought one letter from the senior Inverness Law Officer expressing his pleasure in 'watching the career of a Scotsman in whom we may all be proud'.[46] His successor as leader of the Unionist opposition, Andrew Bonar Law, was a man of very different stamp. Like Campbell-Bannerman, he too was educated at Glasgow High School, but then became an iron merchant in the city.[47] He conformed to an English notion of what an earnest, hardworking, graceless Scot should be. Some historians have found it surprising that the city of Glasgow should produce Prime Ministers of Great Britain.

This important Scottish presence in Downing Street was also matched at ministerial level. What did it signify? It clearly suggested that 'Scots' could reach the highest political office in the British state without much impediment arising from their Scottish connection. It was not easy, however, even for men with property north and south of the border, to be prominent figures in both England and Scotland. Naturally, this was particularly the case for the Scottish Secretaries. His biographer suggests that one of them, Lord Balfour of Burleigh, was assisted in maintaining his Scottish identity in England by his total imperviousness to music and colour, at least in worship.[48]

It is the appointment of Bonar Law, however, which is most significant for our theme. Unlike all his Scottish predecessors as party leaders in British politics, his background and formative influences owed nothing to England. His conduct of the Opposition before 1914, often found mystifying, cannot be explained without reference to this fact. He came to the west of Scotland at the age of twelve from New Brunswick where his father, who hailed from Portrush in Ulster, was a Presbyterian minister. From Bonar Law's perspective, it was London which stood at the edge of the British world. Glasgow was the core of the northern transatlantic British Empire. English contemporaries and subsequent historians have not been able to accept a temporary moment when the second city appeared first. Joseph Chamberlain did spot it. Significantly it was to Glasgow and Greenock that he came in October 1903 to launch his tariff campaign throughout Britain. He was even prepared to recognize Glasgow as the second city of the Empire.[49]

46. M. Egremont, *Balfour* (London, 1980), p. 80.

47. R. Blake, *The Unknown Prime Minister: The Life and Times of Andrew Bonar Law* (London, 1955); Professor Donald Cameron Watt has many stimulating comments to make on the transatlantic relationship but it is surprising that an Anglo-Scot should write that the Tories were 'discarding the scion of the Salisburys for a Scots Canadian shipping magnate'. D. Cameron Watt, *Succeeding John Bull: America in Britain's Place, 1900–1975* (Cambridge, 1984), p. 29; M. Bentley, *Politics Without Democracy, 1815–1914* (London, 1984), p. 315.

48. Lady Frances Balfour, *A Memoir of Lord Balfour of Burleigh* (London, n.d.), p. 201.

49. R. Jay, *Joseph Chamberlain: A Political Study* (Oxford, 1981), pp. 285ff.; C.W. Boyd, ed., *Mr Camberlain's Speeches*, ii (London, 1914), pp. 140–64; Chamberlain urged his audience 'to consolidate the British race'. J. Amery, *The Life of Joseph Chamberlain*, vi, *1903–1968* (London, 1968), p. 453, completely misses the point of Chamberlain's magnanimous opening concession that Glasgow and not Birmingham was the 'second city of the Empire' by bestowing that accolade upon Liverpool.

One further significant feature of these decades was the appearance of English politicians in Scotland in pursuit of constituencies rather than fishing. Receiving the Freedom of Edinburgh in 1910, H.H. Asquith recalled how, when he first invaded Scotland twenty-five years earlier, 'a ferry-boat conveyed me and my carpet-bag across the turbulent and treacherous waters of the Forth to the adjacent Kingdom of Fife, which has been my political home ever since'.[50] For a time he shared the kingdom with Augustine Birrell. When East Fife failed Asquith in 1918, it was Paisley which rescued him, though only temporarily, a few years later. John Morley had 'reluctantly' accepted the Montrose constituency: a diffident traveller, he did not excessively favour the burghers of Montrose with his presence.[51] Winston Churchill was compelled to flee to Dundee. This English Liberal presence in Scotland combined with the Scottish Liberals to form, in the Cabinets before 1914, a most pronounced Scottish colouring to a degree which has not since been exceeded. It did not pass undetected. One of Sir Edward Grey's early biographers described him as 'a typical Englishman' in his 'simple straightforwardness', which contrasted with the Irishmen, Scotsmen, and Welshmen who played, some Englishmen thought, 'so disproportionate a part in the affairs of the United Kingdom'.[52] Even Sir Edward came from dangerously near the border. Were it not for the Scottish leadership of the Opposition at this juncture, the Tory party might have played the English card more strongly than it did. That there was an undercurrent of feeling can be noted, for example, in Sir Cecil Spring-Rice's private reference to Lloyd George as 'a Celt from the lower regions', and in the memorandum circulated by John Gretton, the midlands brewer and MP, in November 1910 in which he detected 'a widespread movement on foot among the Celtic elements in the U.K. to assert predominance over the Anglo-Saxon. An understanding exists between the principal Irish, Welsh and Scottish parties to cooperate at the right time'.[53] Commentators on the general elections of 1910 thought they saw a pronounced geographical aspect to British politics though, significantly, did not quite interpret it in the same way. Beatrice Webb commented on the 'dividing of England into two distinct halves each having its own large majority for its own cause', while J.A. Spender drew a distinction between the Liberal north, Scotland, and Wales on the one hand, and the Unionist south of England on the other.[54] The extent to which

50. H.H. Asquith, *Occasional Addresses* (London, 1918), p. 139. In marrying Margot Tennant, Asquith established another Anglo-Scottish connection.

51. D. Hamer, *John Morley* (Oxford, 1968), p. 320.

52. Anon., *Sir Edward Grey K.G.* (London, 1915), p. 11.

53. S. Gwynn, ed., *The Letters and Friendships of Sir Cecil Spring-Rice*, ii (London, 1929), ed., 159–60; J. Vincent, ed., *The Crawford Papers* (Manchester, 1984), p. 169.

54. Cited in N. Blewett, *The Peers, the Parties and the People: The General Elections of 1910* (London, 1972), pp. 380–89; the areas S. Macintyre identifies as being most sympathetic to Marxist influences between the wars – central Scotland, non-coastal south Wales, the north east of England – share a similarity which derives from comparable socio-economic experiences. They have more in common with each other than with the nation or even region of which they are a part. S. Macintyre, *A Proletarian Science: Marxism in Britain, 1917–1933* (Cambridge, 1980).

the division was within England rather than between England and Scotland and Wales has a bearing on the claim that the Tory Party owed eventual success to 'the highlighting of national differences between England and the Celtic regions'.[55]

The mention of Lloyd George, and his emergence as the first Welsh-speaking Prime Minister of Great Britain, is a reminder of the extent to which the common nineteenth-century habit of referring simply to England and Scotland, or 'the two Kingdoms', was no longer adequate. The Welsh dimension in British history could not be ignored. In one sense of the word, the Welsh had a distinctive claim to be 'British'. Iolo Morganwg dreamed on Primrose Hill of the bards of Britain. Lloyd George himself in 1881 eyed the Houses of Parliament 'in a spirit similar to that in which William the Conqueror eyed England on his visit to Edward the Confessor, the region of his future domain'.[56] Welshmen had felt the same way since the sixteenth century. Welsh city life before the industrial revolution was London life. It was there that the first Welsh books were published. The societies of Welshmen in London maintained a close contact with Wales, but Welshmen were not a 'minority' living in separate ghettos. The nineteenth century, of course, saw major changes in Wales itself. A sense of national identity required institutional recognition in the shape of a national university and library. On the other hand, the Welsh language lost ground sharply, though the erosion was not as catastrophic as in the case of Irish. Wales was able to retain the bulk of its expanding population. There was even substantial immigration into southeast Wales from southwest England. Cardiff emerged as a substantial town with aspirations.[57] Wales as a whole was less remote and inaccessible from England than at any time in its history. The later Cardinal Vaughan expressed a youthful desire 'to get away from civilization altogether' which he thought might mean becoming 'a solitary priest at a seaside town in Wales'.[58] As he wrote, the arrival of the railway and the steady expansion of holiday-making meant that not even seaside towns in Wales were safe from civilization. One might meet Mr Gladstone or Mr Bright.[59] It was not easy to assess the impact of these developments for Welsh–English relations in the context of Britain. Cardiff, widely thought in Welsh/English circles to be 'unwelsh', hardly constituted the core of Welsh life. Quite apart from other considerations, geography and communication flows

55. R. Taylor, *Lord Salisbury* (London, 1975), p. 189.
56. W.R.P. George, *The Making of Lloyd George* (London, 1976), p. 101.
57. M.J. Daunton, *Coal Metropolis: Cardiff, 1870–1914* (Leicester, 1977).
58. Cited in E.R. Norman, *The English Catholic Church in the Nineteenth Century* (Oxford, 1984), p. 358.
59. J.K. Walton, *The English Seaside Resort: A Social History, 1750–1914* (Leicester, 1983), includes Wales and the Isle of Man within its scope; K.G. Robbins, 'Palmerston, Bright and Gladstone in North Wales', *Transactions of the Caernarvonshire Historical Society*, xli (1980), 129–52.

made that unlikely.[60] In the north, it was Liverpool, with its substantial Welsh community, which frequently served the Welsh hinterland. In the northwest, on the periphery, the slate industry seemed to be prospering.[61] Ships came to Porthmadog, where Lloyd George was a young solicitor, from across the globe. Even so, he at least would not be satisfied with local reputation and modest fortune. He wrote in 1884 that as for any higher object — fame — London was the place for that. His private description of Wales as 'this stunted principality' was not flattering.[62] Other Welshmen, less drawn to the prospect of power in London, continued with the task of inventing a national past at home.[63]

The same task was also found engrossing in Ireland.[64] In 1913, listening to the debate on the Home Rule Bill, Leo Amery lamented that no speaker felt 'that the United Kingdom really is a nation and that Irish nationalism in any shape or form means the end of United Kingdom nationalism'. He believed that if only a single name had been invented for the United Kingdom in 1800, and the Viceroyalty abolished, Home Rule would never have been considered.[65] Whatever the plausibility of that contention, the Act of Union certainly complicated the dimensions of Britain yet further. Some Irishmen did glory in the description of 'West Briton', but that terminology was unlikely to prove generally acceptable. Irish identity was too complex to be subsumed under that formula, or indeed perhaps under any. But since, by definition, the evolving Britain of the nineteenth century was an amalgam, was there no place for Irish/British? That possibility was confronted by the alternative vision of a Gaelic nation. 'Celts' and 'Anglo-Saxons' apparently opposed each other as though a thousand years had not passed and as though the populations of Ireland or Britain could be accurately fitted into either category.[66] There

60. The establishment of a University of Wales was a case in point. Henry Bruce, Lord Aberdare, wrote in 1863 strongly supporting the establishment of such a scheme if it were attached to 'some considerable town', such as Swansea or Cardiff. But he wondered whether the north and the south could ever unite for such a purpose or agree upon the site. *Letters of the Rt Hon. Henry Austin Bruce, Lord Aberdare of Duffryn* (Oxford, 1902), pp. 203–4.

61. M. Jones, 'Notes from the Margin: Class and Society in Nineteenth Century Gwynedd', in D. Smith, ed., *A People and a Proletariat: Essays in the History of Wales, 1780–1980* (London, 1980), pp. 199–214. However, when the English-educated Irishman H.R. Reichel was appointed as the first Principal of the University College at Bangor a century ago he had to admit that he had never, until that point, heard a Welsh hymn tune and did not know that such a beast as a red dragon existed.

62. George, *The Making of Lloyd George*, p. 115.

63. P.T.J. Morgan, 'From a Death to a View: The Hunt for the Welsh Past in the Romantic Period', in E. Hobsbawm and T. Ranger, ed., *The Invention of Tradition* (Cambridge, 1983), pp. 43–100.

64. R.F. Forster, 'History and the Irish Question', *Transactions of the Royal Historical Society*, 5th ser., xxxiii (1983), pp. 169–92.

65. J. Barnes and D. Nicholson, ed., *The Leo Amery Diaries i, 1896–1929*, (London, 1980), p. 92.

66. H.A. MacDougall, *Racial Myth in English History: Trojans, Teutons and Anglo-Saxons* (London, 1982); R.R. Davies, *Historical Perception: Celts and Saxons* (Cardiff, 1979).

was an Irish and Irish-descended population in Britain which was almost approaching the 'Irish' population in Ireland. It was not only their Atlantic perspective that linked Liverpool, an 'English' city, and Glasgow, a 'Scottish' city, but the fact that both contained between a quarter and a half of their populations who were 'Irish', and the same was true in lesser degree of other British cities.[67] Not that this influx had been without tension. Alarm amongst many Scottish Presbyterians, for example, reinforced a solidarity with the Scots-Irish of Ulster.[68] The failure of Gladstonian Home Rule had left unresolved on what basis Ireland might continue to exist alongside or within the 'British' world. It had also revealed the hazards that might attend any attempt to suppose that Ireland was a homogeneous entity.

It is, in part, this complex process of intermingling which makes ill-advised the ready and prevalent willingness to talk about any part of the United Kingdom (before or after 1922) outside England as a 'Celtic' land, region or unit. Even more so is this the case with that portmanteau favourite, the Celtic fringe.[69] It is not clear precisely when it came into use, but now seems to be thought indispensable. 'Celtic' in this connection is a good word at twilight, but historians should be wary of its use in modern British history. Of course, enthusiasm for matters Celtic occurred in the most diverse places in the nineteenth century, encouraged by the writings of such varied figures as Matthew Arnold and the invalid uncle and namesake of Charles de Gaulle. The notion of 'sinking the differences between the different members of the great Celtic family' was aired. However, a Celtic League, designed to promote the common political objectives of the Scottish Highlands, Ireland, and Wales, foundered. The hard difficulty was that the religious and linguistic differences within the 'Celtic family' were acute.[70] Not only that, to categorize any of the non-English units of Britain as 'Celtic' *tout court* was, and is, a misleading description both of their past and of their nineteenth-century present. The 'Celtic' element was of undeniable significance but had ceased to be, indeed had rarely been, the whole. The use of the term 'the Celtic fringe' also sometimes posits some underlying 'peripheral' solidarity against the core of

67. P.J. Waller, *Democracy and Sectarianism: A Political and Social History of Liverpool, 1868–1939* (Liverpool, 1981); B. Aspinwall, *Portable Utopia: Glasgow and the United States, 1820–1920* (Aberdeen, 1984); M.A.G.O. Tuathaigh, 'The Irish in Nineteenth-Century Britain: Problems of Integration', *Transactions of the Royal Historical Society*, 5th ser., xxxi (1981), pp. 149–73; C. Holmes, ed., *Immigrants and Minorities in British Society* (London, 1978); K. Lunn, *Hosts, Immigrants and Minorities* (Folkestone, 1980).

68. See above, pp. 99–100.

69. M. Hechter, *Internal Colonialism: The Celtic Fringe in British National Development, 1536–1966* (London, 1975), is a general exposition, but many other authors use the phrase. R.J. Hind, 'The Internal Colonial Concept', *Comparative Studies in Society and History*, xxvi, part 3 (July 1984), pp. 543–68.

70. R. Bromwich, *Matthew Arnold and Celtic Literature: A Retrospect, 1865–1965* (Oxford, 1965). For Arnold to have died in a Liverpool street was, from one standpoint, quite incongruous, but from another it was quite appropriate. B. Crozier, *De Gaulle: The Warrior* (London, 1973), p. 18; J. Hunter, 'The Gaelic Connection: The Highlands, Ireland and Nationalism, 1873–1922', *Scottish Historical Review*, liv (1975), p. 185.

England, yet there is little evidence for any such phenomenon. The very few bilateral studies that exist of relations between Ireland and Scotland, Ireland and Wales, and Wales and Scotland disclose no fundamental affinity which links them with each other in a way which separates them from England.[71] The problem of Ulster is in itself a sufficient obstacle to any such notion.[72]

In the decade before the First World War, the Liberals and some other commentators comtemplated the possibility that the relationships within the British Isles might best be catered for in terms of 'Home Rule All Round'.[73] Sir Edward Grey had declared in 1912 that harm would come from pretending that there were no separate units in the United Kingdom and no differences of national opinion. Devolution all round on a quasi-federal basis seemed to him to offer the best hope for the future. It would have the advantage that central government could concentrate upon external and imperial matters.[74] There was no lack of schemes — but no lack of difficulties. Churchill, who had been dabbling in this area for a decade, came forward with a plan to divide the United Kingdom into ten units which had regard to geographical, racial, and historical considerations.[75] The problem, however, was that to have regard to one of these factors might produce a very different result from that which could emerge from paying attention to others.

The First World War, at least as far as Ireland was concerned, changed the mood and nature of the discussion, but it resumed in 1919.[76] A Speaker's Conference met in October and produced comprehensive proposals in the following Spring. The problem of Britain appeared intractable, both at the core and periphery. London, with the English Parliament, was the historic core of what by expansion and union had become the United Kingdom. If its four constituent countries were each to have a Parliament, was it really conceivable that a separate English Parliament would be set up alongside what would remain as the United Kingdom Parliament? Balfour in 1913 had not been able to conceive that such a Parliament would accept subordination, since England's resources would be so much greater that there could be no parity between the four units.[77] If, in addition, Ireland were to have

71. L.M. Cullen and T.C. Smout, ed., *Comparative Aspects of Scottish Economic and Social History, 1600–1900* (Edinburgh, 1977); C. O'Rahilly, *Ireland and Wales: Their Historical and Literary Connections* (London, 1924). See below, pp. 271–80.

72. F.S.L. Lyons, *Culture and Anarchy in Ireland, 1890–1939* (Oxford, 1979); J.C. Beckett, *Confrontations: Studies in Irish History* (London, 1972); D. Fitzpatrick, 'The Geography of Irish Nationalism, 1910–1921', *Past and Present*, 78 (1978).

73. J.E. Kendle, 'The Round Table Movement and "Home Rule All Round"', *Historical Journal*, xi, part 2 (1968).

74. *Home Rule from the Treasury Bench: Speeches During the First and Second Reading Debates* (London, 1912).

75. Cited in H.J. Hanham, *The Nineteenth-Century Constitution, 1815–1914* (Cambridge, 1969), pp. 131–33.

76. V. Bogdanor, *Devolution* (Oxford, 1979), is a general discussion and one somewhat overtaken by events at the moment of publication.

77. Wan-Hsuan Chiao, *Devolution in Great Britain* (New York, 1926), remains the best discussion. It must be a matter of speculation whether, as the author hoped, this study of devolution in Britain contributed to the constitutional development of China.

two Parliaments, that would only accentuate the disparity. The solution of Halford Mackinder, the English geographer and Glasgow MP, was to divide England into three parts: London, agricultural England and the industrial North.[78] Only a geographer could think such a plan was feasible. Other commentators thought that England might return to the days of the heptarchy, but that did not seem very plausible. One correspondent had told Churchill before the war that the so-called 'provinces' just would not work — 'the points of the compass have no traditions and excite no enthusiasm'.[79] In 1919, Balfour argued that it was illogical to be contemplating treating England on a regional basis while purporting to deal with Ireland, Scotland and Wales on a 'national' basis. If there was a case, on administrative grounds, for establishing provincial administrations, then that should be done treating the United Kingdom as a whole and not being hindered by boundaries inherited from the past. 'England', 'Scotland', 'Wales' and 'Ireland' could not survive such treatment, but perhaps that did not matter. In its place might come a rationally organized 'Britain' which truly reflected the historical process of integration.

The impetus behind the consideration of 'Home Rule all Round' derived not from Scotland, Wales, or England but from the crisis in Ireland. When the Irish question was settled, for the time being, the idea of a more general constitutional reordering of Britain dropped from view. The new institutions of Northern Ireland were anomalous and sprang from peculiar circumstances. They were not for general emulation. How far and to what degree the citizens of the United Kingdom in Northern Ireland were 'British' was, in the last analysis, a matter of sentiment and conviction. For the majority, Irishness and Britishness were not mutually exclusive categories.

The severing of Ireland closely coincided with the advent of democratic politics in Britain. The Anglo-Scottish aristocracy which had played such a part in the government of Britain lost its dominance although, in a curious way, the new Labour Party mirrored the elite which it sought to replace. Its early parliamentary leadership also contained a disproportionate share of Scotsmen — Keir Hardie and Ramsay MacDonald most notably.[80] Even Arthur Henderson was born in Glasgow. Scottish and Welsh Home Rule was part of Hardie's rhetoric, but the party as a whole had little enthusiasm for such schemes. Henderson had even battled against the idea that the Labour Party itself should have a 'national' element in its organizational structure.[81] Like Lloyd George, Ramsay MacDonald aspired to power at the centre of the British state. The geographical spread of the Labour Party's support repeated the pattern which had confronted the Liberal Party before 1914. To win power

78. W.H. Parker, *Mackinder: Geography as an Aid to Statecraft* (Oxford, 1982), p. 45.

79. Sir Thomas Elliott to W.S. Churchill, 28 October 1901. I am grateful to Sir Hugh Elliott for allowing me to see and use this letter.

80. K.O. Morgan, *Keir Hardie: Radical and Socialist* (London, 1975); D. Marquand, *Ramsay MacDonald* (London, 1977).

81. R. McKibbin, *The Evolution of the Labour Party* (London, 1974), pp. 168–69, 205.

it needed support outside J.A. Spender's periphery of 1910, but if it failed to gain that support it might diminish its chances on another occasion by its very 'peripheral' appearance. The fact that all Labour Prime Ministers since MacDonald have been English may be more than accidental.[82]

It is noteworthy, however, that when discussion between the wars turned to projection of the national image abroad, those concerned still thought in English terms. The book which, indirectly, was to lead to the establishment of the British Council, Sir Stephen Tallents' *The Projection of England*, purported to concern itself with 'the standing raw material of England's esteem in the world'. Sir Stephen thought that meant the Derby and the Grand National, Henley and the Boat Race, Wimbledon, Test Matches, Trooping of the Colour, the Lord Mayor of London, Piccadilly, Bond Street, the Metropolitan Police, Big Ben, London omnibuses and underground railways, *The Times* and *Punch*. Momentarily lifting his eyes to the periphery of England he included the *Manchester Guardian*, Oxford and Edinburgh.[83] It was in the same spirit that Sir Robert Vansittart felt no inhibition in writing to the Prime Minister, Ramsay MacDonald, asking him for a short article for distribution abroad which would 'do something to promote better knowledge of English manners and customs and of the ideals on which our particular culture is based'.[84] It must be admitted that MacDonald had refused patronage for a 'Come to Scotland' movement on the ground that 'the mere tourist, up to now at any rate, is disgusting and disquieting . . .'[85]

The Battle of 1940, however, was for Britain. Once again, the western seaboard, including Northern Ireland, was of critical importance. Scotland resumed a pivotal role in the North Atlantic Triangle, with Prestwick airport taking one to the land of Mackenzie King. Even more than in 1914–18, it was the core that was exposed to the threat from Europe while the periphery preserved the vital connections across the Atlantic. Even so, elements of the past remained. Churchill was suspicious of Glasgow, writing in October 1939 that 'there are plenty of Irish traitors in the Glasgow area' who would be supplying details of shipping movements to the German ambassador in Dublin.[86] With victory achieved, however, Professor Namier in 1948 was writing of the 'British island community' and of a historical process which had produced 'a British island nationality'.[87] A quarter of a century later Professor

---

82. After Attlee, Gaitskell, and Wilson, Messrs Callaghan, Foot and Kinnock have sat for Welsh constituencies and their personal ancestry is not straightforwardly English, though only Kinnock is partially of Welsh descent.

83. P.M. Taylor, *The Projection of Britain: British Overseas Publicity and Propaganda, 1919–1939* (Cambridge, 1981), pp. 212–13.

84. Ibid., p. 236. MacDonald's biographer thinks it appropriate to write about him in the following terms: 'He had never been a cheerful Anglo-Saxon extrovert. He was a black and moody Celt, with a Celt's long memory and a Celt's capacity to cherish his grievances.' Marquand, *Ramsay MacDonald*, p. 408.

85. Marquand, *Ramsay MacDonald*, p. 401.

86. M. Gilbert, *Winston S. Churchill, vi, Finest Hour, 1939–1941* (London, 1983), p. 71.

87. L.B. Namier, *Vanished Supremacies* (London, 1962), p. 47.

Seton-Watson was among those who believed that this was ceasing to be true, indeed might already have ceased.[88]

There suddenly appeared to be convincing reasons why this might be so. 'Britain' had only existed in the common enterprise of Empire, and that vital overseas focus was being removed.[89] Simultaneously, the creation of a European Community raised questions about the appropriate units in such a community. As early as 1923 Mackinder had written in *Britain and the British Seas* that 'we Europeans will have to see ourselves massed into a single crowd'.[90] Now it appeared to be happening. Within such a crowd, the nation-states of the nineteenth century might no longer be appropriate. A new core might be emerging in Europe to which the whole of the United Kingdom was peripheral. From another angle, Britain might seem on the periphery of an English-speaking world now dominated by the United States.[91] In such contexts, domestic difficulties multiplied. The Northern Ireland settlement collapsed in protracted violence. A linguistic and cultural crisis in Wales, coinciding with industrial restructuring, appeared likely to be resolved in some form of self-government. A crisis of confidence and the advent of North Sea oil seemed to suggest the same outcome in Scotland. The solution attempted in the late 1970s was to bypass the problem of England and attempt legislation for Scotland and Wales (eventually separate legislation). The proposals did not receive the stipulated endorsement when the people of Scotland and Wales were consulted in a referendum. The English electorate was not given an opportunity to express a view on a development which would have changed the structure of Britain. On this occasion, at least, to attempt to restructure Britain would have produced as many anomalies and imperfections as the existing status quo.

'It is impossible to forecast the destinies of the human race', stated Lord Dufferin at a banquet in honour of Charles Dickens at St George's Hall, Liverpool, in April 1869, 'but there are some conjectures which may be hazarded without presumption, and perhaps one of them is that in God's good providence it is intended that a large portion of the habitable globe should pass under the domination of an English-speaking people.'[92] Lord

---

88. H. Seton-Watson, *Nations and States* (London, 1976), p. 42.

89. See below, pp. 281–92; after a lifetime spent travelling and writing on the history of the British Empire, Sir Reginald Coupland turned latterly to writing a book on Welsh and Scottish nationalism which he published in 1954. In 1950 he could write to Thomas Jones, 'As it happens I don't know a single Scot either in the universities or in the administration or in business'. Sir Reginald Coupland to T. Jones, 16 March 1950, Jones Papers, National Library of Wales, Aberystwyth.

90. Cited in Parker, *Mackinder*, p. 80.

91. D. Cameron Watt, *Succeeding John Bull*, *passim*; R. Jeffreys-Jones, 'The Inestimable Advantage of Not Being English: Lord Lothian's American Ambassadorship, 1939–40', *Scottish Historical Review*, lxiii, (April 1984), pp. 105–10.

92. H. Milton, ed., *Lord Dufferin's Speeches and Addresses* (London, 1882), pp. 86–90; Sir A. Lyall, *The Life of the Marquis of Dufferin and Ava*, 2 vols (London, 1905).

Dufferin, an English-educated Ulster aristocrat, anciently of Scottish descent, who refused to be called an Englishman but gloried in the service of Britain, went on to serve the Crown as Governor-General of Canada, Viceroy of India, and Ambassador to St Petersburg and Paris. He remained, however, a man of the west, a perfect choice to unveil the inscription on Bristol's memorial Cabot Tower. Earlier, sailing up the splendid coastline of British Columbia, he knew that, in one sense, he was at the furthermost boundary of Britain. So, in another sense, was he when he received both a rapturous send-off and return home in the Ulster Hall, Belfast, *before* going on to London, the edge of the Atlantic world which he knew so well. He was well aware, however, that there was nothing static in the relationships within the British Empire. The core and the periphery, he implied, might so shift that the writings of Mr Charles Dickens might hold sway over the English-speaking community when all the more imposing political structures of the age had passed away.

18

Varieties of Britishness

Once upon a time, the story goes, there was an Englishman, an Irishman and a Scotsman. However, in this story there were not three people but one: the Englishman, the Irishman and the Scotsman was Arthur Conan Doyle. His name, life and career make him difficult to define. Was he British?

It is perhaps appropriate that the thoughts of a historian on 'varieties of Britishness' are offered by an Englishman who has not had a home in England for two decades. Do not let us suppose that historians, with only minor exceptions, are disembodied beings whose writing has no relation to their own lives and experiences. Our perception of the past is inevitably filtered through our grasp of the present. I was brought up in the West of England, went to University in Oxford, had my first academic post in the North of England, and have since been in professional appointments in North Wales and the West of Scotland for roughly a decade each. This is by no means my first visit to Northern Ireland. Such peregrination inevitably leads to a concern with 'Britishness' from a perspective not invariably shared by the legions of historians who have written on 'British history' without pausing to consider what they mean by the term.

I realise that my topic may have a certain connexion with a notion of necessary political and cultural balance. Reflections on cultural diversity in Ireland must be followed by reflections on cultural diversity in Britain. Difficult and delicate though it is, therefore, we must address ourselves at the outset to this implied contrast. On the one hand, there is 'Irishness', and on the other there is 'Britishness' — which may be no more than an empty can — of worms rather than beans.

If we are to get anywhere with this basic problem we must establish our spatial and chronological perspectives. In May 1987 I was privileged to be one of a group of historians invited to attend the first ever international conference in the People's Republic of China exclusively devoted to British History.[1] Scholars came from all over China to attend and fraternize with the foreign delegation. It was part of my task to inform them of recent developments in British historiography and at the same time to explain many features of British political, social and cultural life to people who had never left China. Such an exercise in cross-cultural communication was both

---

1. The conference has been published, in Chinese, under the title *British History and the Modernisation of China* (Nanjing, 1989).

stimulating and exhausting. In these circumstances, talk of widely diverging cultural traditions within the small group of islands off mainland Europe lacked a certain plausibility. From the massive perspective of China, the differences between 'England', 'Ireland', 'Scotland' and 'Wales' — tiny blobs on the map — seemed modest and manageable. Cultural traditions which we may suppose to be distinct, self-contained and sometimes mutually hostile within Ireland/Britain appeared to be mere rifts within a common inheritance of political discourse or religious conviction when viewed from China in the late twentieth century. And, insofar as an 'Irishness' or a 'Britishness' could be discerned, it might seem little more than a version, no doubt the original version, of a culture encountered in the 'English-speaking world', from Australia to the United States. It was illuminating and rather quaint for Chinese scholars to learn about the origins of institutions and conventions now more frequently encountered elsewhere, though frequently transformed in the process of implantation and adaptation. Distance, of course, lends distortion as well as enchantment to the view, and I am not suggesting that my experience in a southern Chinese city renders this conference redundant. It may help, however, to remind ourselves that our 'authentic' and well-manicured cultural traditions frequently seem indistinguishable or cross-bred to 'outsiders'.

It is not surprising, therefore, that there is a growing disposition among some historians in the United States, in particular, to write about the history of Great Britain and Ireland from a perspective which attempts to grapple with the totality of these complex insular relationships. They aspire to embrace the 'Atlantic Archipelago' and in so doing to 'recognise a physical reality which was and is a community of island-dwellers whose political lives have ever been closely related'.[2] They resort to this ungainly terminology simply because any other has inherent problems of acceptance. To speak of 'the British Isles' in this connexion would presuppose the answer we are exploring. Nevertheless, this American author does speak of the 'island-dwellers' — and there is, of course, a vast diversity of islands that can be included within the Archipelago — as 'a community'. That is what it looks like, apparently, from Salt Lake City. It is, too, the Atlanticism of the Archipelago which receives emphasis. On the other hand, present political tendencies push an enigmatic 'Europeanness' to the fore. From Brussels, for example, the new hub of the European Community, we could perceive 'off-shore' islands, all in some sense 'European' but also closer together in their very insularity, with all that entails, than would be readily admitted in the islands themselves.

I have learnt much from these distant vistas and am convinced that we would all benefit from a greater awareness of where others now often locate us, however we continue to define ourselves. I am not, therefore, in talking about 'Britishness', committing myself to the view that it exists as a discrete phenomenon to be sharply differentiated from 'Irishness' at every conceivable

---

2. Richard S. Tompson, *The Atlantic Archipelago: A Political History of the British Isles* (Lewiston, NY, 1986), p. 1.

point. I do not believe that 'Irishness' is confined to the physical island of Ireland or that 'Britishness' is confined to Britain, either in the past or the present. I think it is obvious that much of what I say about 'Britain' has application in Northern Ireland, but I will not pause at each relevant point to say so.

'Britain' has had a troubled history as a term and a brief glance helps us to begin to understand the problems of 'Britishness'. 'Britain' might have lapsed after the withdrawal of the Romans and the defeat of the 'Britons' at the hands of Saxon 'proto-English' invaders if it had not been for the fact that the regal style *rex Britanniae* had an appeal to certain Saxon kings. William the Conqueror also liked to be regarded as monarch '*totius Britanniae*'. During the middle ages there was considerable disparity of usage. Sometimes 'Britannia' was taken to be synonymous with that precociously united country of England but some Scots writers took exception to the fact that many Englishmen and foreigners used 'Britain' both as the name for the Roman province and also for the whole island. At the beginning of the sixteenth century, however, the Scottish writer John Major declared: 'At the present there are, and for a long time have been, to speak accurately, two kingdoms in the island; the Scottish kingdom, namely, and the English . . . Yet all the inhabitants are Britons . . . all men born in Britain are Britons, seeing that on any other reasoning Britons could not be distinguished from other races'. It was James VI and I in 1604 who proclaimed his assumption of the style 'King of Great Britain, France, and Ireland'. In the subsequent century, however, the new title was very contentious and only gained final acceptance after the Anglo-Scottish Union of 1707.[3]

'Britain' therefore has a very lengthy but also rather awkward pedigree. On both sides of the northern border, men had been accustomed to think of themselves as English or Scots (though we cannot be precise about what sense of 'nationality' accompanied these descriptions). They continued to do so and it seemed odd, though not unknown, to be referred to as a 'Briton'. The term 'North Britain' gained status in Scotland but its acceptability was disappearing at the end of the nineteenth century and 'Scotland' returned.

The English had felt no serious temptation to adopt 'South Britain' and to describe themselves as 'South Britons'. Indeed, speaking generally, Englishmen were not inclined to consider themselves 'Britons' at all. 'Rule Britannia', which asserted that they would never be slaves, was probably the only occasion on which Englishmen collectively referred to 'Britons' — and of course the words were written by a Scotsman. The English were John Bull characters who tended to suppose that 'England' really included everybody. The juvenile members of the Primrose League in Croydon in 1900 were asked to complete a question paper which talked about 'the English Parliament' without any hesitation. Continentals referred to 'England' and frequently still do.[4]

3. I owe this paragraph to Denys Hay's appendix 'The Use of the Term "Great Britain" in the Middle Ages' in his *Europe; The Emergence of an Idea* (Edinburgh, 1968), pp. 128–44.

4. See in general R. Colls and P. Dodd, ed., *Englishness: Politics and Culture, 1880–1920* (London, 1986); M. Pugh, *The Tories and the People, 1880–1935* (Oxford, 1985), p. 214.

Likewise, by the end of the nineteenth century, Welsh identity (Mid-West Britain?) no longer permitted simple talk of 'the two kingdoms' (England and Scotland); there had to be a place for the principality and that hybrid 'England and Wales' was under threat.[5]

These reassertions pointed to the demise of 'Britain' as the universally-accepted all-purpose name of the country. England, Scotland, Wales and Ireland could not be relegated to oblivion. It was perhaps fortunate, in these circumstances, that the Postmaster-General had had the foresight to make sure that no name was attached to the country on postage stamps. Likewise, when the Historical Association was founded in 1906, it was decided that it would be best not to give any hint about its nationality. Matters never went so far as to require any change in the regal style to make, say, King Edward VII, monarch of 'England, Scotland, Ireland and Wales' rather than of 'Great Britain', but 'Great Britain' had become, and was to remain, problematic.

I have written elsewhere of *Integration and Diversity* in nineteenth-century Britain, altered (wisely?) in the paperback version to *Nineteenth-Century Britain; England, Scotland and Wales; The Making of a Nation*.[6] I tried in those lectures to examine those pressures which made for 'integration' and those for 'diversity'. The field of my enquiry ranged from religion and politics to music and sport. As I have already suggested, I do not believe that a British 'cultural conformity' was the outcome of this interactive process. It was scarcely to be expected, in a century of enormous economic and industrial change, that 'cultural traditions' would remain untouched from Sussex to Sutherland, but nonetheless a plurality of identities remained, both within and between England, Scotland and Wales.

If, therefore, we position ourselves for a moment in that critical decade before 1914, when so much happened that shaped the future alignments of these islands, it would perhaps have appeared puzzling to have been speaking about 'Varieties of Britishness'. It was rather that the very term 'Britishness' implied the existence of cultural and, to some extent, political diversity.

A visitor to Perth would not have supposed that he was still at home in Exeter — strange banks and strange banknotes would be one problem, but there would also be striking differences in vernacular architecture. Place names and personal names reinforced a sense of 'foreignness', yet the visitor could communicate, although sometimes with a certain difficulty. The common language purported to be English, though doubtless extensive conversation would have revealed unfamiliar words and different ways of constructing sentences. 'Britishness' presupposed an English, more or less 'standard' and a *lingua franca*, rendering feasible the transmission of 'cultural inheritance' throughout the kingdom. Dickens could be read in Edinburgh and Scott in

5. K.O. Morgan, *Wales: Rebirth of a Nation, 1880–1980* (Oxford and Cardiff, 1981).
6. K.G. Robbins, *Nineteenth-Century Britain: Integration and Diversity* (Oxford, 1988) and paperback as *Nineteenth-Century Britain; England, Scotland and Wales: The Making of a Nation* (Oxford, 1989). See also id above, pp. 239–58.

London, although no one could doubt where the authors 'belonged'. The transmission of such a 'British culture' did not preclude the existence of a literature which was more specific and limited in appeal to particular region or nation, either by virtue of language or of cultural context. The English reader, for example, might not find it altogether easy to 'tune in' to the local ecclesiastical and political world exemplified in the novels of John Galt, and a Scottish reader might experience a comparable difficulty with say Trollope or Hardy.

Likewise, a visitor to Caernarfon would not have supposed that he was still at home in Canterbury. In this case, the existence of another language in everyday use would have become immediately apparent as a mark of difference in the cultural milieu. The local MP, David Lloyd George, endeavoured to pass on a few words of Welsh to the Prince of Wales. Royal visitors who came to the town for the installation could not fail to notice that this was a distinctive *Kulturgebiet* (region of culture). Canterbury, by contrast, seemed to be deeply expressive of the cultural atmosphere of small-town provincial England, with the cathedral, 'the heart of the Anglican Communion', towering above it. Travellers throughout the length and breadth of Britain could therefore not avoid a certain 'culture shock'.

Yet, despite the variety of landscape and people, it was not necessary to conclude that there was no unity. A common 'political culture' was expressed in a party system which extended throughout Britain with the same labels Whig/Tory, Liberal/Conservative, Liberal Unionist/Labour, even if the flavour of party identity might be different. British Governments depended for their existence on a majority of seats gained throughout Britain — with, of course, the Irish MPs also a significant factor. Yet to put matters so baldly is to oversimplify. The Liberal Party in Wales and in Scotland sought to present itself as the 'national' party and Welsh and Scottish Liberals sometimes pressed for 'Home Rule'. Such aspirations never reached fruition, largely because 'Home Rule' raised as many questions about Welsh or Scottish identity as it claimed to solve. In any case, there was no doubt that Welshmen and Scotsmen could play their full part in British Government. In addition, because there was a disposition among the English to vote Conservative, the Liberal Party needed all the voting strength it could get outside England to be able to form a government. One might therefore regard the last decade of Liberal Government as the high point of a 'British political culture'. The administration, in the person of Campbell-Bannerman, Haldane, Lloyd George and others, contained a disproportionate number of non-Englishmen in its ranks, as was sometimes noted with dismay in England. The territorial dimension of British politics could not infrequently mean that a non-Conservative Government in Britain could exist against the wishes of the majority of English MPs and a Conservative Government could exist against the wishes of the majority of Scottish and Welsh MPs. The 'common British political culture' did exist, but tensions were by no means merely latent in preserving it.

A common 'religious British culture' was expressed in the existence through-out of three major ecclesiastical communities — Roman Catholic, Anglican/Episcopalian and Presbyterian/Free Church. These features gave a certain homogeneity to the British scene, at least at one level. However, religious allegiance was not uniform throughout Britain. There was little left, for example, of indigenous English Presbyterianism. Presbyterianism, in its divided condition, was essentially Scottish in numerical strength and stature. Welsh Calvinistic Methodism had rather different roots. Anglicanism was comparably essentially English, and Scottish and Welsh Episcopalians had to defend themselves against the charge that they belonged to 'alien' churches. Methodism, in its various forms, was everywhere, but nowhere dominant and this was also true of the other Dissenting or Free Churches. The Church of Scotland was 'established', though not in the same way as the Church of England in England. The Anglican Church in Wales was about to be disestablished. In these circumstances, we both can and cannot speak of 'British religion'. The denominational ingredients, as it were, existed throughout Britain, but in sharply different proportions.[7]

In all three countries, churches expressed, created and transmitted a certain sense of identity. At the beginning of the nineteenth century one could have spoken unequivocally of the British self-image as 'Protestant'. For many, a century later, this conception remained, whatever its particular ecclesiastical expression. However, it was in practice modified by the growth of the Roman Catholic community, ubiquitously if far from uniformly. Roman Catholicism grew as a result both of conversions and of Irish immigration. As a result, notably in major urban centres, there was a substantial Roman Catholic presence.[8] It scarcely needs to be said that a major issue was the extent to which that church should consciously strive to perpetuate Irish community feeling amongst its members or how far it should seek to establish itself as an authentically British tradition. It is probably fair to suggest that the prevailing wisdom both desired and accepted a 'marginal' position which was not commensurate with its growing strength. However, it was already apparent to discerning observers in all denominations that 'Non-Churchgoing' was a well-established phenomenon. The question of the twentieth century might not be whether a Protestant tradition remained in the ascendancy but whether the nature of British identity might be transformed by a marginalization of all Christian traditions.

The final point which I wish to make about this period is that the identity of Britain was predominantly conceived as 'imperial'. The British Empire was frequently stated to be the logical expression of British greatness. It was the goal to which all previous British History had pointed. It was an empire in the administration and control of which all the peoples of Britain shared. It

---

7. See above, pp. 85–104.
8. Edward Norman, *The English Catholic Church in the Nineteenth Century* (Oxford, 1984); Roger Swift and Sheridan Gilley, ed., *The Irish in Britain, 1815–1939* (London, 1989).

was their common achievement and gave an added *raison d'être* for their political unity. The maintenance of unity in Britain during the First World War, despite stresses and strains, seemed to testify both to the vitality of the British empire — Greater Britain — and the cohesion of Britain. In the latter case, of course, the United Kingdom of Great Britain and Ireland was in process of anguished dissolution. The eventual constitutional settlement, however, gave the appearance of strengthening a sense of 'Britishness'. The absence of a major bloc of anti-Union Irish MPs from Westminster brought the welcome disappearance of 'national' issues, however much the existence of the Irish Free State gave rise to certain security anxieties. Devolved government in Northern Ireland had the consequence of very substantially removing Irish issues altogether from the concern of British MPs. Of course, Northern Ireland remained part of the United Kingdom but its internal affairs and cultural distinctiveness did not impinge on Britain. I believe I am right in stating that only the rather exceptional figure of Lord Londonderry served in both a Northern Ireland and a Westminster Cabinet in the inter-war period.

In a general sense, this condition lasted for nearly half a century. Successive governments in London in the 1920s gave fresh emphasis to the British Empire as a place in which ex-servicemen, in particular, should settle. There were all the splendours of the Empire Exhibition at Wembley in the mid 1920s and Glasgow still thought it was in the right mood when it organised Scotland's Empire Exhibition in 1938.[9] In the meantime, however, colonial nationalism had become more demanding and specific recognition of the equal status of the self-governing Dominions had been made at the 1926 Imperial Conference (to be codified in the 1931 Statute of Westminster). There were also stirrings in India which led, eventually, to the 1935 Government of India Act. It was a measure bitterly opposed by Churchill, who feared the disappearance of the brightest jewel in the imperial crown. There was a growing awareness of the many challenges being presented to Britain's position as a world power. It was one element in the policy of 'Appeasement'.[10] In the end, however, the British government soberly and apprehensively went to war in 1939. The Prime Minister suspected that, even if Britain did 'win', the price it would have to pay would undermine the British Empire. Churchill, a few years later, declared that he had not become the King's first Minister to preside over the liquidation of the British empire — but by the year of his death, 1965, that empire had virtually passed away.

It is not necessary, here, to go through the stages of that process in detail nor to decide whether it was forced upon a reluctant government or was a splendid act of statesmanship. By any standards, however, the transformation in status and power through which Britain passed in the quarter of a century after the end of the Second World War was of major significance. Of course, the British Empire was, in a sense, transmuted into

9. Bob Crampsey, *The British Empire Exhibition of 1938* (Edinburgh, 1988).
10. K.G. Robbins, *Appeasement* (Oxford, 1988).

the British Commonwealth (subsequently merely the Commonwealth) but the belief that the Commonwealth could still 'project' Britain in the world had to be abandoned, in private if not in public. Decolonization had many difficult moments, but it did not precipitate the kind of domestic crisis which led, in France, to the fall of the Fourth Republic. Even so, it would be unwise to underestimate the profound psychological adjustments which governments and people had to make to this changed condition. The famous words of Dean Acheson — that Britain had lost an empire and not found a role — were strongly resented at the time, but were apposite.

Britain had reached a point when the hopes and myths which had sustained and underpinned national existence — the imperial destiny — no longer had validity. This moment had also been reached at a time when the Cold War dominated international politics and when Western European countries were growing more prosperous and assertive. They seemed determined to press for some kind of 'European Community'. The British economy itself seemed sluggish, to say the least. It is difficult in all these developments to establish what is cause and what is effect. The result, however, was that a protracted discussion of 'Britishness' commenced which has not yet come to an end.

One school of thought has discerned, often with approval, the break-up of Britain. It was argued that 'Britain' had meaning and purpose in a different world from that which now existed. 'Britishness' was a diminishing commodity world-wide as the pattern of immigration into Australia changed dramatically and Canadian governments sought to cope with the French problem by espousing 'multiculturalism'. It was also a wasting asset in these islands. In both Wales and Scotland nationalist parties had been founded in the interwar period. Plaid Cymru's primary concern was with linguistic and cultural issues as it became clear that the Welsh language was steadily losing ground. The Scottish National Party had a broader concern for what it considered to be the erosion of Scotland's individuality. Both parties had an appeal to certain intellectuals, but did not gain mass support, though the SNP briefly won a by-election at the end of the Second World War. Only in the mid 1960s did they begin to present a serious political challenge in certain constituencies. The discovery of oil in the North Sea prompted the demand that 'Scotland's Oil' should be used for Scotland's benefit. Gwynfor Evans of Plaid Cymru and Winifred Ewing of the SNP reached Westminster pledged to seek independence. By the middle seventies, the SNP seemed to be 'setting the agenda'. There had to be a Royal Commission on the Constitution. The Labour Government, in increasingly difficult circumstances, moved towards measures which would give substantial devolution of power to both Scotland and Wales. In the event, the electorate in both Wales and Scotland did not give the proposals sufficient support, in the former case emphatically rejecting the scheme. The incoming Conservative Government set its face firmly against 'devolution'. A phase in modern British history had apparently come to an end.[11]

11. I have discussed these issues at greater length above, pp. 227–38.

It is not easy to interpret the significance of these developments. On the one hand, the referendum results could be held to show that there was more attachment to 'Britishness' than had been frequently alleged by partisans in the debate. In Wales, in particular, the 'cultural tradition' had proved a source of division rather than unity. Non-Welsh-speakers, particularly in South Wales, alleged that in a Wales with a devolved administration Welsh-speakers would gain hegemony. It was quite possible to have a Welsh identity which did not depend upon knowledge of the language. Welsh-speakers frequently asserted, on the contrary, that in the longer term it could not survive the death of the language. The political divisions in the principality remained. The substantial political successes of Plaid Cymru in the ensuing decade were confined to north-west Wales and thus reinforced the notion that it was the vehicle for localised cultural defence rather than a party capable of 'liberating' Wales as a whole from the 'British' embrace. In Scotland, however, although political fortunes have fluctuated, the SNP has continued to be a substantial political presence, although now with the slogan of 'Independence in Europe', reversing a previous hostility to the European Community. The Labour Party in Scotland has in turn supported a rather different measure of devolution to be introduced if Labour ever forms another British Government.

It seems self-evident, therefore, from this discussion, that 'Britishness' is a capacious concept. Understandably, political scientists have great difficulty in finding a definition of Britain's essential character. From certain points of view it is a 'multi-national' state, from other points of view it is a 'national' state. In some respects it is a unitary state, but in others it permits a considerable and confusing diversity. The distinctive cultural attributes — musical, linguistic, educational — have all received additional emphasis and central funding. For many, it remains undesirable to seek an integral nationalism which obliterates all traces of 'Britain' in a headlong pursuit of 'Balkanisation', though such a course is not without its attractions for others. From time to time, there is revived talk of a 'Federation of Britain' or of some structure which would be capable of satisfactorily embracing the totality of relations within these islands. It is reminiscent of talk of 'Home-Rule-All-Round' before 1914.

It is entirely consonant with my general line of reasoning that the two greatest Ulstermen of the nineteenth century — James Bryce and William Thomson, Lord Kelvin — both matured in Glasgow and then proceeded to Oxford and Cambridge. It was Bryce, as you would expect, who addressed himself to the question of 'England' and 'Ireland' in 1884 and concluded, from his perspective and background, that 'the Irish, according as you look at them from this side or from that, are and are not a part of the British nation'. My argument, a century later, is that this formulation now appears to give to the concept of 'the British nation' a concreteness and coherence which it lacks. In this respect, however, it is not vastly different from the concept of 'the Irish Nation'. The yearning for an Ireland (and particularly a Northern Ireland) with 'Brits out' does as much injustice to the complexities of individual identity as simply unqualified assertion that 'Ulster is British'. I do not need to bombard you with studies, both historical and contemporary, which attempt to establish what portion of the population considers itself to be 'British', what proportion 'Irish' and what proportion 'Ulster'. Whenever I read these analyses I find the hardness of these definitions deceptive. My experience suggests that it is only in particular contexts such labels have significance. Divisions occur as much within individuals as between peoples.

Speaking personally, therefore, I regard 'Britain' as a house with many mansions which can and should contain 'Ulster' within the United Kingdom for so long as this remains the wish of most of its inhabitants. It should be self-evident that this does not mean that 'Ulster' can or should be a 'little England' or a 'little Scotland'. It is transparently *sui generis*, a thing in itself. It is, of course, very unfashionable in many academic and other quarters to speak favourably of 'the United Kingdom'. Yet, despite particular grievances which some of us may feel, I believe that the endless quest for unity — not uniformity — is as necessary as the proper assertion of individuality. Neither the study of the past nor of the present offers much ground for supposing that this is easy. It seems to me that the new situation in 'these islands' since the 1960s — which may or may not be the consequences of living in a post-imperial society — is that the reconciliation of these imperatives within Ulster (and within Ireland) can now be seen to be not a peculiar feature of a peripheral outpost, uncertainly articulated to a homogeneous mainland, but perhaps the central issue confronting the United Kingdom conceived still as a state but now itself within a European Community which also has this task before it.

Then, as now, however, the fundamental problem is England and 'Englishness'. Peripheral peoples of the state have long experience of schizophrenetic identity, with all its joys and difficulties. The English, speaking generally, have not had that experience. The solid antiquity of the English state is remarkable. It has dominated *totius Britanniae* in various forms with varying degrees of consent and coercion. It has not been conquered or subjected to assimilation into what has been perceived to be a norm by any aliens. England has remained massively the most populous and powerful element within these islands. There may be some tension between 'North' and 'South' but no support for the restoration of the Anglo-Saxon heptarchy in order to make each unit on a par with Scotland or Wales. However, it is in England that 'British' institutions exist, such as, for example, the British Museum. There are national museums, libraries and galleries in Scotland and Wales but there is nothing that is 'English national' in this sphere. It is England that has absorbed, and continues to absorb, hundreds of thousands of Irish, Scottish and Welsh families. It is not too much of a paradox to suggest that it is in England that the 'blending of Britain' has historically occurred. However, it may be the case that 'Englishness' will revive and lose interest in 'Britain' altogether. Just as the British Empire has contracted to 'Britain', so England will return to the *fons et origo* of the entire enterprise. There was, for example, considerable impatience, in the late 1970s, with the amount of time and energy devoted to the proposed Welsh and Scottish legislation. It is not impossible to hear expressed the view that 'the Scots' and 'the Welsh' want to have their cake and eat it and that they should be made to choose which it is they really want. An 'English backlash' hovers in the background.

One further factor should also be mentioned as of great significance in all these matters. Our discussion has centred on the patterns of interaction between what might be described as the 'indigenous' cultural traditions of these islands. However, the decades since the 1950s have seen very substantial immigration from the West Indies, the Indian sub-continent, and many other parts of the world. Immigration of various groups — Jews, Poles, Germans and others — has not been a novelty. However, the scale of recent immigration and the range of cultural tradition that has accompanied it raises issues about 'Britishness' which would not have been conceivable at the beginning of the century. Is 'Britishness' a complex of political and civic values, now detached from any specific anchorage in Christianity, to which all citizens must assent? Can 'Britishness' permit/encourage/tolerate beliefs, values and practices which may have their own logic but which can be remote from those which have informed the legislation and social arrangements which have come to prevail in these islands? At what point is the cultural gap so wide that society cannot function?

This is speculation, but it draws attention to the changed and changing perceptions of power and identity across our offshore islands. Use of that term reminds us that in the contemporary world no island is a continent entire in itself. It is the English who have now to struggle with the fact that they are but one of many European varieties. They have to accommodate themselves to being part of a wider whole, even if one of uncertain structure and destination. The 'varieties of Britishness' have historically flourished or suffered in a context where ultimately the 'norm' has rested in London. It is not clear that this will continue to be the case, but the pace of change is such that it is equally not clear what the nature of our common European home is going to be.[12]

12. This lecture has also drawn on material to be found in such diverse sources as Anthony P. Cohen, ed., *Belonging; Identity and Social Organisation in British Rural Cultures* (Manchester, 1982); Anthony P. Cohen, ed., *Symbolising Boundaries; Identity and Diversity in British Cultures* (Manchester, 1986); D.H. Akenson, *Small Differences; Irish Catholics and Irish Protestants, 1815–1922: an International Perspective* (Kingston and Montreal, 1988); A.H. Birch, *Nationalism and National Integration* (London, 1989); Ulf Hedetoft, *British Colonialism and Modern Identity* (Aalborg, 1985); John Darwin, *Britain and Decolonisation: The Retreat from Empire in the Post-War World* (London, 1988); E. Tonkin et al., *History and Ethnicity* (London, 1989); K.G. Robbins, *The Eclipse of a Great Power: Modern Britain, 1870–1975* (London, 1983).

19

Wales and the Scottish Connexion

I like to think that a historian who is neither a Welshman nor a Scot can bring to this topic a friendly but detached curiosity. As far as I am aware, there is nothing in print that discusses 'Wales and the Scottish Connexion'. One conclusion that might be drawn from this omission is that it is a non-subject. Indeed, in his *Word from Wales*, published in 1941, Wyn Griffith made the following remark as he attempted to describe the condition of the Welsh people, painfully emerging, as he saw it, from a nineteenth-century puritan heritage: 'It may be that Scotland is in much the same condition, but Wales and Scotland never meet except upon the Rugby football field — there is no cultural contact between the two countries.'[1] As I hope to show, some instructive 'cultural' points can be made even about such muddy encounters, but his central assumption has been echoed elsewhere and seems to be the orthodoxy. Much depends, of course, on what is meant by 'cultural contact', but that is a border country which I will leave with Raymond Williams.

On the other hand, some of the writers on modern British history seem to presuppose some underlying similarity in the cultural formation of Scotland and Wales. In his most recent book on the 1945 Labour government, and elsewhere, for example, Kenneth Morgan writes of 'the two Celtic nations of Scotland and Wales'.[2] Evidently he assumes some sense of common feeling or identity by such a reference. Other writers presumably have something similar in mind when, in this context, they talk about the 'Celtic fringe' and believe Scotland and Wales to be part of it.

My own approach is somewhat different. I hope to suggest, while not being exhaustive or comprehensive, that the contacts between Wales and Scotland have been greater, at various levels, than Wyn Griffith allowed. On the other hand, I confess that I have some difficulty in grasping what is meant by talk of 'Celtic lands'. There is, I believe, a relationship between Wales and Scotland which is not without contemporary political significance. There have been occasions, notably in the recent past when, for better or for worse, their fates

1. Wyn Griffith, *Word from Wales*, (London, 1941), pp. 29–30.
2. K.O. Morgan, *Labour in Power, 1945–1951* (Oxford, 1984), p. 306. It is interesting to note, too, that in the *Oxford Illustrated History of Britain* (Oxford, 1984), p. 539 referring to Nonconformity he writes: 'Even in their strongholds in Wales and Scotland, the chapels were in steady retreat.' This betrays a misunderstanding of the ecclesiastical position in the two countries. In Scotland, the term 'chapel' is reserved exclusively for Roman Catholic places of worship and the Church of Scotland was and is in no sense Nonconformist.

have been linked, but even so such *conjonctures* have not directly arisen from some fundamental similarity. They may be held to spring rather from certain features of the modern industrial structure of the two countries. In such a context, particularly in contemporary terms, their relationship is as likely to be competitive as collaborative.

To start with, the obvious point needs to be made that Wales and Scotland do not share a frontier. Both literally and metaphorically, England stands in between. Thus it is rarely possible to see Wales and Scotland in straightforward bilateral terms. Of course, it was not ever thus. If we turn back to earlier periods, before 'Wales' or 'Scotland' could be said to exist, the sea-culture of the 'Irish' Sea produced close links between Gwynedd and Strathclyde which lasted while Brythonic Celtic survived in Strathclyde. The complexities of philological research into these matters are beyond my competence to judge. Nevertheless, the contacts and connexions were such that it was entirely natural for St Kentigern (or St Mungo), patron saint of Glasgow, to seek refuge in Wales at a time when he was experiencing certain local difficulties in the valley of the Clyde, though no one now seems to believe that he had any connexion with the diocese of St Asaph.[3] Sea traffic, indeed, may still be held a significant means of contact along the west coast of Britain long after the collapse of particular polities in North Wales and the West of Scotland. There was a shipping fraternity which brought Scotsmen and Welshmen together.

In subsequent centuries, over which I must necessarily pass summarily, the kingdom of Scotland was slowly consolidated, but such was the fusion of elements which went to make it — Gaelic, Pictish, 'Scots', Norse, 'Anglo-Norman' — that at almost any stage the broad categorization of 'Celtic' seems to me quite inappropriate. Its cohesion was at best fragile and the authority of the crown over the whole of 'Scotland' tentative. The line of control fluctuated, but it can hardly be claimed that the polity that developed in the Lowlands was essentially or even substantially 'Celtic'. The heartland of Gaeldom in the Highlands and Islands still contrived to go its own way, resisting, so far as possible, the tentacles of Perth or Edinburgh. Indeed, during the centuries of its existence as a separate state, the rulers of Scotland found the Highlanders intractable. While it is an exaggeration, even a distortion, to regard 'Scotland' as a kind of marcher lordship that 'got away with it', there is an element of truth in the notion. Medieval historians will know that there has been considerable interest in these and kindred questions in an essay by Professor Geoffrey Barrow.[4] We must not forget, too, the role of Welshmen in the English campaigns in Scotland. It would not be fitting for me to attempt to disentangle these complex questions of allegiance and identity in

3. Kenneth Jackson, 'The Sources for the Life of St Kentigern' in N.K. Chadwick et al., *Studies in the Early British Church* (Cambridge, 1958); E.G. Bowen, *Saints, Seaways and Settlements* (Cardiff, 1969).

4. G.W.S. Barrow, 'Wales and Scotland in the Middle Ages', *Welsh History Review* (1980–81), pp. 302–19.

the middle ages, except to suggest that there appears to be little manifestation of 'Pan-Celticism'. Nor do I intend to linger in the early modern period, except to add the obvious point that after the Act of Union with England there was no possibility of a totally distinct and independent Welsh relationship with Scotland, even if it had been desired.

It might be said, in the seventeenth century, though scarcely to applause all round, that sooner or later the corollary of the Union of the Crowns in 1603 was the Union of Parliaments. When that union was achieved in 1707, without pausing to examine how it was achieved, I thought it might be interesting to look at a Welsh comment. I chose a sermon by the Rev. Daniel Williams, a 'thanksgiving sermon', though I recognize that other pulpits might have produced different utterances. Daniel Williams, though born and brought up near Wrexham, ministered outside Wales — in Ireland and England. He described the Union as in itself a great mercy, fully consonant with the will of God. 'England', he noted 'is agrandized by the ingrafture of a Nation, so famous for Warriors and Men of Sense; and which is more, a People noted among Foreign Churches for Purity of Religion, eminent for Glorious Martyrs, and for Men enjoying the most intimate Communion with God'. He observed that 'Further Marks of Divine Providence may be expected in Britain United: if not prevented by future Backslidings'.[5] There is no mention of 'Wales' or 'Celtic' in the address. Two years later, Daniel Williams received Doctorates of Divinity from both Glasgow and Edinburgh. On his death, he left the substantial fortune he had acquired through marriage for educational and religious purposes which, as we shall see, have over the centuries, brought about a connexion between Wales and Scotland. The details of the bursary, open to applicants from South Britain, still appear in the Glasgow University *Calendar*.

Under the 1707 Act of Union, of course, Scotland retained its own distinctive legal, ecclesiastical and educational systems. Its ancient universities remained intact and, arguably, stood on the brink of their most distinguished period in the age of Adam Smith and David Hume. The Bank of Scotland was founded in 1695 and other Scottish financial institutions followed. Westminster, however, did not find it difficult to discover Scottish 'managers' who could handle the baffling intricacies of Scottish politics. Scottish peers jostled eagerly for the privilege of being the 'representative' peers who could attend the House of Lords. The 1745 rebellion briefly brought into question this process of accommodation but, with only few exceptions, it served to reinforce the 'North Britishness' of the Lowland centres. The Highlanders who followed Bonnie Prince Charlie were seen, in a sense, as a 'threat' to 'Scotland'. It was well that they were defeated. It has been suggested that the Scottish eighteenth-century pioneering work in what we would now call sociology or

---

5. Daniel Williams, *A Thanksgiving Sermon occasioned by the union of England and Scotland preach'd at Hand-Alley, May the 1st, 1707* (London, 1707).

social anthropology was stimulated by the awareness of a different culture close at hand — a culture to be studied but not emulated. The nineteenth century naturally saw substantial shifts in population and brought Highlanders pouring into Greenock and Glasgow, not to mention the arrival of many thousands of Irish families, Catholic and Protestant. It is not my purpose to discuss in detail the consequences of these changes in Scottish life except to suggest that while in a broad sense, the population balance might be held to be more 'Celtic' throughout Scotland than it had been for centuries, it was a segmented influx, both socially and religiously. It had little impact on the determination of nineteenth-century Scotsmen to play a full part, indeed a disproportionately large part, in the general life of the United Kingdom. We need only list the names of Lord Aberdeen, Lord Rosebery, Arthur Balfour, Campbell-Bannerman, even William Gladstone, to see their success at the very highest level. This list could be supplemented by many other names at ministerial level. Nor, early in the nineteenth century, was the educational drift all in one direction. Two Prime Ministers, Palmerston and Melbourne, were students for a time at Edinburgh and Glasgow respectively. Whereas, before the nineteenth century, the student-elected Rectors of Glasgow University had all been local worthies, or at any rate Scotsmen, thereafter, through until the very recent past, every significant major British politician, almost without exception, felt it necessary to accept nomination.

I mention all these matters to point up the contrast, in broad terms, between Scotland and Wales through most of the eighteenth and nineteenth centuries. Wales lacked, indeed had not possessed, those aspects of institutional distinctiveness which Scotland retained. To put it bluntly, Scotland had never been conquered. There was a sense of assurance and self-confidence among the industrial, landed, and political elites of Scotland which was not present in the same form in Wales. Scotsmen had a very significant place in the administration and commerce of the Empire, not to mention the warriors who were the delight of Daniel Williams. Even if all the 'Scottish' Prime Ministers I have so far mentioned were, at one stage or another, educated in England, that did not mean that they ceased to think of themselves as in some sense Scots. Lord Rosebery, of Mentmore and Derby fame, was also at home in Dalmeny outside Edinburgh and successfully pressed for the creation of the office of Scottish Secretary. Psychologically, therefore, amongst men of this class and background, there was no sense of inferiority; indeed one might detect a rather smug sense of superiority. Such an environment was not congenial ground for the development of 'Pan-Celticism'. As Chief Secretary for Ireland, A.J. 'Bloody' Balfour displayed no sign of picking up the infection. The Court of this King Arthur was a rather different affair. An enormous dinner was held in Edinburgh to celebrate this great Scotsman's achievements in Ireland. He was no less determined in dealings with Highland crofters. Nor should the links between Scotland and Ulster be underestimated.

It is not, therefore, surprising that the nineteenth-century contact between Scotland and Wales, modest though it was, reflected some of this arrogance.

A Scotto-Welsh landed aristocracy did exist, even if it was not very extensive. Scrutiny of Bateman's *The Great Landowners of Great Britain and Ireland*, referring to the 1870s, does produce a few relevant names. Earl Cawdor had some 33,000 acres in Carmarthenshire and 17,000 in Pembrokeshire and 46,000 in Nairn and 4,000 in Inverness, and no land in England. The Earl of Crawford and Balcarres also had substantial land in West Wales and the North of Scotland, though he chiefly lived in Wigan. The Mackintosh had 2,000 acres in Glamorgan, ten times that amount in Inverness, and nothing in England. Amongst lesser figures we find Allan Cameron Bruce-Pryce of Cardiff with 3,000 acres in Glamorgan. Augustus Kennedy-Erskine held land equally in Forfar and, through his mother, in Carmarthen and Brecon. The Harries-Campbell-Davis family had substantial land in Brecon, Carmarthen and Argyll, but nothing in England. Sir James Williams-Drummond of Llandeilo had a patch of Midlothian to supplement substantial Carmarthenshire acres. At Penrhyn we find the surname of Douglas-Pennant and, early in the twentieth century, the adoption of the title Lord Aberconway, obscured Charles Benjamin Bright McLaren, son of the Edinburgh radical and nephew of John Bright.

The most wealthy and conspicuous figure, however, was the Third Marquess of Bute, owner of very considerable property in Cardiff and Glamorgan, exceeding, indeed, his land in Scotland. However, his devotion to Catholicism and liturgical scholarship made him somewhat exceptional amongst the ranks of the Scots/Welsh aristocracy. Dr John Davies describes him as a 'fervent Celt', though this quality was not enough to save him from the strictures of the *Western Mail* for spending in Scotland the wealth he gained in Wales. Lord Bute, it must be said, developed a certain fluency in Welsh, and was given to elaborating on the mission of the Celts on Eisteddfod platforms. The Fourth Marquess sustained the cause, speaking Welsh fluently, though it was alleged that he was 'above all' a patriotic Scot. Certainly he became President of the Scottish History Society.[6]

Other Scotsmen 'on the make', with less impressive pedigrees and less given to reflecting on the mission of the Celts, came to Wales with professional or managerial aspirations. They made no small mark in sectors of Cardiff and Newport society in particular. The Boys' Brigade, the youth organization founded in Glasgow in 1883, formed its first company in Wales under the aegis of a Newport draper who had worked in Glasgow.[7] Scotsmen were playing for Newport Rugby Club from its foundation — Uskside International. Were such men 'indigenized'? It is difficult to say. Certainly Captain Angus Buchanan was proudly displayed in the *Welsh Who's Who* as the winner of a VC during the Great War. Take Sir George (later Lord), Riddell, crony of Lloyd

6. J. Davies, *Cardiff and the Marquesses of Bute* (Cardiff, 1981), pp. 27–30.
7. J. Springhall, B. Fraser and M. Hoare, *Sure and Steadfast: A History of The Boys' Brigade, 1883 to 1983* (London and Glasgow, 1983), p. 50.

George and proprietor of the *News of the World*. He is described by one of Lloyd George's biographers as 'another Scotsman [who] had been a successful solicitor in Cardiff',[8] but another writer calls him 'a wily Welshman'.[9] He was born, brought up and educated in suburban London. Or take another figure, a little later, A.J. Cronin — a graduate of Glasgow university. Did he display any particular sensitivity to the Welsh scene deriving from his Clydeside background?[10]

At another level, Scotsmen came to the expanding coal industry in the early twentieth century to work in mines in South Wales. They contributed further to the population mix of those years. And in North Wales, it was a mining background that was to produce, in the mid twentieth century, the rather unlikely combination of Lord Macdonald of Gwaenysgor. And, indeed, it is perhaps in the mining world that the Scottish-Welsh nexus proved, for a time, to be most enduring, with aspects still evident today. It was to Merthyr that Keir Hardie came, steeped, so Kenneth Morgan tells us, in Scottish history and fable, with a sturdy Scottish patriotism undergirding all. His biographer suggests that he was seized of a vision of the regeneration of man comparable to that of another 'unknown Celtic rebel', Lloyd George.[11] As a Scot, Morgan claims, he had a sentimental attachment for Welshmen. It is true that Hardie did proclaim that Welshmen, 'like all Celts' were 'socialists by instinct' and was deeply moved by a miners' choir singing 'Aberystwyth'. He learnt to sing *Hen Wlad fy Nhadau*, but also accepted that at election time there was 'always that undercurrent of Welsh national feeling to be reckoned with, especially in out of the way places where English is a foreign tongue'. To put in a dash of Saxon scepticism, however, it is difficult to see why Hardie (any more than Lord Bute) should be thought a 'Celt' at all. Certainly, there is no need to posit a Celtic affinity whenever Welshman meets Scotsman. Ramsay MacDonald, for example, may have a better claim to 'Celtic' ancestry. David Marquand, his biographer, sees fit to write in these terms: MacDonald was 'a black and moody Celt, with a Celt's long memory and a Celt's capacity to cherish his grievances'.[12] Obviously, he was made for Wales. Yet we find that he did not get on at all well when he was MP for Aberavon and sought refuge in County Durham. Indeed, the only Welshman with whom MacDonald seems to have got on was that expatriate railwayman from Swindon, J.H. Thomas. And, to put my point in even sharper focus, consider the marriage of Aneurin Bevan and Jennie Lee. There is nothing like detail to deflate generalizations. In her *My Life with Nye*, Jennie recounts that, as a good Scots girl should, she had been having what might be termed a loquacious altercation with her father in

8. D.M. Cregier, *Bounder from Wales* (London, 1976), pp. 136–7.
9. M. Goulden, *Mark My Words!* (London, 1978), pp. 90–1.
10. Cronin graduated MB, ChB from Glasgow University in 1919 and was in general practice in South Wales from 1921 to 1924. His *The Citadel* was published in 1937.
11. K.O. Morgan, *Keir Hardie: Radical and Socialist* (London, 1975), pp. 7, 113, 118, 229.
12. D. Marquand, *Ramsay MacDonald* (London, 1977), p. 408.

Nye's presence. A little later Bevan took her on one side: 'Don't you ever again dare talk to your father like that'. His voice, she recounts, was one of cold, hard hostility to her. She was stunned. Nye had been scared out of his wits by the encounter. Later, she came to understand that her manner of speaking seemed barbarous and northern. The episode, she claimed, utterly changed her relationship with her father — for the worse.[13]

What of the traffic in the opposite direction, from Wales to Scotland? Its primary nineteenth-century nexus was educational. The universities of Scotland offered attractive possibilities for non-Anglican Welshmen of modest means. For those specifically contemplating the ministry, Dr Williams's Bursaries facilitated the path of many and there were intending doctors in abundance. I mention merely a few names from the registers of the University of Glasgow:[14] David Daniel Davis of Carmarthen, physician accoucheur to the Duchess of Kent at the birth of Queen Victoria; Evan Keri Evans, Professor of Logic at UCNW in the early 1890s; Benjamin Thomas Williams whose *The Desirableness of a University for Wales* (1853) was the direct product of his Glasgow years and was not without influence. Two late nineteenth- and early twentieth-century figures are worth a little more comment. The first is Sir Henry Jones who, over decades, flitted in various roles and positions between his native North Wales and Scotland, latterly in Glasgow.[15] Sir Henry Reichel was awarded an honorary LL.D. by the University of Glasgow. Although his philosophical mode is out of fashion, Jones is a man whose career and connexions repay further study. Better known is Tom Jones, 'T.J.' In his *Welsh Broth* he says he was unable to recall what precisely attracted him to Glasgow — except perhaps that Sir Henry Jones was lecturing there. It was a twelve-hour journey from Rhymney, but he found the city lively and stimulating.[16] It might be said that all the academic foundations of his subsequent successful administrative career were laid in Scotland.

Outside the university in Glasgow there was a small Welsh community and, I believe, a Welsh chapel. Certainly in the later decades of the nineteenth century Welshmen came up to work in various specialist aspects of the Clydeside industrial scene. There was, for example, a 'Welsh Row' in Coatbridge.[17] None achieved the fame of a Robert Owen during his twenty-four years at New Lanark at the beginning of the century, but we have to note that Owen left Wales for England as a small boy to be apprenticed, somewhat unbelievably, to a 'Scotch pedlar' in Stamford who had pretensions as a draper. In the ecclesiastical sphere, how far, and to what extent, Welsh Calvinistic Methodists were really Presbyterians was doubtless a more than

13. J. Lee, *My Life with Nye* (London, 1980), pp. 117–18.

14. W. Innes Addison, *A Roll of the Graduates of the University of Glasgow, 1727–1897* (Glasgow, 1898).

15. H.J.W. Hetherington, *The Life and Letters of Sir Henry Jones*, (1924).

16. T. Jones, *Welsh Broth* (London, n.d.), chapter 1, 'Glasgow, 1900–1910'.

17. A.B. Campbell, *The Lanarkshire Miners: A Social History of their Trade Unions, 1775–1874* (Edinburgh, 1979), p. 156.

passing topic of conversation in many a kirk session. Certain Scotsmen were not happy with Eglwys Bresbyteraidd Cymru and doubted whether it was the genuine article. James Moffat's book on Presbyterianism in the late 1920s hints darkly about the defective form of the General Assembly in Wales.[18] At another level, I understand that Scottish divinity had a considerable impact on theological thought and writing in Welsh. It was also possible, however, for divinity students from Wales to be deflected into Scottish pulpits. This could even happen amongst the well-bred congregations of Kelvinside in the West End of Glasgow. In the 1980s both the minister of Glasgow Cathedral and the Principal of the University of Glasgow, Sir Alwyn Williams, were graduates of the University of Wales.

The impact of Welsh politicians in Scotland has not been great, but deserves some mention. The call of duty has brought them north of the border from time to time but, with a few exceptions, they have not lingered unduly. Lloyd George seems not to have found many Celtic responses — his visit to Glasgow during the Boer War and again during the First World War could hardly have ranked amongst his most pleasurable. It was Englishmen, from Asquith to Churchill, who were drawn, to no small extent, into Scottish politics. The few Welsh exceptions as members of parliament for Scottish constituencies derived their positions from somewhat exceptional circumstances. Emrys Hughes represented Ayrshire South, largely a mining constituency, and his acceptability in the constituency derived not from Welshness or some intuitive understanding of Scottish matters but from an awareness of mining in general. Sir David Hunt records that Churchill found Emrys Hughes as a Scottish MP difficult to believe and referred to him as 'the Black Welsh'. On one occasion, he momentarily stopped the loquacious 'Scottish' member in his tracks by retorting an execrably delivered, but rehearsed 'dim o gwbl' (nothing doing) in answer to a tiresome question.[19] The second exception is Roy Jenkins, formerly MP for Glasgow Hillhead. He does mention his Welsh origins but it might be thought that his acceptability in the constituency derives in part from the fact that neither in style nor in substance does he seem 'typically Welsh'[20]

In Wales, however, there is the former leader of Her Majesty's Opposition, in succession to Michael *Mackintosh* Foot, the Rt Hon. Neil Gordon Kinnock, normally described as a Welshman. He is, of course, the product of a Scottish-Welsh union. However, mention of Mr Kinnock does, for some reason, turn one's mind back to the days of the debate over devolution. I do not wish to dwell on either its substance or its outcome but simply to mention several points. In the light of much of what I have said, it comes as no surprise to

---

18. J. Moffat, *The Presbyterian Churches* (London, 1928), p. 72.

19. Sir David Hunt, *On the Spot* (London, 1975), p. 72: William Knox, 'Emrys Daniel Hughes' in W. Knox, ed., *Scottish Labour Leaders, 1918–1939* (Edinburgh, 1984), pp. 144–48. Hughes's father was a Calvinistic Methodist minister.

20. One of Mr Jenkins's Conservative predecessors as MP for Hillhead was Sir Robert Horne, a Glasgow graduate, who began his career as a philosophy lecturer at UCNW Bangor in its early years before going into business and politics.

remember that when the original single Scotland and Wales Bill was proposed, the debates on Scottish aspects took precedence. This was no mere alphabetical listing. It was Scotland which seemed to give the whole matter fundamental urgency; Wales followed on. This can be seen to repeat the pattern of so many administrative and other developments. It was a standard argument for some years that a Welsh Office and a Secretary of State of Wales was logical 'to make Wales like Scotland' (something the Scottish Office was not altogether happy about). It was an irony, therefore, that the first Welsh Secretary was a Scotsman, Sir David Maxwell-Fyfe, even if he was transformed into 'Dai Bananas'. Speaking of the late 1970s, one recent book concludes that 'the details of the proposed Scottish Assembly intruded more into the Welsh debates than the merits of the Welsh case necessitated and thus became significant issues in the passage of the Wales Bill that were nothing to do with Wales'. That, of course, is a matter of opinion. It can be suggested that even if on this occasion aspects of the Scottish Bill had 'nothing to do with Wales' in formal terms, in practice, as we have seen, Scotland had in many ways constituted something of a model or precedent for Wales.[21] At this particular juncture, Scotland and Wales might appear to be working together, but the other side of the coin should never be forgotten. There have been and are circumstances in which Wales and Scotland are in direct competition in the context of Britain as a whole. Steel-making is one example. In the end Ravenscraig did not survive, while the industry continues in South Wales.

I began this essay by referring to Wyn Griffith's remarks and I hope that I have at least shown their inadequacy even if I have not wanted to suggest that Scotland looms *very* large in the life of Wales. You may recall, however, that he made one qualification — 'except on the Rugby Football field'. I can think of no better way to end this lecture than to run on to the pitch. Some material from the Smith and Williams history of the Welsh RFU has the advantage not only that it is, I think, amusing but it also happens to highlight, somewhat unexpectedly, some points made in the body of the essay. It was 1888 before Wales first defeated Scotland, when the defeat was taken poorly. It was a blow to Scottish conceit — the Welsh press had already noted how well dressed Edinburgh crowds were. In 1900, having suffered their fourth defeat in six encounters, the Scots felt that something was wrong with the natural order in the relationship between the two countries. Welsh commentators detected that Scotland could accept defeat 'by her sister country Ireland' and by England 'for the sake of sport', but that Wales has 'got upon her national nerves'. Allegations of commercialism were made — into which murky subject we shall not go. In 1903, however, the treasurer of the Irish Rugby Football Union noted in his report that, the previous year, in Ireland, the Welsh

21. D. Foulkes, J.B. Jones and R.A. Wilsford, *The Welsh Veto: The Wales Act 1978 and the Referendum* (Cardiff, 1983), pp. 45–46.

fellows had broken into the ground and smashed things up. Higher prices would keep them away. He also drew the attention of his committee to the fact that the dinner for the visiting Scotsmen had come to £50 but that for the Welshmen had come to only £30. There was, it seems, a simple explanation. Champagne was given to the Scotsmen but only beer (though plenty of it) to the Welshmen. The latter, it was said, liked the drinks they were used to. The Scotsmen were gentlemen and appreciated a good dinner. By the 1930s, relations between the two countries had improved, perhaps because Wales succeeded in fielding some university-educated men. Ten thousand and more Welshmen flocked to Murrayfield in these years. In 1938, Smith and Williams tell us that some 20,000 Welshmen seemed likely to appear in the capital of Scotland and the LMS went to the lengths of drafting Welsh-speaking railwaymen who would guide these fellows through the station and act 'as interpeters when necessary'. However, several years previously, eight colliers from the Rhondda Fach had chartered a special plane, adorned its front with the Prince of Wales feathers, a leek and daffodil, and took off for Murrayfield. Problems with the compass meant that they ended up watching a soccer match in Portsmouth.[22]

22. D. Smith and G. Williams, *Fields of Praise* (Cardiff, 1980), pp. 123–25, 208, 283.

20

'This Grubby Wreck of Old Glories': The United Kingdom and the End of the British Empire

Over recent decades, when the United Kingdom appeared to some observers to be on the brink of dissolution, it has been fashionable to see this supposed development as an inevitable concomitant of the loss of Empire. 'In 1976', wrote Hugh Seton-Watson,

> the United Kingdom was not united ... The centuries-long process of union of Saxon-Danish, Anglo-Celtic and Celtic-Norse territories into one kingdom appeared in the first half of the twentieth century to have been rather successful. It also seemed to have been accepted by the Celtic Welsh; and the wounds left by the separation and partition of Ireland seemed to be healing. A quarter century later none of this was as true.[1]

Contemporary historians, however, have the difficult task of adjusting to changing moods and situations. The two unsuccessful referendums held in Scotland and Wales on 1 March 1979 brought this particular mood to an end. In the 1980s it was difficult to believe that the United Kingdom was on the point of collapse. However, the problem of the governance of Britain has not disappeared. The place of 'region' in the European Community has added a new dimension to the issue. The fluctuating outcome of the voting in England and Wales shows that it is unwise to conclude, in a rather bland fashion, that the United Kingdom is disunited and that a centuries-long process of union had been brought to an end. It might be argued that historians and politicians both allowed themselves to be persuaded of a reality from which the people were only spared by a referendum. The different results in Scotland and Wales also indicate that it is most unwise to assume that the devolution exercise was part of some grand, uniform historical phenomenon with an inevitable success. In Scotland, the proposals received a narrow endorsement on the part of those who voted, but the opposition was strong. The figure of 40 per cent was not achieved. Six Scottish regions (Central, Fife, Highland, Lothian, Strathclyde and The Western Isles) were in favour of the Scotland Act and six against (The Borders, Dumfries and Galloway, Grampian, Orkney, Shetland and Tayside). In Wales, a weaker set of proposals was decisively defeated and

1. H. Seton-Watson, *Nations and States* (London, 1976), p. 42.

not a single Welsh county voted in favour.[2] For better or worse, therefore, it would appear that, at the lowest, the present structure of the United Kingdom has more support than any alternative. To assert that firmly is, of course, not to deny the existence of important segments of opinion in Scotland and Wales who do wish to establish separate states. These groups may wax and wane in the years to come. Devolution, if it ever comes, may, as some of its supporters argue, prove the stepping-stone to an independent Scotland or it may, as other supporters argue, strengthen the United Kingdom. At present, however, it remains hyperbole to speak of the United Kingdom as 'disunited'. Indeed, in 1976, Seton-Watson did try to reduce the force of his own assertion by arguing that 'loyalty to a common British homeland, devotion to the British crown and pride in the British form of civilisation' were not dead and were not confined to the middle-aged or the middle class. In a footnote, he further revealed his personal opinion that the break-up of the United Kingdom would be a disaster.[3] So, perhaps, he was momentarily giving way to a bout of pessimism.

When the United Kingdom was believed to be coming to an end, it was fashionable to see a connexion with the end of the British Empire. During the devolution campaign, for example, Jan Morris, who has written extensively on the British Empire, contributed an article with the impressive, if untrue title, 'The Hills are Alive with the Sound of Devolution'. She argued that

> In the days of the never-setting sun all the pride of Empire was there for the sharing, and to be part of one of the most vital and exciting of the world's Powers was certainly a compensation. But who gets satisfaction from the present state of the Union? Who is really content with this grubby wreck of old glories? Is there anyone, except those with a vested interest in the thing, who does not yearn for a new beginning?[4]

Such a piece was, of course, avowedly persuasive and polemical, but the thesis is one which had wide acceptance. Seton-Watson appeared to accept the connexion when he added that not only was the United Kingdom not

---

2. In response to the question 'Do you want the provisions of the Scotland Act, Wales Act 1978, to be put into effect?' the totals were:

In Scotland:	Yes	=	1,230,937	(32.85 per cent)
	No	=	1,153,502	(30.78 per cent)
In Wales:	Yes	=	243,048	(11.9 per cent)
	No	=	956,330	(46.9 per cent)

It is too early yet to assess the significance of the Scottish result, but it is difficult to reconcile it with the assumption, based on apparently 'hard' data that 'the level of support for devolution or home rule of some sort has stood at around 75 per cent for a very long time: from the period before the large increase in the nationalist vote.' If there has been 'a gradual restructuring of the political consciousness of the Scottish electorate in such a way that they began to perceive themselves as Scots in terms of their political interests rather than as, for example, members of the working class', it is surprising that a different result was not achieved. See J. Brand, *The National Movement in Scotland* (London, 1978), pp. 300–1.

3. Seton-Watson, *Nations and States*, pp. 42 and 487.

4. *The Daily Telegraph*, 24 February 1979.

united but 'Great Britain was no longer great, due to the actions not of its enemies but of its own citizens.' We are not concerned here with the second clause in that statement, but with the implied assumption that Great Britain and the British Empire were interdependent structures; together they fell. It is this assumption that is questioned in what follows, though it is recognized that, in the nature of things, proof is not possible.

It is incontestable that in the thirty years after 1947 the British Empire was dismantled and, as part of the same process, the influence of the United Kingdom in world affairs slumped. Of course, self-government for India and Pakistan did not come as a totally unexpected development; quite the contrary. While few forecast the rapid decolonization elsewhere which did occur, the vital principle had been conceded. The end of empire was clearly in sight, but in 1948, in his essay on 'Nationality and Liberty', Namier spoke confidently of 'a historical process, operating within a geographically determined framework' which had 'produced a British island nationality which comprises the English, Scots and Welsh, and to which Ulster adheres . . . The political life of the British island community centres in its Parliament at Westminster which represents men rooted in British soil.'[5] As those words almost indicate, the United Kingdom had just emerged from a war which had been conducted without any apparent political strain between its constituent parts. A few nationalists in Wales and Scotland described the war as the 'English' war, but their comments carried little weight. Thirty years later, when the Empire was indeed no more, that 'British island nationality' also seemed, to some, no more. Did not the chronology fit very snugly and make inference unavoidable?

Clearly, the fact that two developments seemed to be happening at the same time does not, in itself, establish a connexion. Chronology, if a necessary basis for such a hypothesis, is not a sufficient one. Discussion of other post-imperial metropolitan societies, may disclose a tendency to political disintegration on regional, ethnic or linguistic lines. But even if such a pattern does occur, one would still need to move from the general to the particular and to demonstrate that the United Kingdom's development was a part of a general process, part of the 'imperial hangover'. Of course, an enquiry which confined itself to ex-imperial states would be of limited value. Broad political tendencies must be looked at on a world-wide basis for comparison to be helpful. If centrifugal or fissiparous tendencies were only apparent in states which had recently ceased to be the possessors of substantial empires, then indeed it would seem likely that the special circumstances of decolonisation might be held responsible for these developments. Clearly, in the contemporary world there are many conflicts revolving round the relative position of linguistic or cultural communities within states which have not undergone the experience of loss

5. L.B. Namier, *Vanished Supremacies* (London, 1962), p. 47.

of empire. The present crisis in the Canadian federal system, for example, does not arise from the loss of an imperial role. Even in Switzerland, tension between French and German speakers has led to the establishment of a new canton. In Spain, the problems in relationships between Basques, Catalans and Madrid arose afresh with the change of regime, but can hardly be said to be 'post-imperial' in character. It would also be rather dubious to suggest that the deterioration in relations between Flemings and Walloons arose from the demise of Belgium's rather curious colonial empire. Where there is a revolt of the regions against the centre, it occurs in states which have never had empires as much as in former imperial powers. The phenomenon of the 'new federalism' in the United States cannot be adequately explained in terms of 'loss of empire'.[6]

To argue that the loss of imperial glory naturally created a situation of hostility to the concept of the United Kingdom seems to involve the belief that the Empire must have been a vital cement of that unity. However, it is difficult to see that the late nineteenth and early twentieth-century constitutional structure of the United Kingdom had a very close connexion with the fact of Empire. The United Kingdom was not created in order to form a basis for overseas expansion. English colonisation overseas began before the consolidation of the United Kingdom. It is also misleading to suppose that the imperial era saw an inexorable process of internal fusion. The partial break-up of the United Kingdom occurred at a time when the British Empire still appeared to have considerable vitality. The 'scramble for Africa' did not prevent the emergence of the Irish Home Rule movement and the development of greater national consciousness in Scotland and Wales. Imperialists were very alarmed about the implications of these developments for the future of the Empire, because if one central government was thought inadequate for the United Kingdom of Great Britain and Ireland, how could the Empire as a whole be kept together? It seemed that internal divisions might precipitate the loss of Empire rather than the other way round.

Yet, to stress that some well-placed commentators felt that the whole United Kingdom was about to break up in the mid 1880s when the Empire was still expanding, does not settle matters completely. After all, the United Kingdom did not disintegrate, and the fact of empire may have been a reason why it did not do so. It is certainly true that all four 'home' countries had a stake in the overseas expansion. The Empire provided an area of common settlement, though this did not mean that in Canada, Australia or New Zealand the distinct origins of United Kingdom settlers did not still manifest themselves. In relation to their total proportion of the United Kingdom, the Irish and the Scots settled within the Empire to a larger extent than the English or Welsh. Contacts with Ireland and Scotland were strongly maintained, but it was a world in which the existing colonists and the new settlers were all, in some

6. V. Bogdanor, *Devolution* (Oxford, 1979), p. 1.

sense, British. It would not have made sense, at least in the period before the First World War, to think of a relationship between Scotland and Australia which could exist without reference to the United Kingdom as a whole. Scotland and Australia were both part of the ill-defined but nevertheless real 'British family of nations'.

However, if aspirations towards self-government had developed more strongly in Scotland in the late nineteenth century, it is difficult to believe that possible implications for Scots overseas would have been a decisive consideration in the minds of most Scots. It did not deter the Irish. Unfortunately, Irish attitudes towards the British Empire in the late nineteenth century have not been the subject of much research, but Irishmen undoubtedly participated in the functioning of the imperial system and had a certain pride in it. Such participation did not prevent the demand for Home Rule or, latterly, for full self-government. The existence of the British Empire facilitated continuing contact between Irishmen at home and abroad, but it was not vital for the maintenance of such contacts. Irish Australians in 1914 were willing to fight with their fellow-Australians in the common cause of the British Empire. However, the opposition to conscription in Australia was substantially assisted by Irish-Australian criticism of the British treatment of those involved in the 1916 rising. The relative indifference of Irishmen to Empire and their willingness to put themselves in the position of the colonized was, however, rather special. In Great Britain, there was little doubt that the British Empire was an important common enterpise. The government of that Empire was the most challenging task that politicians or administrators could aspire to. In this sense, it may be admitted that in this era the Empire did strengthen the unity of the United Kingdom but the Empire did not create that unity nor did its mere existence sustain it.

'I am more inclined for a London career', wrote a young North Wales solicitor in early 1884, 'a fellow may make a successful lawyer down here and amass a tidy — tho' not a large fortune; but as for any higher object — fame — London is the place for that.' He wished fervently to achieve a reputation as a public speaker, but that would be an impossibility in Wales where there were so many good public speakers already. Besides, he would have to speak in Welsh, and his reputation thereby would be confined to this 'stunted principality'. Six years later, the lawyer, David Lloyd George, was elected to what his brother called 'the historic English parliament'.[7] By 1910 he was in the forefront of British politics — a piece of Celtic infiltration which was not universally welcomed. Noting that for years Germany had been content to be governed by a 'denationalized mountebank' like Bülow, in permitting the advance of a 'Celt from the lower regions' Sir Cecil Spring-Rice felt that the English were following a fashion.[8] After another six years, it was as Prime

---

7. W.R.P. George, *The Making of Lloyd George* (London, 1976), pp. 115, 171.
8. S. Gwynn (ed.), *The Letters and Friendships of Sir Cecil Spring-Rice* (London, 1929), ii, pp. 159–60.

Minister that David Lloyd George presided over the destiny of the British Empire at its most perilous hour. Everything depended upon a representative of the 'five-foot-five' nations. Strangely, the Archbishop of Canterbury, a Scot, wrote to Lloyd George about the moment being very critical for 'English history'.[9] It seemed that English, Irish, Scots and Welsh came together without reserve in defence of an empire which was an expression of their 'Britishness'. Wales registered a higher proportion of troops to population then either England or Scotland.[10] The Welsh Guards were formed as was the Welsh Division. Scotland was already amply endowed with distinguished regiments of the British Army. Even the military contribution from Ireland was not inconsiderable. Wales even supplied another Empire leader — William Hughes, Prime Minister of Australia. It would not be an exaggeration to say that the First World War brought about the mixing together of men from all parts of the United Kingdom in a way that had never before been achieved. Had it not been for the Easter Rising in Dublin, the picture of unity might have been complete.

It would be wrong, however, to assume that a common sharing in empire was accompanied by a belief that strong centralized government in the United Kingdom was an inevitable corollary. Indeed, in the decade before the First World War, it was often argued that the Empire could not properly be governed unless Westminster was relieved of much domestic business by a system of devolution. Sir Edward Grey, the Foreign Secretary, declared in the Commons on 2 May 1912,

> The problem we have to deal with is how, under modern conditions, with a population far bigger than any population of one State in history before, with a civilisation so developed, with political problems more complex than ever existed before, with all the invention of modern science, concentration of everything, by telegraph and every conceivable means, in the centre, to liberate and free ourselves from congestion caused by that unparalleled and unprecedented condition of affairs.[11]

Others were of a similar view. It was still possible for the ardent spirits of the *Round Table* to think in terms of a federation of the Empire. Earl Grey, Governor-General of Canada, wrote to Lionel Curtis at the end of 1909 that

> Before the road is cleared for the Federation of the Empire we have to put the United Kingdom straight. The time is approaching, if it is not already here, for getting this work done . . . Provincial Legislatures of the Canadian rather than the South African type for 1. Ireland 2, Scotland 3. Wales 4. England (4. North?

9. G.K.A. Bell, *Randall Davidson* (London, 1952), pp. 793–94.
10. K.O. Morgan, *Wales in British Politics, 1868–1922* (Cardiff, 1970), p. 275.
11. *Home Rule from the Treasury Bench Speeches during the First and Second Reading Debates* (London, 1912), p. 166.

5. South?) with a Federal Parliament armed with powers of disallowance sitting in London. Each provincial unit to be represented in the Federal Parliament in proportion to its population . . .[12]

In 1911 the Foreign Secretary wrote to his relative in Canada that '. . . the Federal Idea made great progress during the last General Election. We shall, I hope, save the House of Commons by delegating local affairs within the limits of the United Kingdom, the reform of the Second Chamber and a permanent adjustment of the relations between the two Houses.'[13] It was Empire, in other words, which made fundamental constitutional change within the United Kingdom imperative. Such a reorganization should recognize the diversity of the United Kingdom. 'I do not believe we can do anything but harm', Sir Edward Grey argued in a speech in May 1912, 'by attempting to make out that there are no separate units in the United Kingdom and no difference of national opinion. There is an Irish national feeling and there is national feeling in other parts of the United Kingdom. You cannot help it. The thing is there, and if you deny its existence you will only intensify it.' There was no incompatibility between such national feeling and Empire.[14]

Such concern was widely shared. As early as 1901 Winston Churchill had prepared a scheme of devolution on the grounds that 'the reputation and efficiency of Parliament almost entirely depends upon its being cleared of the over-press of minor duties on which so much time is wasted, and which prevents any detailed and effective criticism being brought to bear on the affairs of a world-wide Empire.' He and Lord Hugh Cecil floated a scheme for 'Provincial Councils' for scrutiny by Sir Thomas Elliott, a leading civil servant. Elliott was not very impressed, fastening on the problem of trying to define the 'Province' or 'Provinces' of England. To some extent, Churchill took the point.[15] In a Cabinet paper a decade later, he argued that it was 'absolutely impossible that an English Parliament, and still more an English Executive, could exist side by side with an Imperial Parliament and an Imperial Executive, whether based on separate or identical election. Imperial affairs could not in practice be separated from English party politics . . .'[16] Churchill proposed instead to divide the United Kingdom into ten areas, each of which would have legislative and administrative bodies possessing limited powers. However, despite a great deal of discussion in the years before the First World War no comprehensive scheme of devolution could be produced. Many of the problems which were encountered have again been encountered over the last decade.

12. J.E. Kendle, 'The Round Table Movement and "Home Rule All Round"', *The Historical Journal*, xi, (1968), p. 334.

13. Sir Edward Grey to Albert, Earl Grey, 27 January 1911, Grey Papers.

14. *Home Rule from the Treasury Bench*, p. 185.

15. W.S. Churchill to Sir Thomas Elliott, 22 October 1901; Sir Thomas Elliott to W.S. Churchill, 28 October 1901. I am indebted to Sir Hugh Elliott, Bt, for allowing me to use these letters.

16. Cited in H.J. Hanham, *The Nineteenth-Century Constitution, 1815–1914* (Cambridge, 1969), pp. 131–33.

The First World War changed the context of the devolution discussion in several important respects. Firstly, it dampened the enthusiasm for it on the part of those for whom 'putting the United Kingdom straight' was merely the first step towards the Federation of the Empire. The imperial federation began to look increasingly distant. The pressure from the self-governing dominions for clarification of their constitutional status pointed in quite the opposite direction. In such circumstances, they lost interest in tinkering about with the structure of the United Kingdom. Secondly, the developments in Ireland meant that no solution on the lines of a local parliament with local powers would be acceptable. In the 'Articles of Agreement for a Treaty', Lloyd George was forced to concede that the status of Ireland would be like that of Canada within the Empire rather than akin to the status of a Canadian province within the United Kingdom. Many British politicians had come to the conclusion that Irish history over the previous thirty years had demonstrated that 'Home Rule' was little more than a half-way stage to complete self-government. There was no middle way. This also seemed to be the lesson of events in contemporary Europe. The war had seen a general championing of 'self-determination'. The notion that the Habsburg Monarchy would be replaced by a central European federal state proved only a dream. The transition seemed to be from sovereign multi-national states to sovereign national states. In this light, the immediate post-war debates seemed to show a hardening in favour of a British national state. In the House of Lords in March 1919, Lord Brassey advocated a scheme which would secure the indefeasible supremacy of the Imperial Parliament but permit extensive devolution in the areas of local government, education, agriculture and licensing. Birkenhead replied that parliamentary congestion would not be overcome by such a scheme. There was, in his opinion, only one way in which the matter might be resolved — 'namely that there must be a statutory definition of the powers of each inferior Legislature. This is an immense revolution in all our habits of thought'.[17] A Speaker's Conference was established in October 1919 to investigate these problems.

When the conference reported in 1920, the Speaker announced a surprising degree of unity among its members. However, they were divided on the perhaps crucial point of the composition of the proposed separate legislatures and whether members of these legislatures should also be members of the United Kingdom parliament. Lloyd George was not moved to take any action, nor were his successors. Despite the existence of some backbench support for Home Rule both for Scotland and Wales, no government could be persuaded to embark on a programme of constitutional reconstruction. Devolution was indeed bestowed, rather strangely, on Northern Ireland, but Stormont was not monitored with great interest and enthusiasm.[18] In many respects it had been Ireland which had fuelled the discussion in the pre-1914 period, but the Irish

---

17. Wan-Hsuan Chiao, *Devolution in Great Britain* (New York, 1926).
18. R.J. Lawrence, *The Government of Northern Ireland* (Oxford, 1965).

question had seemingly been solved. Even if there had been greater pressure from Scotland and Wales, the problem of what to do with England would have made progress difficult. It was commonly argued that if ever a specifically English Parliament was established — perhaps outside London — it would inevitably carry more weight in a federal system than the parliaments of Scotland, Wales or Northern Ireland. Balfour had considered this point back in 1913. 'A collision with an Irish Parliament', he argued 'would be bad enough. A collision with a Scottish Parliament is not a desirable thing to think of. But conceive a collision with an English Parliament! I believe that directly you face the question of England's position in your ideal federal system you will see the utter absurdity of it.'[19] Lord Bryce returned to the same point in 1919. The preponderant population of England made such a scheme unworkable. An alternative was to contemplate the regionalization of the United Kingdom as a whole, with approximately equal units. Bonar Law argued that 'from the point of view of the integrity of the country as a whole, the very worst way in which you can set up devolution is by putting it on a national basis'.[20] But how did you establish English 'provinces'? No one knew.

It was, nevertheless, in the inter-war period, when political issues seemed to be discussed in a firmly British framework, that new nationalist parties emerged in Scotland and Wales. The Welsh Nationalist party was founded in 1925 — a fusion of groups previously active at the University Colleges in Bangor and Aberystwyth. The central concern of the founders was with the vigour and survival of the Welsh language and culture. By the thirties, they saw 'self-government', whatever that quite implied, as a necessary condition for that survival. It was hoped that Welsh would become the only official language of Wales. The party decided to fight elections at an early stage in its history, but by 1945 this had only been done on a small scale and with little success. It had gained some publicity from the burning of an RAF bombing school on the Llŷn peninsula in 1936. The task was undertaken by three leading members of the party. This action brought it increased support from Pacifists and Nonconformists, though the actual outbreak of war somewhat modified this mood. The prospects for an electoral break-through appeared slim, but by-elections in 1946 in industrial South Wales gave some ground for encouragement. When Labour was securely in power, voters might feel able to protest 'against the present misrule of Wales by an English party'. There was, however, no consistent pattern of electoral progress. Plaid Cymru's share of the vote rose from 1.1 per cent of the Welsh electorate in 1945 to 5.2 per cent in 1959, but a parliamentary seat still eluded it. However, the fortunes of the plaid should not be taken as the only index of political support for some institutional recognition of the distinctiveness of Wales. A 'Parliament for Wales' campaign was launched in July 1950. Such a parliament was to

19. Chiao, *Devolution in Great Britain*, pp. 146–47.
20. Ibid., p. 141.

have adequate legislative authority in Welsh affairs within the framework of the United Kingdom. It had some Labour and some Liberal support. A quarter-of-a-million signatures were collected by 1956, some 14 per cent of the Welsh electorate, but no parliament for Wales emerged — only six out of thirty-six Welsh MPs supported it. Even so, in the post-war decade, starting with the 1948 Council for Wales and Monmouthshire, increasing attention was paid to the distinctive claims of Wales. It was not clear how far these administrative and political changes would go. It was already clear, however, that 'nationalism' was something which profoundly divided Welshmen. The 'Parliament for Wales' campaign had been strongest in the areas where those who could speak Welsh were in a majority. Arguments about the essence of 'Welshness' proliferated and, by the end of the fifties, were beginning to become more strident. In 1966, the party's leader, Gwynfor Evans, gained a by-election victory at Carmarthen, and Plaid Cymru did well in other industrial seats in South Wales. In 1974, however, although it won three parliamentary seats, it only achieved just over 10 per cent of the Welsh vote, and twenty-six out of thirty-six candidates lost their deposits. Nevertheless, it was in some degree to head off possible further progress by Plaid Cymru that the Labour government embarked on the abortive scheme of devolution for Wales. This history, sketchy though it must be, would seem to argue that the emergence of some pressure for Home Rule for Wales has little to do with 'loss of Empire'. Hostility to the British state antedated imperial decline, and there has not in fact been a dramatic increase in that hostility since that decline has become manifest. The fate of the Welsh language and culture would have had political implications in Wales, imperial state or non-imperial state. It is frequently stated that a new Lloyd George, in the absence of empire, would find nothing in London to tempt him out of the 'stunted principality', but there is little evidence for this hypothesis. To judge by the prominence of Welsh MPs or Welshmen in the most recent Labour government, the attractions of operating in a British context are greater than those of operating simply in a Welsh context.[21]

In Scotland in the interwar period, nationalist politics seemed to be more confused than in Wales, at least in organizational terms. It was not until 1934 that the Scottish National Party was formed from a fusion of hitherto rival groups. There had been a good deal of bickering over the previous decade about the ultimate objective of Scottish nationalism, not to mention conflicts between leading personalities. The involvement of literary figures like Hugh MacDiarmid and Compton Mackenzie, amongst others, naturally led to a great deal of attention being given to the question of a distinctively Scottish culture; but there was little agreement about its essence. While there was much agony about the propriety of writing in English or Scots or Gaelic, this cultural preoccupation was not as universal as was discussion of linguistic matters in Plaid Genedlaethol Cymru. The originating programme of the SNP declared that its object was 'self-government for Scotland on a basis which will enable Scotland as a partner in the British Empire with the same status as England to develop its National Life to the fullest advantage'.[22] This statement reflected a degree of self-confidence and a breadth of horizon lacking in comparable Welsh statements of the same period. The quest for Scottish self-government would not be at the price of losing Scotland's share in the management of the British Empire. That share, in the fields of education, commerce and administration, was large. The case for self-government was to be argued irrespective of whether there was an Empire. Such an attitude was not universal. Left-wing elements in nationalist circles took a critical attitude to empire both before and after the Second World War, and saw a link between colonial freedom and Scotland's freedom which eluded most of their follow-countrymen.

Between 1945 and 1959, the SNP never gained more than 1.3 per cent of the Scottish vote at a general election. In 1966 it gained 5 per cent, and the following year won a by-election at Hamilton and performed very well in other by-elections. In 1970 its share of the Scottish vote went up to 11 per cent. In February 1974 it gained 21.9 per cent of the votes and won seven seats, and in October 1974 won 30.4 per cent of the vote and won 11 seats, becoming in the process the second largest party in Scotland, overtaking the Conservatives in percentage terms. Hanham's book was published in 1969 before these heights had been scaled, and he invoked, in general terms, the 'loss of empire' hypothesis. 'Now that the Empire is dead,' he wrote,

> many Scots feel cramped and restricted at home. They chafe at the provincialism of much of Scottish life and at the slowness of Scottish economic growth, which is related to that provincialism. To give themselves an opening to a wider world the Scots need some sort of outlet, and the choice appears at the moment to be between emigration and re-creating the Scottish nation at home.[23]

Once again, however, one wonders whether the concept will really bear the explanatory weight which is placed upon it. Did the death of empire really cause so many Scots to feel cramped and restricted at home? How many Scots in its wake saw the situation in terms of a stark choice between emigration and the 're-creation' of the Scottish nation? While accepting that many Scots took pride from their share in the 'great imperial adventure', the antithesis between imperial and post-imperial life seems too sharply drawn.

In principle, therefore, there seems no reason why 'loss of Empire' should be specifically invoked to explain the conflicts and tensions which have manifested

22. Cited in H.J. Hanham, *Scottish Nationalism* (London, 1969), p. 163.
23. Ibid., p. 212.

themselves in the United Kingdom over the last decade or so. In one form or other the problem of the most satisfactory constitutional relationship between the component parts of the United Kingdom has been present for over a century.[24] That unity has throughout been precarious because it has never been a uniformity. Attempts at devolution in order to meet the needs of Imperial Britain were very similar to attempts to meet the needs of post-Imperial Britain, and neither have succeeded. The Empire did not in fact obscure tensions within the United Kingdom between town and country, between peripheral and core regions, within as well as between England, Ireland, Scotland and Wales. The balance obtaining at any one moment owed much more to such complex matters as class allegiance and identity, religious loyalty, linguistic stability and the ever-shifting pattern of economic and industrial development. It still does. To accept that 'loss of empire' played a critical part in determining the degree of unity or disunity is to overemphasize the part that Empire played in establishing Namier's 'British island nationality'. It is only a hundred or so years since Gladstone became the first politician to establish a real personal following in England, Scotland and Wales, and even in Ireland — the first British politician. 'Britishness' has always been an elusive concept, but it would be a mistake to suppose that its comprehensive capacity is exhausted.

24. A.H. Birch, *Political Integration and Disintegration in the British Isles* (London 1977); B. Porter, *The Lion's Share* (London, 1975), pp. 353–54.

Index